My wife had a baby!!!
To think I'd actually get to be a
dad! I'm hugely grateful to my wife
for working so hard, and to my
daughter for being born!!!

—*Yūki Tabata, 2019*

YŪKI TABATA

was born in Fukuoka Prefecture
and got his big break in the 2011
Shonen Jump Golden Future Cup
with his winning entry, *Hungry
Joker*. He started the magical fantasy
series *Black Clover* in 2015.

BLACK CLOVER
VOLUME 22
SHONEN JUMP Manga Edition

Story and Art by YŪKI TABATA

Translation ❃ TAYLOR ENGEL,
HC LANGUAGE SOLUTIONS, INC.

Touch-Up Art & Lettering ❃ ANNALIESE CHRISTMAN

Design ❃ KAM LI

Editor ❃ ALEXIS KIRSCH

Printed in the U.S.A.

Published by VIZ Media, LLC
P.O. Box 77010
San Francisco, CA 94107

10 9 8 7 6 5 4 3 2 1
First printing, August 2020

Lumiere

Licht

Black ✤ Clover

YŪKI TABATA · 22 · DAWN

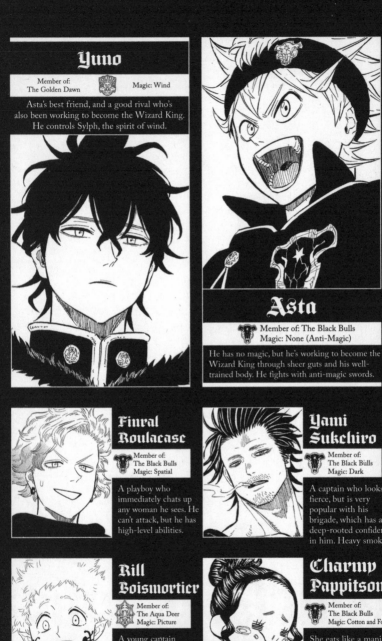

Yuno

Member of: The Golden Dawn

Magic: Wind

Asta's best friend, and a good rival who's also been working to become the Wizard King. He controls Sylph, the spirit of wind.

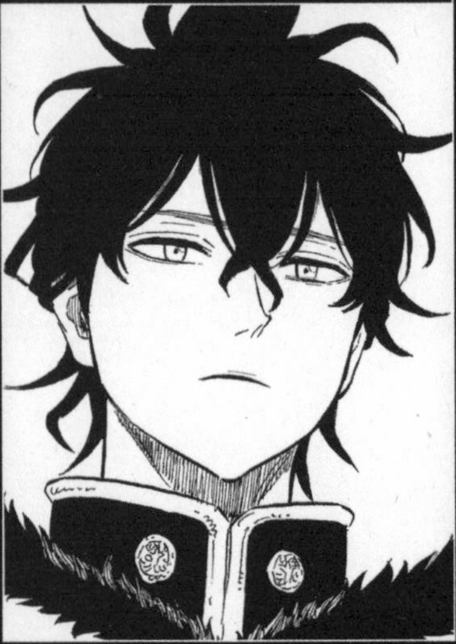

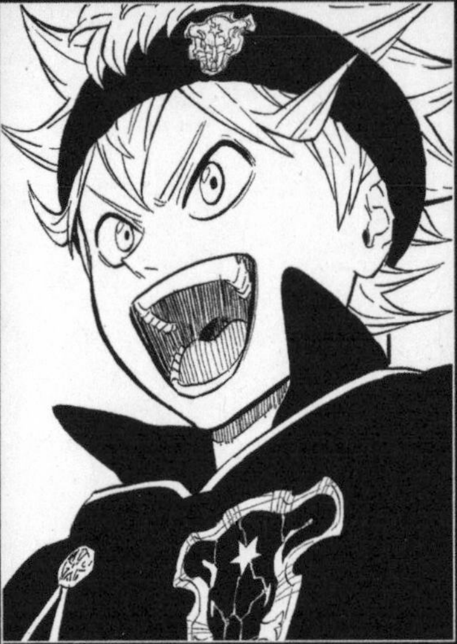

Asta

Member of: The Black Bulls
Magic: None (Anti-Magic)

He has no magic, but he's working to become the Wizard King through sheer guts and his well-trained body. He fights with anti-magic swords.

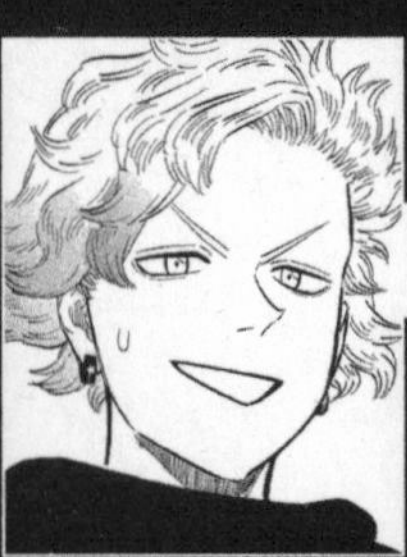

Finral Roulacase

Member of:
The Black Bulls
Magic: Spatial

A playboy who immediately chats up any woman he sees. He can't attack, but he has high-level abilities.

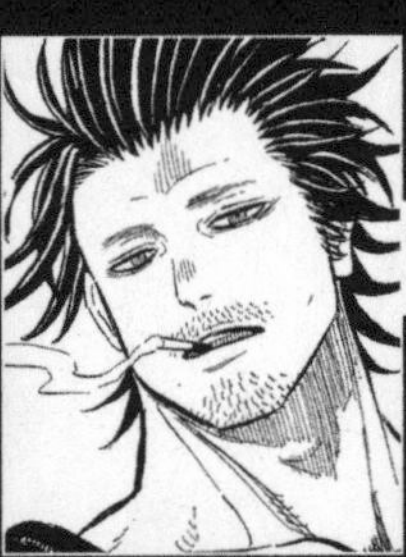

Yami Sukehiro

Member of:
The Black Bulls
Magic: Dark

A captain who looks fierce, but is very popular with his brigade, which has a deep-rooted confidence in him. Heavy smoker.

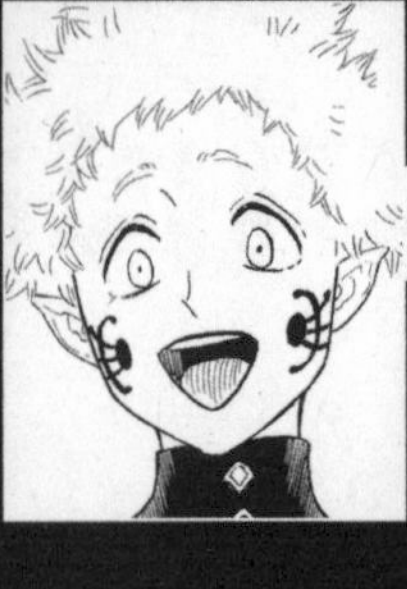

Rill Boismortier

Member of:
The Aqua Deer
Magic: Picture

A young captain with outstanding talent. His body has been taken over by an elf named Lira.

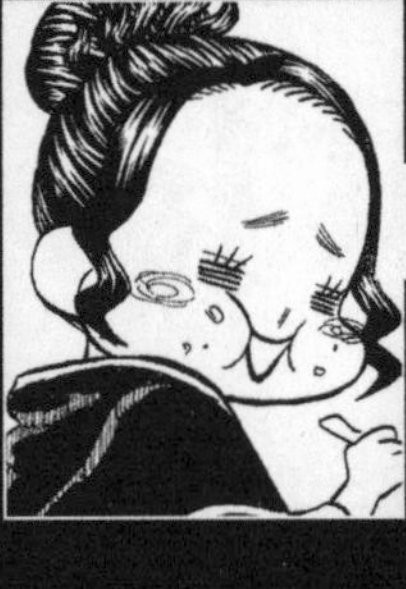

Charmy Pappitson

Member of:
The Black Bulls
Magic: Cotton and Food

She eats like a maniac, and prizes food above all else. She's half dwarf. She has a big crush on Yuno.

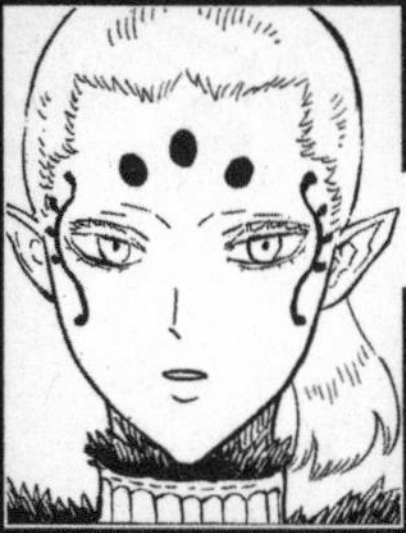

Patry

Magic: Light

He monopolized the body he'd shared with William and completed the reincarnation. His temporary form looks exactly like Licht.

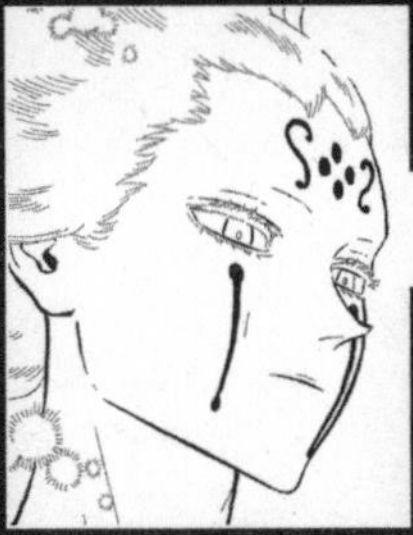

Licht

Magic: Sword

The leader of the elves. He was resurrected by the reincarnation spell, but his mind hasn't returned yet, so he's unstable.

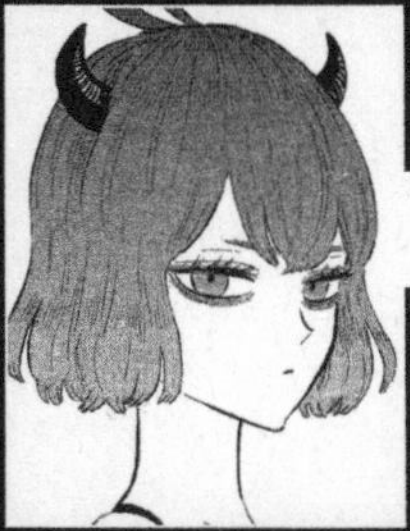

Secre Swallowtail (Nero)

Magic: Sealing

500 years ago, she paid for using forbidden magic by becoming a bird. She watched over Licht's grimoire.

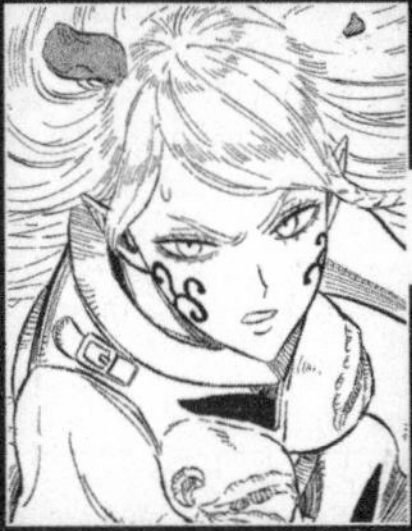

Charlotte Roselei

Member of:
The Blue Rose Knights
Magic: Briar

Has a cold personality, and doesn't like men. Her body is being controlled by an elf named Charla.

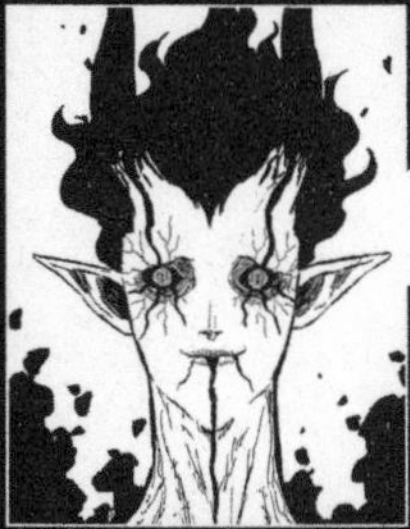

Devil

Magic: Word Soul

The mastermind behind the elves' reincarnation. It took 500 years, but he finally acquired a physical body.

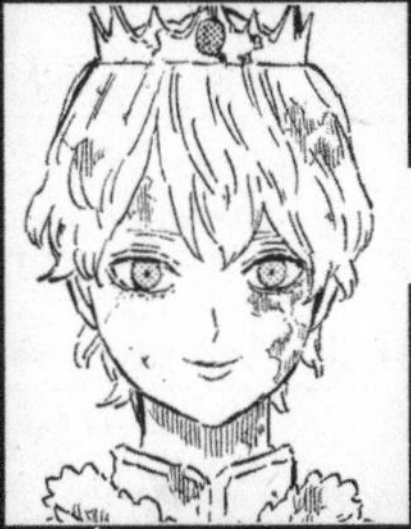

Lumiere Silvamillion Clover

Magic: Light

The first Wizard King. His life was sealed into a stone statue for 500 years in preparation for the devil's revival.

STORY

In a world where magic is everything, Asta and Yuno are both found abandoned on the same day at a church in the remote village of Hage. Both dream of becoming the Wizard King, the highest of all mages, and they spend their days working toward that dream.

The year they turn 15, both receive grimoires, magic books that amplify their bearer's magic. They take the entrance exam for the Magic Knights, nine groups of mages under the direct control of the Wizard King. Yuno, whose magic is strong, joins the Golden Dawn, an elite group, while Asta, who has no magic at all, joins the Black Bulls, a group of misfits. With this, the two finally take their first step toward becoming the Wizard King…

The devil who planted hatred in the elves 500 years ago and engineered their reincarnation has returned! Now that he has a body and a grimoire, Asta and the elves are in serious trouble. But just as hope seems lost, first Wizard King Lumiere, who knew the truth of the nightmare of 500 years ago, awakens from his sealed state and rushes to the Shadow Palace!

CONTENTS

BLACK ❀ CLOVER

22

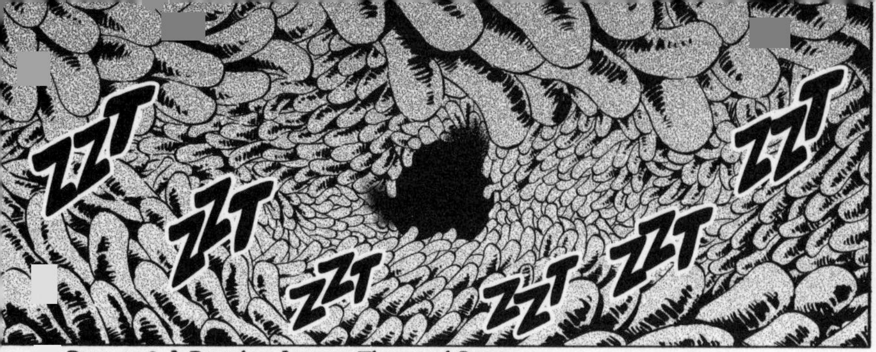
ZZZT
ZZZT
ZZZT
ZZZT
ZZZT
ZZZT

Page 206: A Reunion Across Time and Space

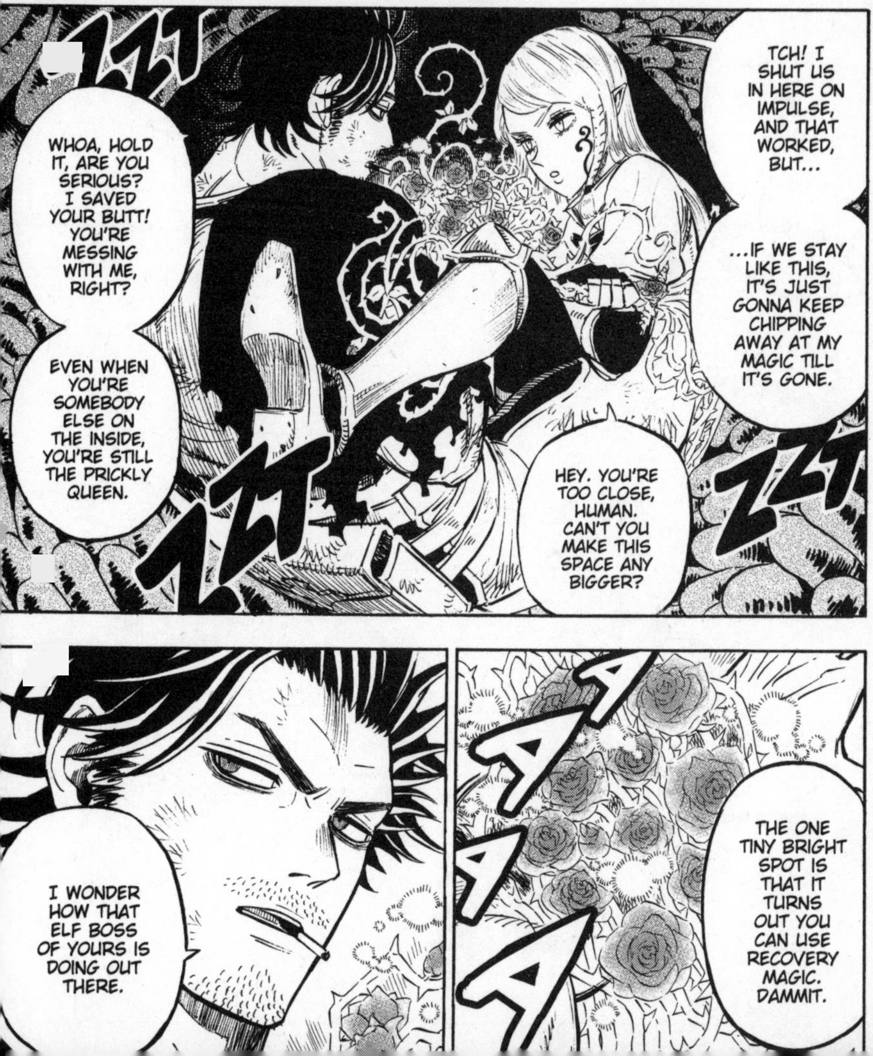
TCH! I SHUT US IN HERE ON IMPULSE, AND THAT WORKED, BUT...
...IF WE STAY LIKE THIS, IT'S JUST GONNA KEEP CHIPPING AWAY AT MY MAGIC TILL IT'S GONE.
ZZZT
HEY. YOU'RE TOO CLOSE, HUMAN. CAN'T YOU MAKE THIS SPACE ANY BIGGER?
ZZZT
ZZZT
WHOA, HOLD IT, ARE YOU SERIOUS? I SAVED YOUR BUTT! YOU'RE MESSING WITH ME, RIGHT?
EVEN WHEN YOU'RE SOMEBODY ELSE ON THE INSIDE, YOU'RE STILL THE PRICKLY QUEEN.
THE ONE TINY BRIGHT SPOT IS THAT IT TURNS OUT YOU CAN USE RECOVERY MAGIC. DAMMIT.
I WONDER HOW THAT ELF BOSS OF YOURS IS DOING OUT THERE.

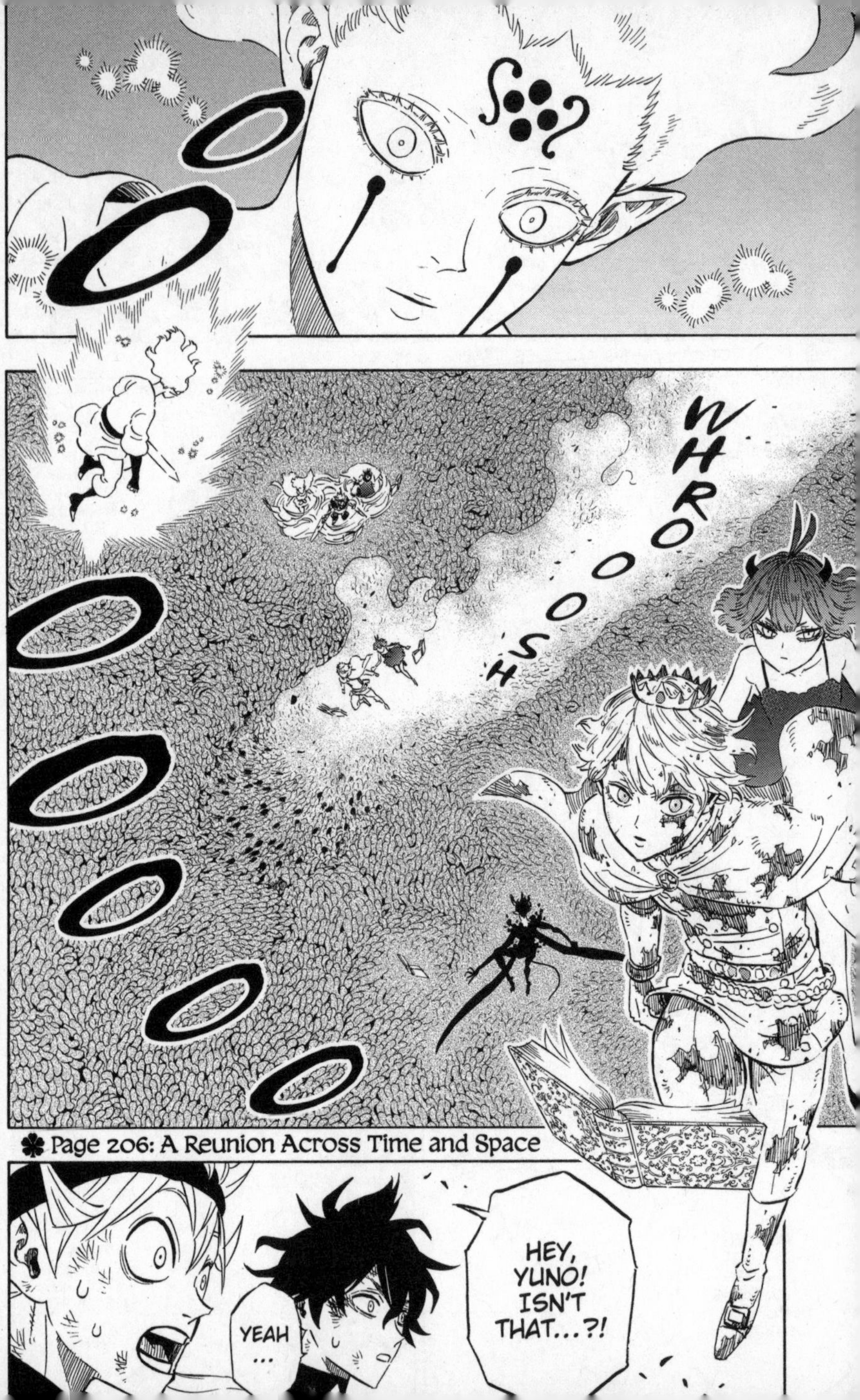
WHROOOOSH
Page 206: A Reunion Across Time and Space
HEY, YUNO! ISN'T THAT...?!
YEAH...

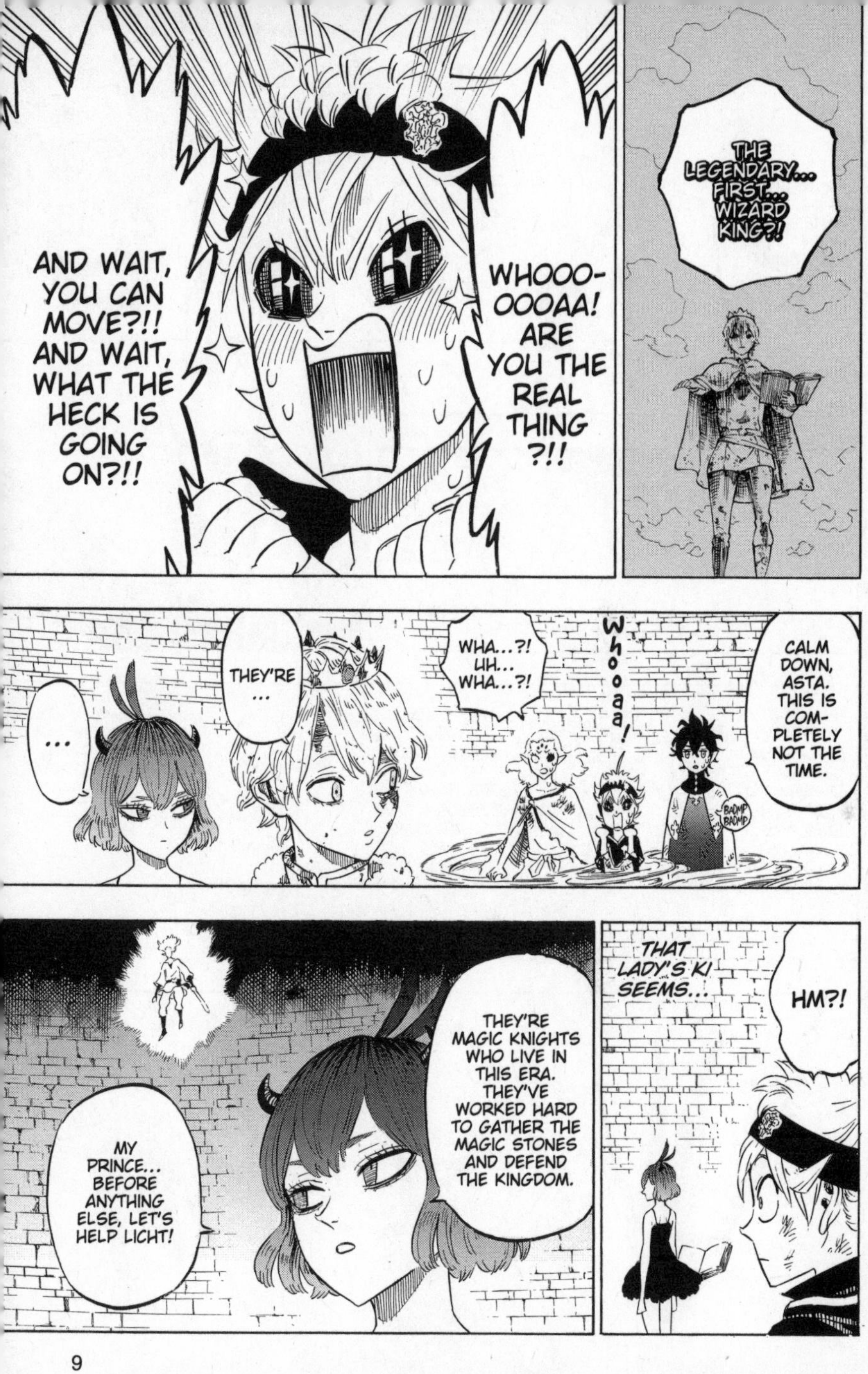
THE LEGENDARY... FIRST... WIZARD KING?!
WHOOOO-OOOAA! ARE YOU THE REAL THING?!!
AND WAIT, YOU CAN MOVE?!! AND WAIT, WHAT THE HECK IS GOING ON?!!
CALM DOWN, ASTA. THIS IS COMPLETELY NOT THE TIME.
BADMP BADMP
Whooaa!
WHA...?! UH... WHA...?!
THEY'RE ...
...
HM?!
THAT LADY'S KI SEEMS...
THEY'RE MAGIC KNIGHTS WHO LIVE IN THIS ERA. THEY'VE WORKED HARD TO GATHER THE MAGIC STONES AND DEFEND THE KINGDOM.
MY PRINCE... BEFORE ANYTHING ELSE, LET'S HELP LICHT!

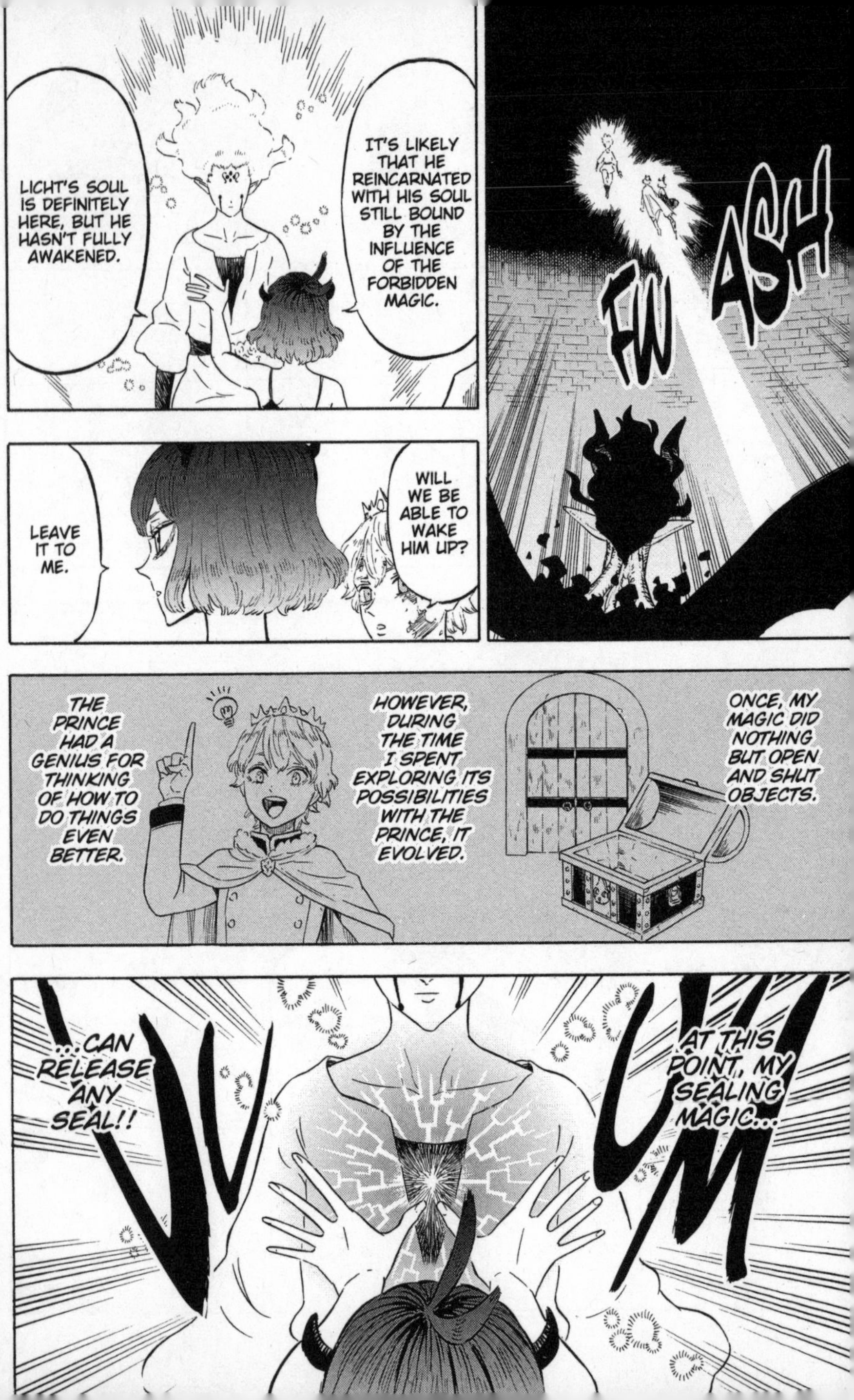
FWASH
IT'S LIKELY THAT HE REINCARNATED WITH HIS SOUL STILL BOUND BY THE INFLUENCE OF THE FORBIDDEN MAGIC.
LICHT'S SOUL IS DEFINITELY HERE, BUT HE HASN'T FULLY AWAKENED.
WILL WE BE ABLE TO WAKE HIM UP?
LEAVE IT TO ME.
ONCE, MY MAGIC DID NOTHING BUT OPEN AND SHUT OBJECTS.
HOWEVER, DURING THE TIME I SPENT EXPLORING ITS POSSIBILITIES WITH THE PRINCE, IT EVOLVED.
THE PRINCE HAD A GENIUS FOR THINKING OF HOW TO DO THINGS EVEN BETTER.
AT THIS POINT, MY SEALING MAGIC...
VWM
...CAN RELEASE ANY SEAL!!

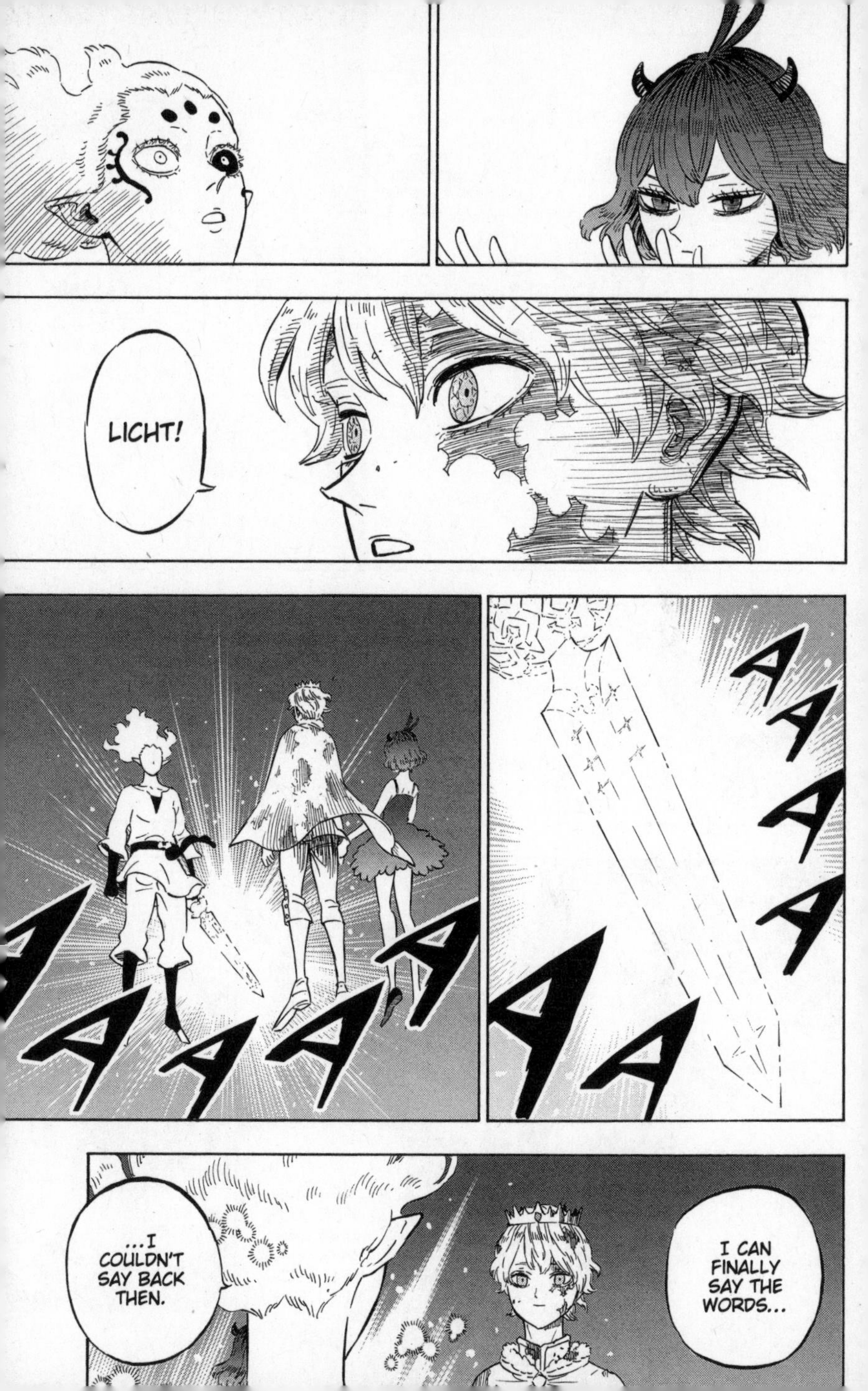
LICHT!
AAAAAA
AAAAAA
I CAN FINALLY SAY THE WORDS...
...I COULDN'T SAY BACK THEN.

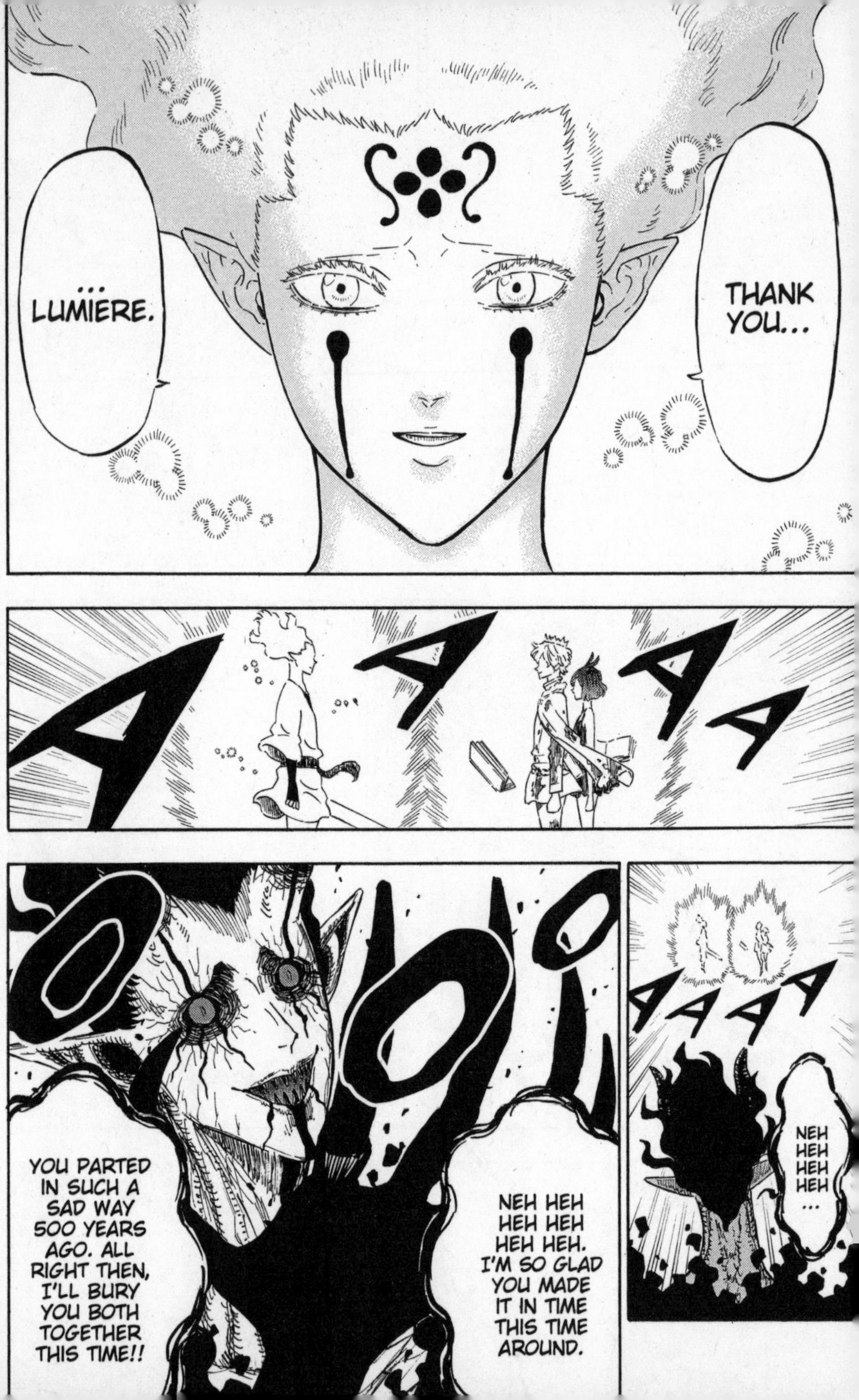
THANK YOU...
... LUMÏERE.
AAAAA
NEH HEH HEH HEH ...
AAAA
NEH HEH HEH HEH HEH HEH. I'M SO GLAD YOU MADE IT IN TIME THIS TIME AROUND.
YOU PARTED IN SUCH A SAD WAY 500 YEARS AGO. ALL RIGHT THEN, I'LL BURY YOU BOTH TOGETHER THIS TIME!!
OOOO

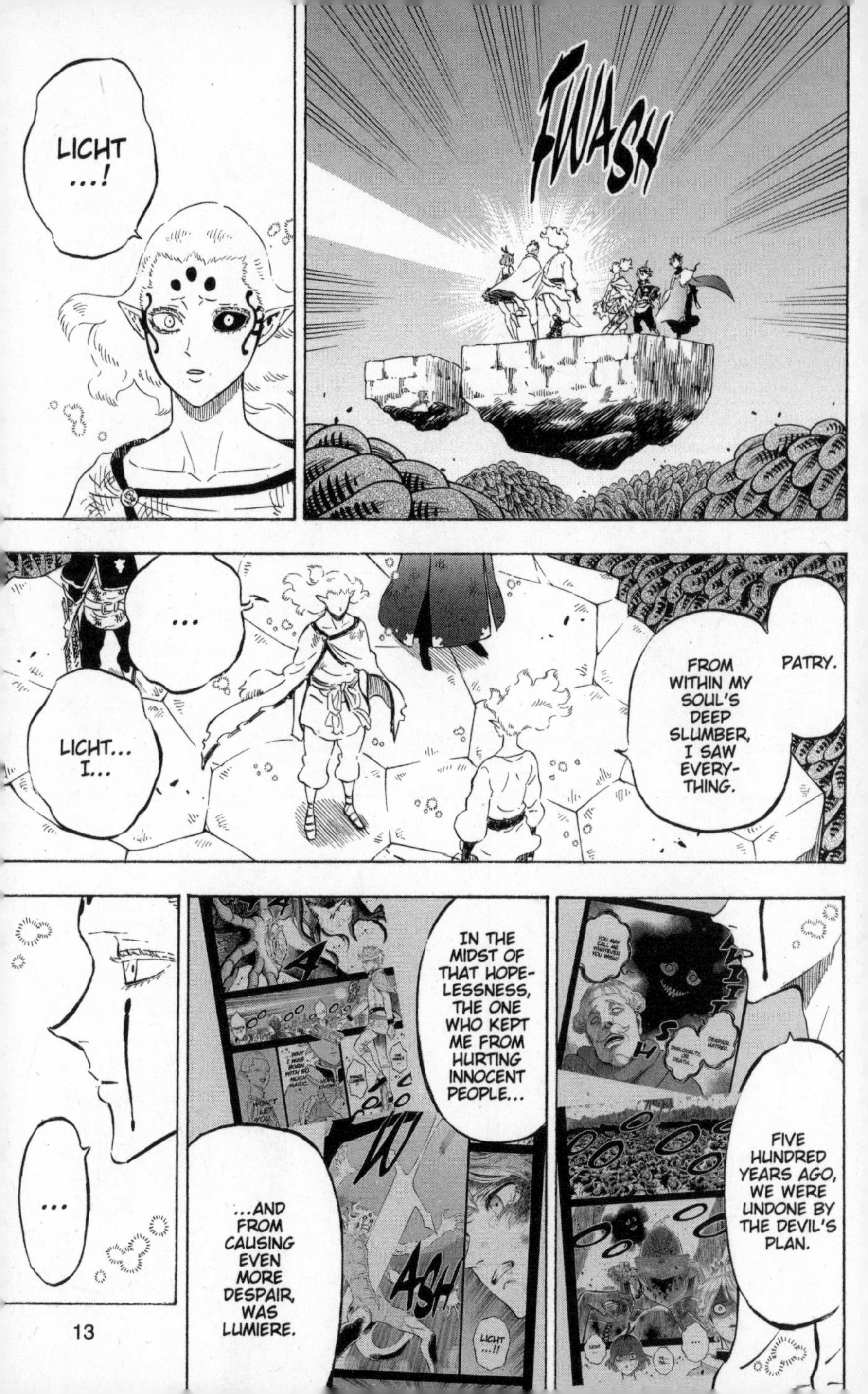
FWASH
LICHT ...!
PATRY.
FROM WITHIN MY SOUL'S DEEP SLUMBER, I SAW EVERYTHING.
...
LICHT... I...
FIVE HUNDRED YEARS AGO, WE WERE UNDONE BY THE DEVIL'S PLAN.
IN THE MIDST OF THAT HOPE-LESSNESS, THE ONE WHO KEPT ME FROM HURTING INNOCENT PEOPLE...
...AND FROM CAUSING EVEN MORE DESPAIR, WAS LUMIERE.
I WON'T LET YOU
LICHT ...!!
...

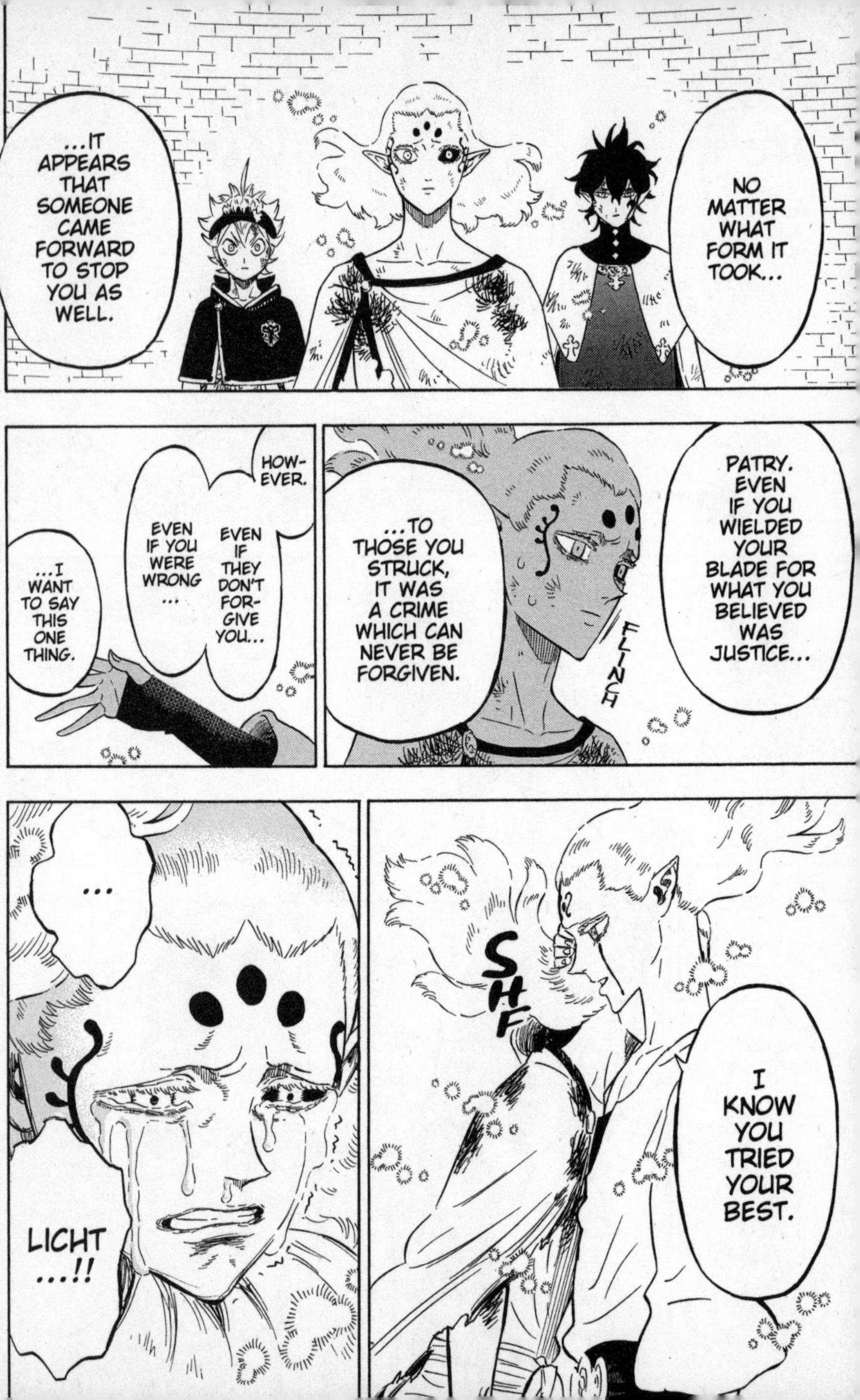
NO MATTER WHAT FORM IT TOOK...
...IT APPEARS THAT SOMEONE CAME FORWARD TO STOP YOU AS WELL.
PATRY. EVEN IF YOU WIELDED YOUR BLADE FOR WHAT YOU BELIEVED WAS JUSTICE...
...TO THOSE YOU STRUCK, IT WAS A CRIME WHICH CAN NEVER BE FORGIVEN.
FLINCH
HOW-EVER.
EVEN IF THEY DON'T FOR-GIVE YOU...
EVEN IF YOU WERE WRONG...
...I WANT TO SAY THIS ONE THING.
I KNOW YOU TRIED YOUR BEST.
SHF
...
LICHT ...!!

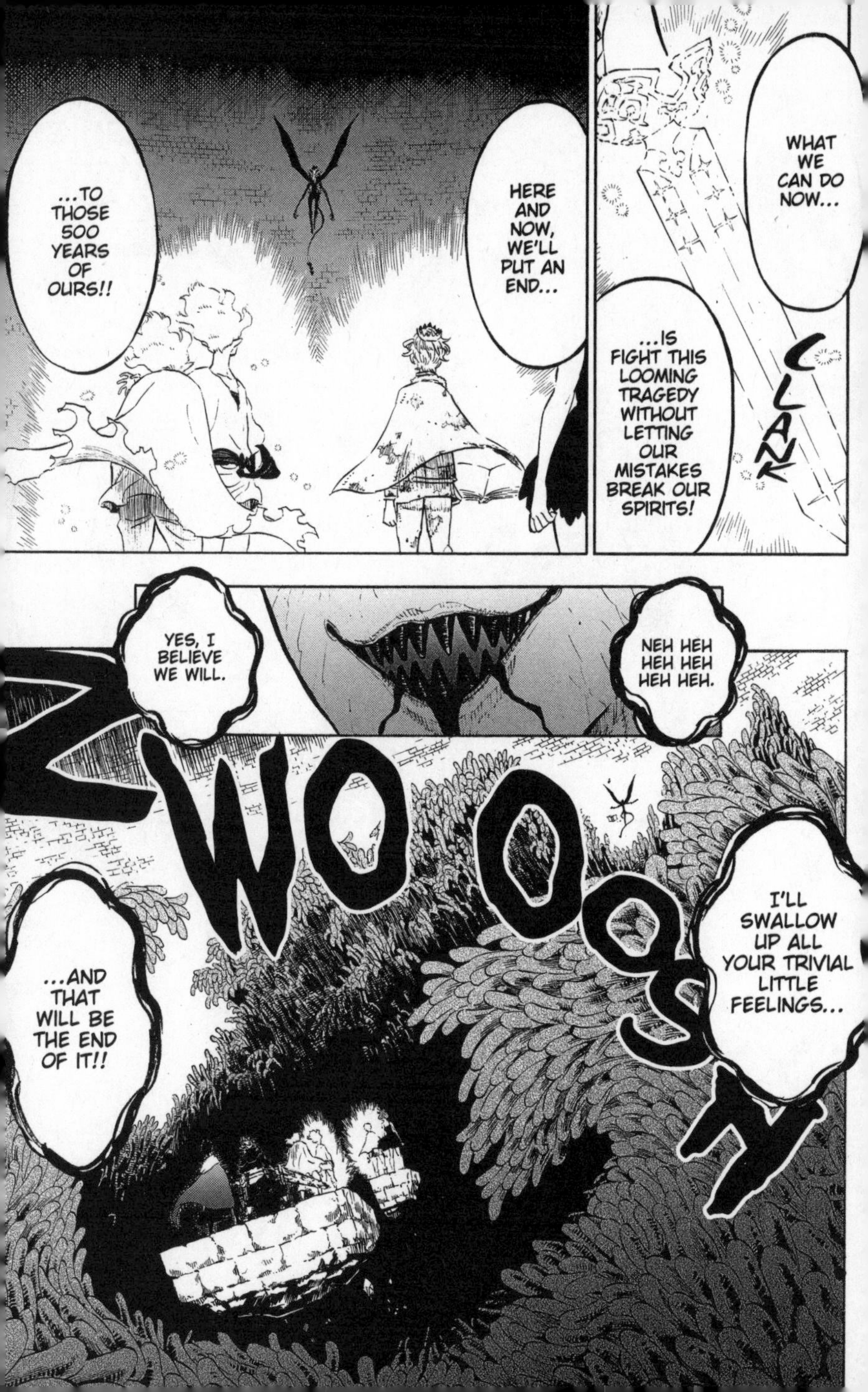
WHAT WE CAN DO NOW...
...IS FIGHT THIS LOOMING TRAGEDY WITHOUT LETTING OUR MISTAKES BREAK OUR SPIRITS!
CLANK
HERE AND NOW, WE'LL PUT AN END...
...TO THOSE 500 YEARS OF OURS!!
NEH HEH HEH HEH HEH HEH.
YES, I BELIEVE WE WILL.
I'LL SWALLOW UP ALL YOUR TRIVIAL LITTLE FEELINGS...
...AND THAT WILL BE THE END OF IT!!
WOOOGH

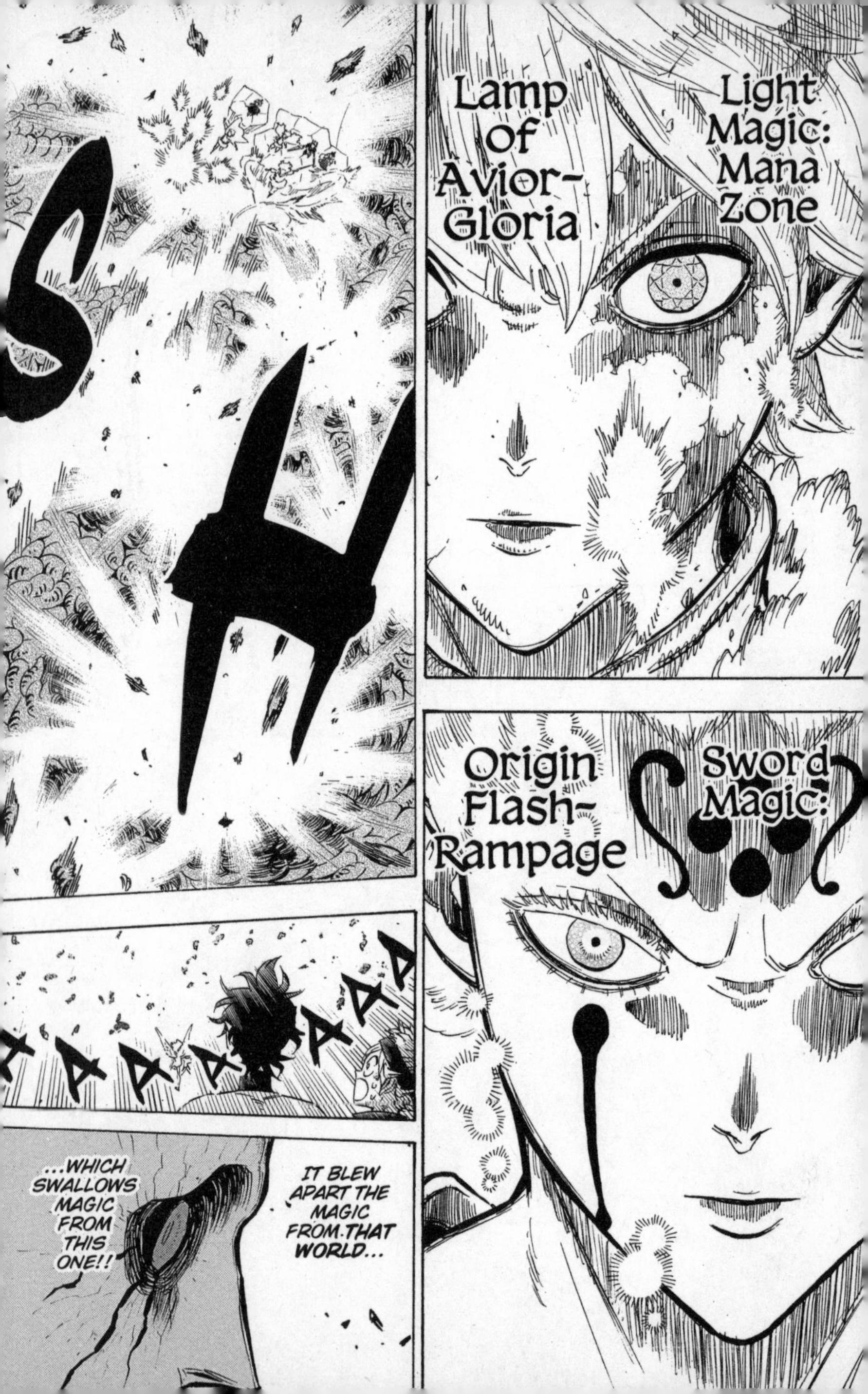
Light Magic: Mana Zone
Lamp of Avior-Gloria
Sword Magic:
Origin Flash-Rampage
SHH
AAAAAAAAAA
IT BLEW APART THE MAGIC FROM THAT WORLD...
...WHICH SWALLOWS MAGIC FROM THIS ONE!!

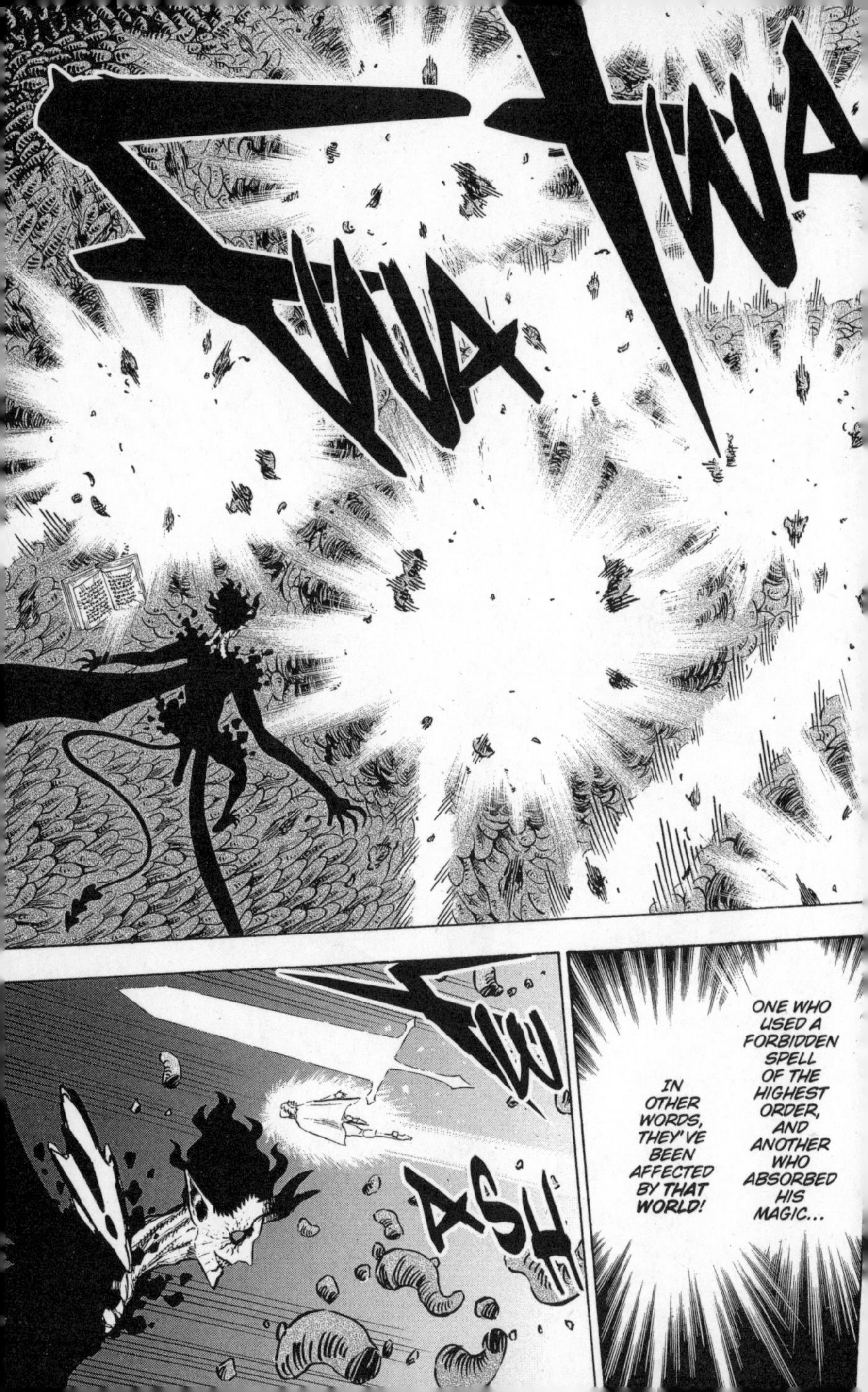
ONE WHO USED A FORBIDDEN SPELL OF THE HIGHEST ORDER, AND ANOTHER WHO ABSORBED HIS MAGIC...
IN OTHER WORDS, THEY'VE BEEN AFFECTED BY THAT WORLD!

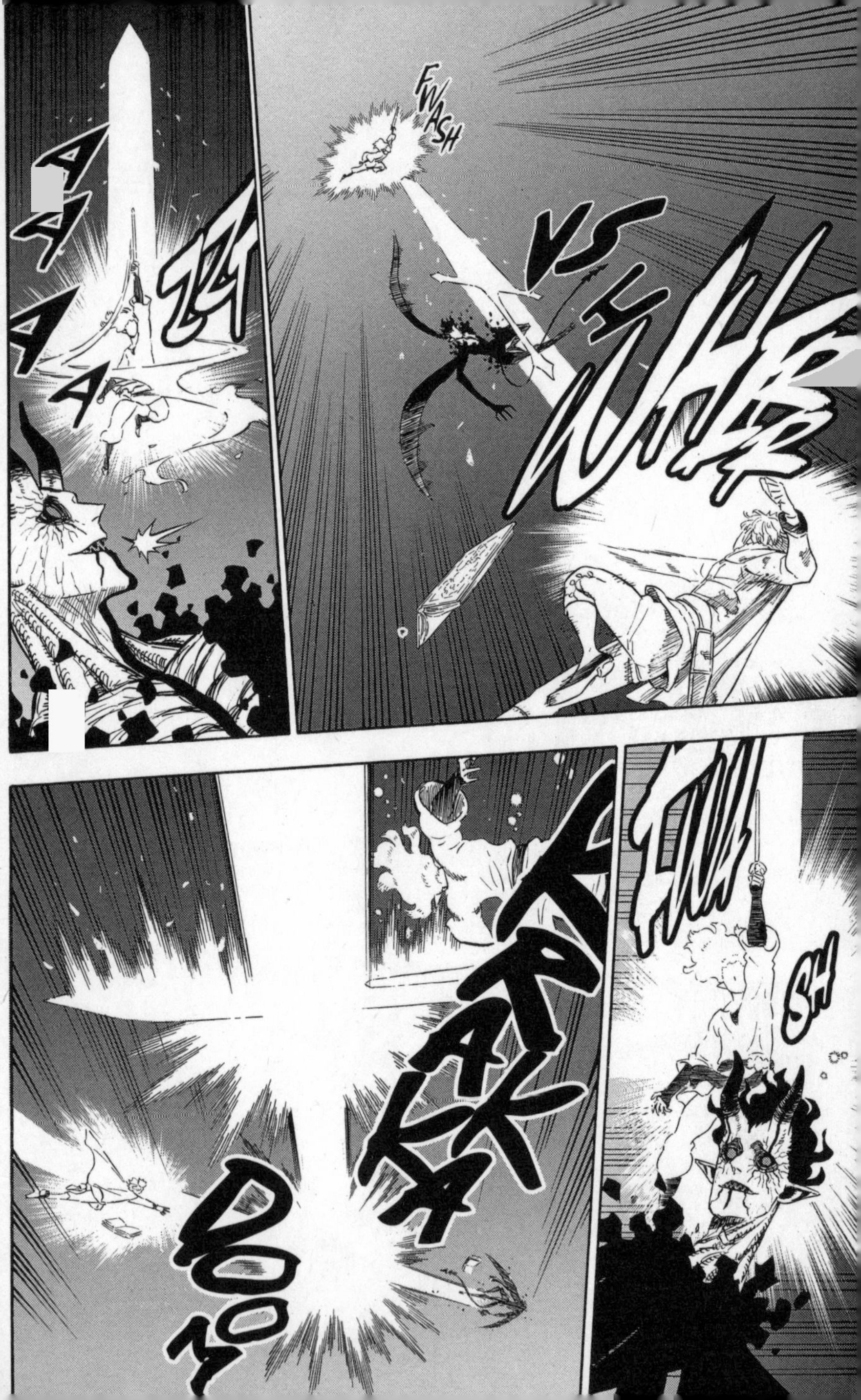
FWASH
VSH
SH
KRAKKA
DOOM

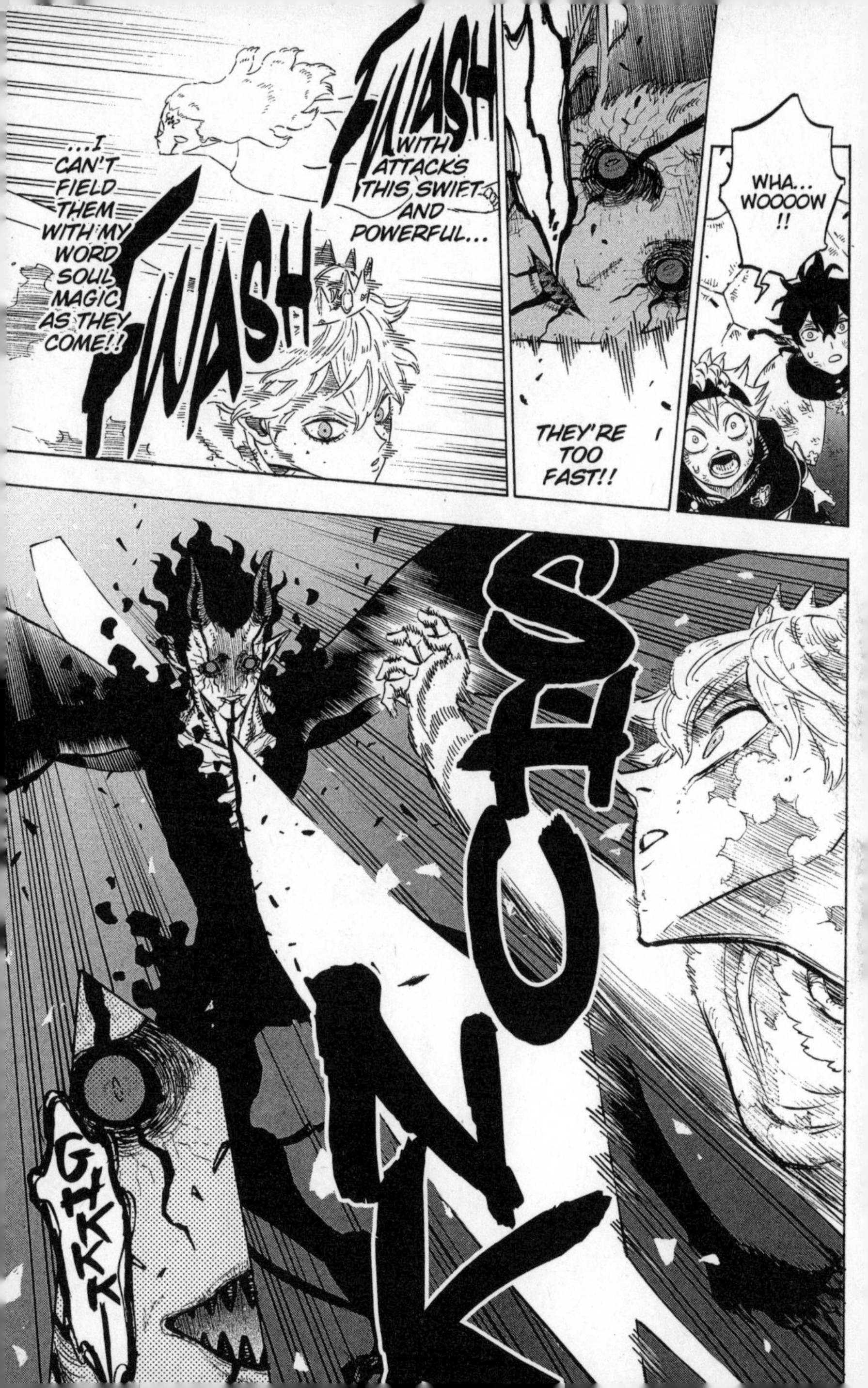
WHA... WOOOOW!!
THEY'RE TOO FAST!!
SWASH
WITH ATTACKS THIS SWIFT AND POWERFUL...
...I CAN'T FIELD THEM WITH MY WORD SOUL MAGIC AS THEY COME!!
SWASH
GHKKK

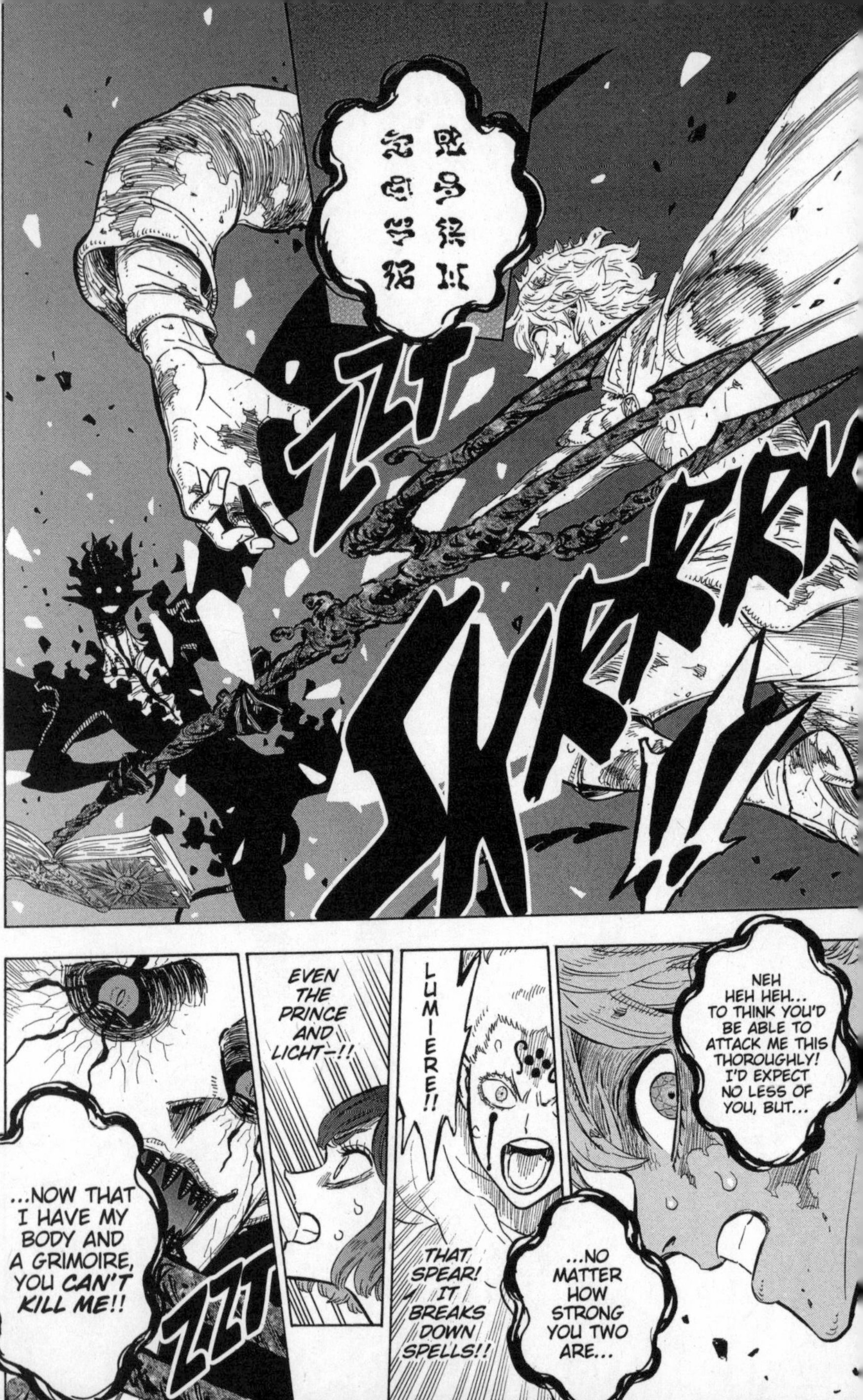
ZZZT
NEH HEH HEH... TO THINK YOU'D BE ABLE TO ATTACK ME THIS THOROUGHLY! I'D EXPECT NO LESS OF YOU, BUT...
...NO MATTER HOW STRONG YOU TWO ARE...
LUMIERE!!
THAT SPEAR! IT BREAKS DOWN SPELLS!!
EVEN THE PRINCE AND LICHT—!!
...NOW THAT I HAVE MY BODY AND A GRIMOIRE, YOU CAN'T KILL ME!!
ZZZT

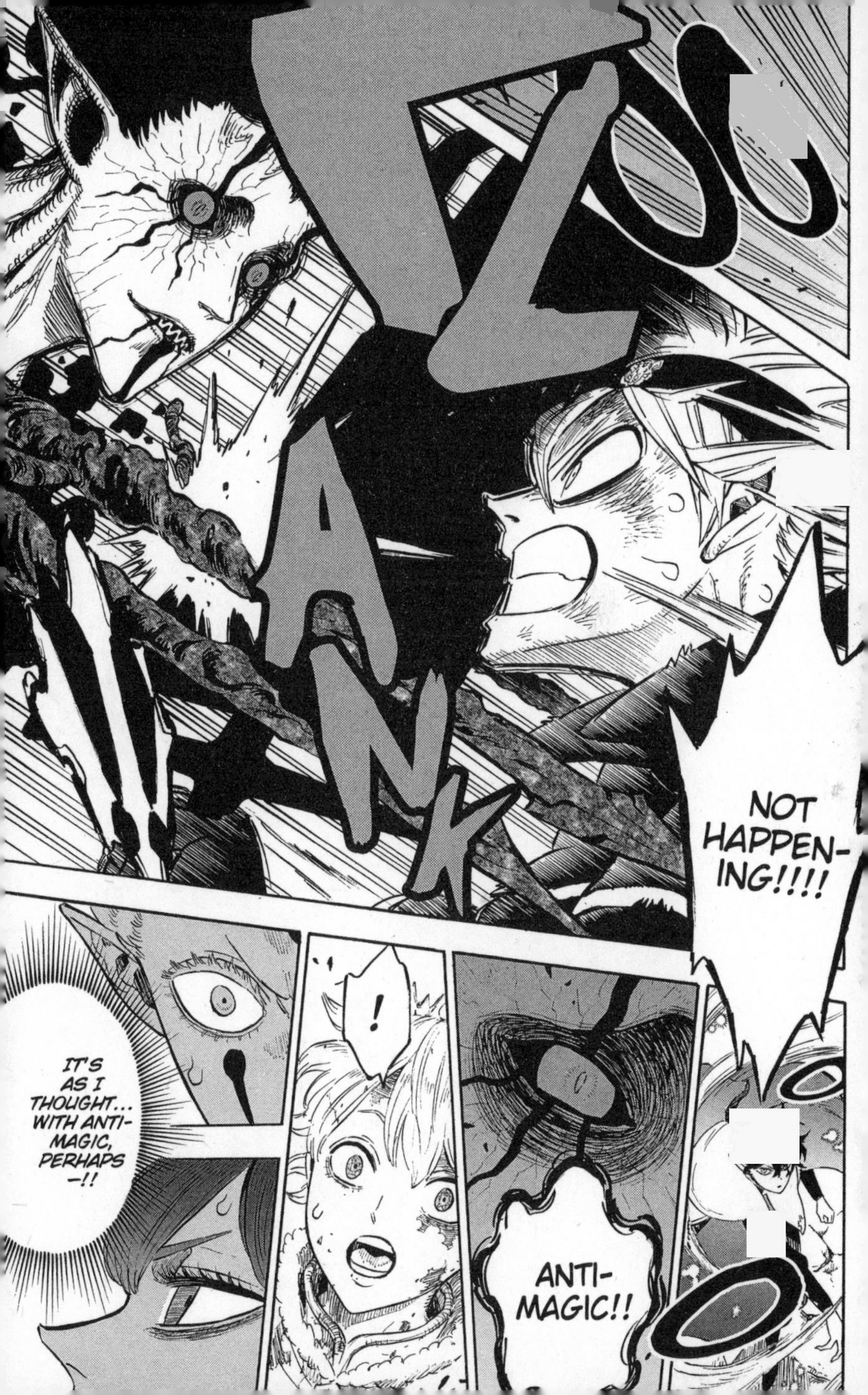
ZANK
NOT HAPPEN-ING!!!!
ANTI-MAGIC!!
!
IT'S AS I THOUGHT... WITH ANTI-MAGIC, PERHAPS—!!

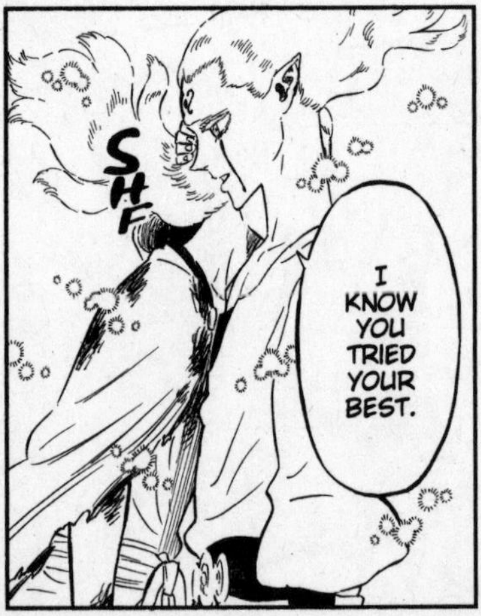
SHF
I KNOW YOU TRIED YOUR BEST.

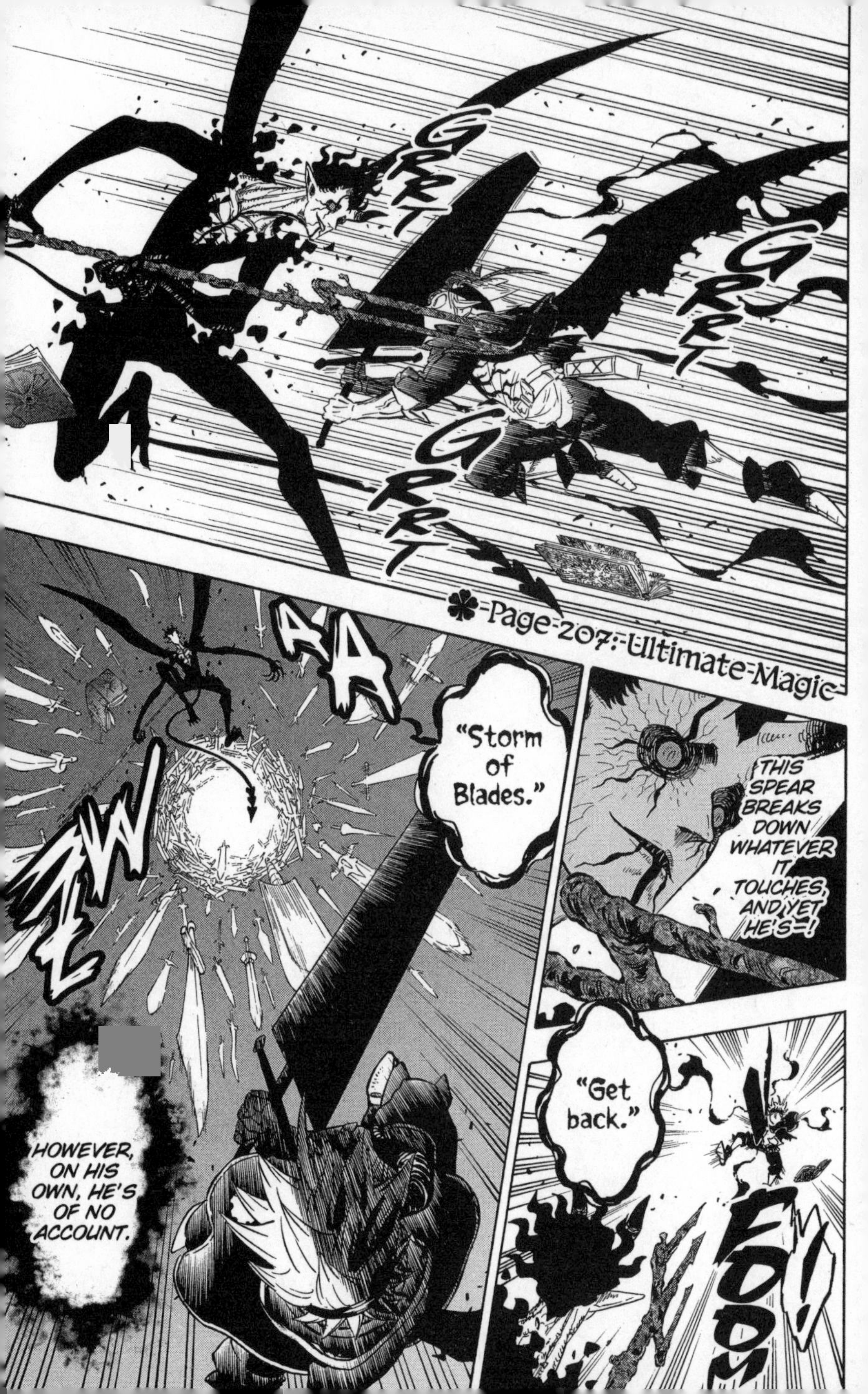
GRRT
GRRT
GRRT
Page 207: Ultimate Magic
THIS SPEAR BREAKS DOWN WHATEVER IT TOUCHES, AND YET HE'S—!
"Get back."
FOOM!
AA
"Storm of Blades."
HOWEVER, ON HIS OWN, HE'S OF NO ACCOUNT.

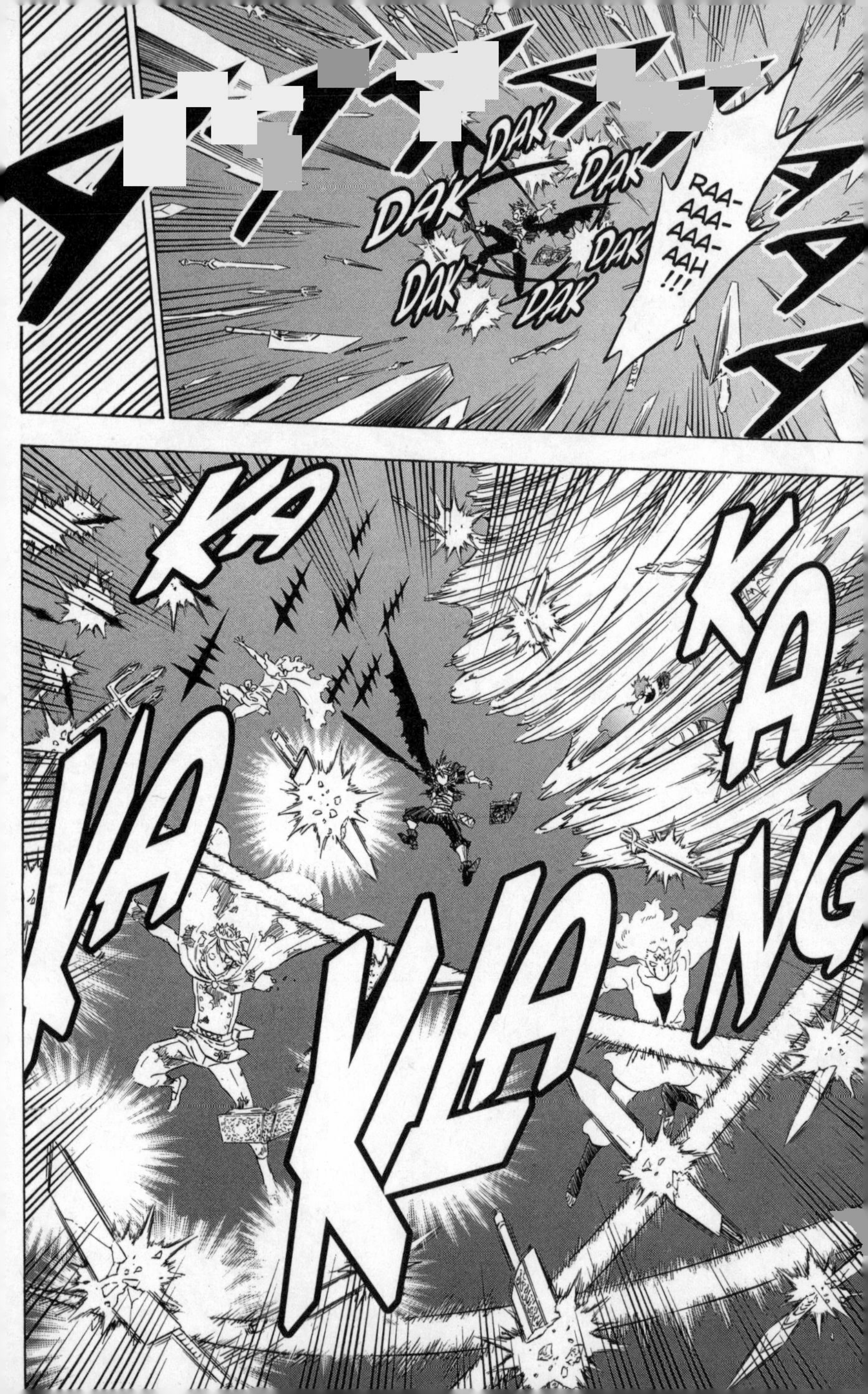
RAA-AAA-AAA-AAH!!!
DAK
DAK
DAK
DAK
DAK
DAK
DAK
KA
KA
KA
KLANG

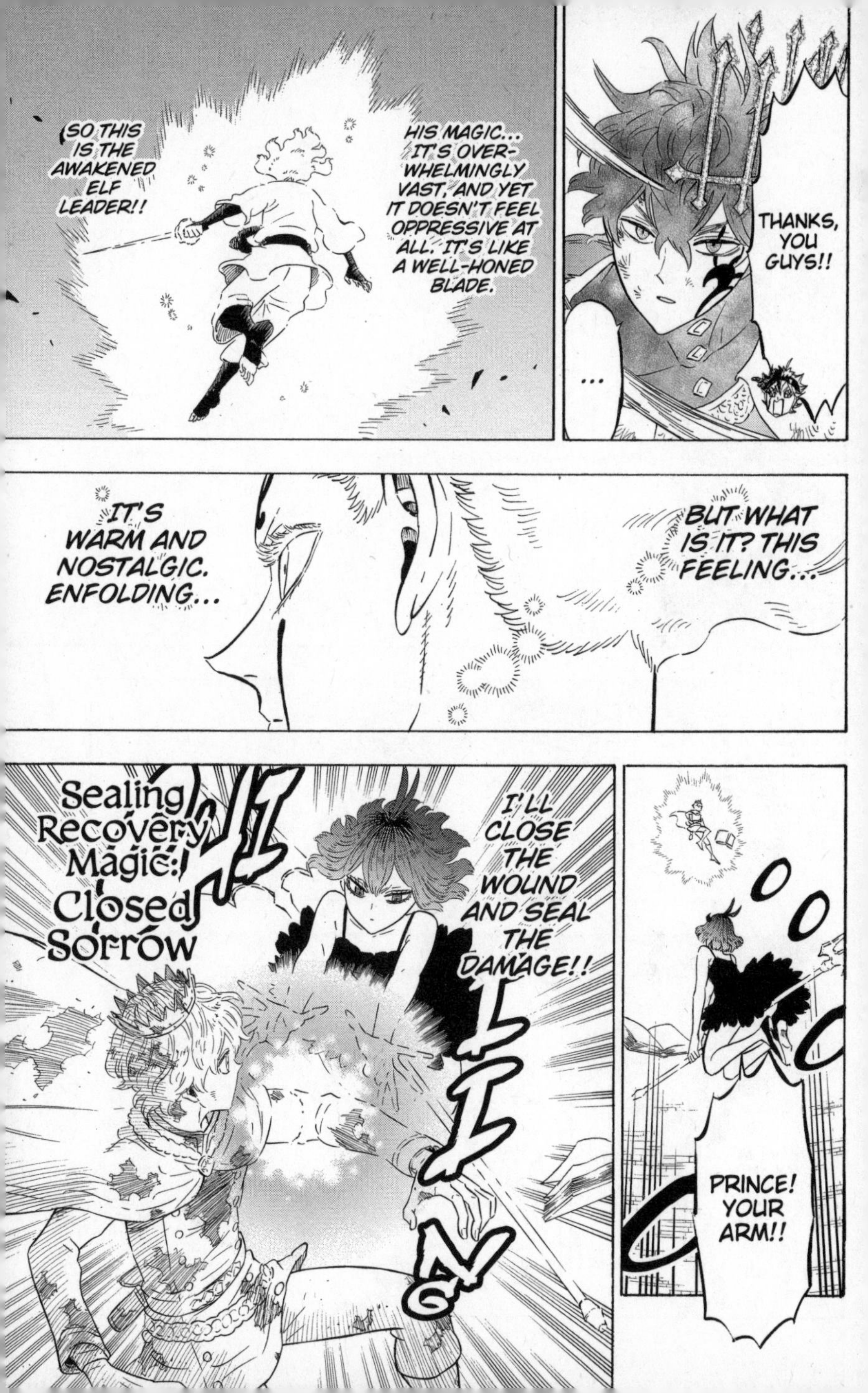
THANKS, YOU GUYS!!
...
HIS MAGIC... IT'S OVERWHELMINGLY VAST, AND YET IT DOESN'T FEEL OPPRESSIVE AT ALL. IT'S LIKE A WELL-HONED BLADE.
SO THIS IS THE AWAKENED ELF LEADER!!
BUT WHAT IS IT? THIS FEELING...
IT'S WARM AND NOSTALGIC. ENFOLDING...
PRINCE! YOUR ARM!!
I'LL CLOSE THE WOUND AND SEAL THE DAMAGE!!
Sealing Recovery Magic: Closed Sorrow

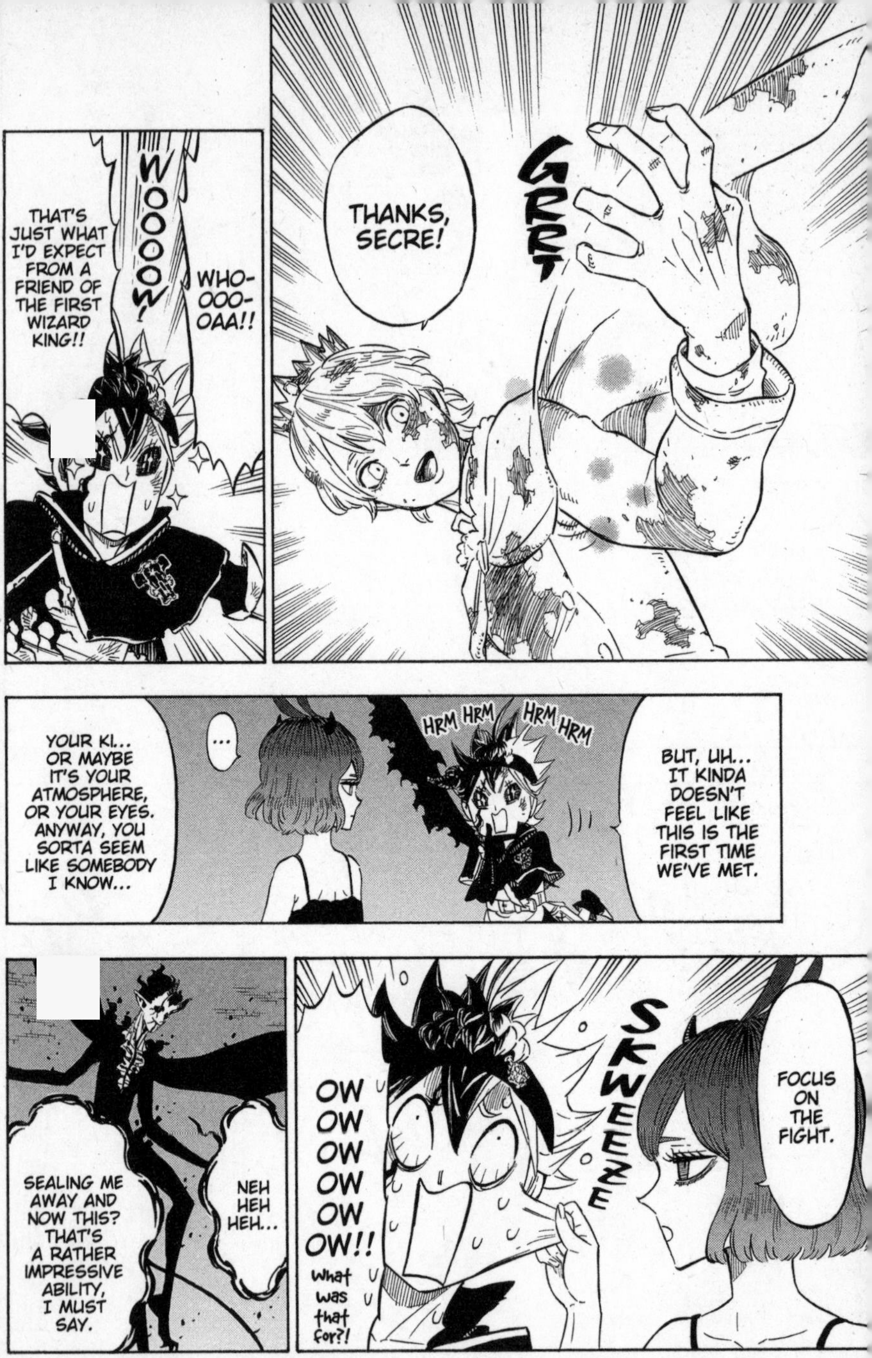
GRRT
THANKS, SECRE!
WOOOOW!
WHO-OOO-OAA!!
THAT'S JUST WHAT I'D EXPECT FROM A FRIEND OF THE FIRST WIZARD KING!!
BUT, UH... IT KINDA DOESN'T FEEL LIKE THIS IS THE FIRST TIME WE'VE MET.
HRM HRM HRM HRM
...
YOUR KI... OR MAYBE IT'S YOUR ATMOSPHERE, OR YOUR EYES. ANYWAY, YOU SORTA SEEM LIKE SOMEBODY I KNOW...
FOCUS ON THE FIGHT.
SKWEEZE
OW OW OW OW OW OW!!
what was that for?!
NEH HEH HEH...
SEALING ME AWAY AND NOW THIS? THAT'S A RATHER IMPRESSIVE ABILITY, I MUST SAY.

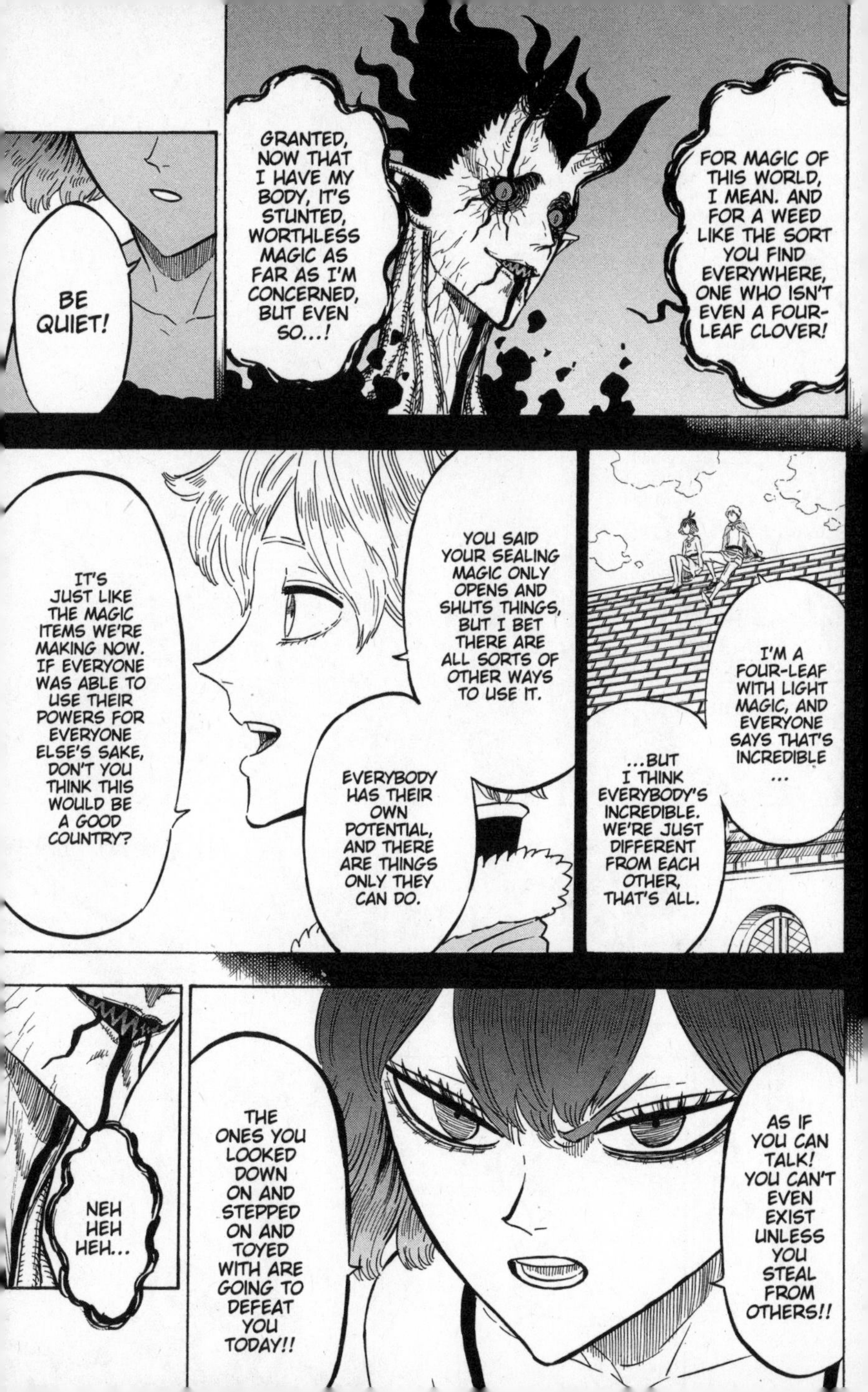

FOR MAGIC OF THIS WORLD, I MEAN. AND FOR A WEED LIKE THE SORT YOU FIND EVERYWHERE, ONE WHO ISN'T EVEN A FOUR-LEAF CLOVER!
GRANTED, NOW THAT I HAVE MY BODY, IT'S STUNTED, WORTHLESS MAGIC AS FAR AS I'M CONCERNED, BUT EVEN SO...!
BE QUIET!
I'M A FOUR-LEAF WITH LIGHT MAGIC, AND EVERYONE SAYS THAT'S INCREDIBLE...
...BUT I THINK EVERYBODY'S INCREDIBLE. WE'RE JUST DIFFERENT FROM EACH OTHER, THAT'S ALL.
YOU SAID YOUR SEALING MAGIC ONLY OPENS AND SHUTS THINGS, BUT I BET THERE ARE ALL SORTS OF OTHER WAYS TO USE IT.
EVERYBODY HAS THEIR OWN POTENTIAL, AND THERE ARE THINGS ONLY THEY CAN DO.
IT'S JUST LIKE THE MAGIC ITEMS WE'RE MAKING NOW. IF EVERYONE WAS ABLE TO USE THEIR POWERS FOR EVERYONE ELSE'S SAKE, DON'T YOU THINK THIS WOULD BE A GOOD COUNTRY?
AS IF YOU CAN TALK! YOU CAN'T EVEN EXIST UNLESS YOU STEAL FROM OTHERS!!
THE ONES YOU LOOKED DOWN ON AND STEPPED ON AND TOYED WITH ARE GOING TO DEFEAT YOU TODAY!!
NEH HEH HEH...

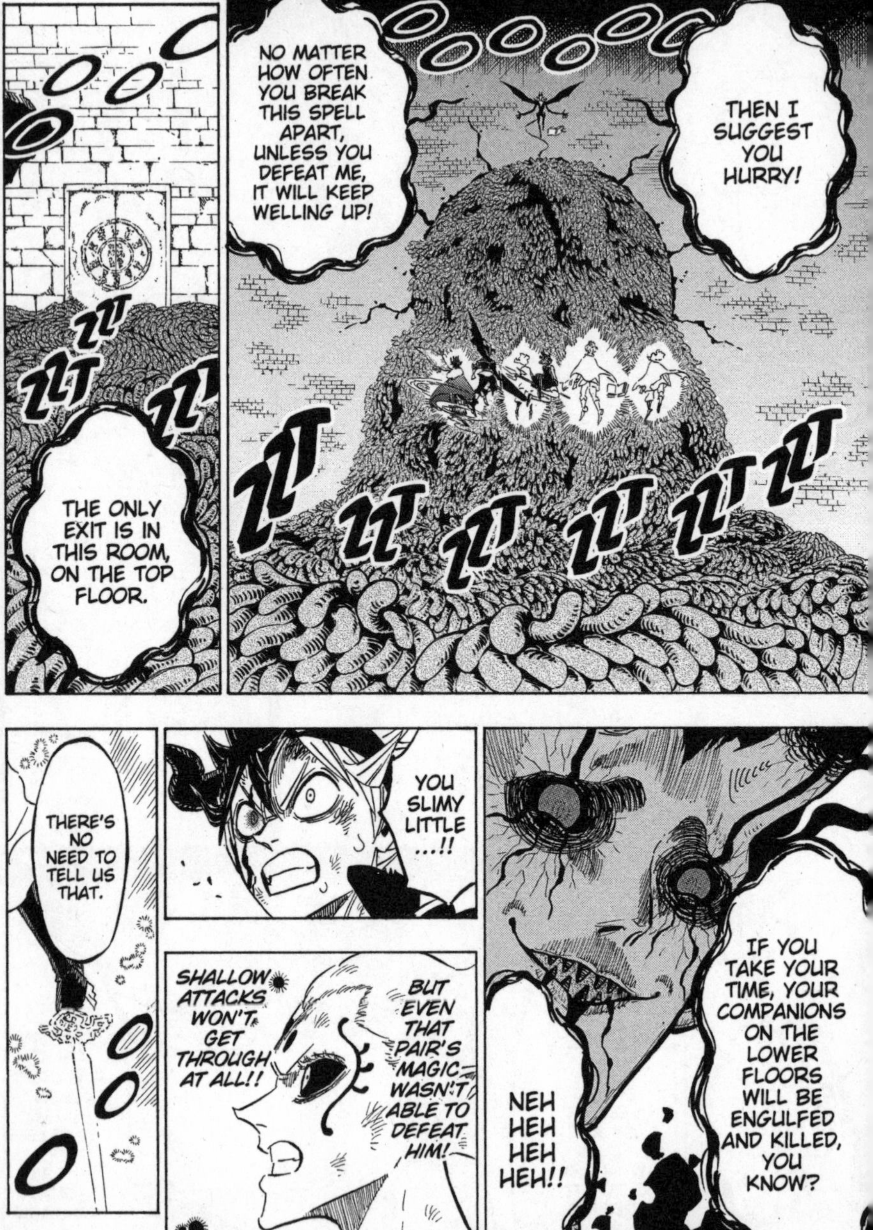
NO MATTER HOW OFTEN YOU BREAK THIS SPELL APART, UNLESS YOU DEFEAT ME, IT WILL KEEP WELLING UP!
THEN I SUGGEST YOU HURRY!
ZZT
ZZT
ZZT
ZZT
ZZT
ZZT
THE ONLY EXIT IS IN THIS ROOM, ON THE TOP FLOOR.
ZZT
ZZT
IF YOU TAKE YOUR TIME, YOUR COMPANIONS ON THE LOWER FLOORS WILL BE ENGULFED AND KILLED, YOU KNOW?
NEH HEH HEH HEH!!
YOU SLIMY LITTLE ...!!
BUT EVEN THAT PAIR'S MAGIC WASN'T ABLE TO DEFEAT HIM!
SHALLOW ATTACKS WON'T GET THROUGH AT ALL!!
THERE'S NO NEED TO TELL US THAT.

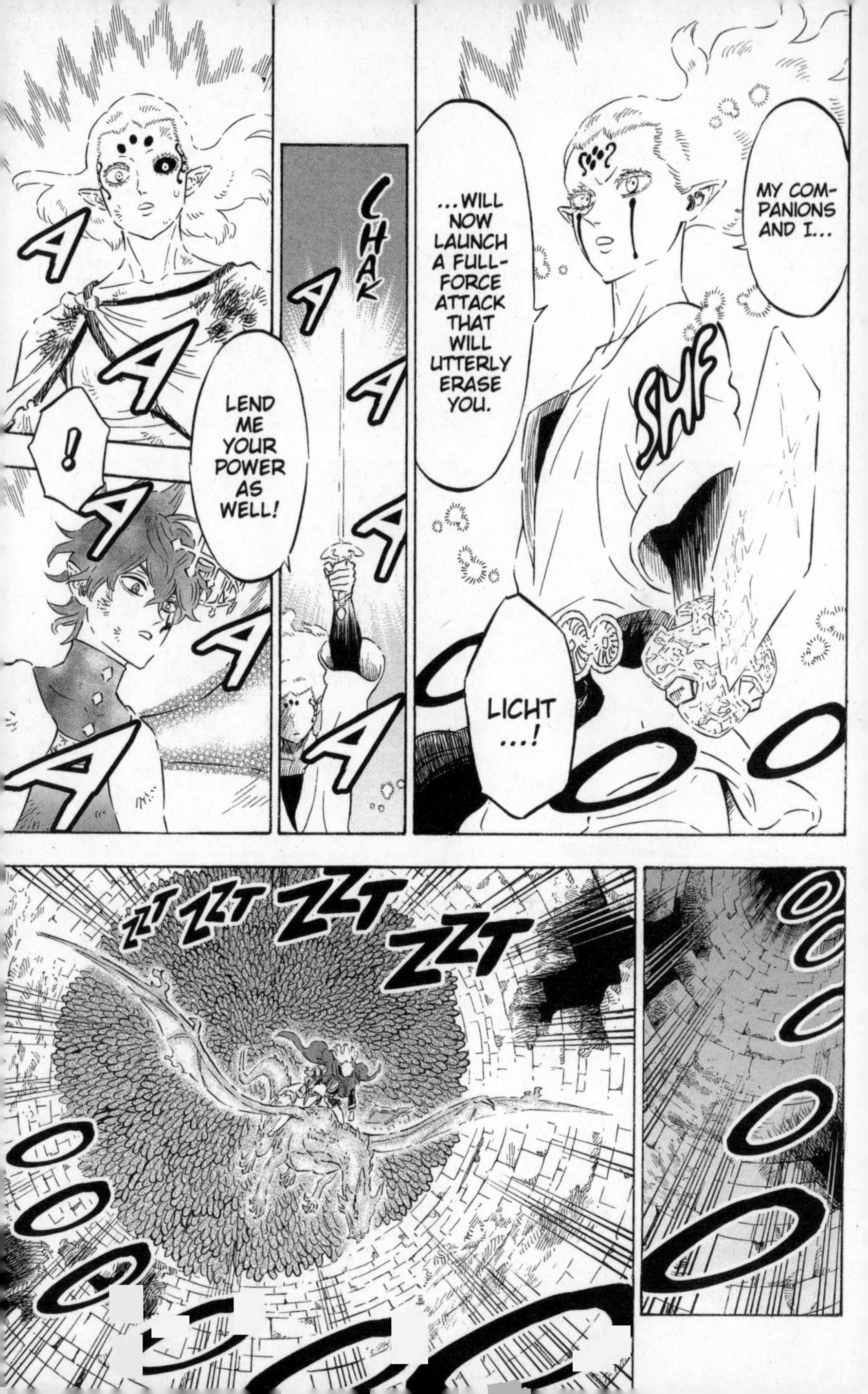
MY COMPANIONS AND I...
...WILL NOW LAUNCH A FULL-FORCE ATTACK THAT WILL UTTERLY ERASE YOU.
SHF
LICHT ...!
OOOOO
CHAK
AAAA
LEND ME YOUR POWER AS WELL!
!
AAAAA
OOOOOOO
ZZT ZZT ZZT ZZT
OOOO

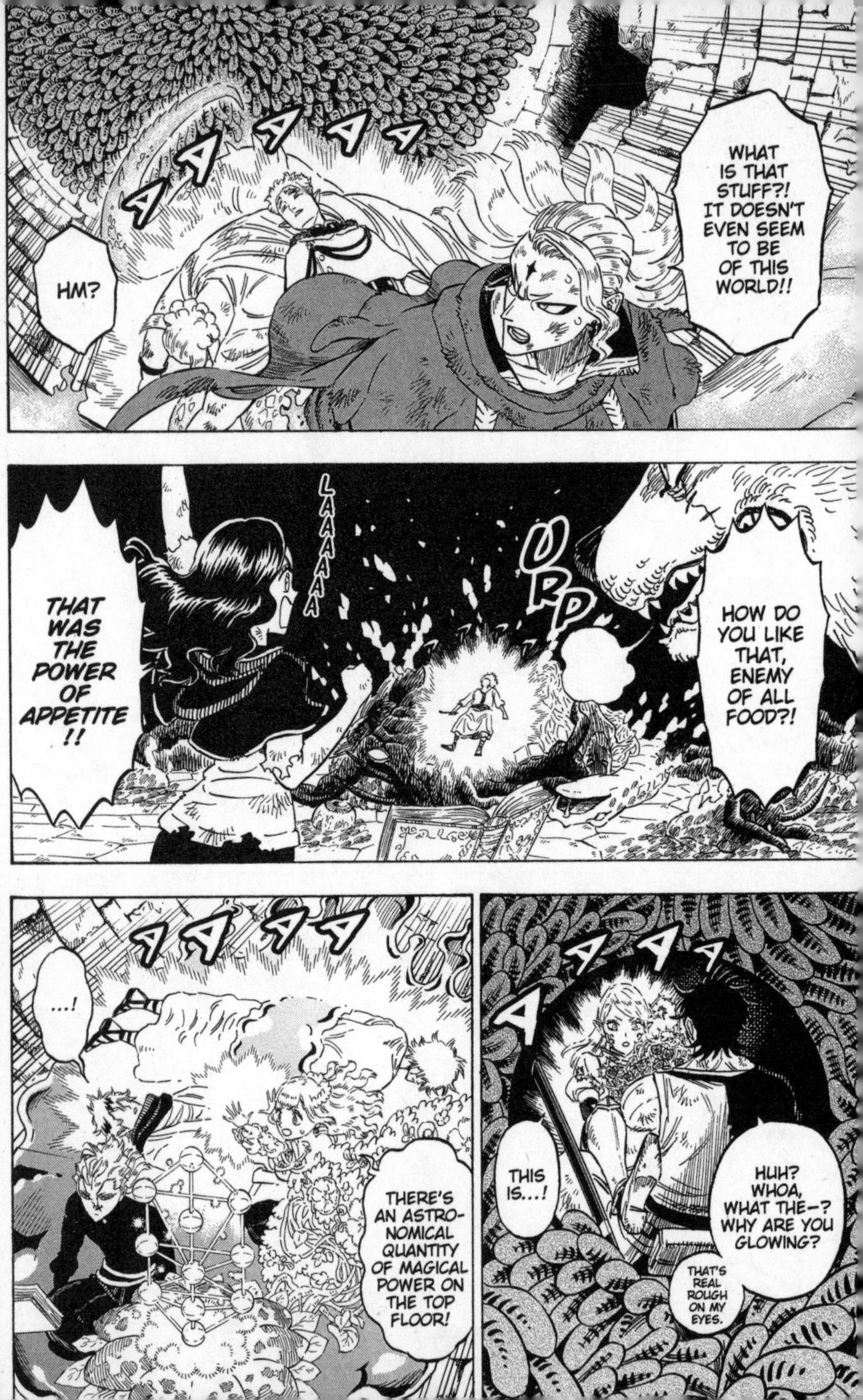
WHAT IS THAT STUFF?! IT DOESN'T EVEN SEEM TO BE OF THIS WORLD!!
AAAAAA
HM?
HOW DO YOU LIKE THAT, ENEMY OF ALL FOOD?!
URP
LAAAAAAA
THAT WAS THE POWER OF APPETITE!!
AAAAA
HUH? WHOA, WHAT THE—? WHY ARE YOU GLOWING?
THAT'S REAL ROUGH ON MY EYES.
THIS IS...!
AAAAA
...!
THERE'S AN ASTRONOMICAL QUANTITY OF MAGICAL POWER ON THE TOP FLOOR!

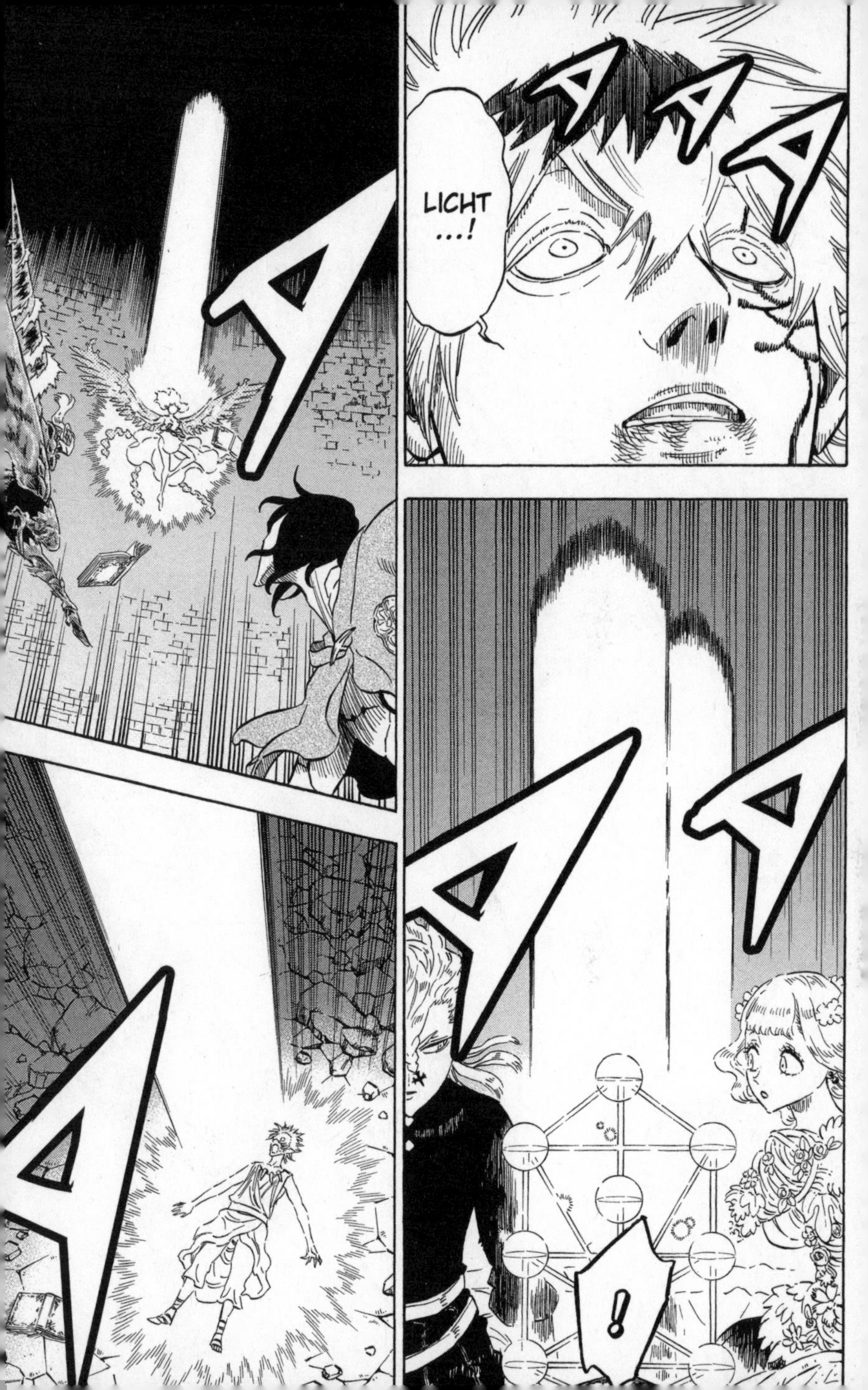
AAAA
LICHT
...!
A
AA
!
A

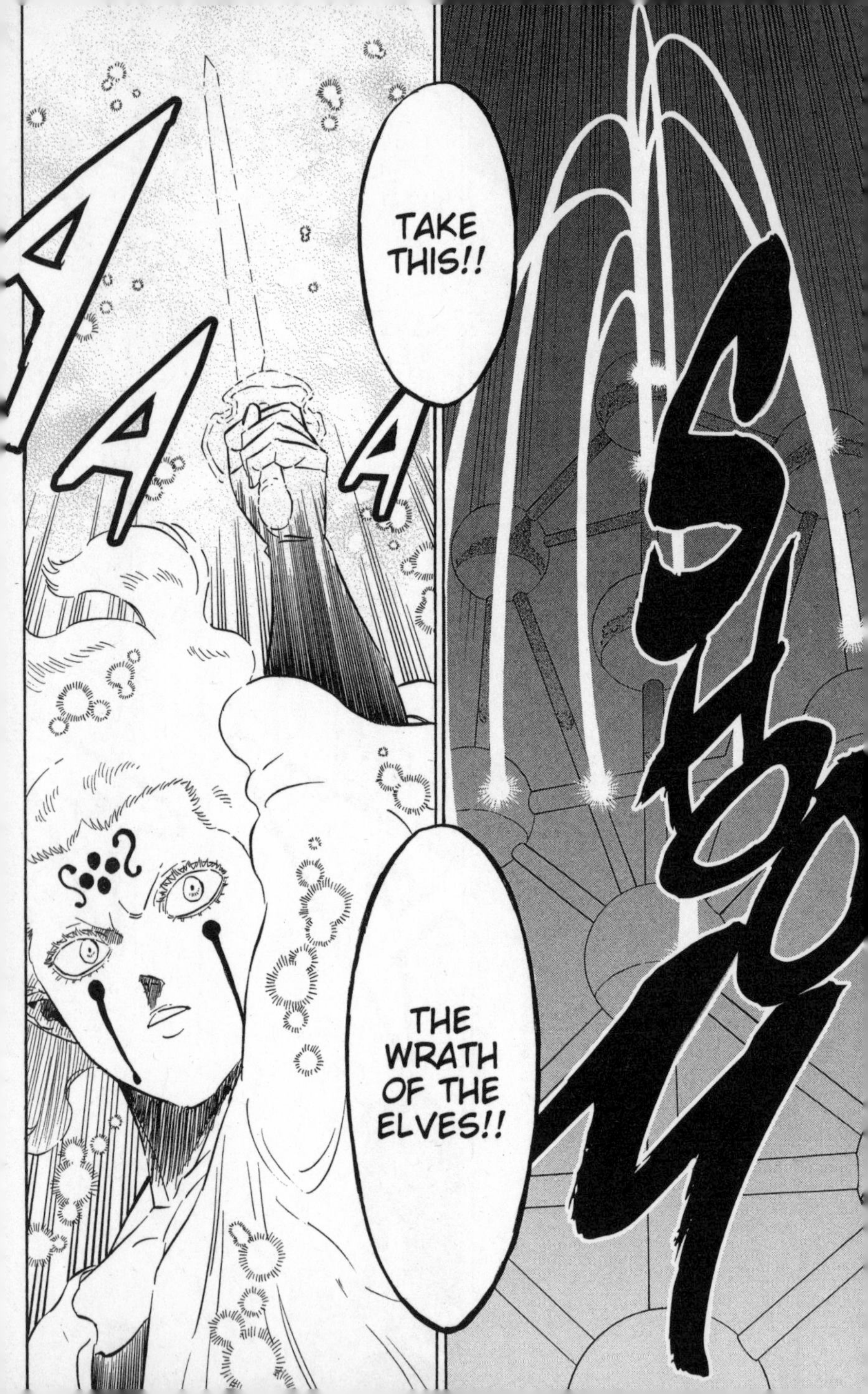
TAKE THIS!!
AAAA
THE WRATH OF THE ELVES!!

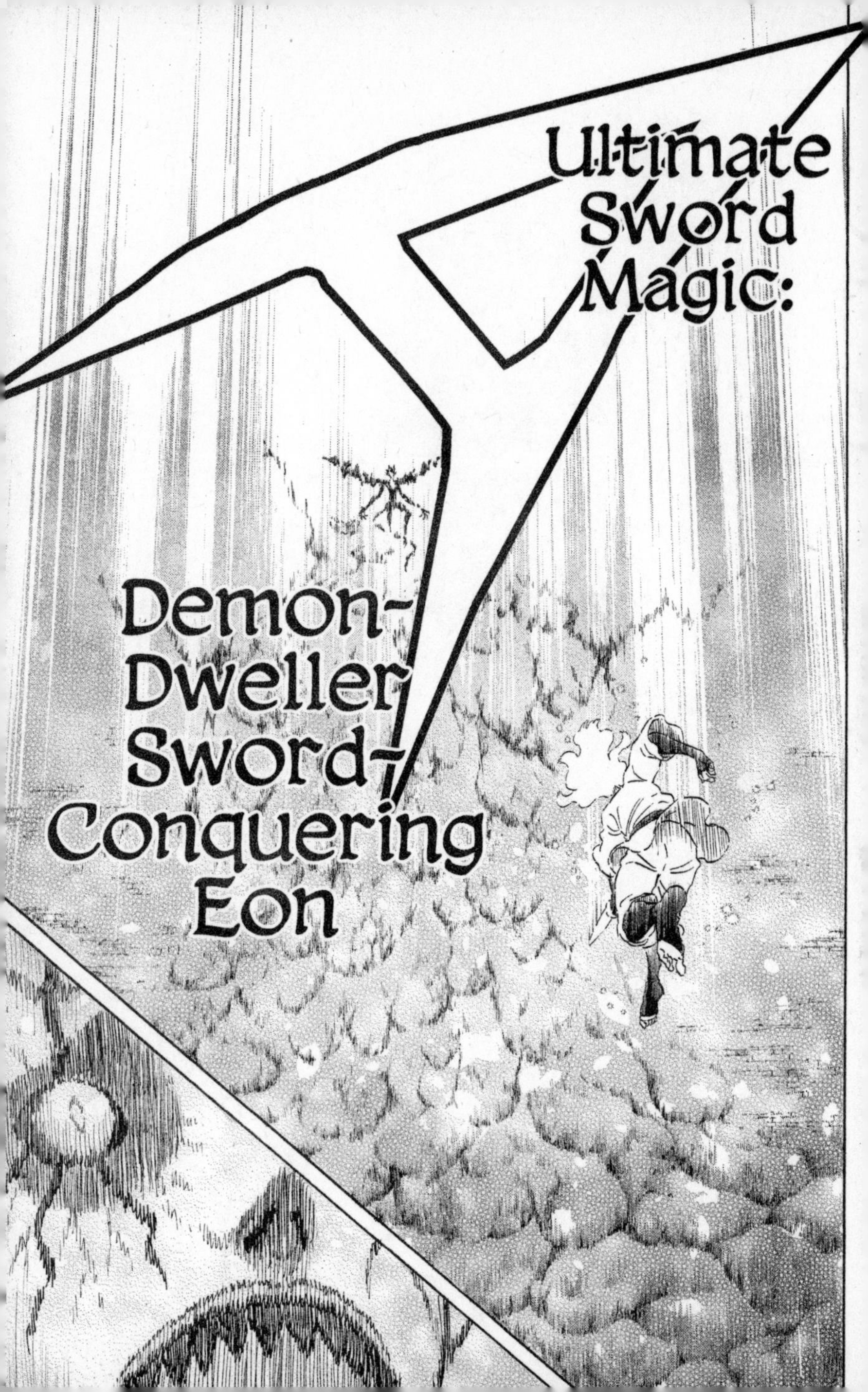
Ultimate Sword Magic:
Demon-Dweller Sword-Conquering Eon

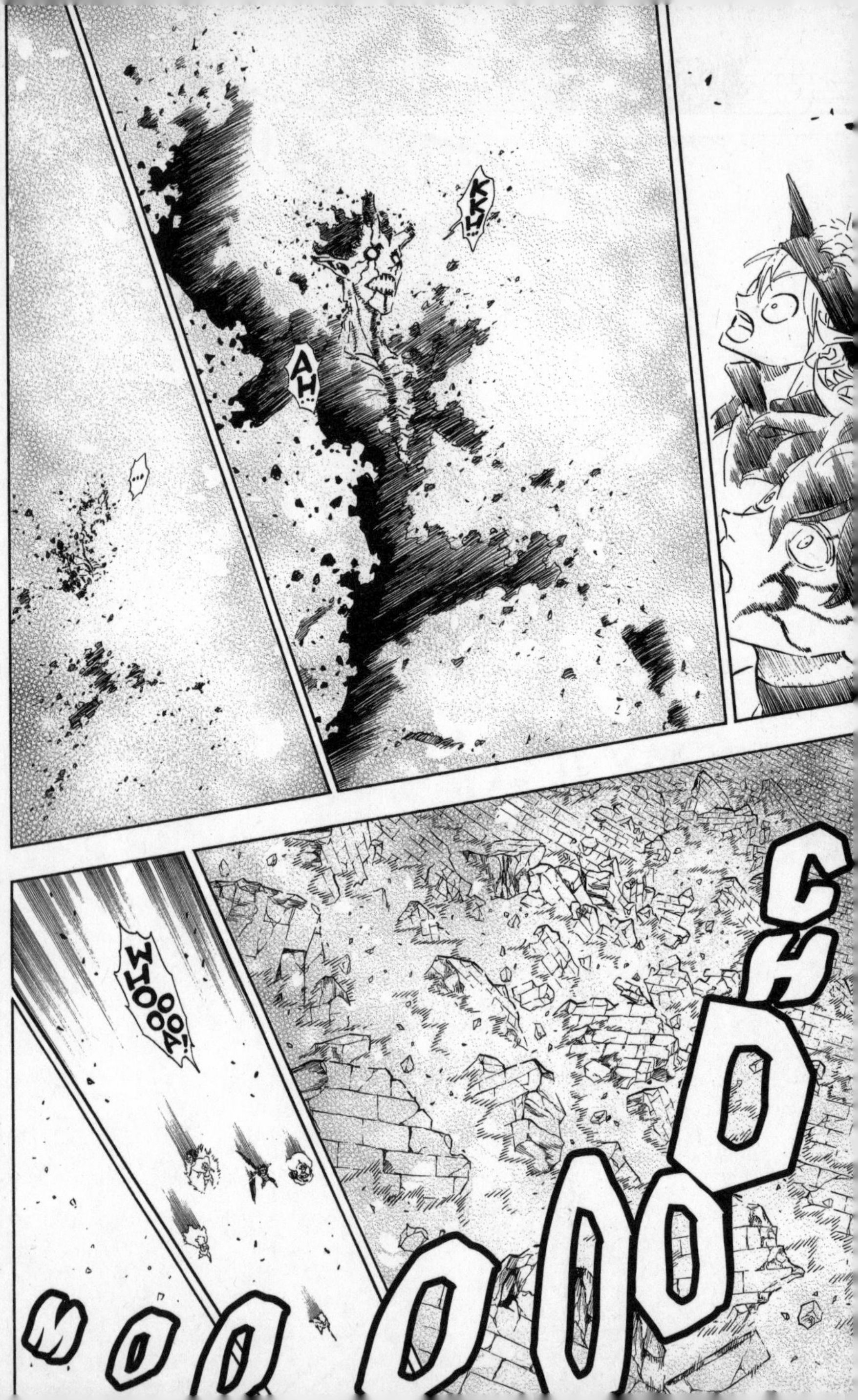
KKH!...
AH...
...
CHDOOOOOM
WHOOOOA!

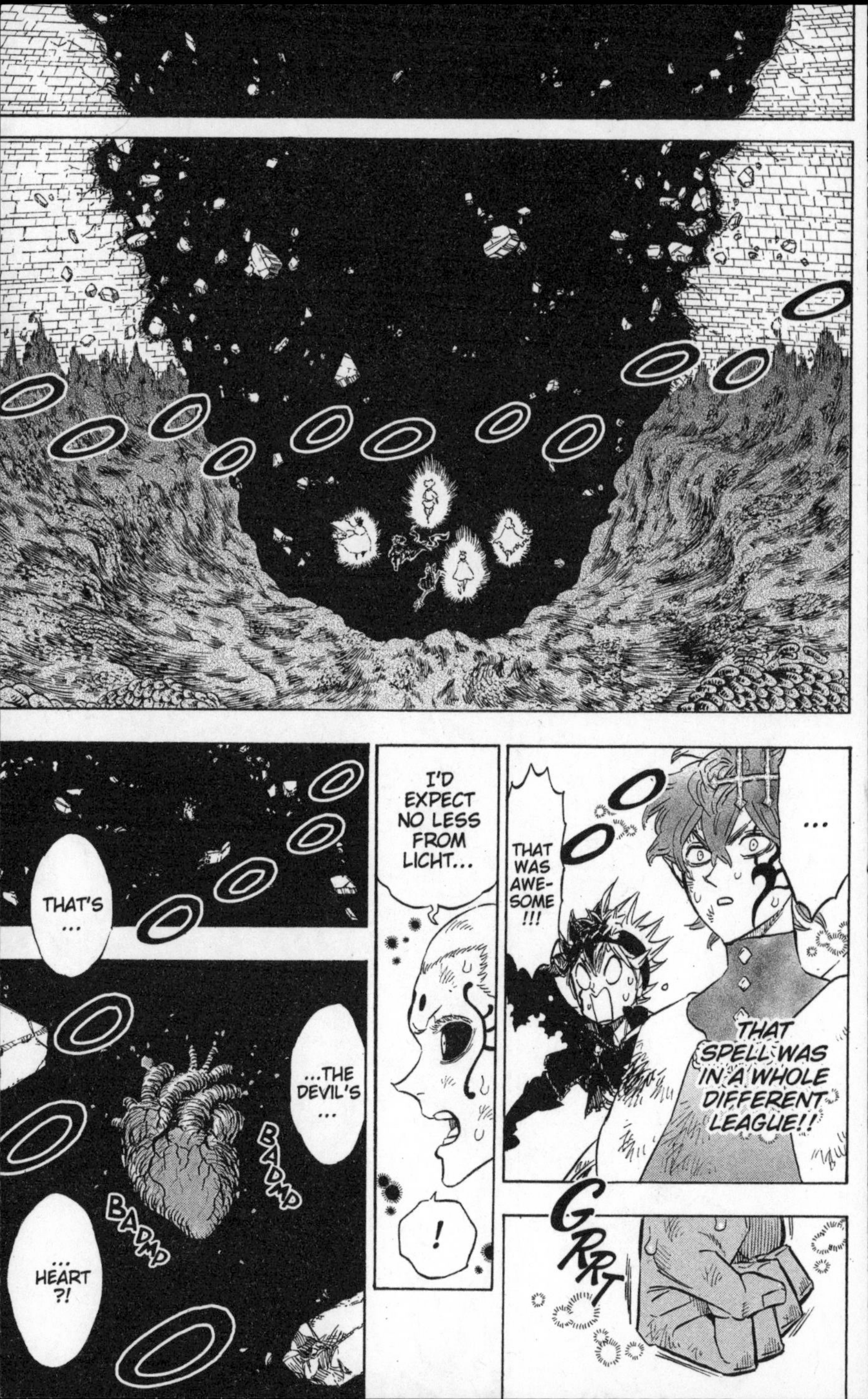
...
THAT WAS AWE-SOME!!!
THAT SPELL WAS IN A WHOLE DIFFERENT LEAGUE!!
GRRRT
I'D EXPECT NO LESS FROM LICHT...
!
THAT'S ...
...THE DEVIL'S ...
BADMP
BADMP
... HEART ?!

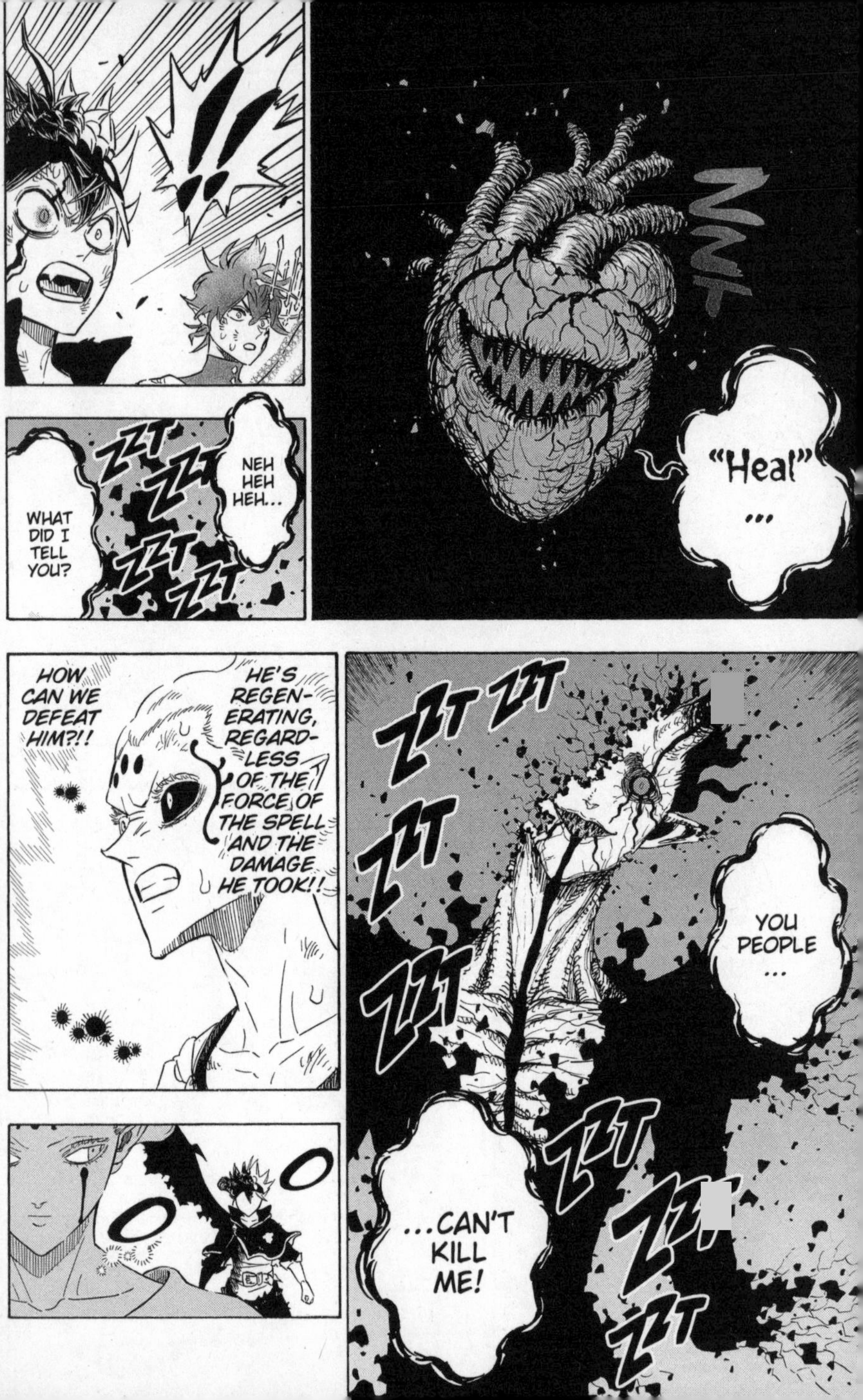
ZZZT
"Heal"...
ZZZT
ZZZT
ZZZT
ZZZT
NEH HEH HEH...
WHAT DID I TELL YOU?
ZZZT ZZZT
ZZZT
ZZZT
YOU PEOPLE...
...CAN'T KILL ME!
ZZZT
ZZZT
ZZZT
HE'S REGENERATING, REGARDLESS OF THE FORCE OF THE SPELL AND THE DAMAGE HE TOOK!!
HOW CAN WE DEFEAT HIM?!!

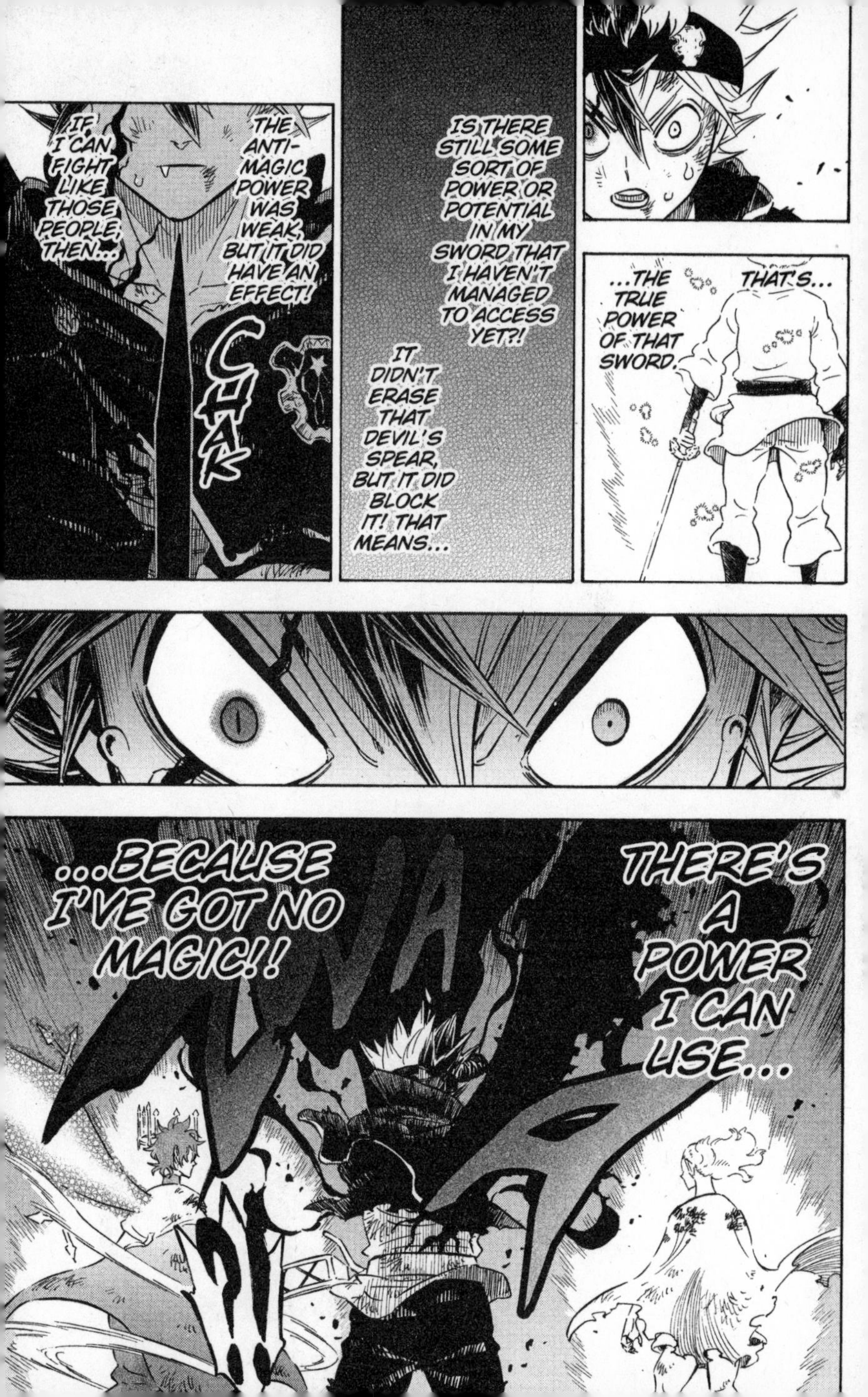
THAT'S...
...THE TRUE POWER OF THAT SWORD.
IS THERE STILL SOME SORT OF POWER OR POTENTIAL IN MY SWORD THAT I HAVEN'T MANAGED TO ACCESS YET?!
IT DIDN'T ERASE THAT DEVIL'S SPEAR, BUT IT DID BLOCK IT! THAT MEANS...
THE ANTI-MAGIC POWER WAS WEAK, BUT IT DID HAVE AN EFFECT!
IF I CAN FIGHT LIKE THOSE PEOPLE, THEN...
CHAK
THERE'S A POWER I CAN USE...
...BECAUSE I'VE GOT NO MAGIC!!

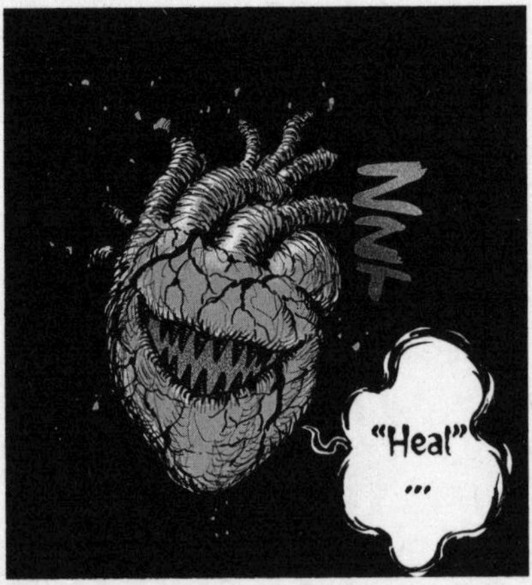
"Heal"
...

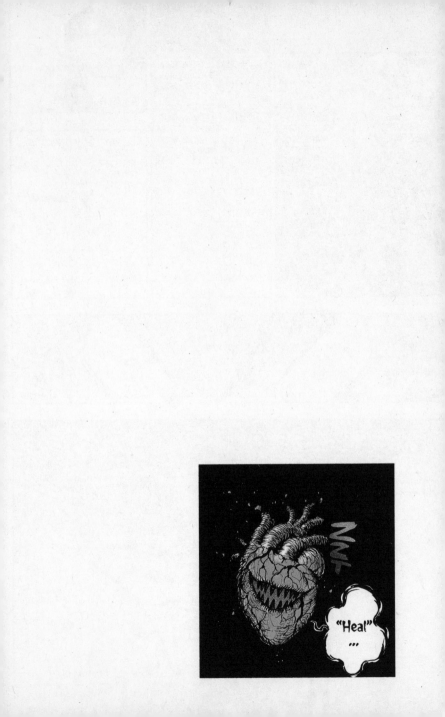

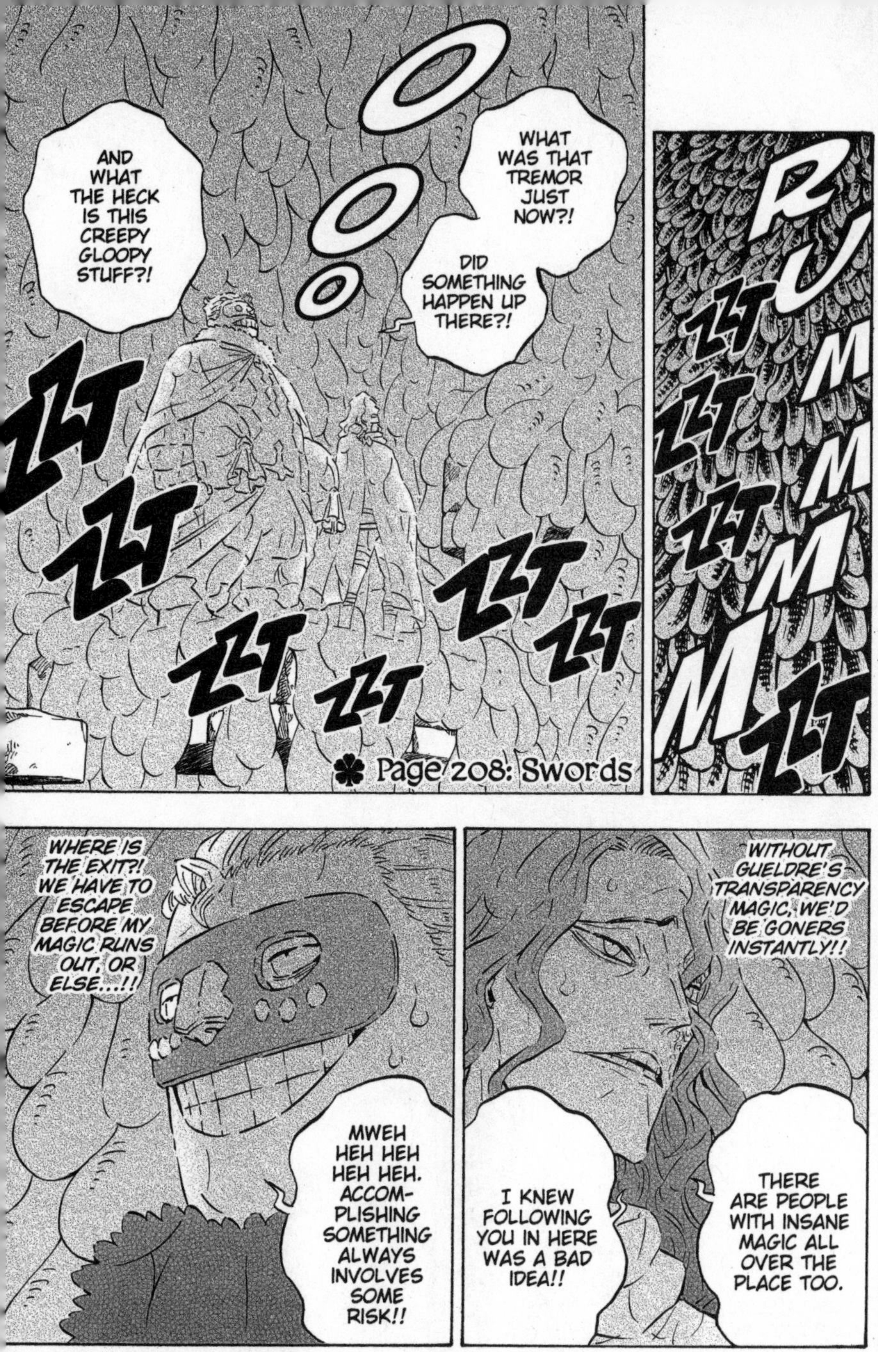
RUMMMMM
ZZZT
ZZZT
ZZZT
ZZZT
WHAT WAS THAT TREMOR JUST NOW?!
DID SOMETHING HAPPEN UP THERE?!
AND WHAT THE HECK IS THIS CREEPY GLOOPY STUFF?!
ZZZT
ZZZT
ZZZT
ZZZT
ZZZT
ZZZT
Page 208: Swords
WITHOUT GUELDRE'S TRANSPARENCY MAGIC, WE'D BE GONERS INSTANTLY!!
THERE ARE PEOPLE WITH INSANE MAGIC ALL OVER THE PLACE TOO.
I KNEW FOLLOWING YOU IN HERE WAS A BAD IDEA!!
WHERE IS THE EXIT?! WE HAVE TO ESCAPE BEFORE MY MAGIC RUNS OUT, OR ELSE...!!
MWEH HEH HEH HEH HEH. ACCOMPLISHING SOMETHING ALWAYS INVOLVES SOME RISK!!

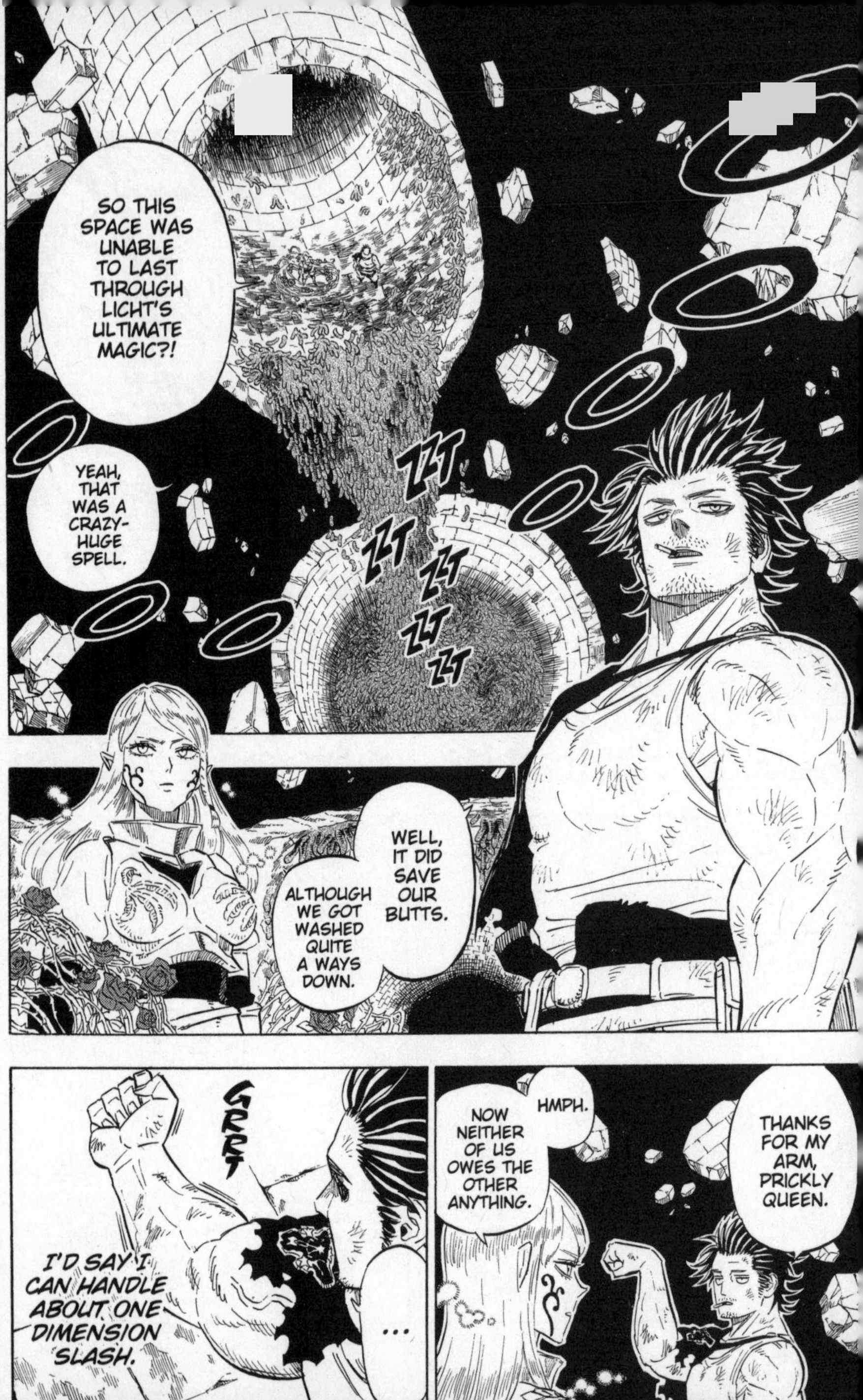
SO THIS SPACE WAS UNABLE TO LAST THROUGH LICHT'S ULTIMATE MAGIC?!
YEAH, THAT WAS A CRAZY-HUGE SPELL.
ZZT ZZT ZZT ZZT ZZT
WELL, IT DID SAVE OUR BUTTS.
ALTHOUGH WE GOT WASHED QUITE A WAYS DOWN.
THANKS FOR MY ARM, PRICKLY QUEEN.
HMPH.
NOW NEITHER OF US OWES THE OTHER ANYTHING.
GRRT
I'D SAY I CAN HANDLE ABOUT ONE DIMENSION SLASH.
...

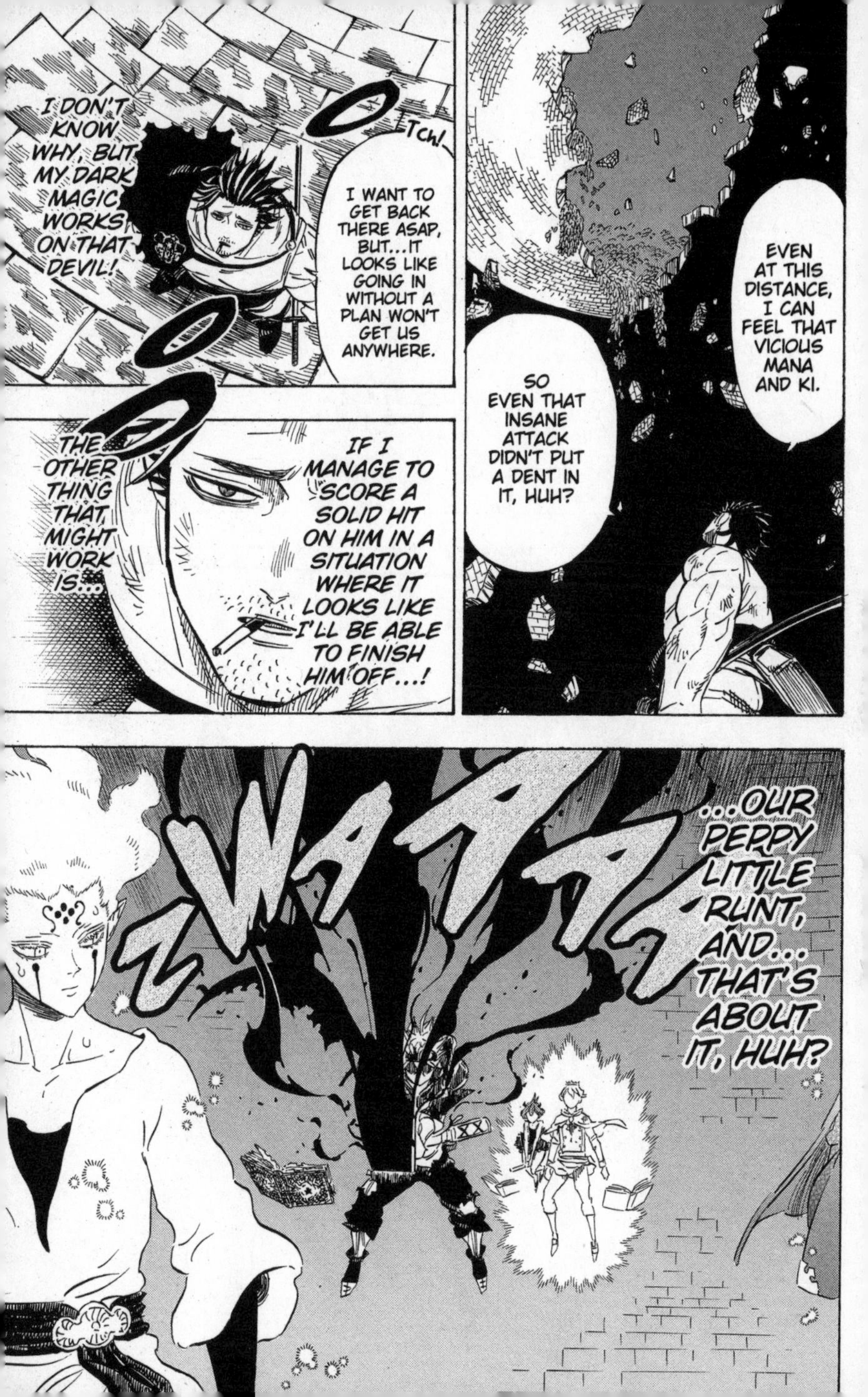
EVEN AT THIS DISTANCE, I CAN FEEL THAT VICIOUS MANA AND KI.
SO EVEN THAT INSANE ATTACK DIDN'T PUT A DENT IN IT, HUH?
Tch!
I WANT TO GET BACK THERE ASAP, BUT...IT LOOKS LIKE GOING IN WITHOUT A PLAN WON'T GET US ANYWHERE.
I DON'T KNOW WHY, BUT MY DARK MAGIC WORKS ON THAT DEVIL!
IF I MANAGE TO SCORE A SOLID HIT ON HIM IN A SITUATION WHERE IT LOOKS LIKE I'LL BE ABLE TO FINISH HIM OFF...!
THE OTHER THING THAT MIGHT WORK IS...
ZWAAA
...OUR PEPPY LITTLE RUNT, AND... THAT'S ABOUT IT, HUH?

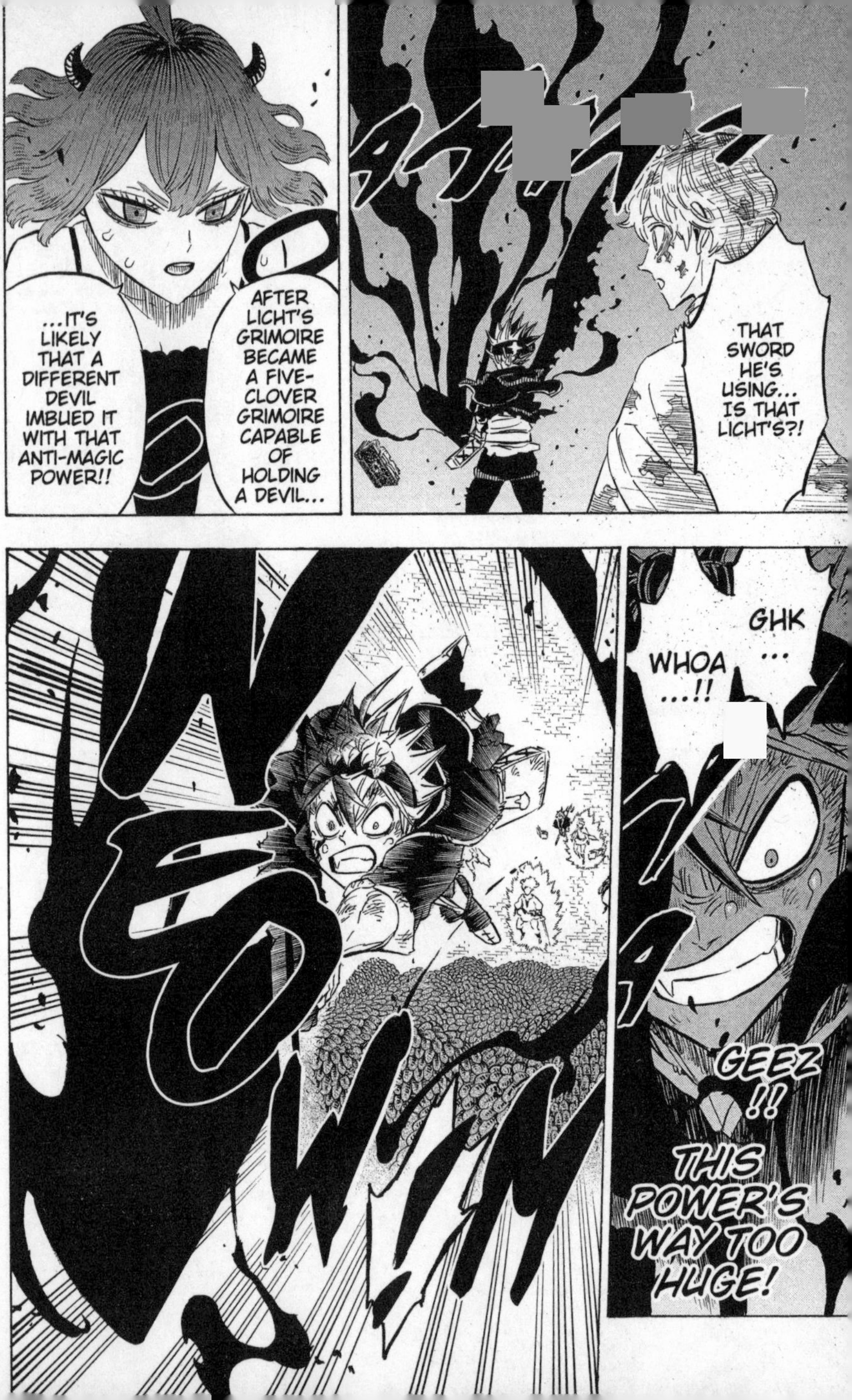
THAT SWORD HE'S USING... IS THAT LICHT'S?!
AFTER LICHT'S GRIMOIRE BECAME A FIVE-CLOVER GRIMOIRE CAPABLE OF HOLDING A DEVIL...
...IT'S LIKELY THAT A DIFFERENT DEVIL IMBUED IT WITH THAT ANTI-MAGIC POWER!!
GHK...
WHOA...!!
GEEZ!!
THIS POWER'S WAY TOO HUGE!

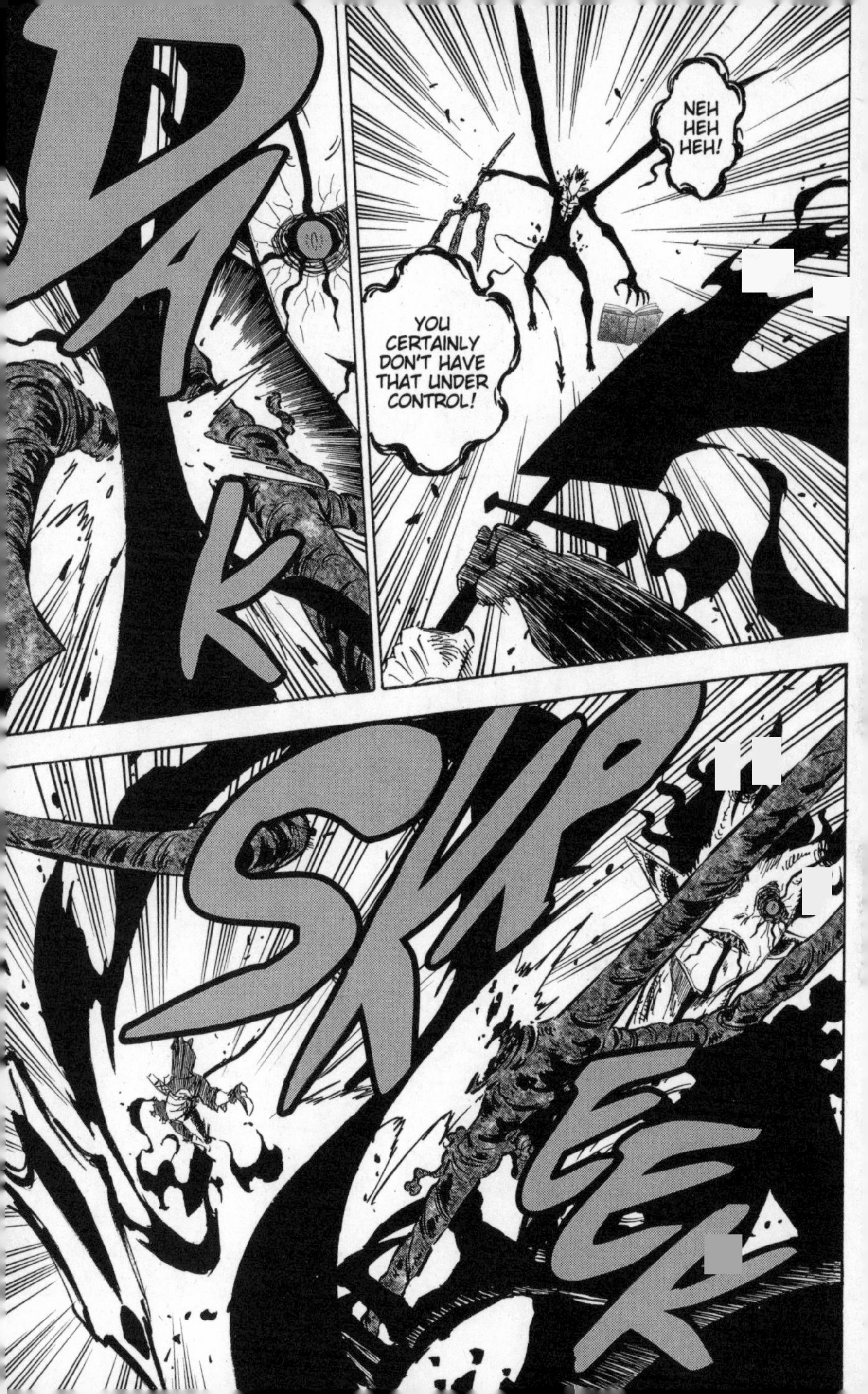
NEH HEH HEH!
YOU CERTAINLY DON'T HAVE THAT UNDER CONTROL!
DAK

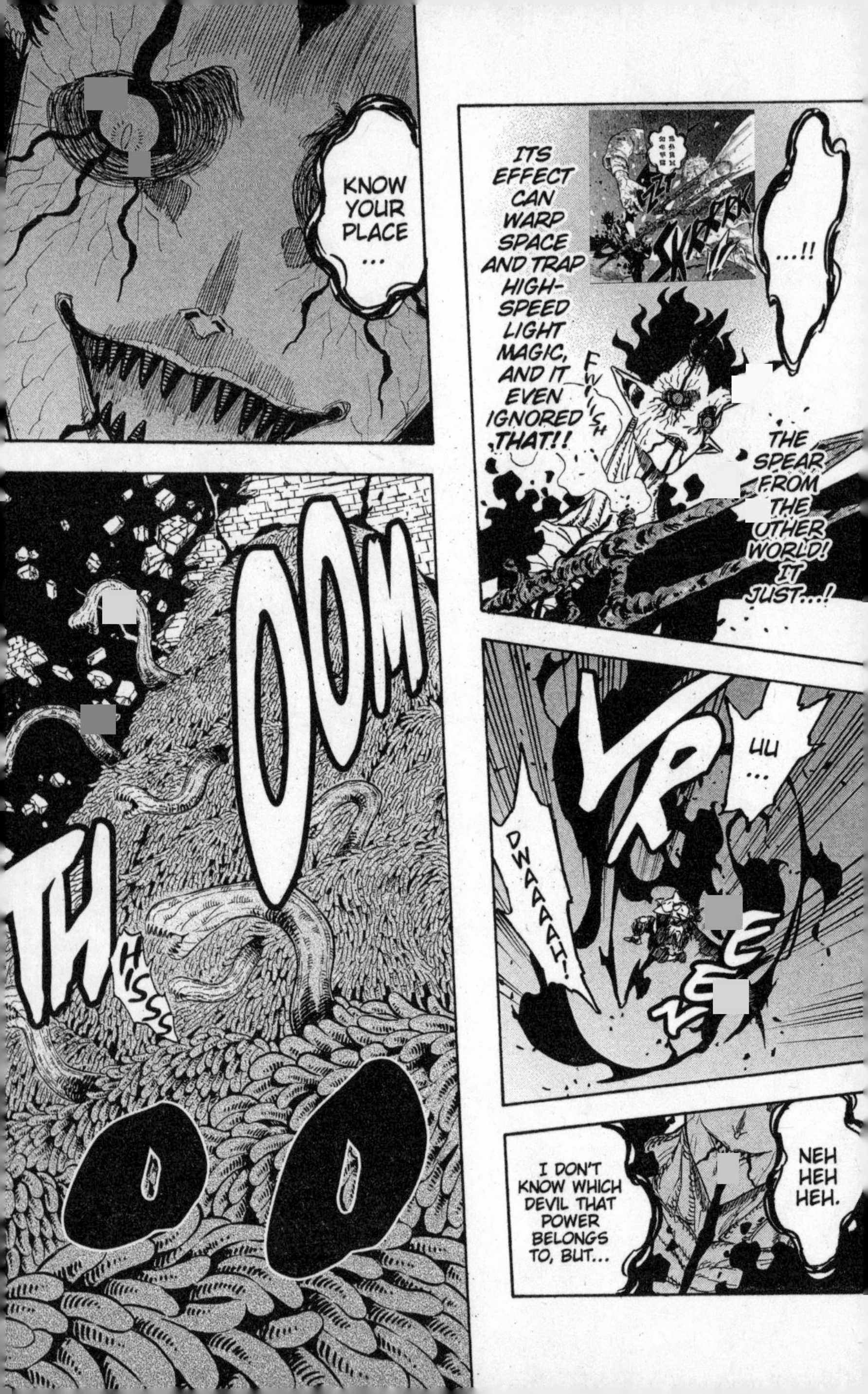
...!!
THE SPEAR FROM THE OTHER WORLD! IT JUST...!
ITS EFFECT CAN WARP SPACE AND TRAP HIGH-SPEED LIGHT MAGIC, AND IT EVEN IGNORED THAT!!
SZZT
SKRRRK
FWISH
UU...
DWAAAAAH!
NEH HEH HEH.
I DON'T KNOW WHICH DEVIL THAT POWER BELONGS TO, BUT...
KNOW YOUR PLACE ...
THOOOOM
HISSS

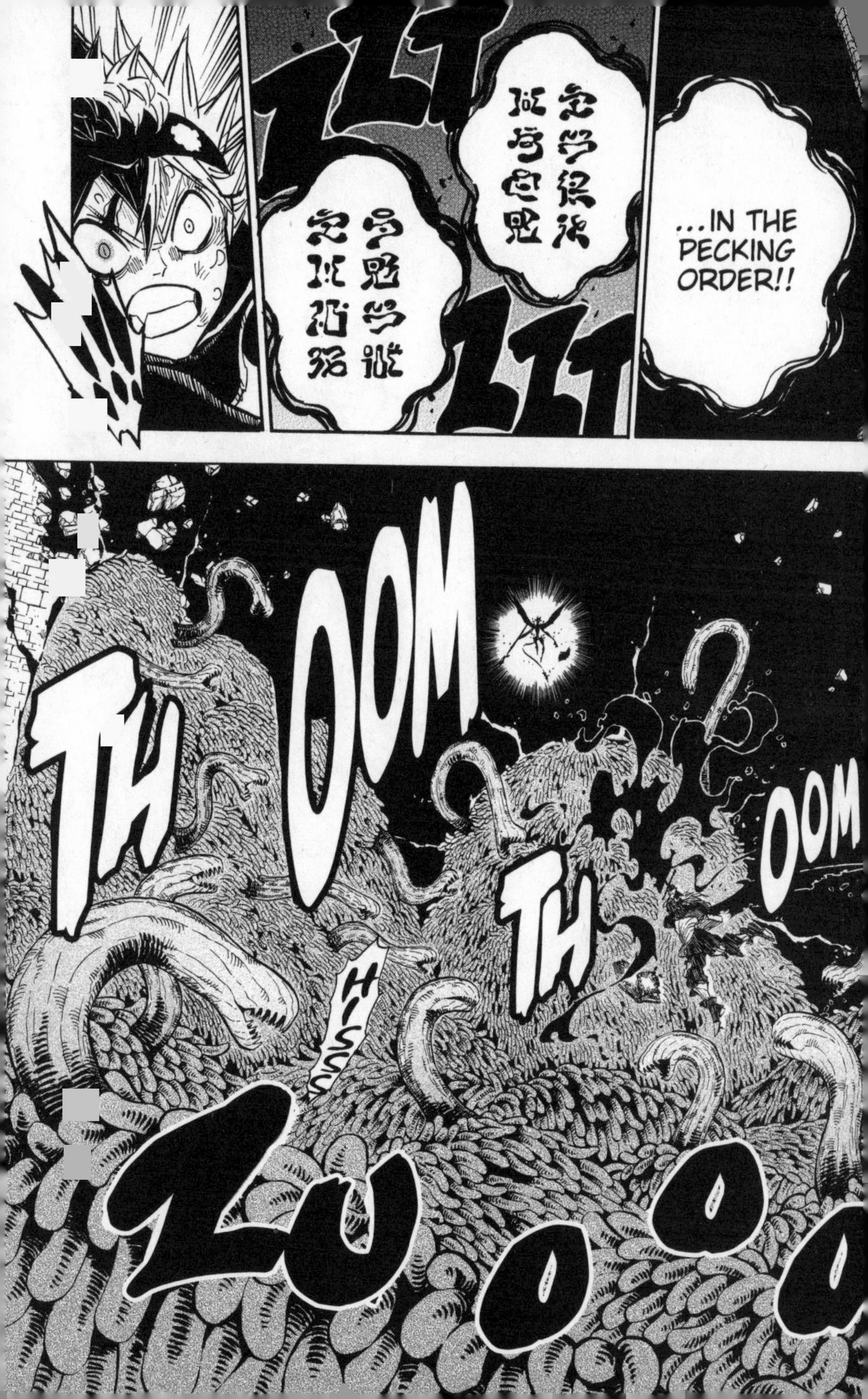
...IN THE PECKING ORDER!!
THOOM
THOOM
HISSSS

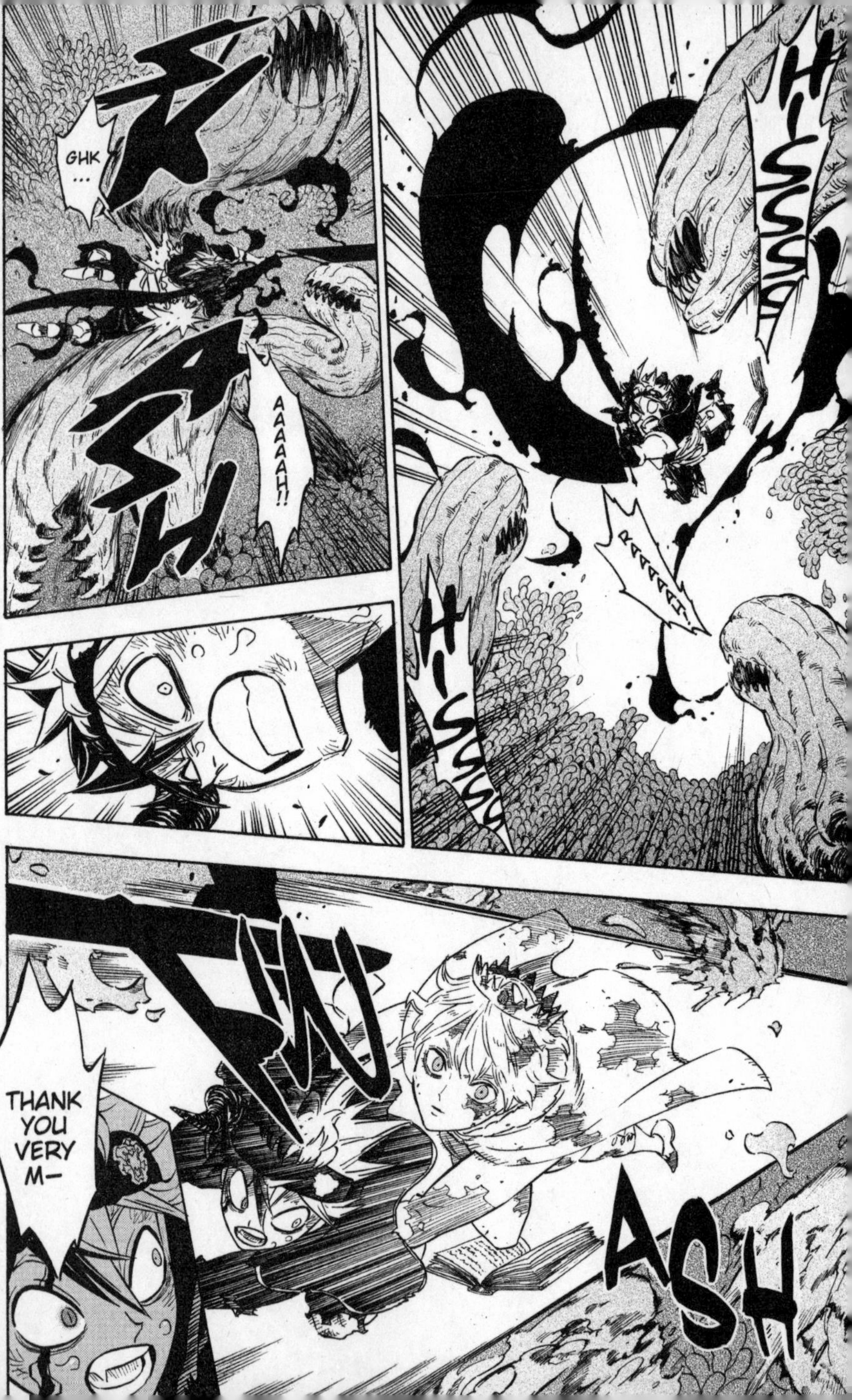
HI-SSSSS
HI-SSSS
RAAAAAH!!
GHK...
AAAAAH!!
THANK YOU VERY M—
ASH

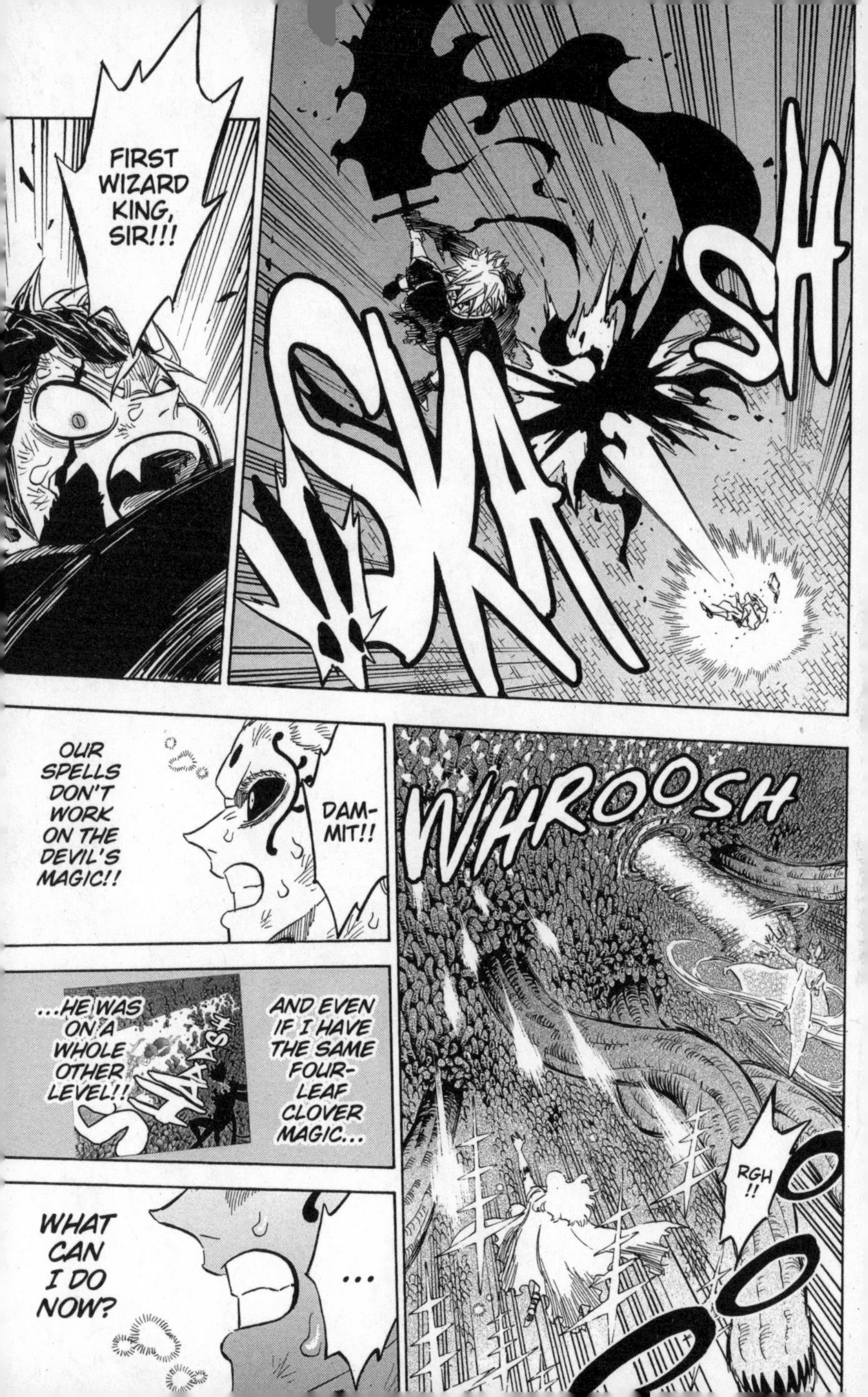
SKASH
FIRST WIZARD KING, SIR!!!
WHROOSH
RGH!!
DAM-MIT!!
OUR SPELLS DON'T WORK ON THE DEVIL'S MAGIC!!
AND EVEN IF I HAVE THE SAME FOUR-LEAF CLOVER MAGIC...
...HE WAS ON A WHOLE OTHER LEVEL!!
...
WHAT CAN I DO NOW?

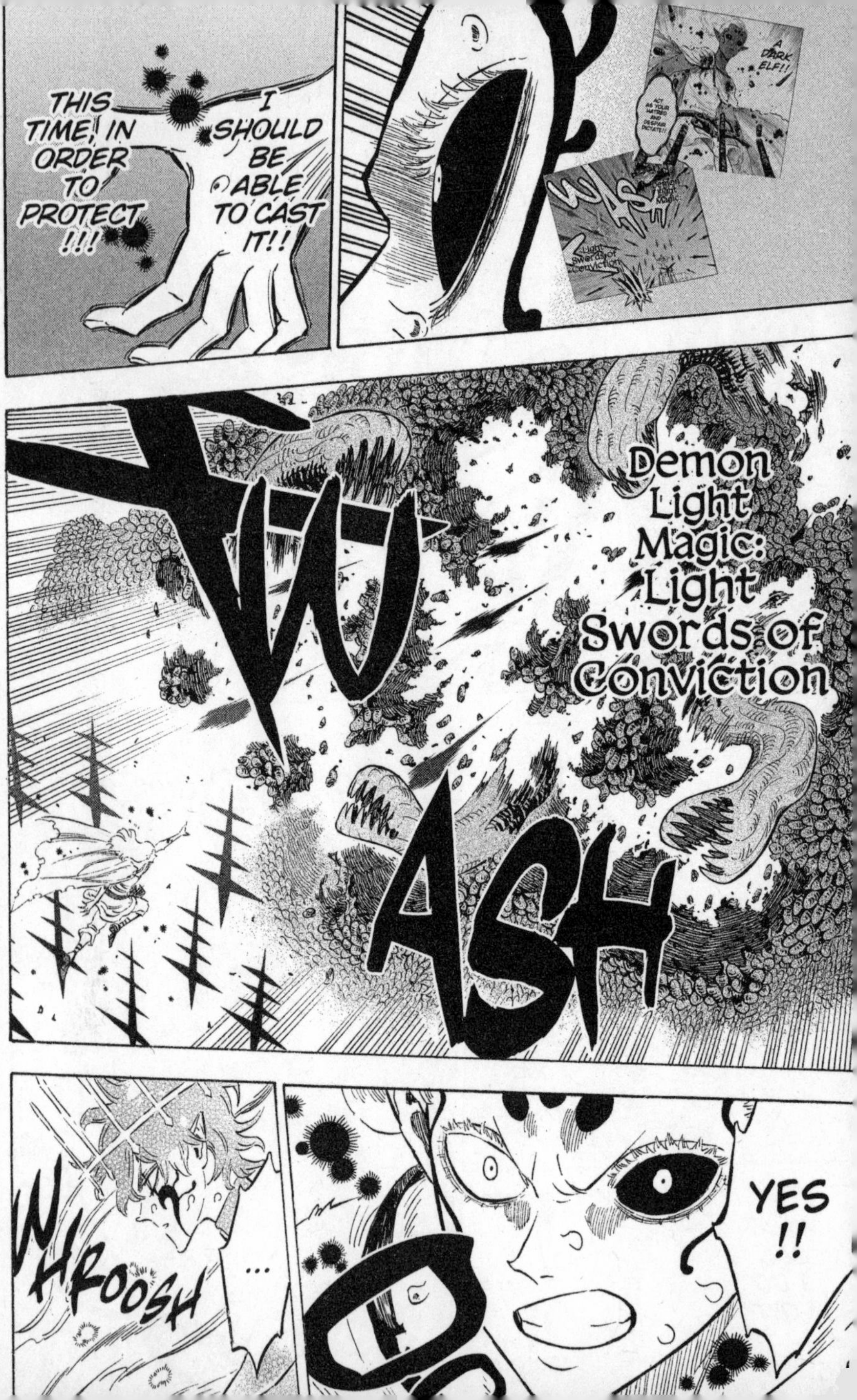
A DARK ELF!!
ACT AS YOUR HATRED AND DESPAIR DICTATE!!
Demon Light Magic:
WASH
Light Swords of Conviction
I SHOULD BE ABLE TO CAST IT!!
THIS TIME, IN ORDER TO PROTECT!!!
SWASH
Demon Light Magic: Light Swords of Conviction
YES!!
...
WHROOSH

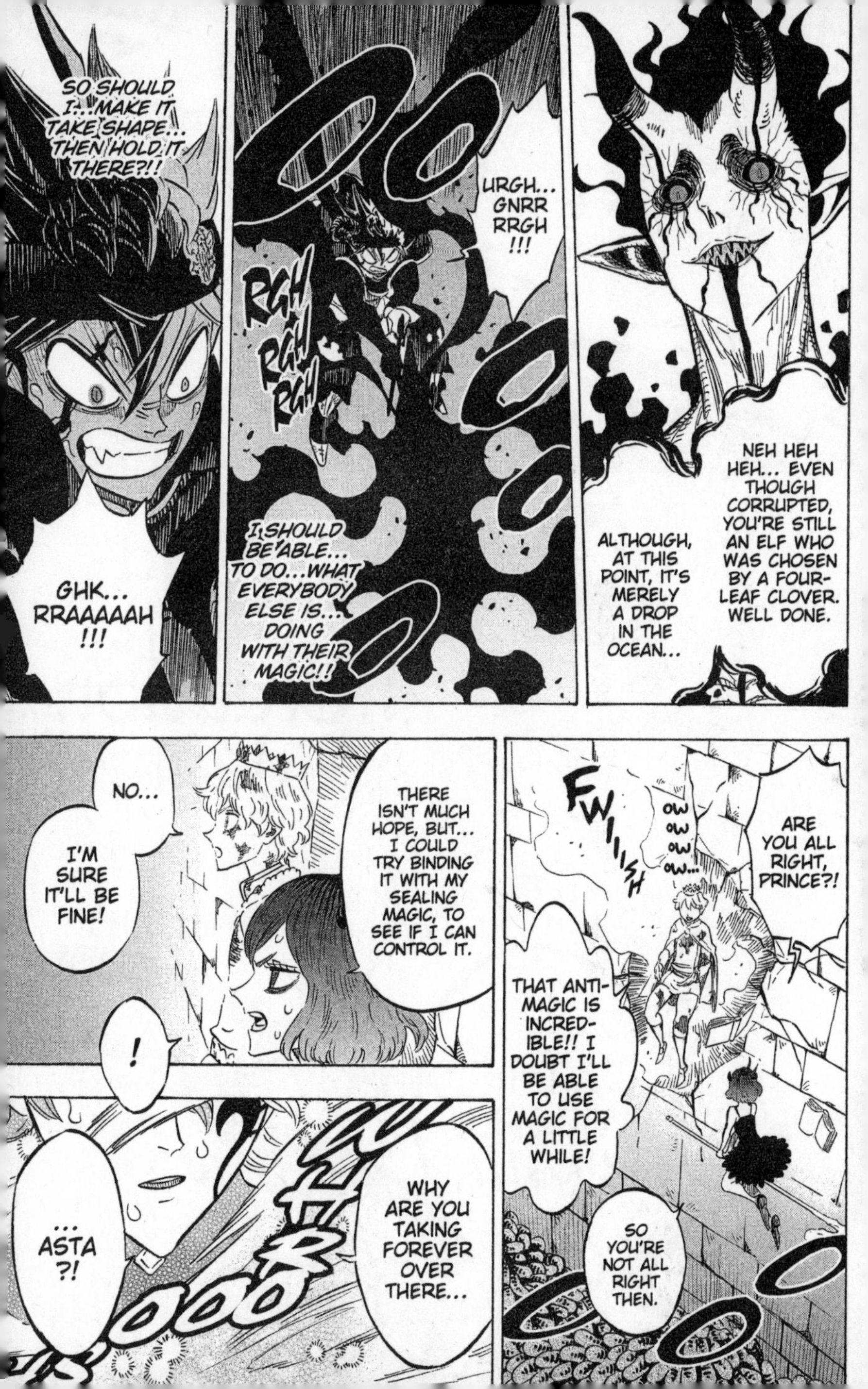
NEH HEH HEH... EVEN THOUGH CORRUPTED, YOU'RE STILL AN ELF WHO WAS CHOSEN BY A FOUR-LEAF CLOVER. WELL DONE.
ALTHOUGH, AT THIS POINT, IT'S MERELY A DROP IN THE OCEAN...
URGH... GNRR RRGH !!!
RGH RGH RGH
I SHOULD BE ABLE... TO DO... WHAT EVERYBODY ELSE IS... DOING WITH THEIR MAGIC!!
SO SHOULD I... MAKE IT TAKE SHAPE... THEN HOLD IT THERE?!!
GHK... RRAAAAAH !!!
FWIIISH
OW OW OW OW...
ARE YOU ALL RIGHT, PRINCE?!
THAT ANTI-MAGIC IS INCREDIBLE!! I DOUBT I'LL BE ABLE TO USE MAGIC FOR A LITTLE WHILE!
SO YOU'RE NOT ALL RIGHT THEN.
THERE ISN'T MUCH HOPE, BUT... I COULD TRY BINDING IT WITH MY SEALING MAGIC, TO SEE IF I CAN CONTROL IT.
NO...
I'M SURE IT'LL BE FINE!
!
WHY ARE YOU TAKING FOREVER OVER THERE...
... ASTA ?!

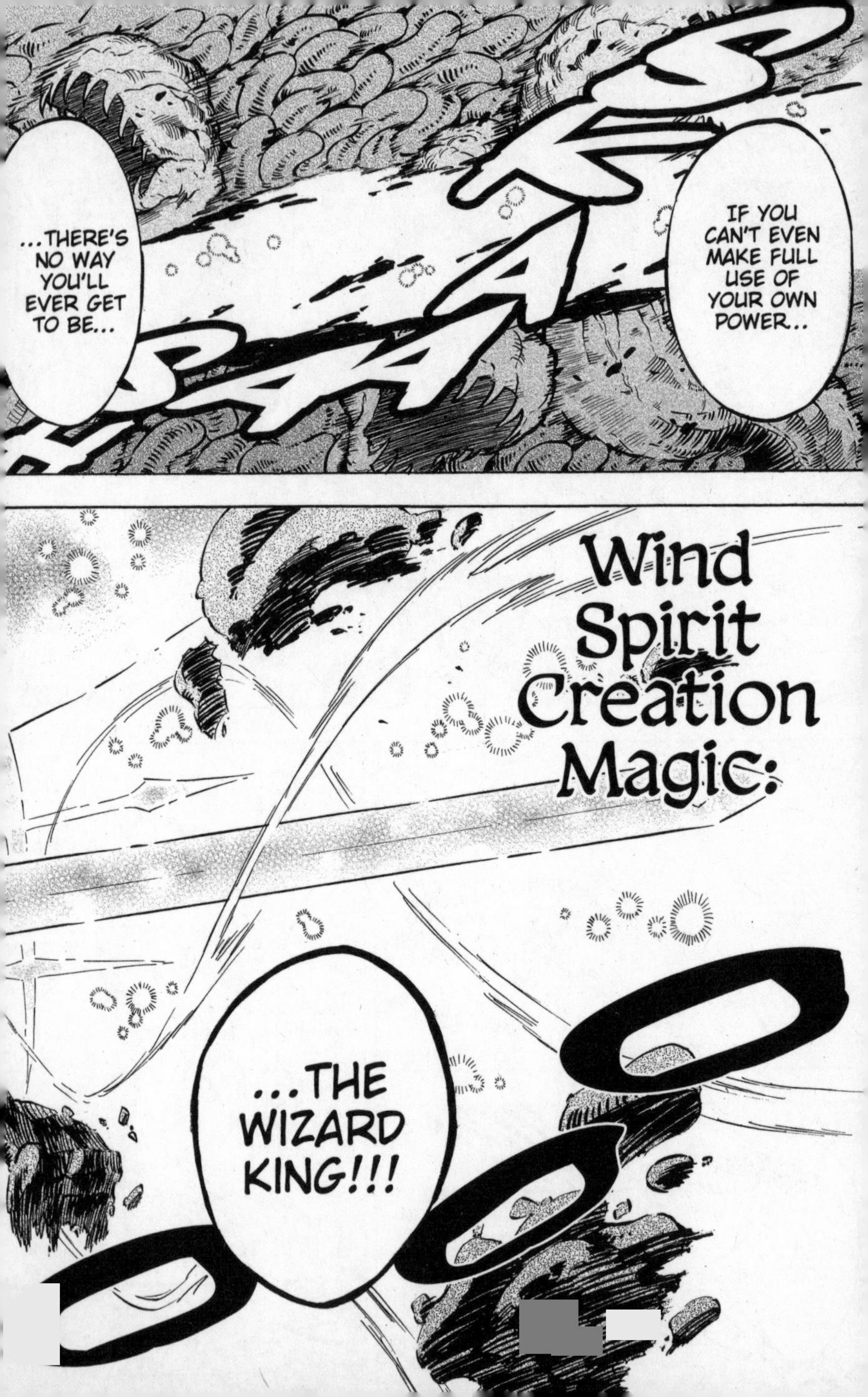
IF YOU CAN'T EVEN MAKE FULL USE OF YOUR OWN POWER..
...THERE'S NO WAY YOU'LL EVER GET TO BE...
Wind Spirit Creation Magic:
...THE WIZARD KING!!!

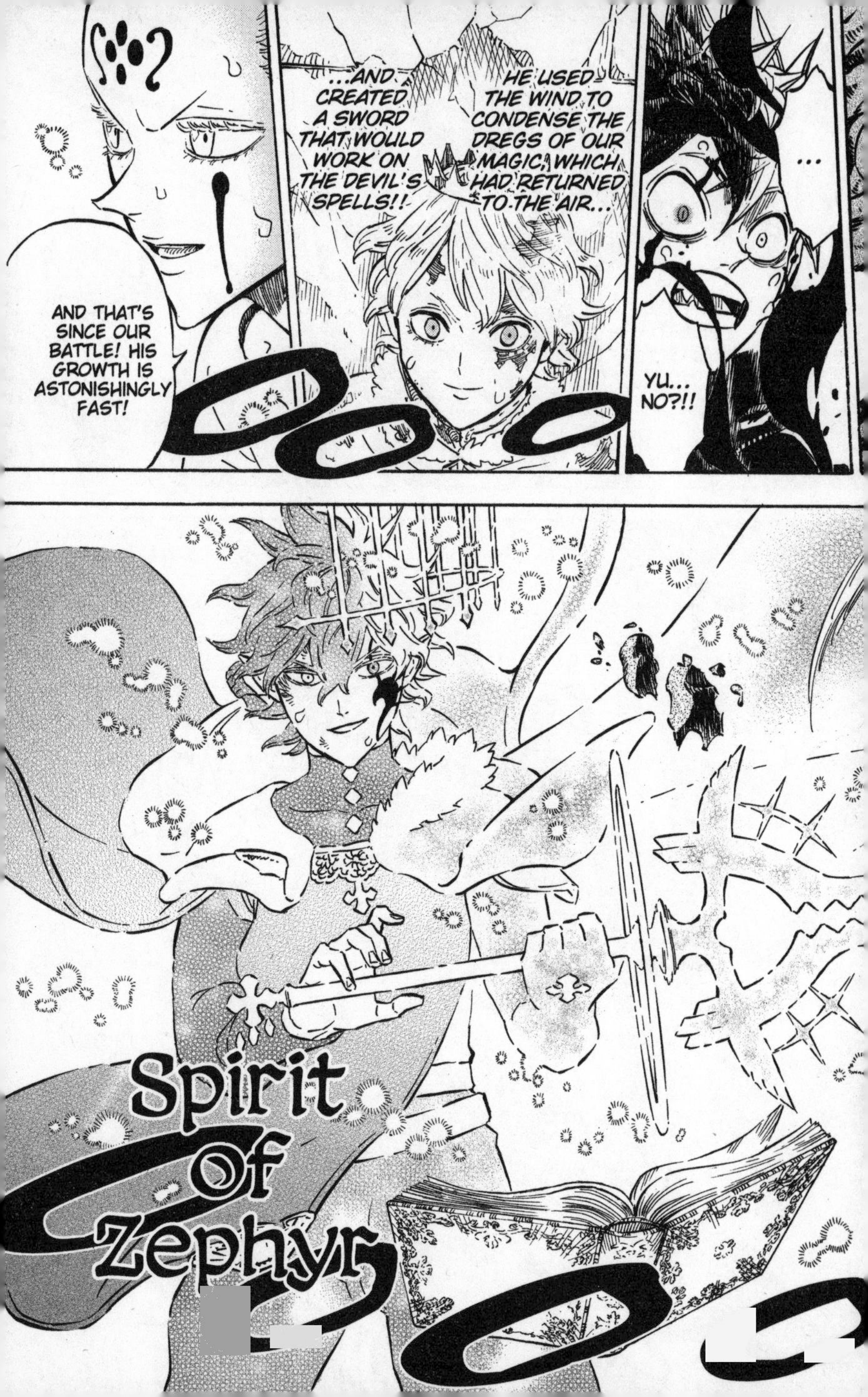
...
YU... NO?!!
HE USED THE WIND TO CONDENSE THE DREGS OF OUR MAGIC, WHICH HAD RETURNED TO THE AIR...
...AND CREATED A SWORD THAT WOULD WORK ON THE DEVIL'S SPELLS!!
AND THAT'S SINCE OUR BATTLE! HIS GROWTH IS ASTONISHINGLY FAST!
Spirit of Zephyr

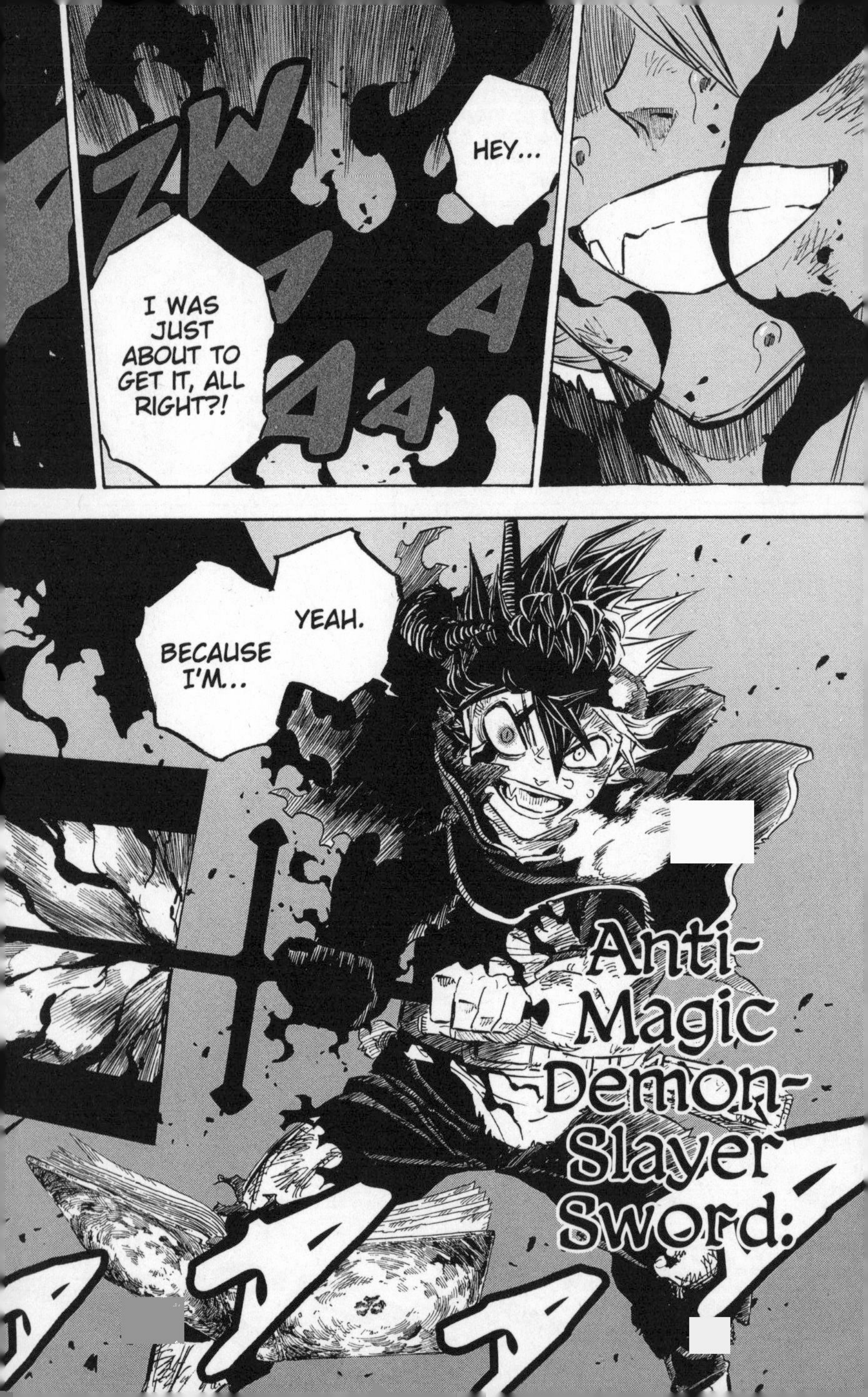
HEY...
ZWAAAAA
I WAS JUST ABOUT TO GET IT, ALL RIGHT?!
YEAH.
BECAUSE I'M...
Anti-Magic Demon-Slayer Sword:

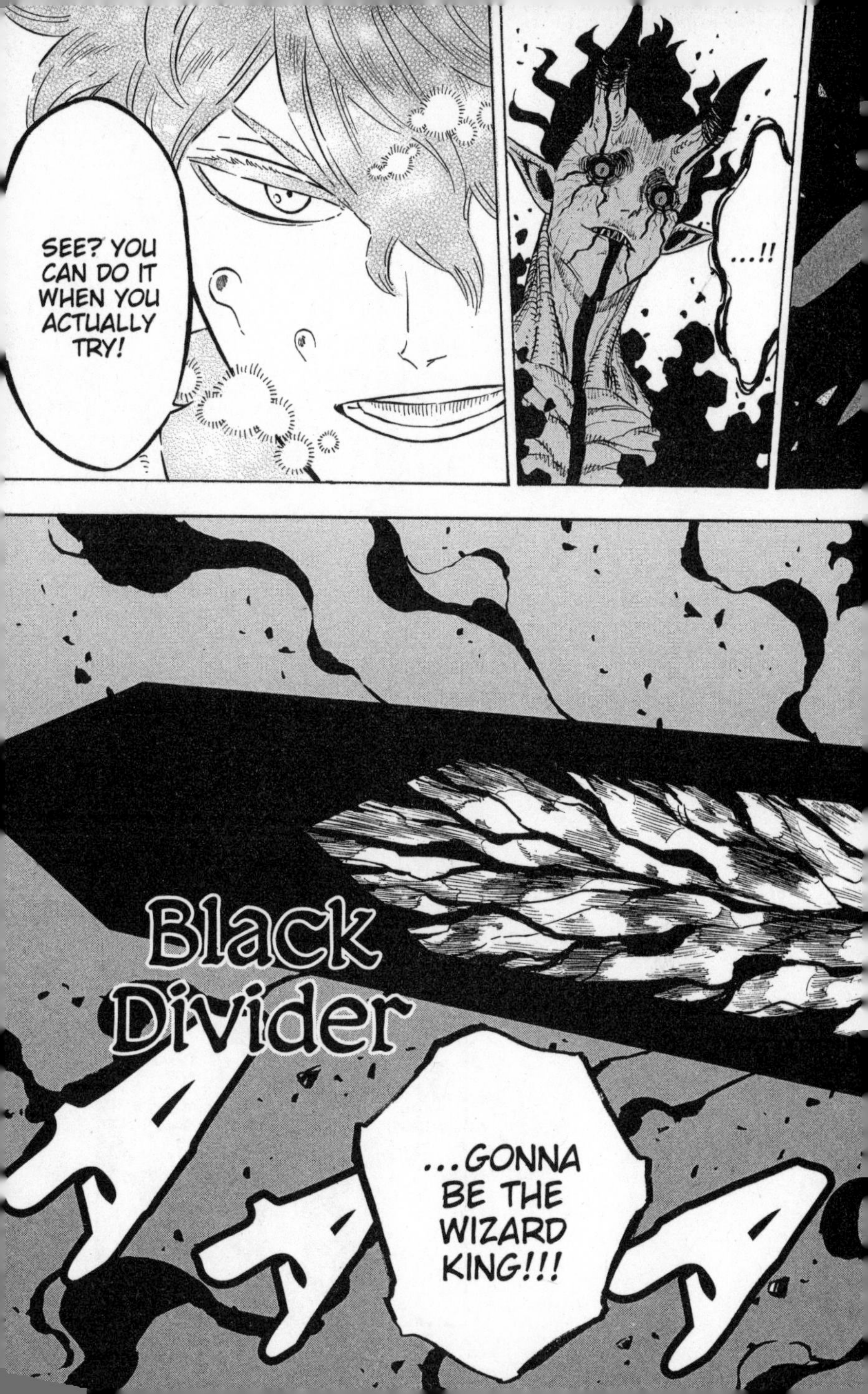
...!!
SEE? YOU CAN DO IT WHEN YOU ACTUALLY TRY!
Black Divider
...GONNA BE THE WIZARD KING!!!

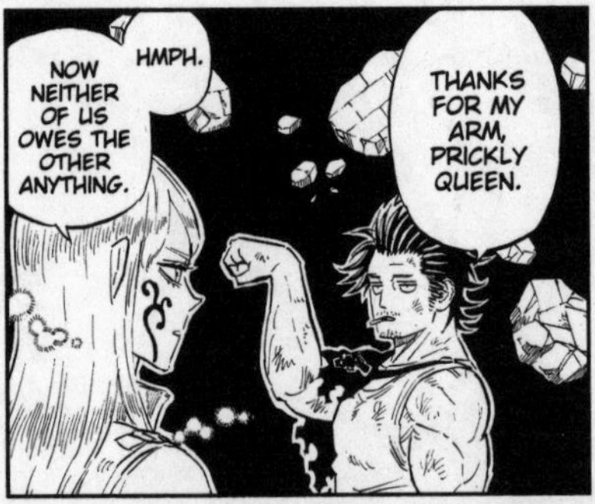
THANKS FOR MY ARM, PRICKLY QUEEN.
HMPH.
NOW NEITHER OF US OWES THE OTHER ANYTHING.

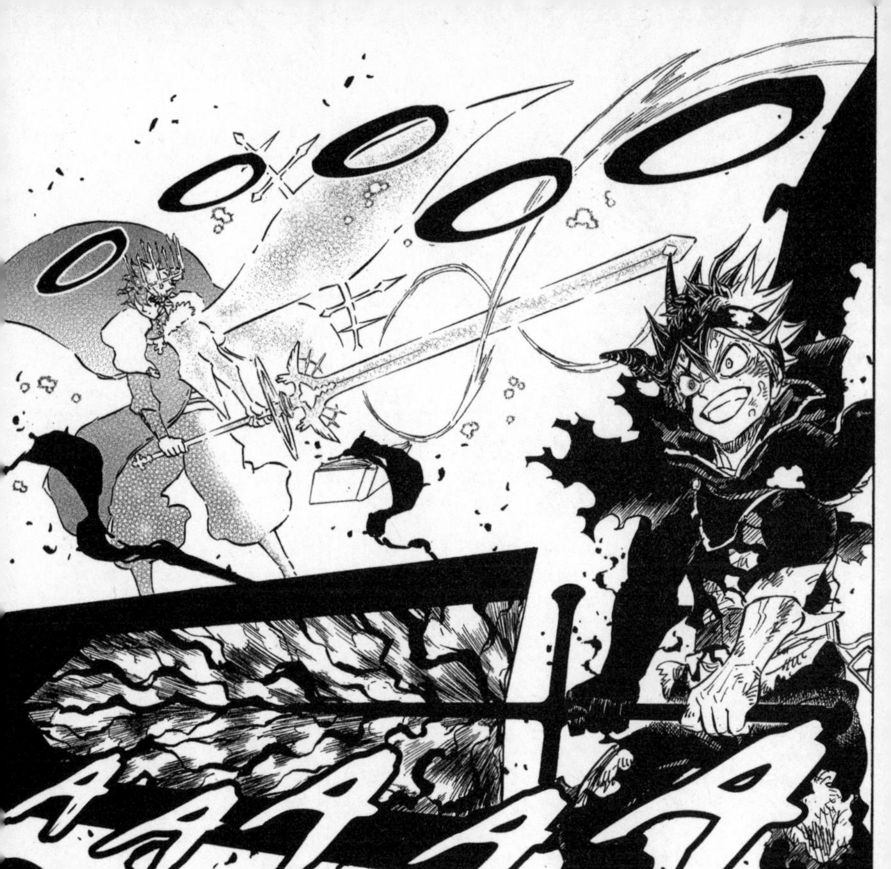
OOOOOO
AAAAA

Page 209: Wish

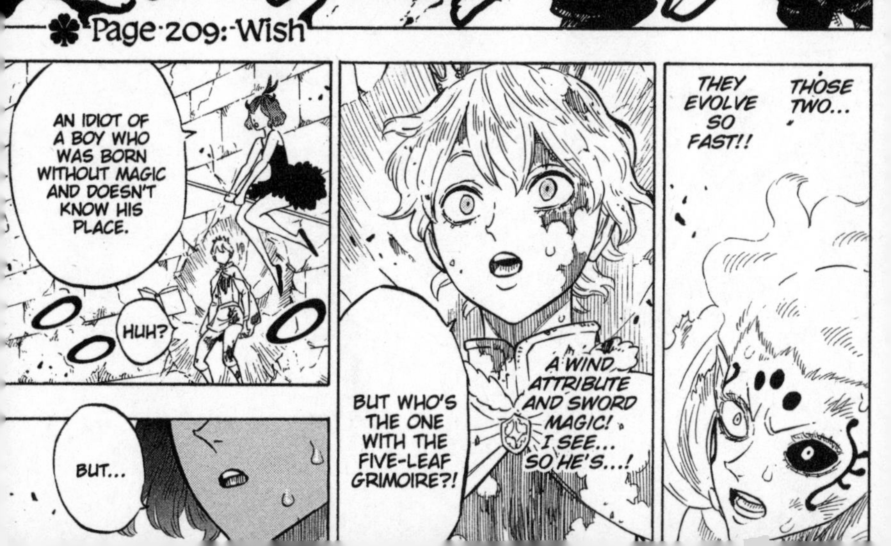
THOSE TWO...
THEY EVOLVE SO FAST!!
A WIND ATTRIBUTE AND SWORD MAGIC! I SEE... SO HE'S...!
BUT WHO'S THE ONE WITH THE FIVE-LEAF GRIMOIRE?!
AN IDIOT OF A BOY WHO WAS BORN WITHOUT MAGIC AND DOESN'T KNOW HIS PLACE.
HUH?
BUT...

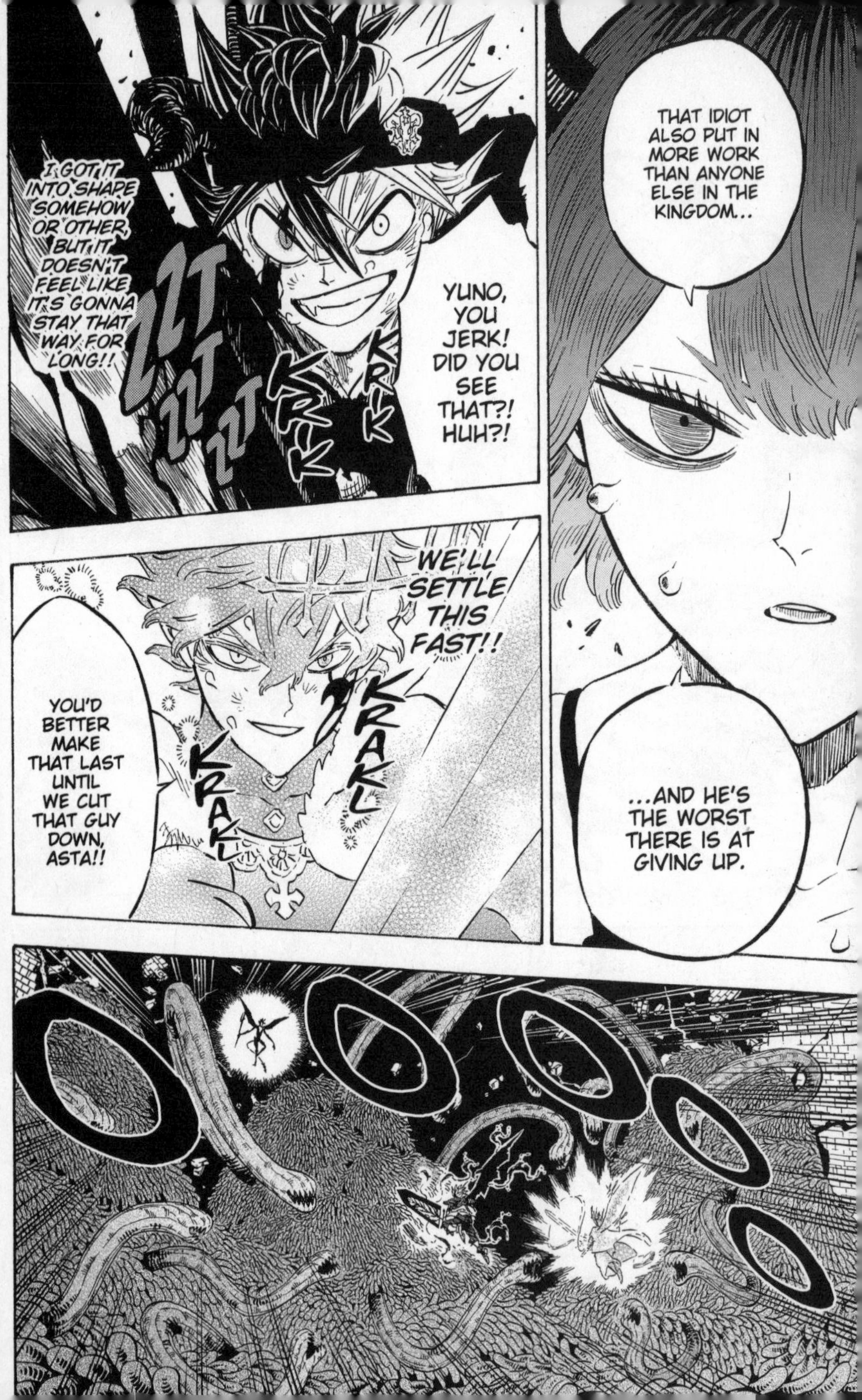
THAT IDIOT ALSO PUT IN MORE WORK THAN ANYONE ELSE IN THE KINGDOM...
...AND HE'S THE WORST THERE IS AT GIVING UP.
YUNO, YOU JERK! DID YOU SEE THAT?! HUH?!
KRIK
KRIK
ZZT
ZZT
ZZT
I GOT IT INTO SHAPE SOMEHOW OR OTHER, BUT IT DOESN'T FEEL LIKE IT'S GONNA STAY THAT WAY FOR LONG!!
WE'LL SETTLE THIS FAST!!
KRAKL
KRAKL
YOU'D BETTER MAKE THAT LAST UNTIL WE CUT THAT GUY DOWN, ASTA!!

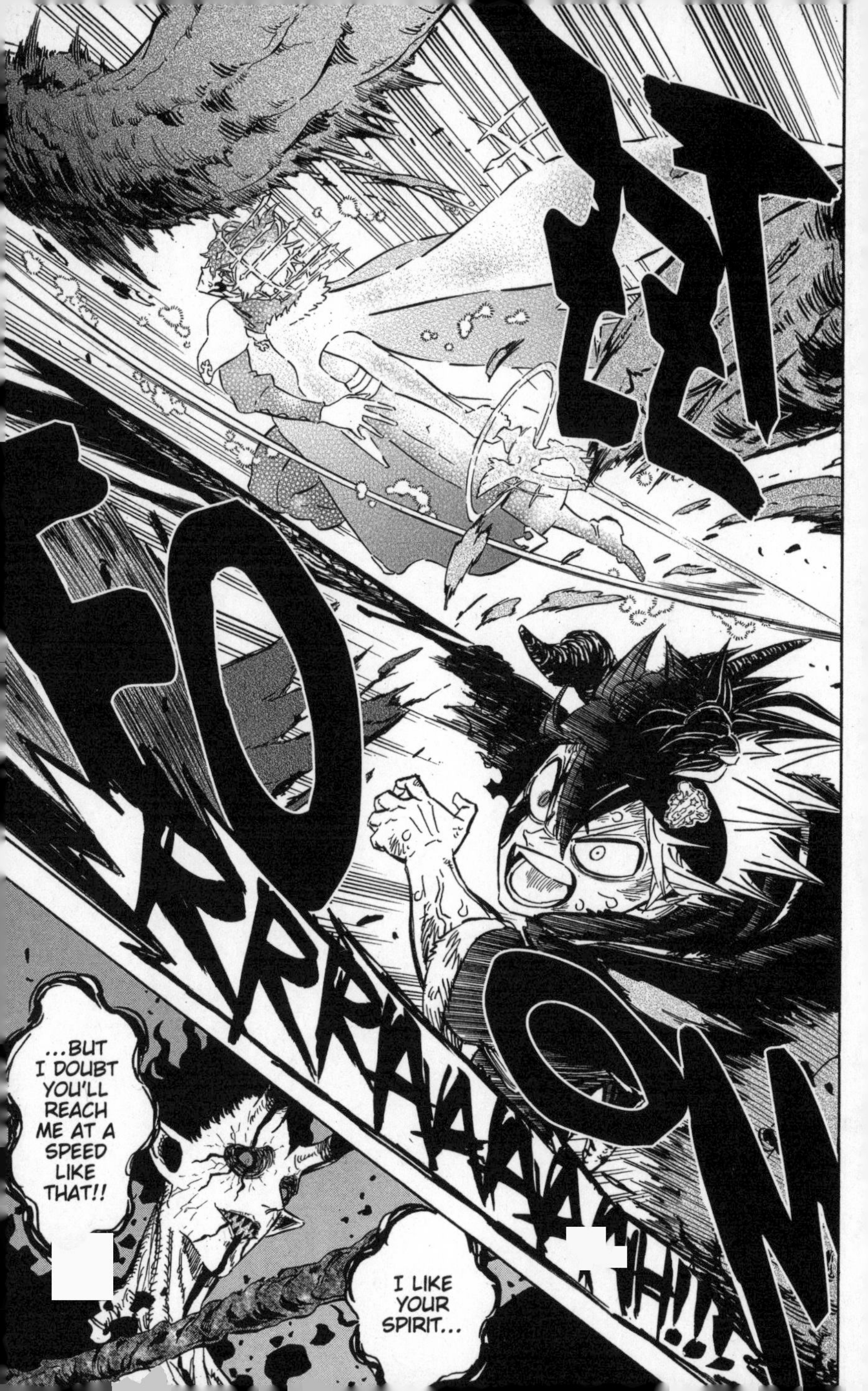
I LIKE YOUR SPIRIT...
...BUT I DOUBT YOU'LL REACH ME AT A SPEED LIKE THAT!!

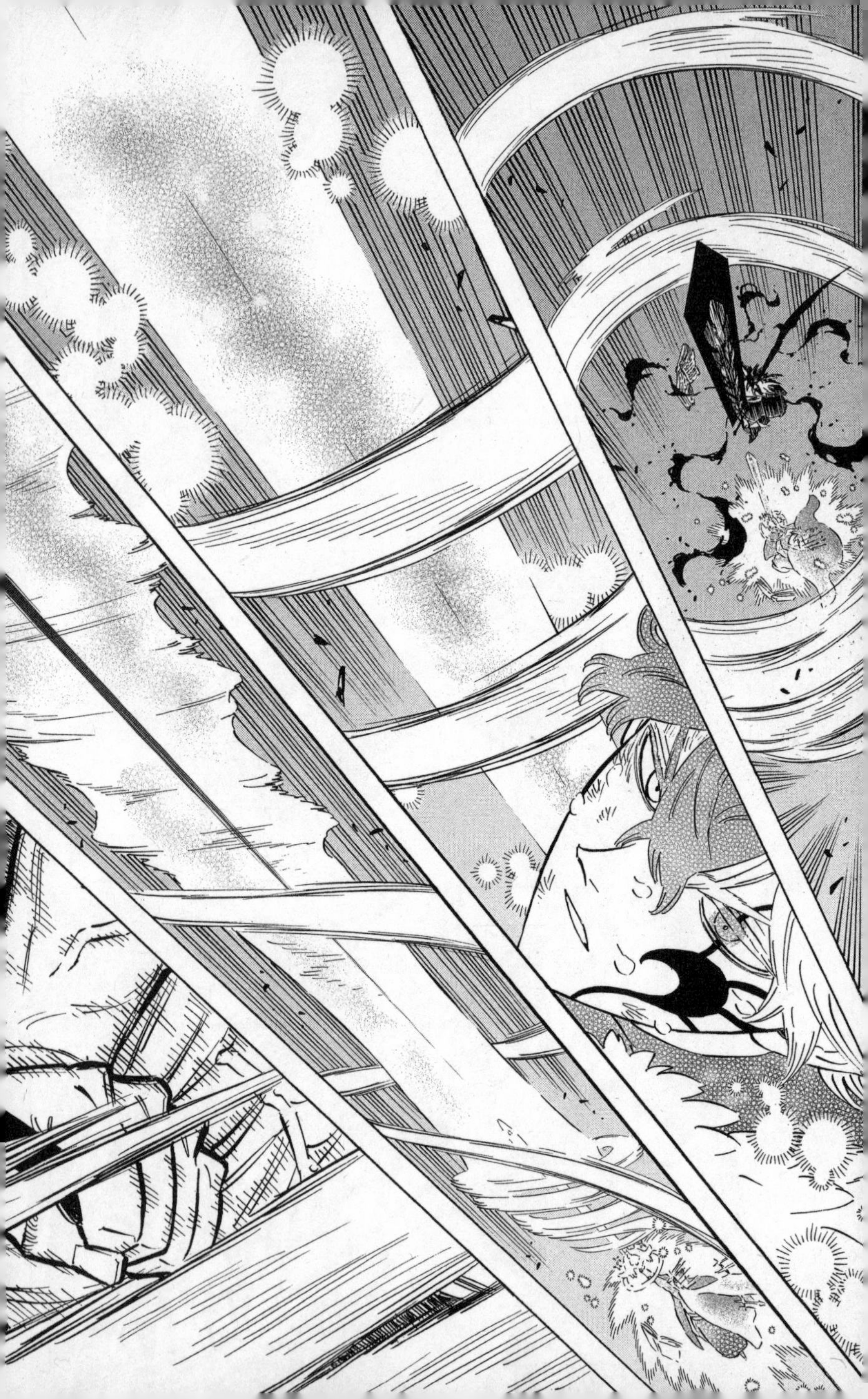

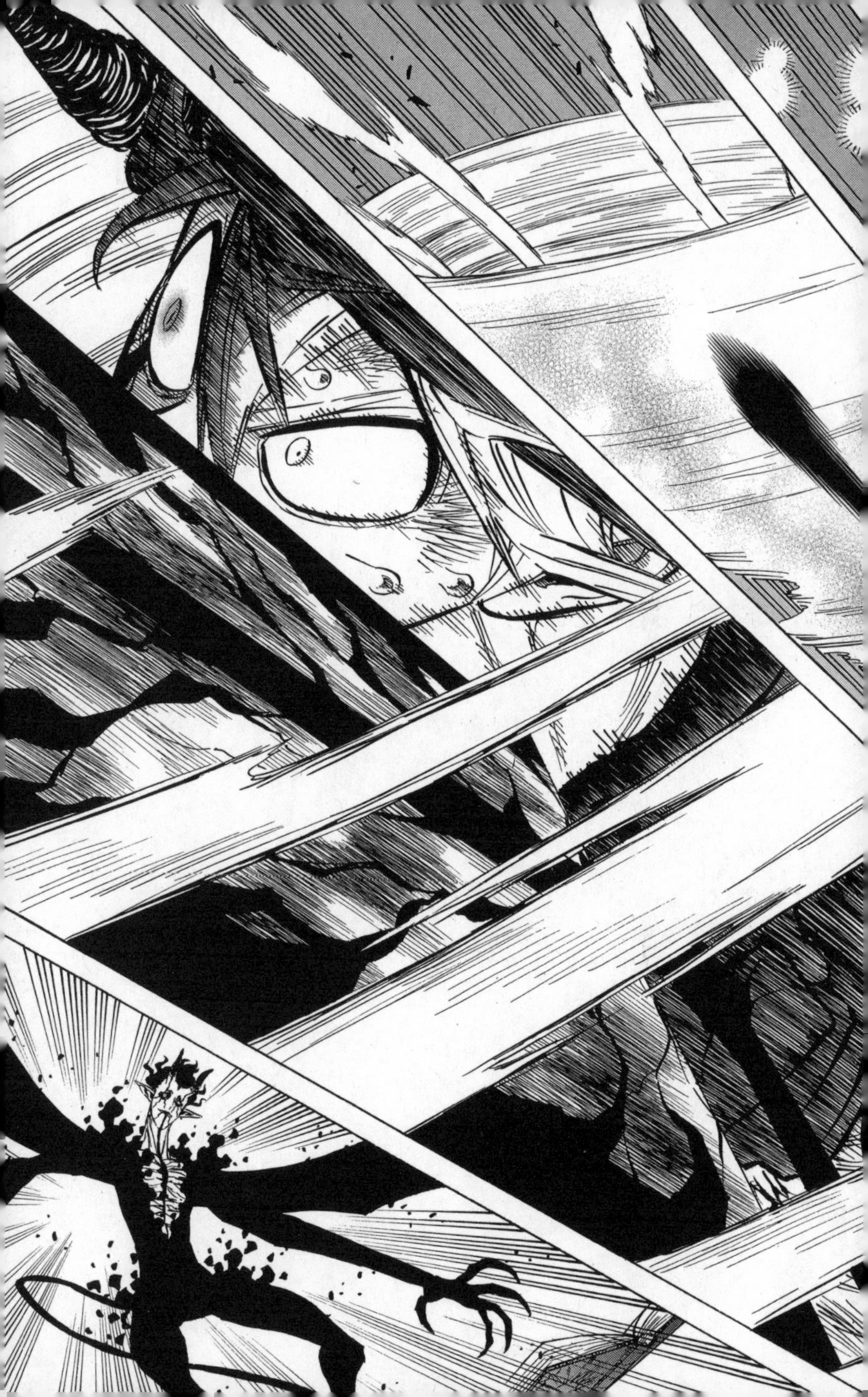

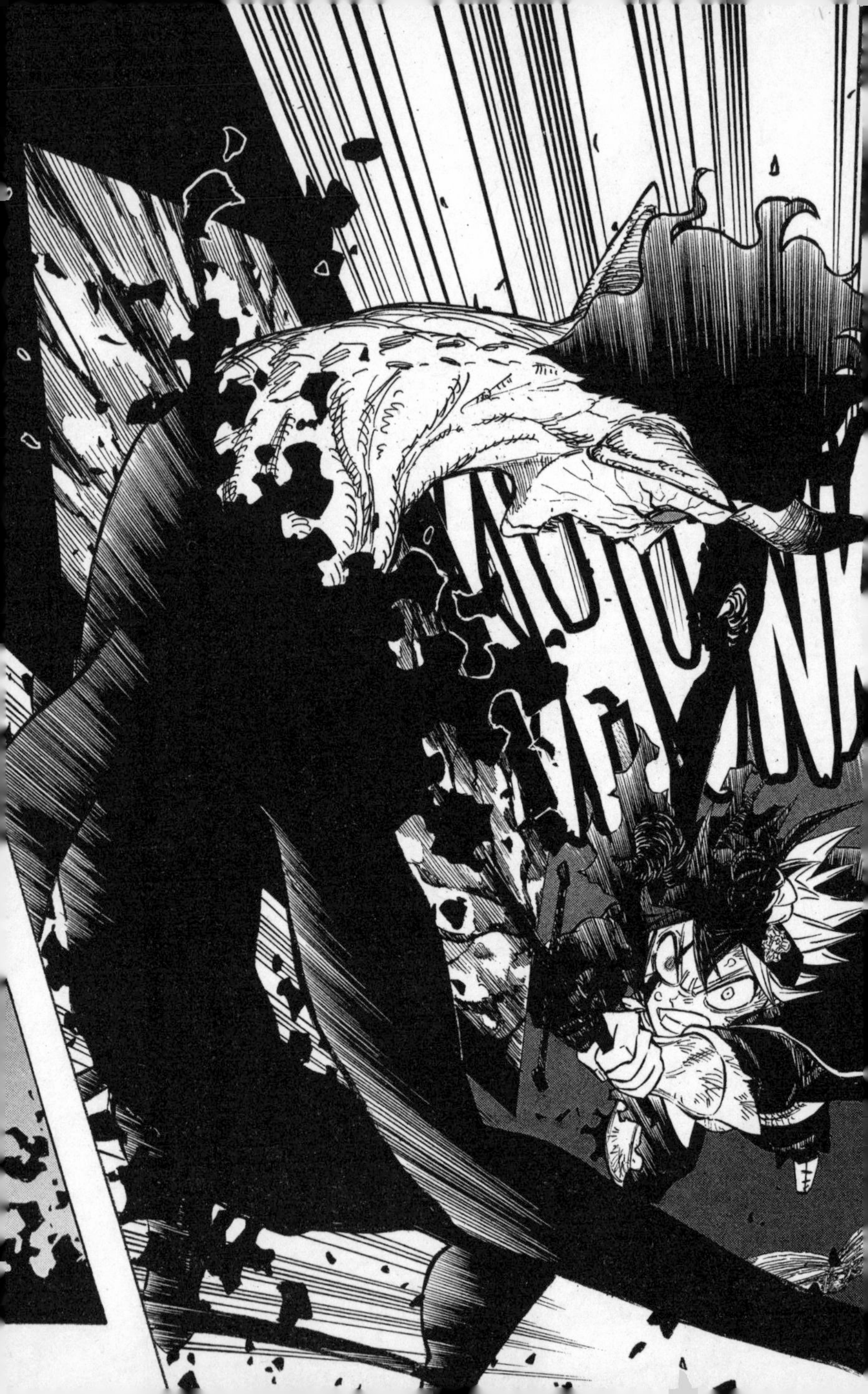

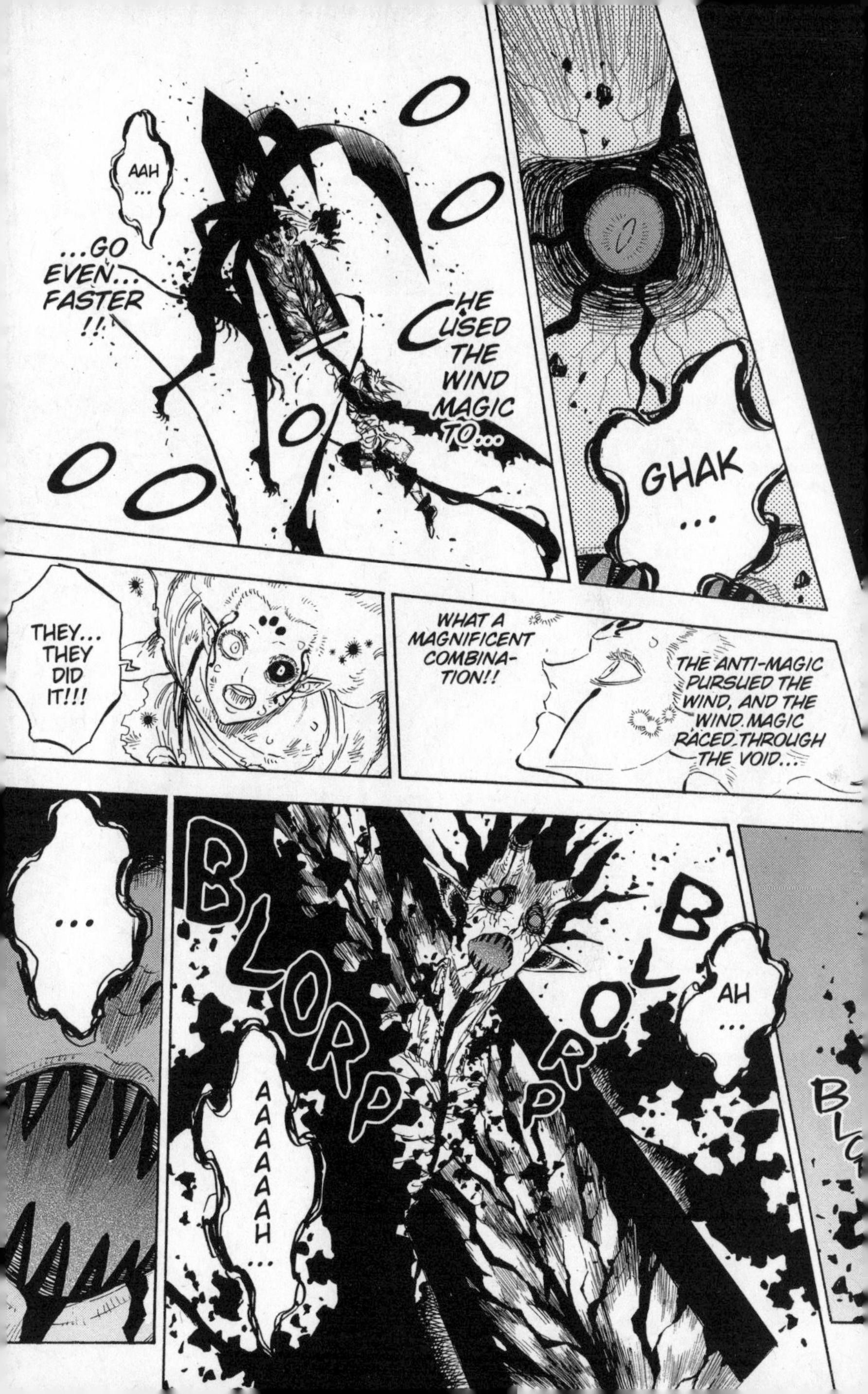
GHAK...
OOOOOO
HE USED THE WIND MAGIC TO...
AAH...
...GO EVEN... FASTER!!
WHAT A MAGNIFICENT COMBINATION!!
THE ANTI-MAGIC PURSUED THE WIND, AND THE WIND MAGIC RACED THROUGH THE VOID...
THEY... THEY DID IT!!!
AH...
BLORP
BLORP
AAAAAAH...
...

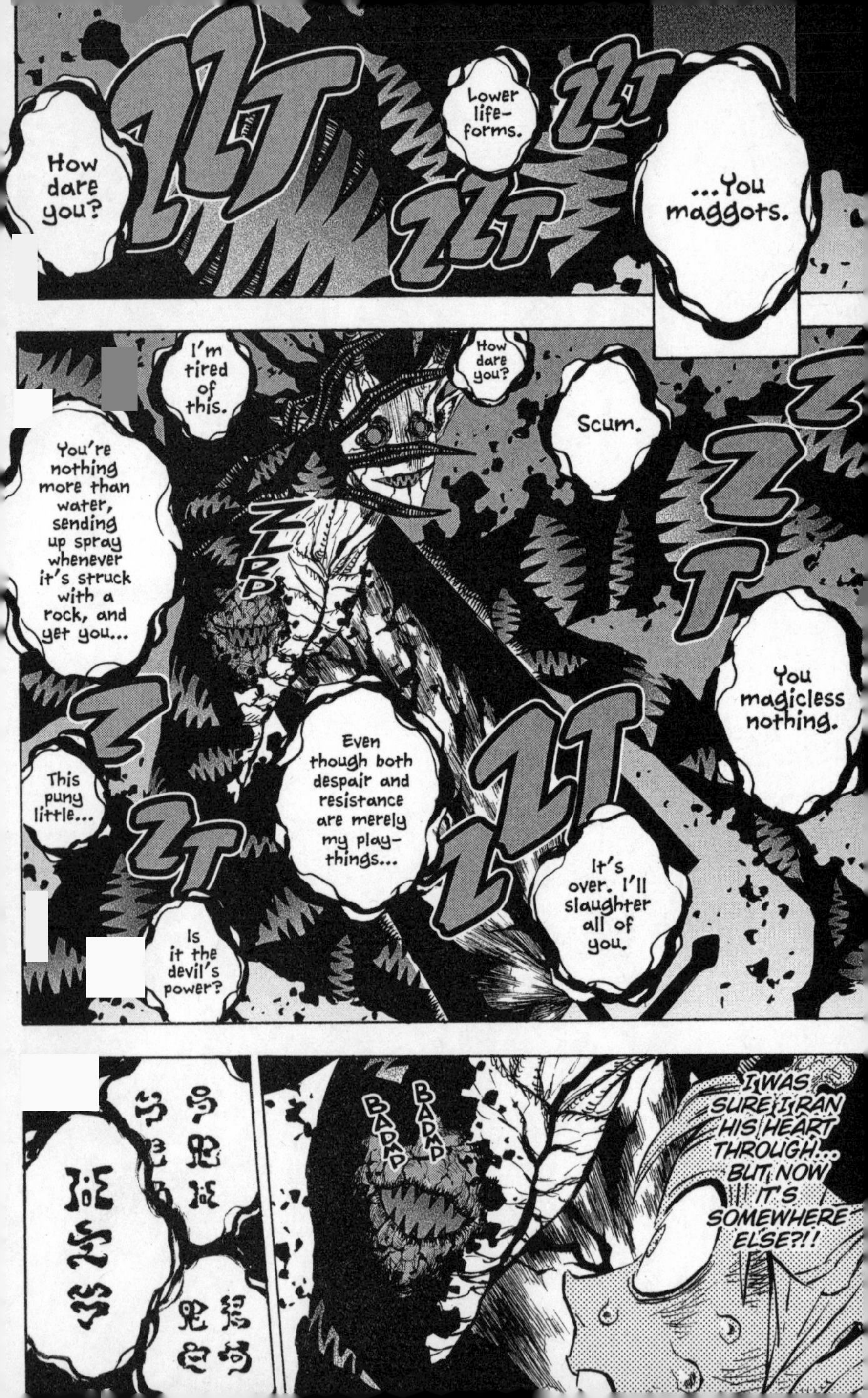
...You maggots.
ZZT
Lower life-forms.
ZZT
ZZT
How dare you?
ZZT
ZZZT
Scum.
How dare you?
I'm tired of this.
You're nothing more than water, sending up spray whenever it's struck with a rock, and yet you...
You magicless nothing.
Even though both despair and resistance are merely my play-things...
ZZT
It's over. I'll slaughter all of you.
ZZT
This puny little...
Is it the devil's power?
I WAS SURE I RAN HIS HEART THROUGH... BUT NOW IT'S SOMEWHERE ELSE?!!
BADMP
BADMP

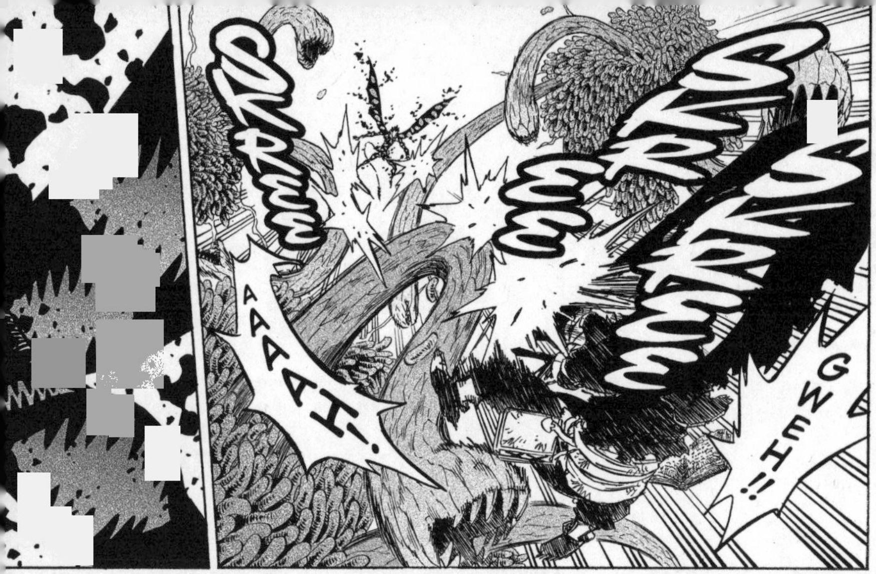
GWEH!!
AAAAH!
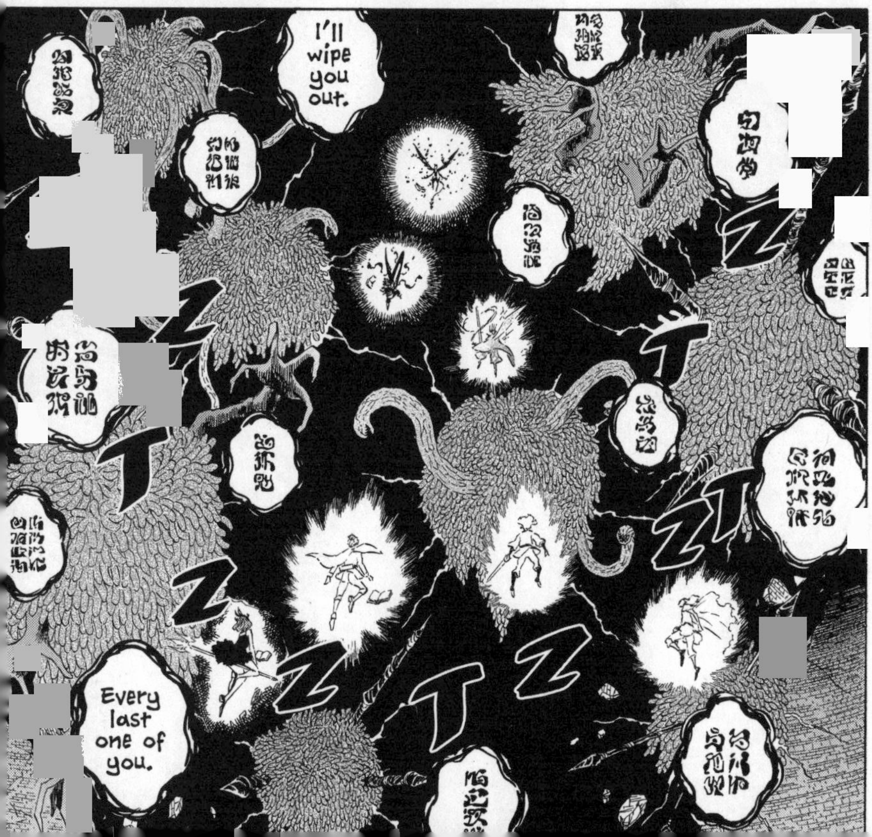
I'll wipe you out.
Every last one of you.

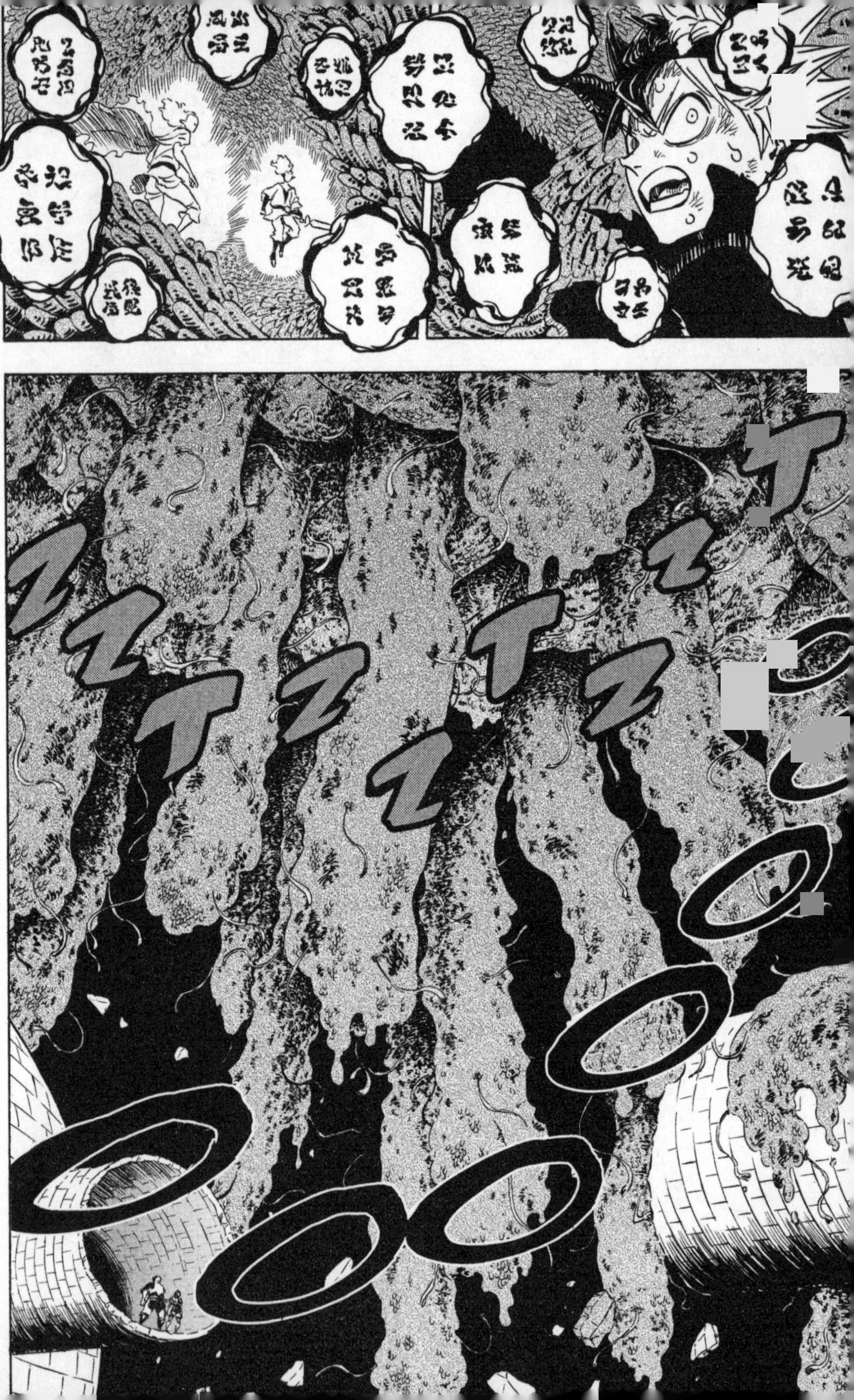

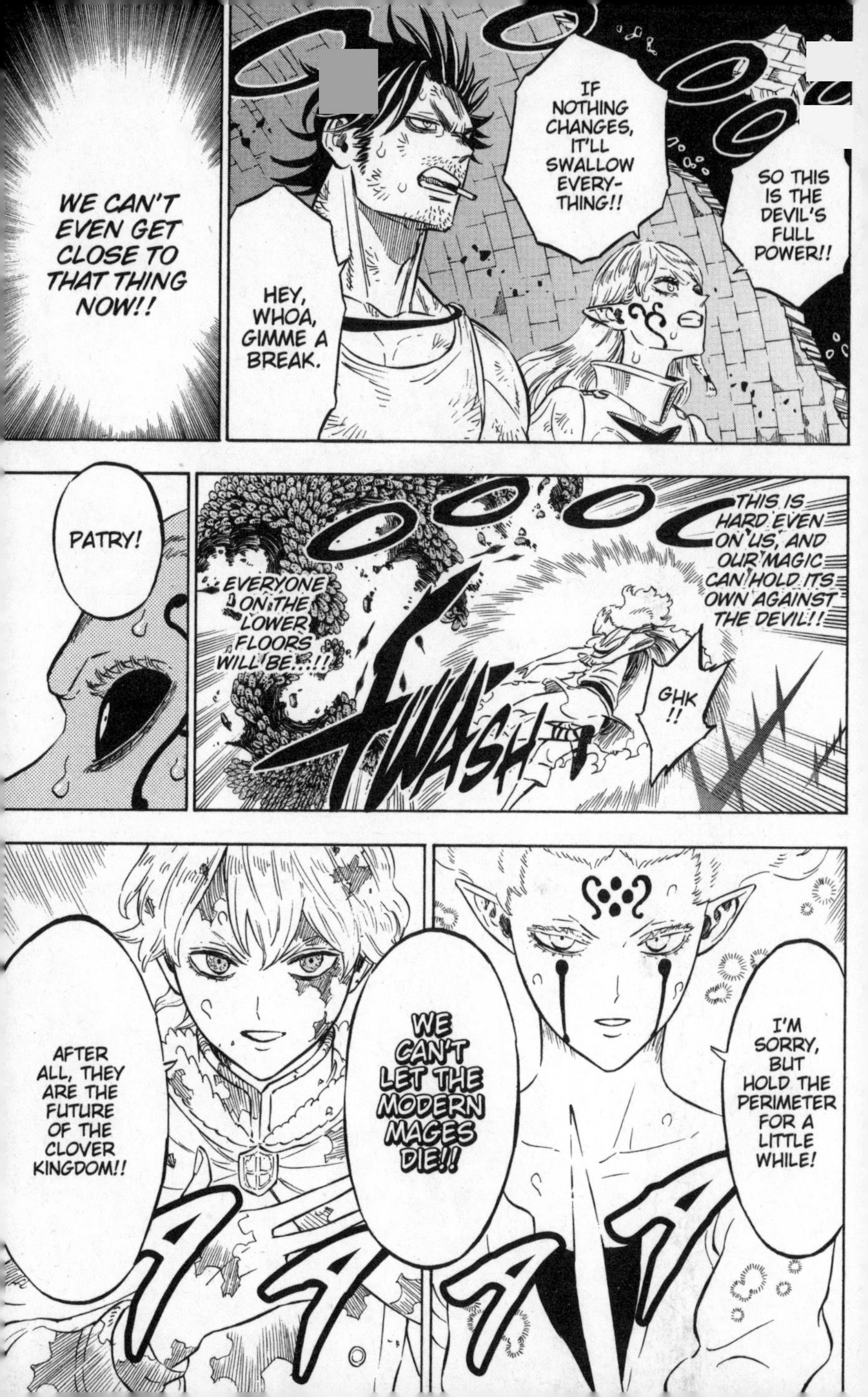
SO THIS IS THE DEVIL'S FULL POWER!!
IF NOTHING CHANGES, IT'LL SWALLOW EVERY-THING!!
HEY, WHOA, GIMME A BREAK.
WE CAN'T EVEN GET CLOSE TO THAT THING NOW!!
THIS IS HARD EVEN ON US, AND OUR MAGIC CAN HOLD ITS OWN AGAINST THE DEVIL!!
GHK!!
SWASH
EVERYONE ON THE LOWER FLOORS WILL BE...!!
PATRY!
I'M SORRY, BUT HOLD THE PERIMETER FOR A LITTLE WHILE!
WE CAN'T LET THE MODERN MAGES DIE!!
AFTER ALL, THEY ARE THE FUTURE OF THE CLOVER KINGDOM!!

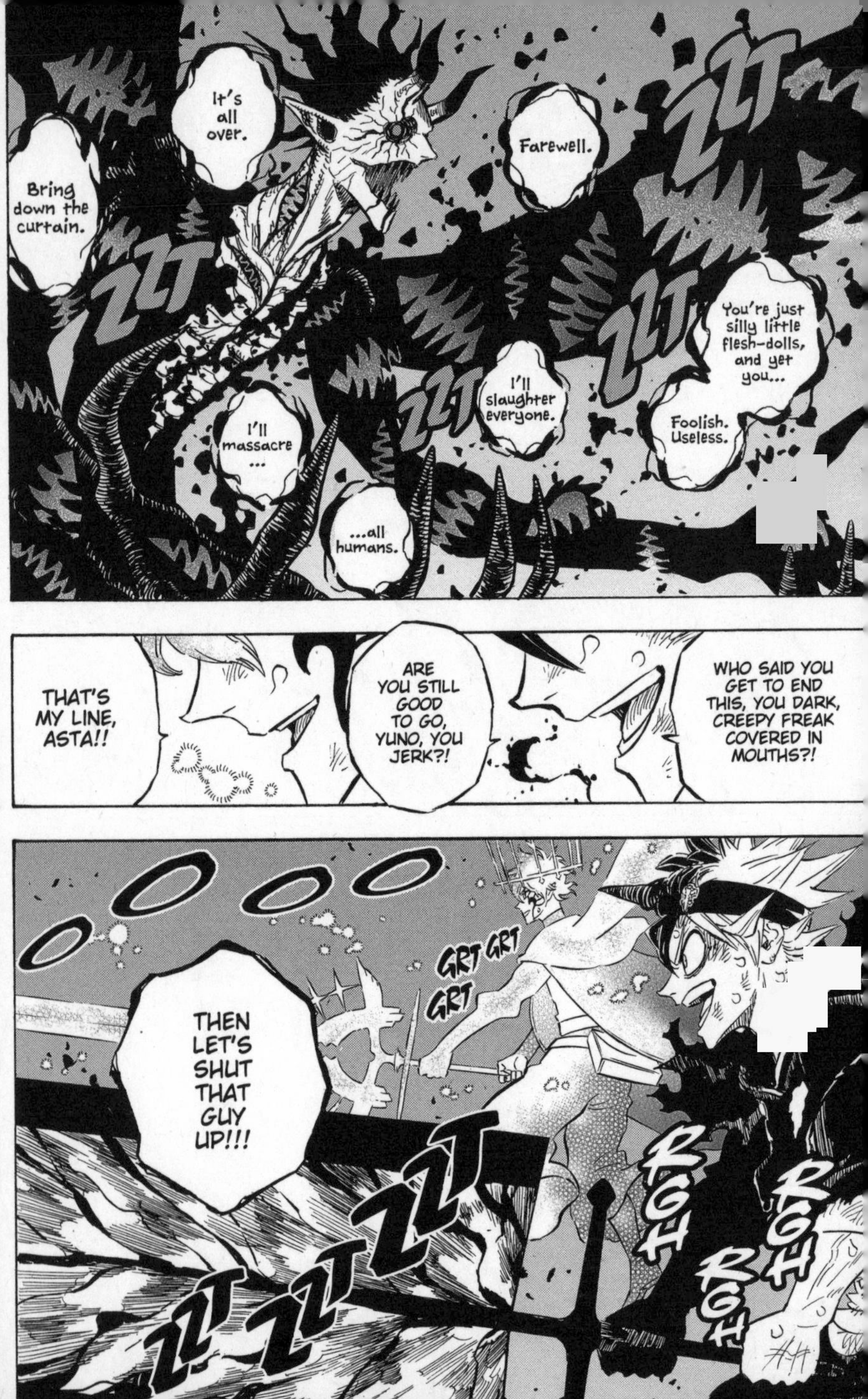
ZZZT
Farewell.
It's all over.
Bring down the curtain.
ZZZT
ZZZT
You're just silly little flesh-dolls, and yet you...
Foolish. Useless.
ZZZT
I'll slaughter everyone.
I'll massacre ...
...all humans.
WHO SAID YOU GET TO END THIS, YOU DARK, CREEPY FREAK COVERED IN MOUTHS?!
ARE YOU STILL GOOD TO GO, YUNO, YOU JERK?!
THAT'S MY LINE, ASTA!!
GRT GRT GRT
THEN LET'S SHUT THAT GUY UP!!!
RGH RGH
RGH RGH
ZZZT ZZZT ZZZT

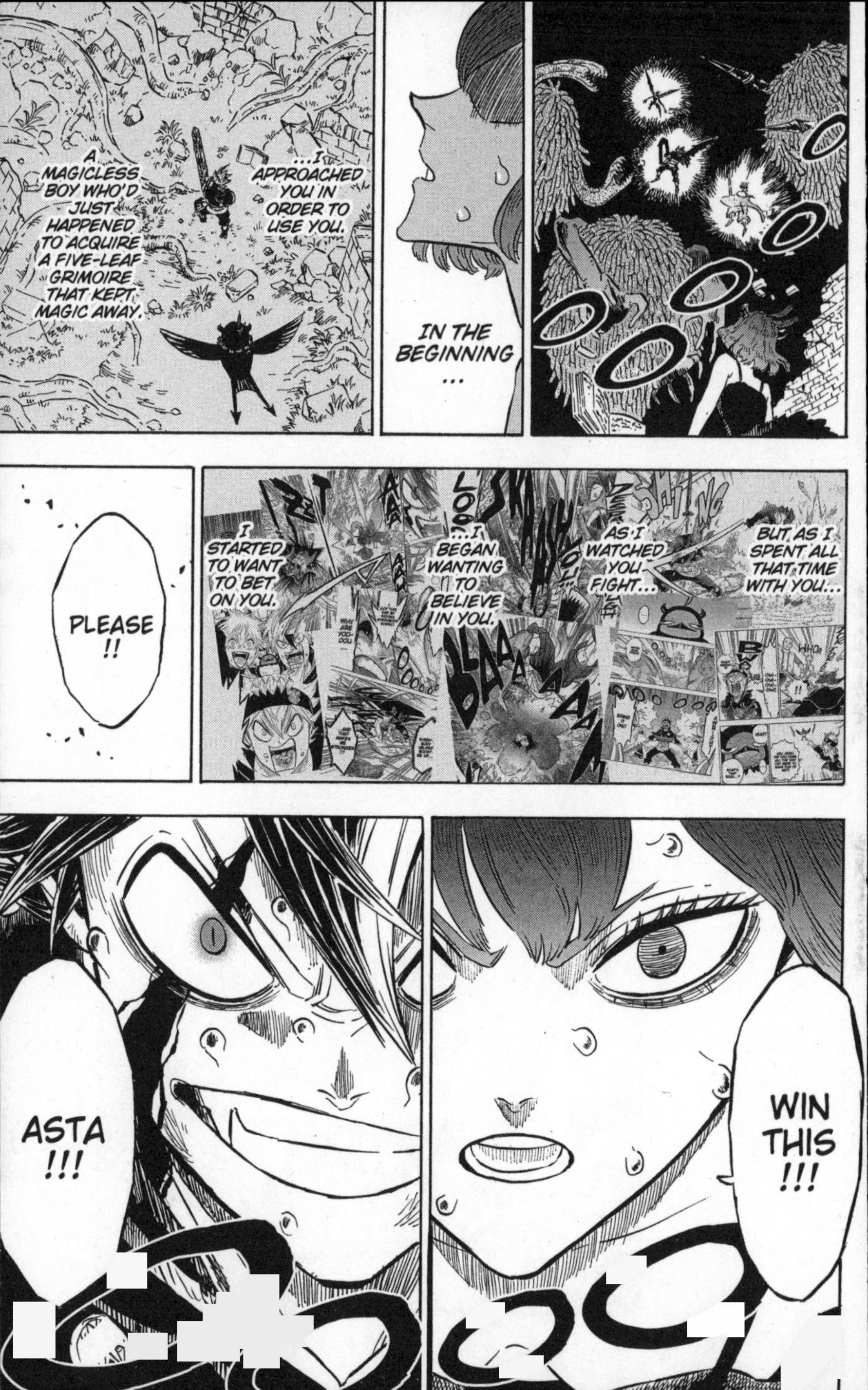
IN THE BEGINNING ...
...I APPROACHED YOU IN ORDER TO USE YOU.
A MAGICLESS BOY WHO'D JUST HAPPENED TO ACQUIRE A FIVE-LEAF GRIMOIRE THAT KEPT MAGIC AWAY.
BUT AS I SPENT ALL THAT TIME WITH YOU...
AS I WATCHED YOU FIGHT...
...I BEGAN WANTING TO BELIEVE IN YOU.
I STARTED TO WANT TO BET ON YOU.
PLEASE !!
WIN THIS !!!
ASTA !!!

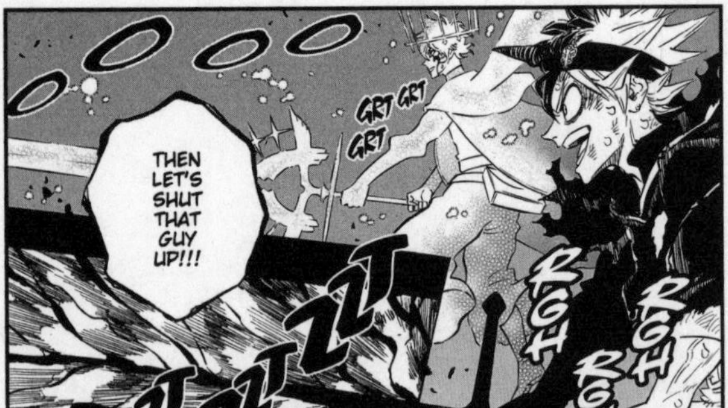

THEN LET'S SHUT THAT GUY UP!!!
GRT GRT GRT
RGH RGH RGH
ZZT ZZT ZZZT

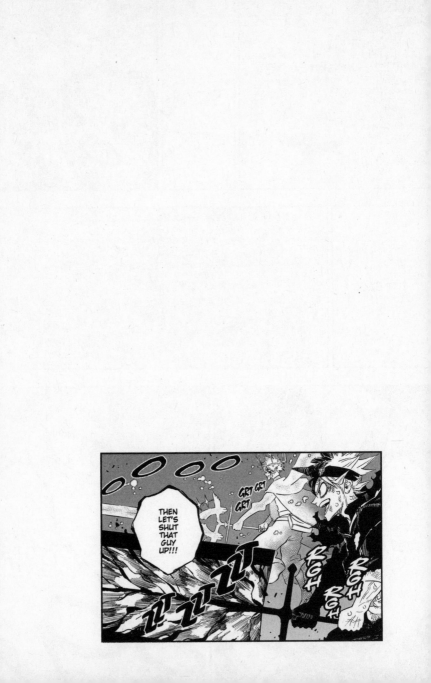

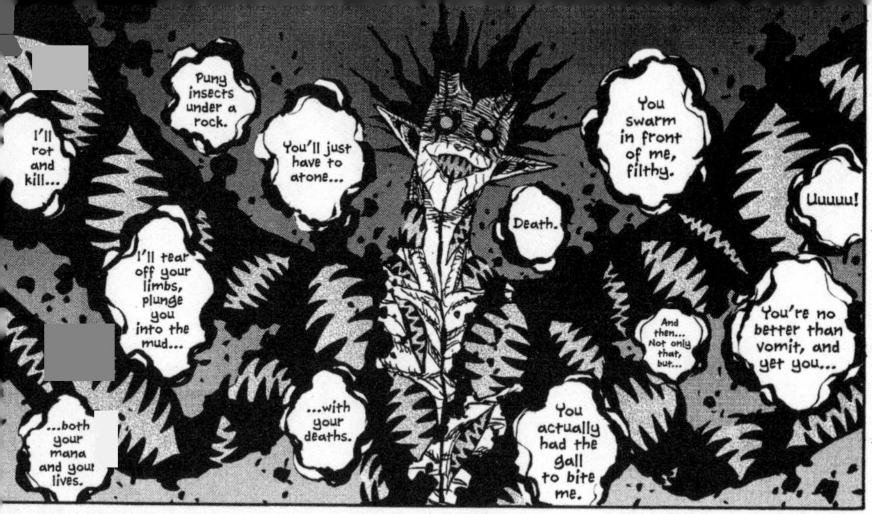
You swarm in front of me, filthy.
Uuuuu!
You're no better than vomit, and yet you...
And then... Not only that, but...
You actually had the gall to bite me.
Death.
Puny insects under a rock.
You'll just have to atone...
I'll rot and kill...
I'll tear off your limbs, plunge you into the mud...
...with your deaths.
...both your mana and your lives.

Page 210: On the Brink

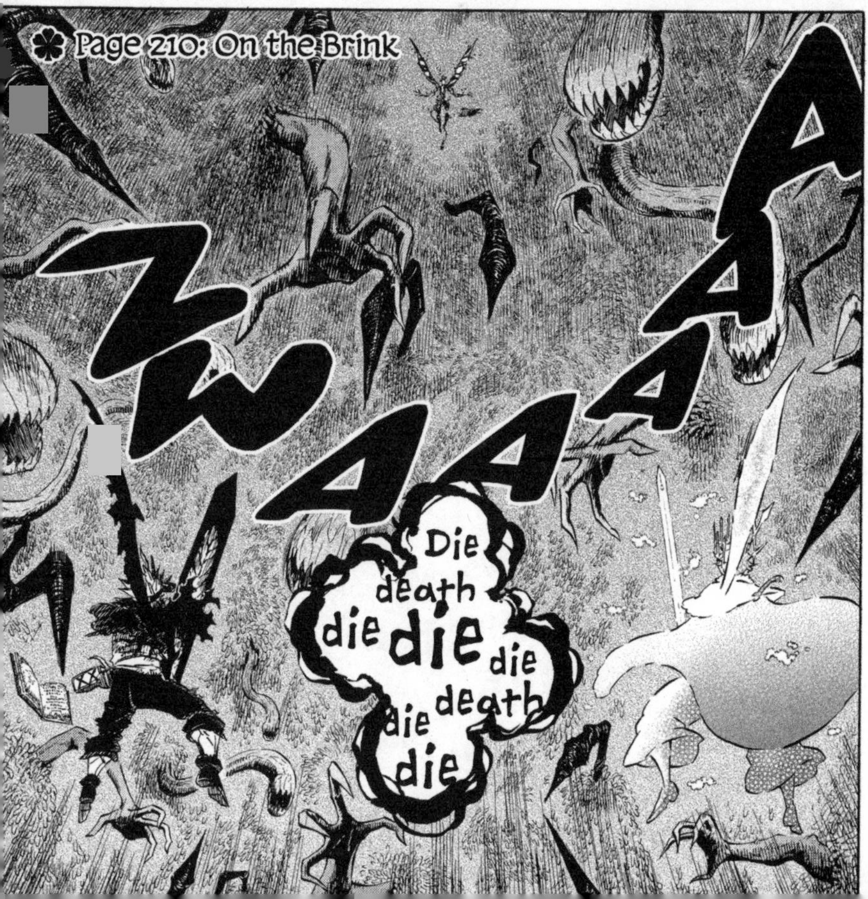
ZWAAAAAA
Die death die die die die death die die

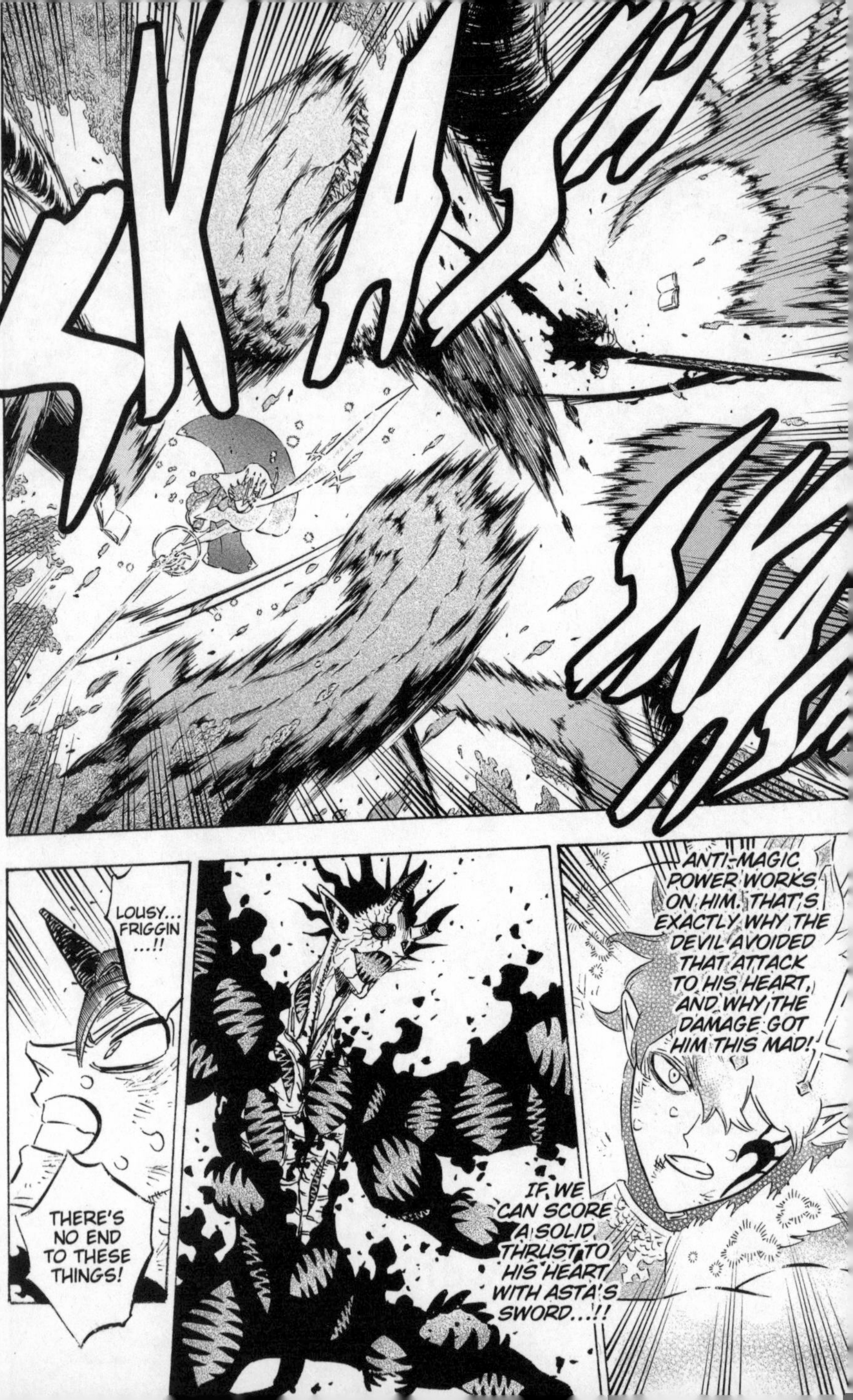
SHASH
ANTI-MAGIC POWER WORKS ON HIM. THAT'S EXACTLY WHY THE DEVIL AVOIDED THAT ATTACK TO HIS HEART, AND WHY THE DAMAGE GOT HIM THIS MAD!
IF WE CAN SCORE A SOLID THRUST TO HIS HEART WITH ASTA'S SWORD...!!
LOUSY... FRIGGIN ...!!
THERE'S NO END TO THESE THINGS!

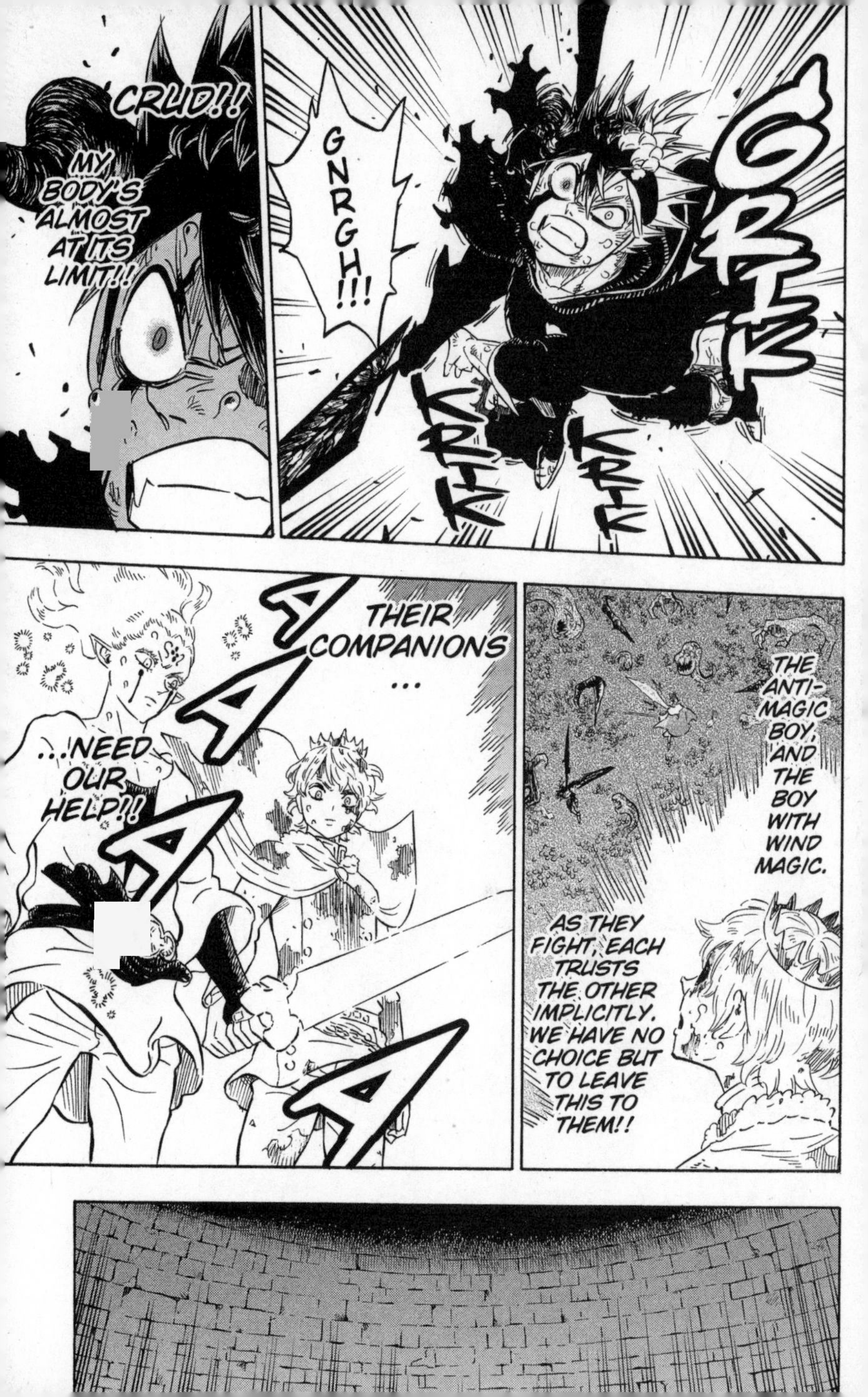

GRIK
GNRGH!!!
KRIK
KRIK
CRUD!!
MY BODY'S ALMOST AT ITS LIMIT!!
THE ANTI-MAGIC BOY, AND THE BOY WITH WIND MAGIC.
AS THEY FIGHT, EACH TRUSTS THE OTHER IMPLICITLY. WE HAVE NO CHOICE BUT TO LEAVE THIS TO THEM!!
A
A
A
A
THEIR COMPANIONS...
...NEED OUR HELP!!

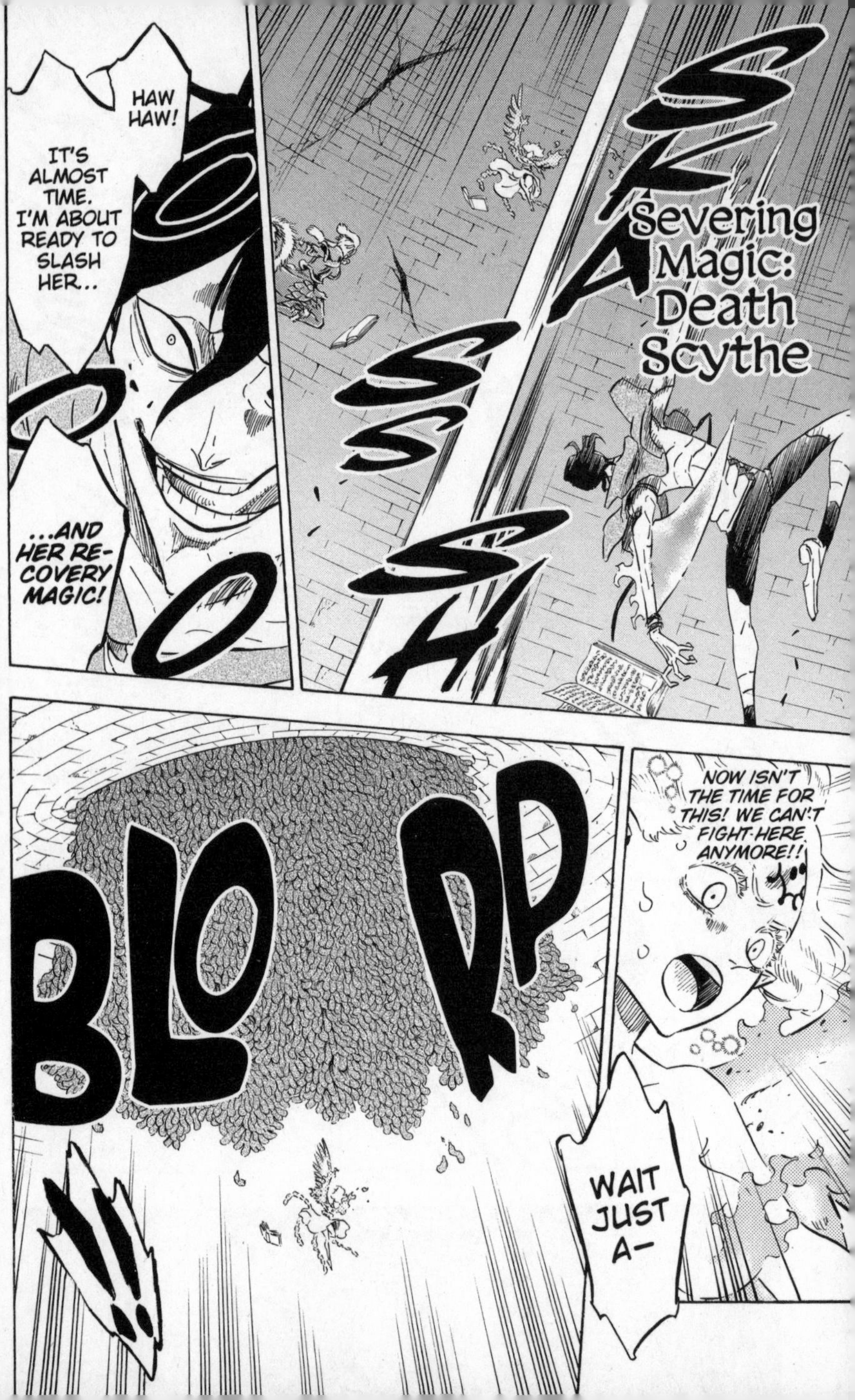
SKA
SSSH
Severing Magic: Death Scythe
HAW HAW!
IT'S ALMOST TIME. I'M ABOUT READY TO SLASH HER...
...AND HER RE-COVERY MAGIC!
NOW ISN'T THE TIME FOR THIS! WE CAN'T FIGHT HERE ANYMORE!!
WAIT JUST A-
BLORP
!!

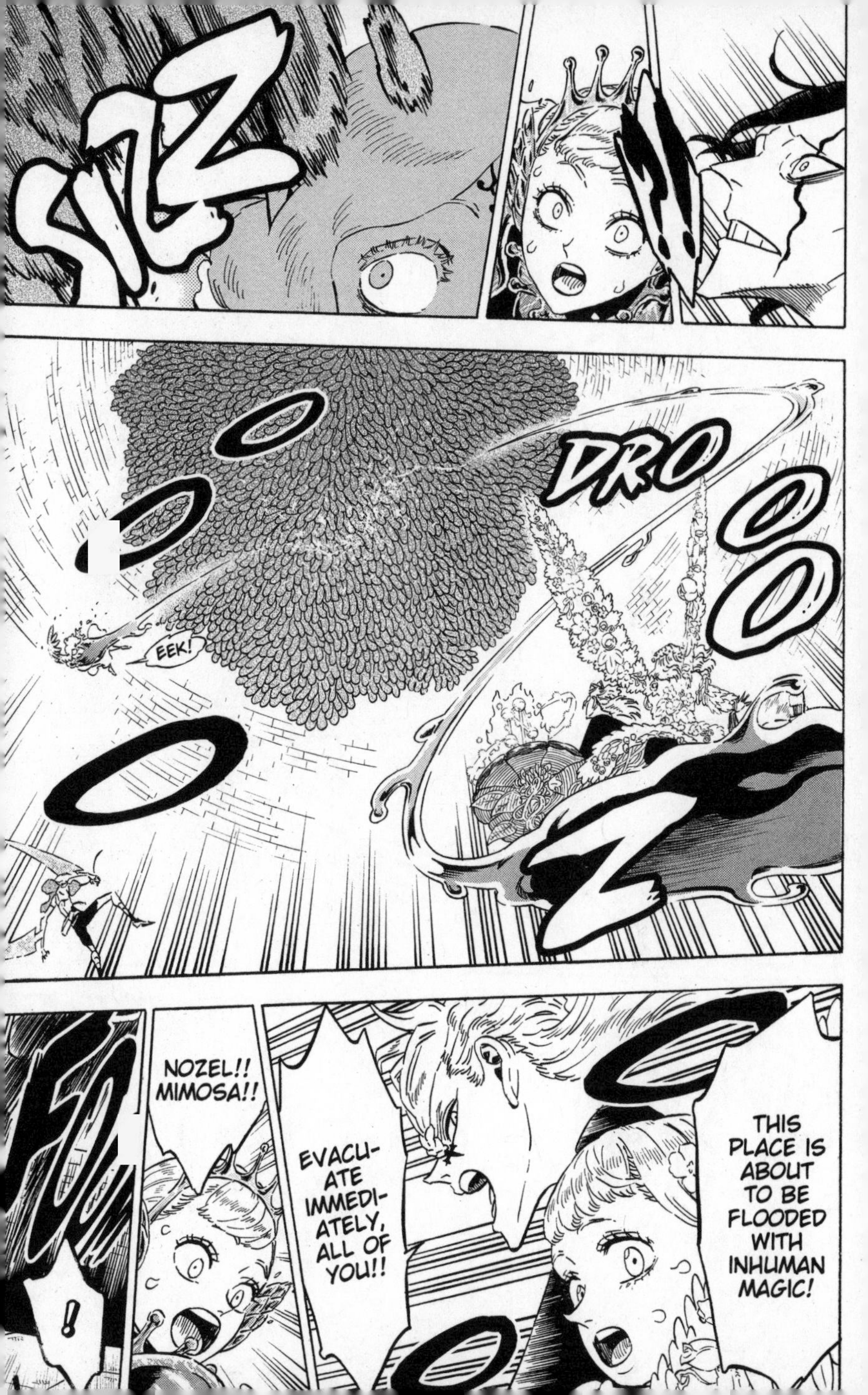
SIZZ
DROOOOOOOZ
EEK!
THIS PLACE IS ABOUT TO BE FLOODED WITH INHUMAN MAGIC!
EVACUATE IMMEDIATELY, ALL OF YOU!!
NOZEL!! MIMOSA!!
!

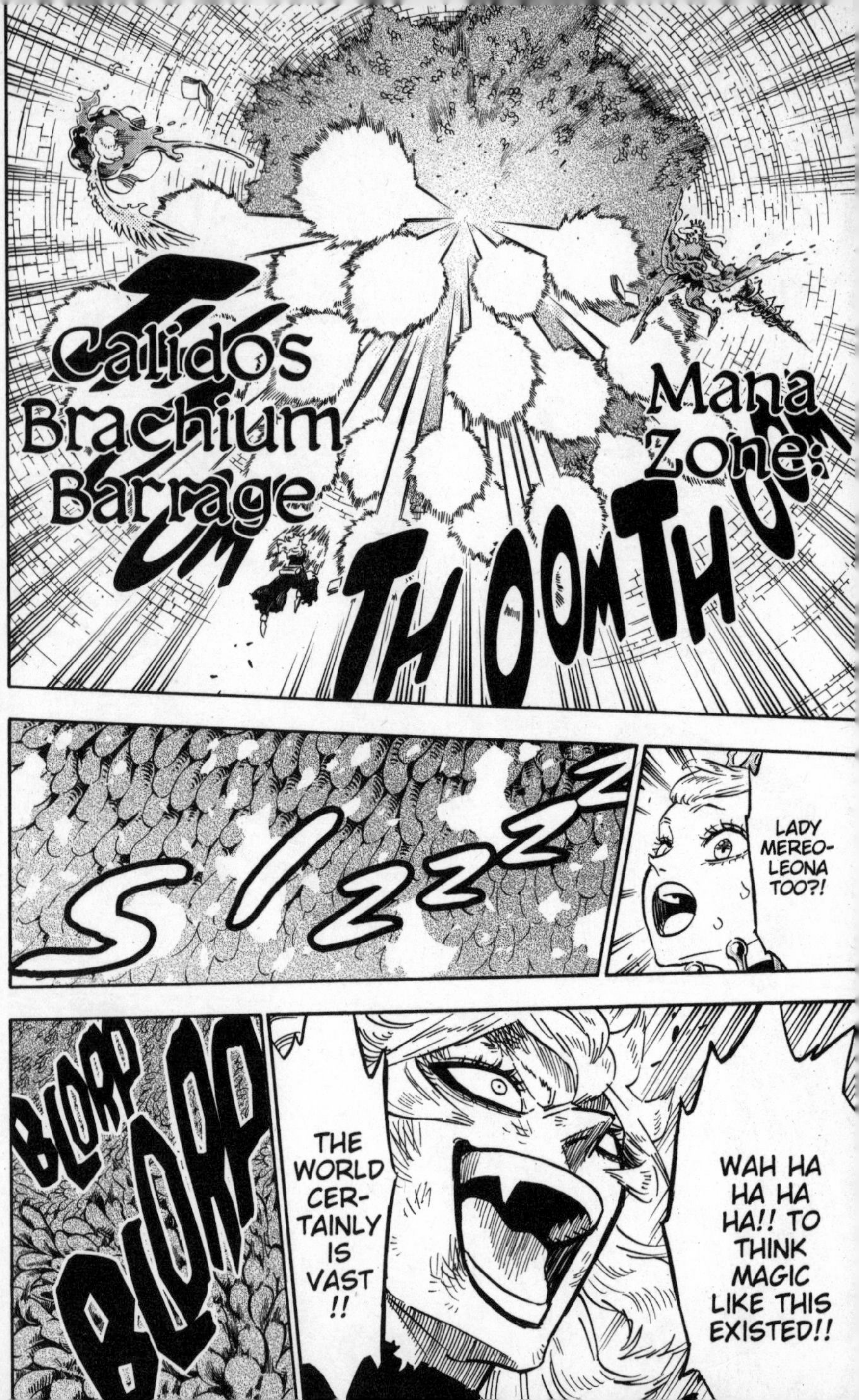

Mana Zone:
Calidos Brachium Barrage
THOOM
THOOM
LADY MEREO-LEONA TOO?!
SIZZZZZ
WAH HA HA HA HA!! TO THINK MAGIC LIKE THIS EXISTED!!
THE WORLD CER-TAINLY IS VAST!!
BLORP
BLORP

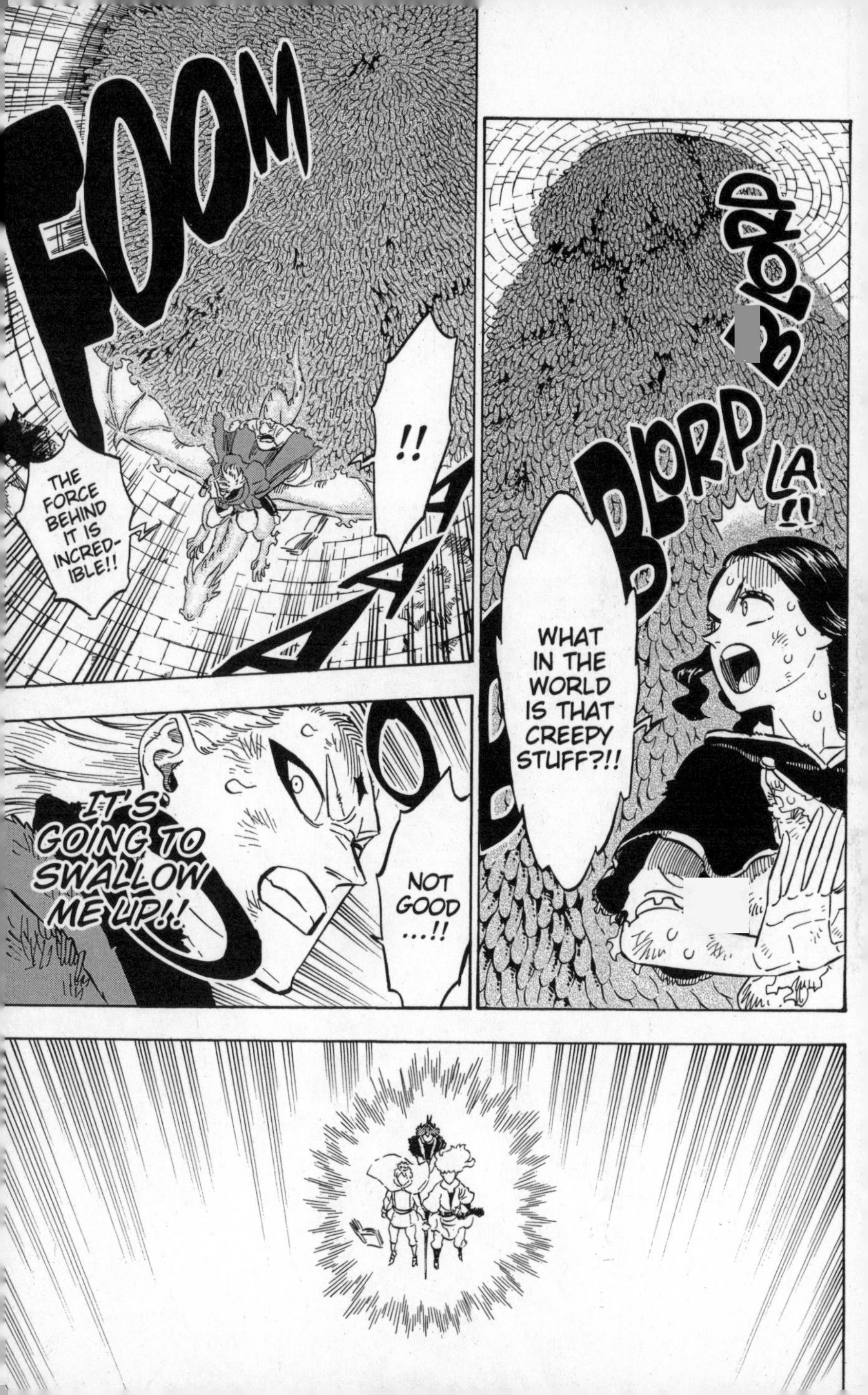
BLORP
BLORP
WHAT IN THE WORLD IS THAT CREEPY STUFF?!!
FOOM
THE FORCE BEHIND IT IS INCRED-IBLE!!
!!
NOT GOOD ...!!
IT'S GOING TO SWALLOW ME UP!!

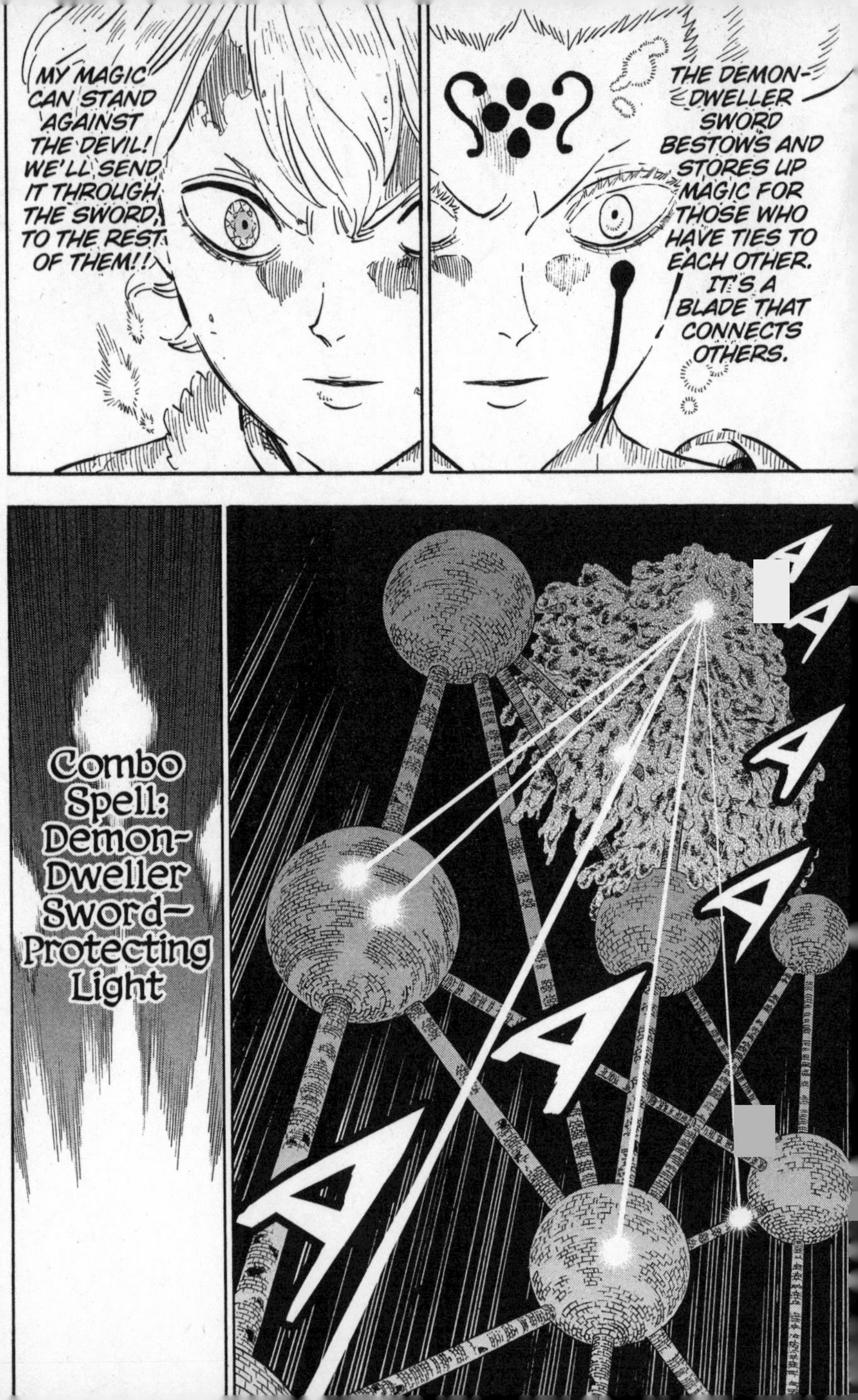
THE DEMON-DWELLER SWORD BESTOWS AND STORES UP MAGIC FOR THOSE WHO HAVE TIES TO EACH OTHER. IT'S A BLADE THAT CONNECTS OTHERS.
MY MAGIC CAN STAND AGAINST THE DEVIL! WE'LL SEND IT THROUGH THE SWORD, TO THE REST OF THEM!!
AAAAAA
Combo Spell: Demon-Dweller Sword—Protecting Light

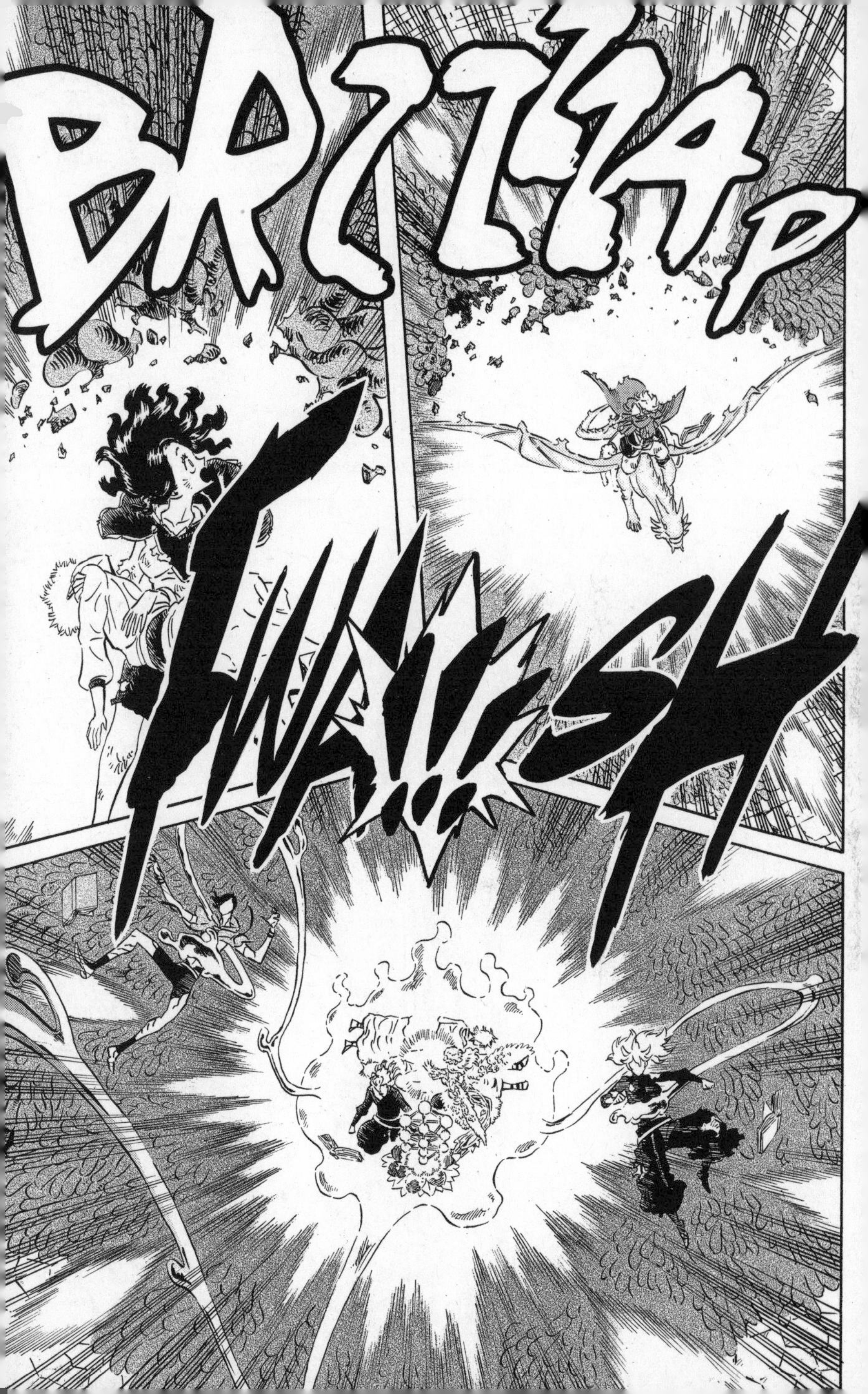
BRZZZAP
SWAAASH

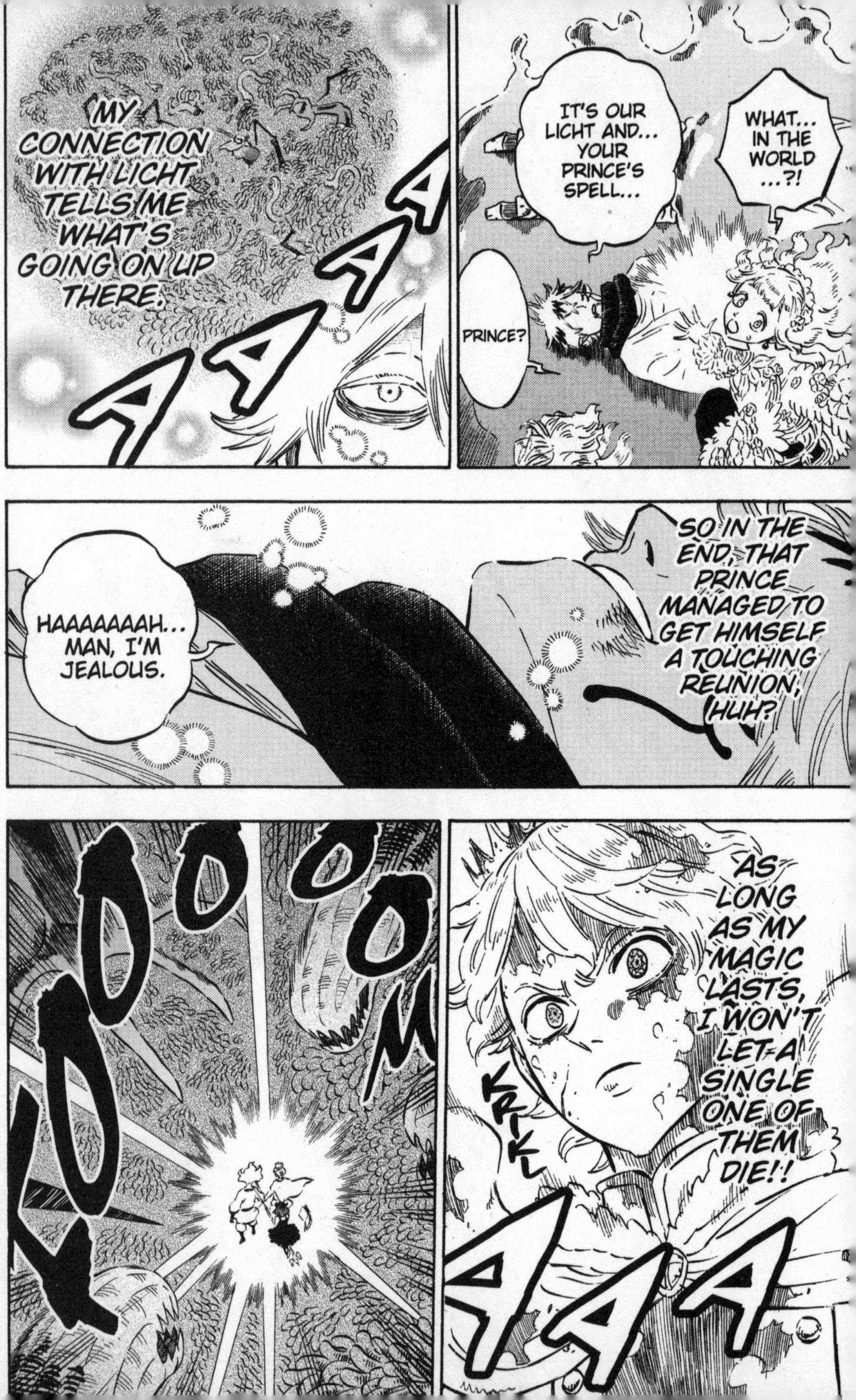
WHAT... IN THE WORLD ...?!
IT'S OUR LICHT AND... YOUR PRINCE'S SPELL...
PRINCE?
MY CONNECTION WITH LICHT TELLS ME WHAT'S GOING ON UP THERE.
AAAAA
SO IN THE END, THAT PRINCE MANAGED TO GET HIMSELF A TOUCHING REUNION, HUH?
HAAAAAAAH... MAN, I'M JEALOUS.
AS LONG AS MY MAGIC LASTS, I WON'T LET A SINGLE ONE OF THEM DIE!!
KRIKL
AAA
DOOOOM

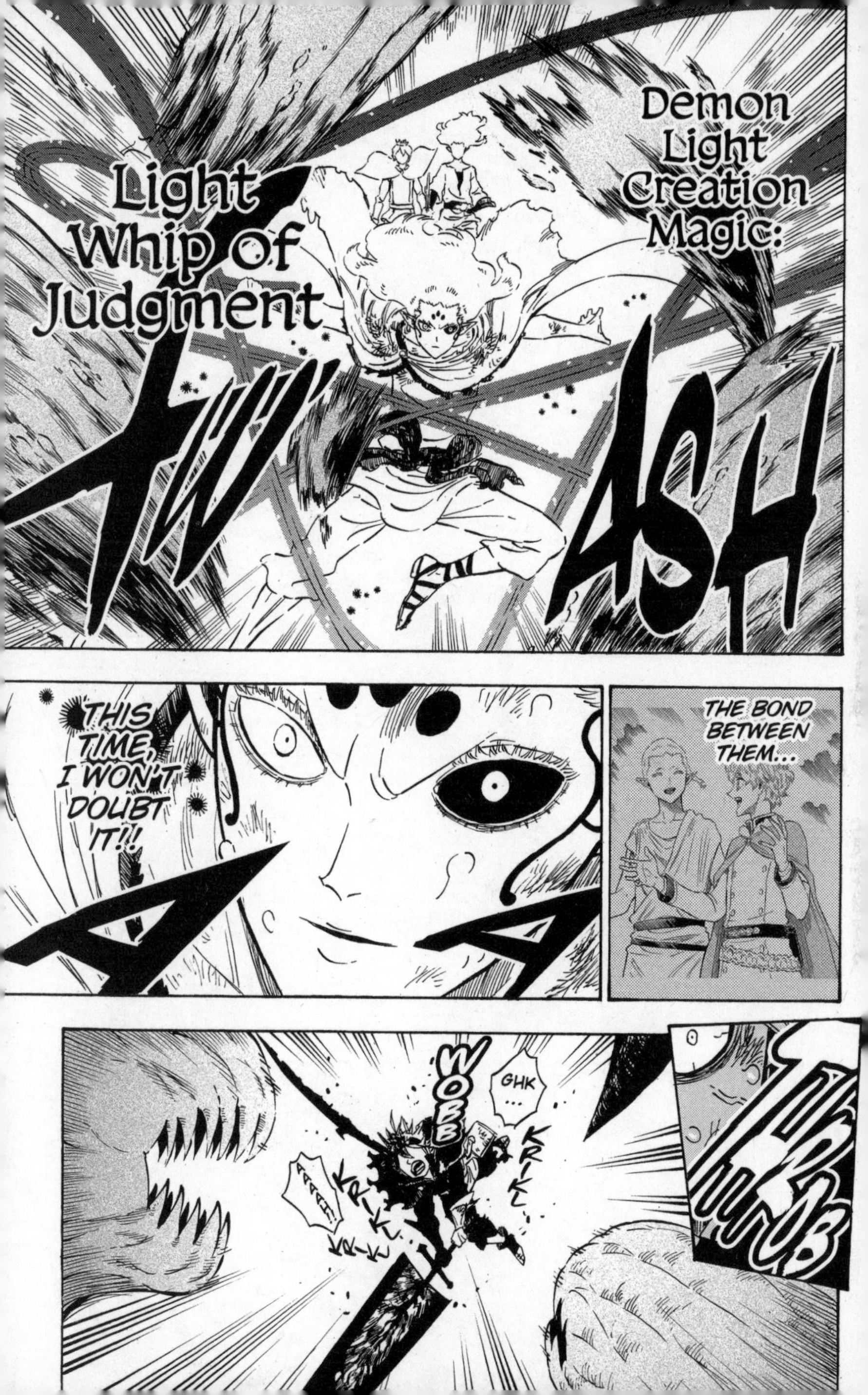
Demon Light Creation Magic:
Light Whip of Judgment
SWASH
THE BOND BETWEEN THEM...
THIS TIME, I WON'T DOUBT IT!!
WOBB
GHK ...
KRIKL

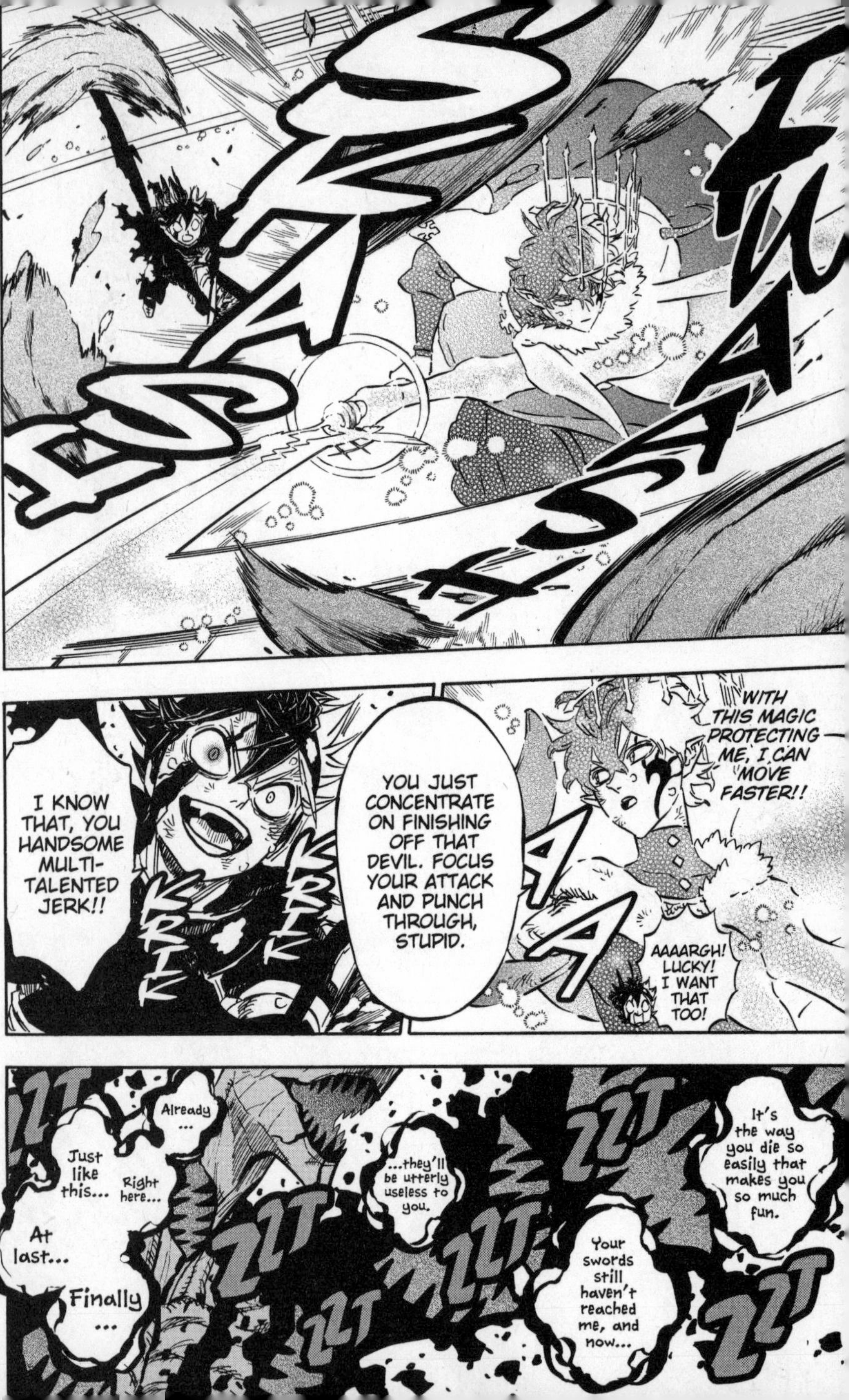
WITH THIS MAGIC PROTECTING ME, I CAN MOVE FASTER!!
AAAARGH! LUCKY! I WANT THAT TOO!
YOU JUST CONCENTRATE ON FINISHING OFF THAT DEVIL. FOCUS YOUR ATTACK AND PUNCH THROUGH, STUPID.
I KNOW THAT, YOU HANDSOME MULTI-TALENTED JERK!!
KRIK
KRIK
It's the way you die so easily that makes you so much fun.
Your swords still haven't reached me, and now...
...they'll be utterly useless to you.
Already...
Right here...
Just like this...
At last...
Finally...
ZZZT

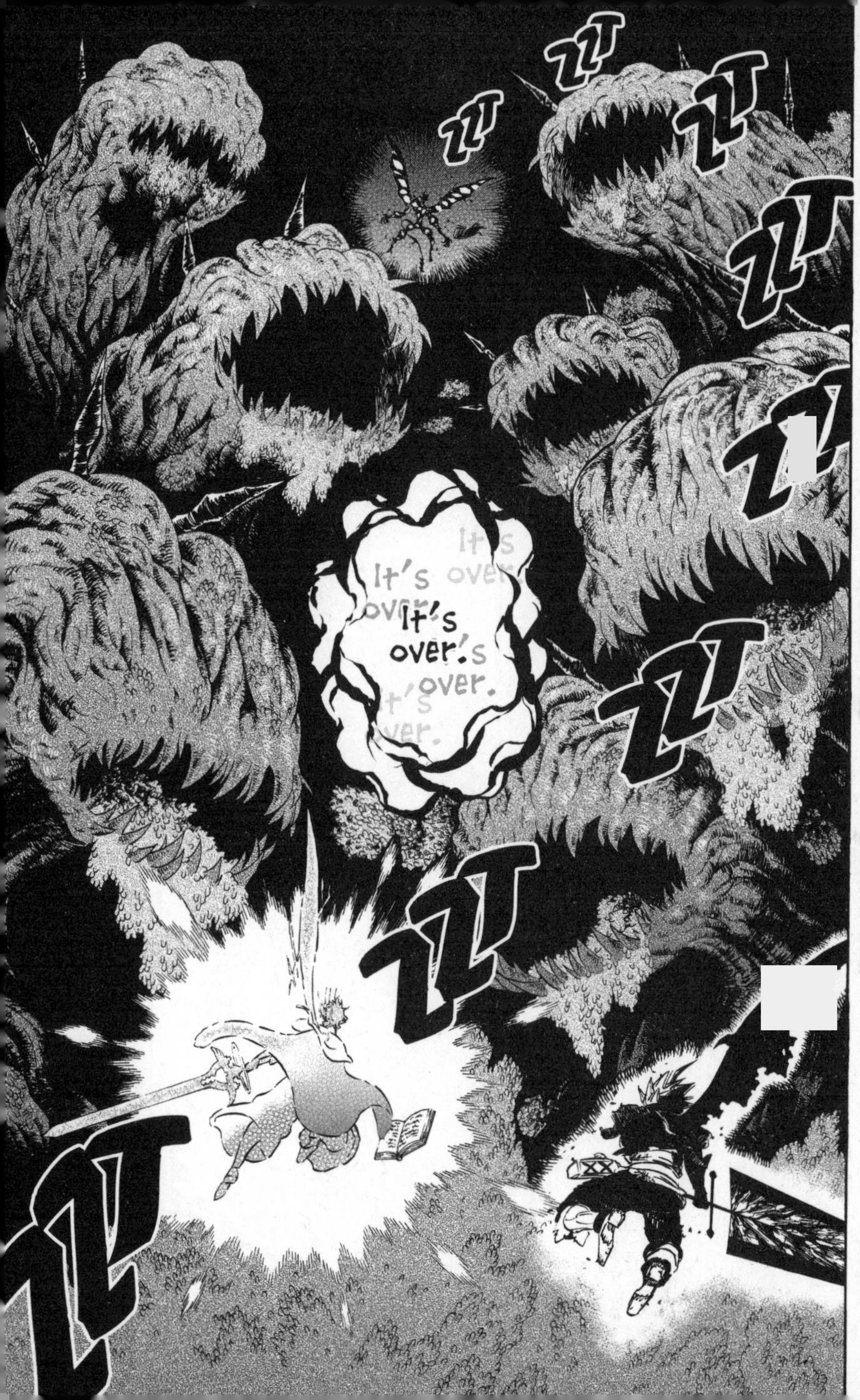
ZZT
ZZT
ZZT
ZZT
It's over.
It's over.
It's over.
It's over.
It's over.
ZZT
ZZT
ZZT
ZZT

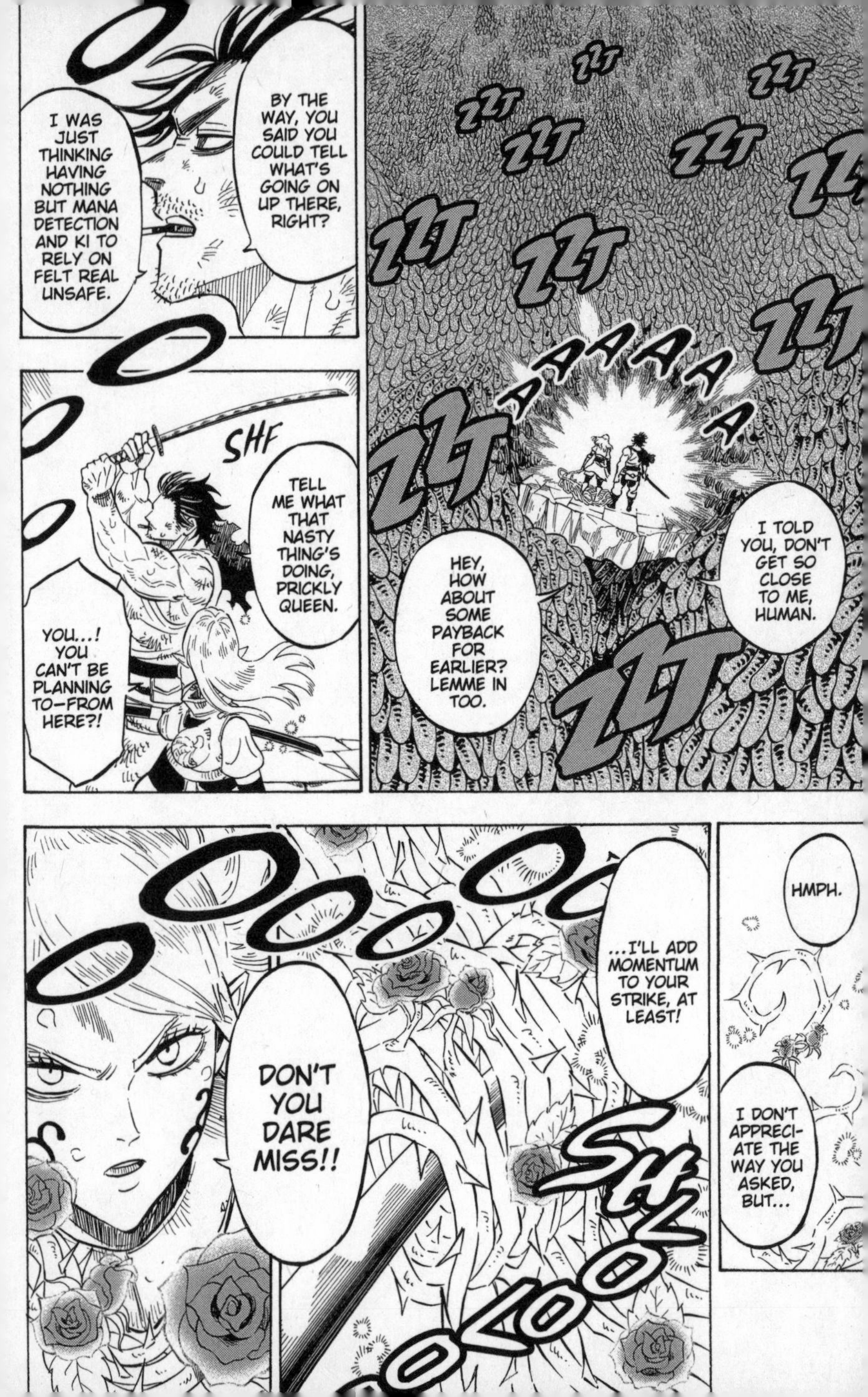
ZZT
AAAAAAA
I TOLD YOU, DON'T GET SO CLOSE TO ME, HUMAN.
HEY, HOW ABOUT SOME PAYBACK FOR EARLIER? LEMME IN TOO.
BY THE WAY, YOU SAID YOU COULD TELL WHAT'S GOING ON UP THERE, RIGHT?
I WAS JUST THINKING HAVING NOTHING BUT MANA DETECTION AND KI TO RELY ON FELT REAL UNSAFE.
SHF
TELL ME WHAT THAT NASTY THING'S DOING, PRICKLY QUEEN.
YOU...! YOU CAN'T BE PLANNING TO—FROM HERE?!
HMPH.
I DON'T APPRECI-ATE THE WAY YOU ASKED, BUT...
SHLOOOO
...I'LL ADD MOMENTUM TO YOUR STRIKE, AT LEAST!
DON'T YOU DARE MISS!!

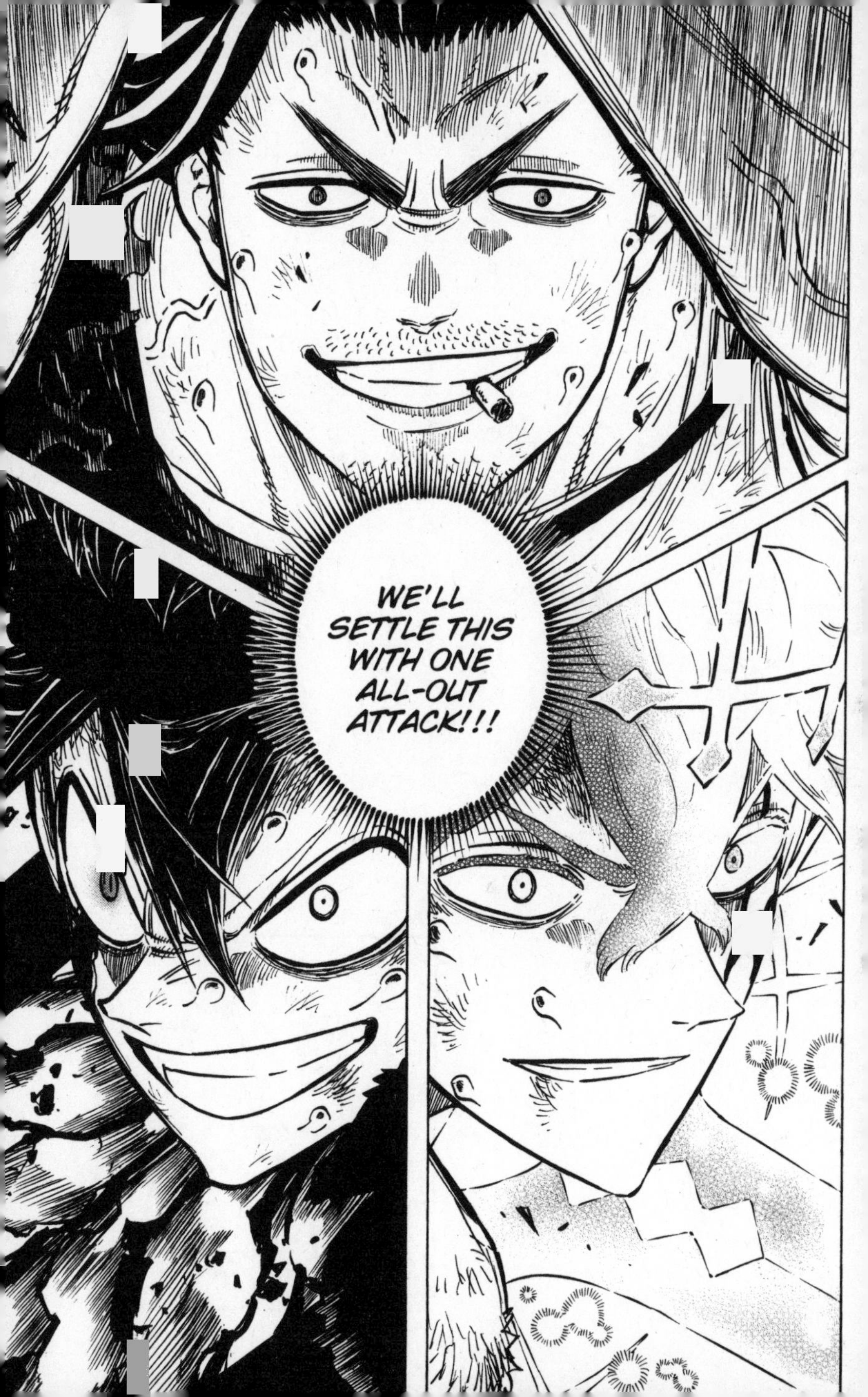
WE'LL SETTLE THIS WITH ONE ALL-OUT ATTACK!!!

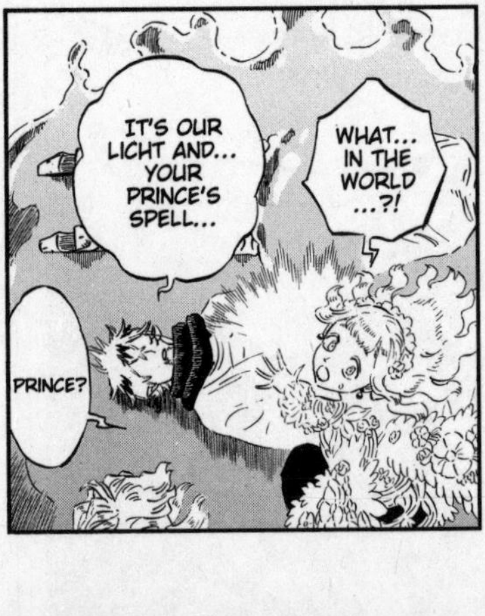
WHAT... IN THE WORLD ...?!
IT'S OUR LICHT AND... YOUR PRINCE'S SPELL...
PRINCE?

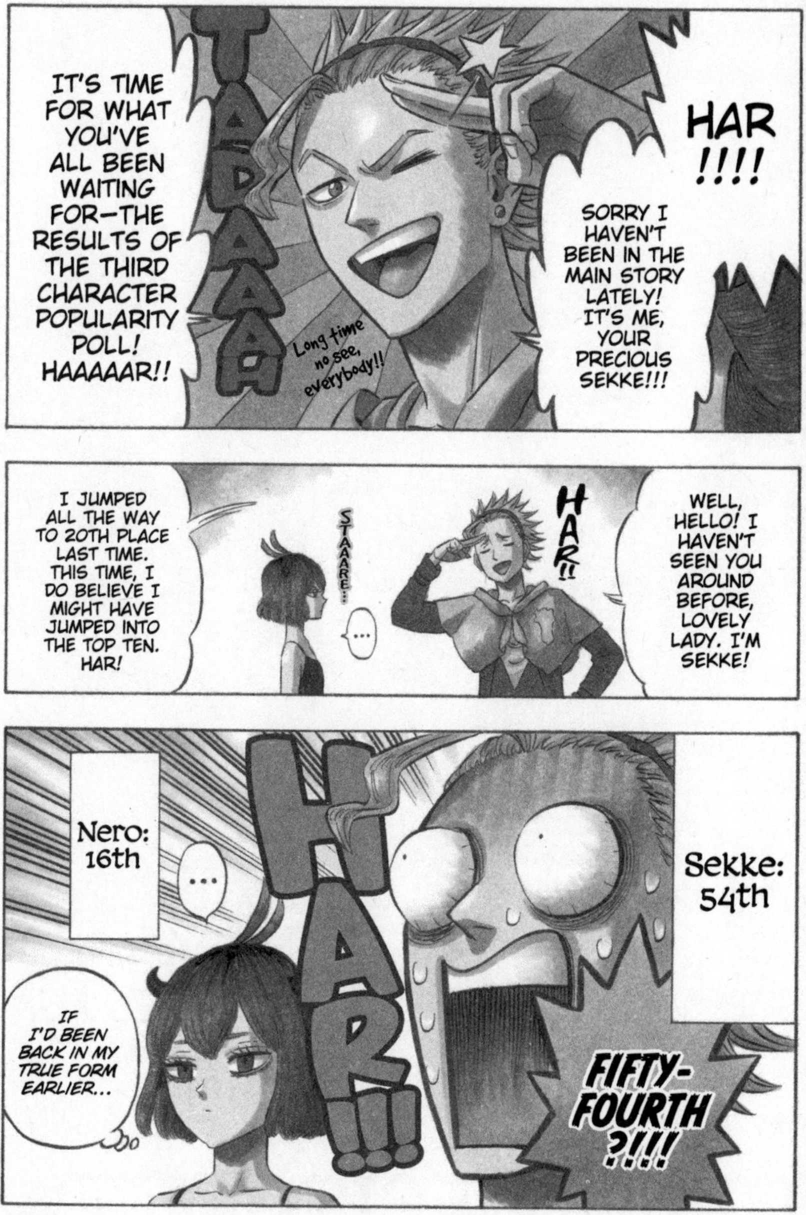
HAR !!!!
SORRY I HAVEN'T BEEN IN THE MAIN STORY LATELY! IT'S ME, YOUR PRECIOUS SEKKE!!!
Long time no see, everybody!!
TADAAAA
IT'S TIME FOR WHAT YOU'VE ALL BEEN WAITING FOR—THE RESULTS OF THE THIRD CHARACTER POPULARITY POLL! HAAAAAR!!
WELL, HELLO! I HAVEN'T SEEN YOU AROUND BEFORE, LOVELY LADY. I'M SEKKE!
HAR!!
...
STAAARE...
I JUMPED ALL THE WAY TO 20TH PLACE LAST TIME. THIS TIME, I DO BELIEVE I MIGHT HAVE JUMPED INTO THE TOP TEN. HAR!
Sekke: 54th
FIFTY-FOURTH?!!!
HAR!!!
...
Nero: 16th
IF I'D BEEN BACK IN MY TRUE FORM EARLIER...

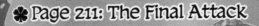

**6th
CHARLOTTE
ROSELEI**
1,156 VOTES

**7th
CHARMY
PAPPITSON**
986 VOTES

4th YUNO
1,628 VOTES

**9th
LUCK VOLTIA**
842 VOTES

**2nd
YAMI
SUKEHIRO**
2,213 VOTES

KNIGHT GENERAL ELECTION!!

Turn to page 88 for the rest!

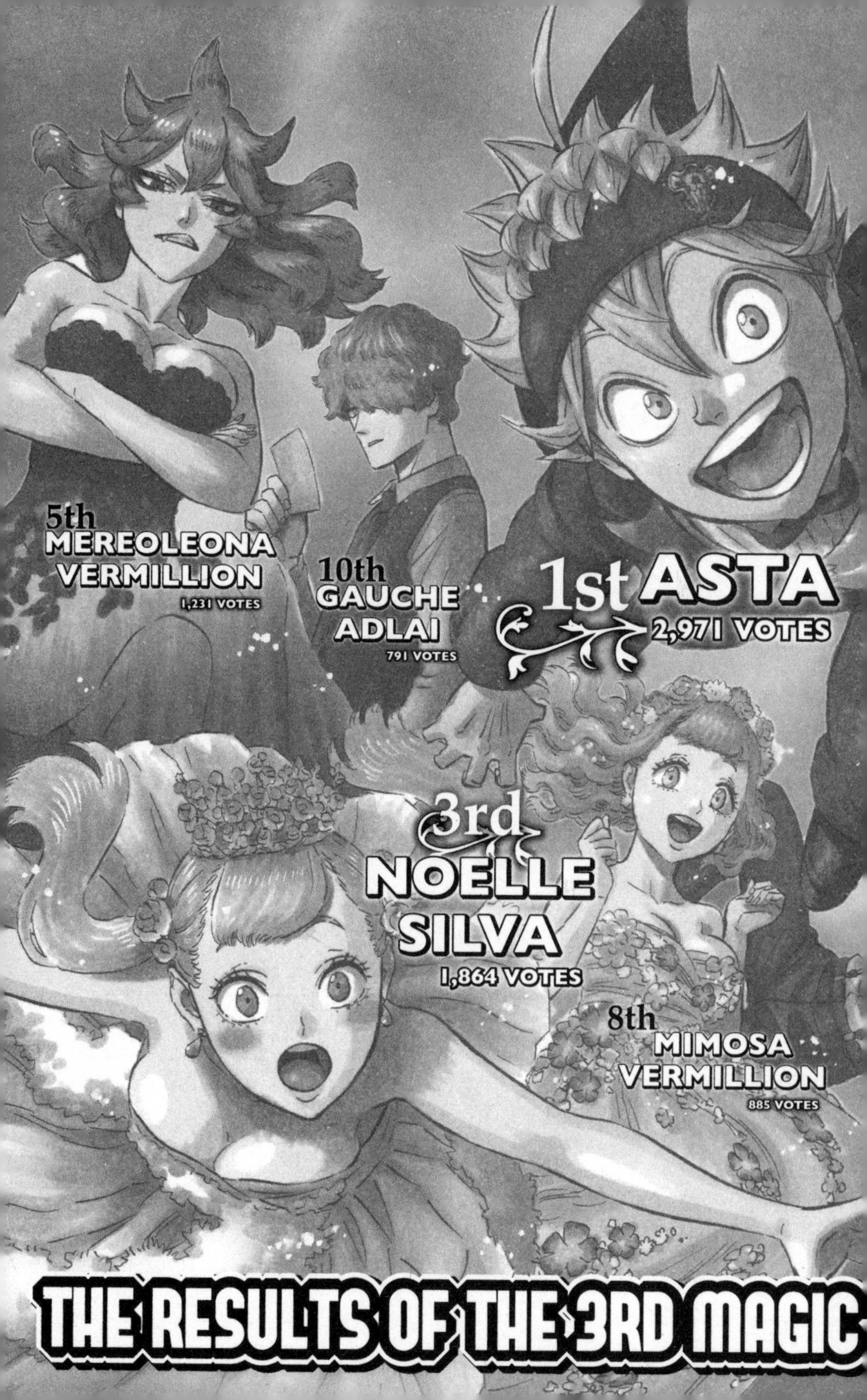
1st ASTA
2,971 VOTES
3rd NOELLE SILVA
1,864 VOTES
5th MEREOLEONA VERMILLION
1,231 VOTES
8th MIMOSA VERMILLION
885 VOTES
10th GAUCHE ADLAI
791 VOTES
THE RESULTS OF THE 3RD MAGIC

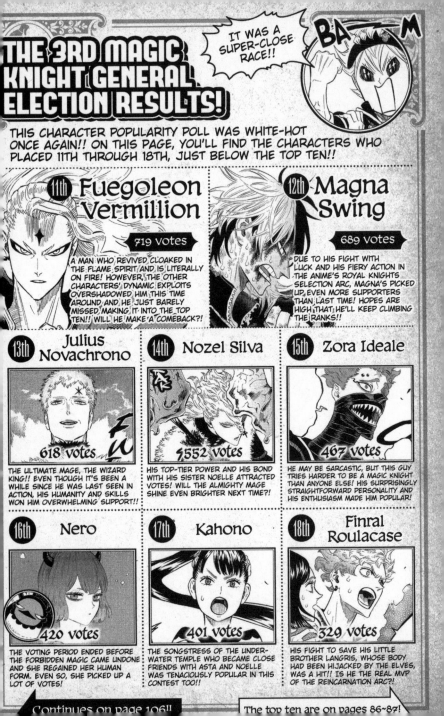

THE 3RD MAGIC KNIGHT GENERAL ELECTION RESULTS!

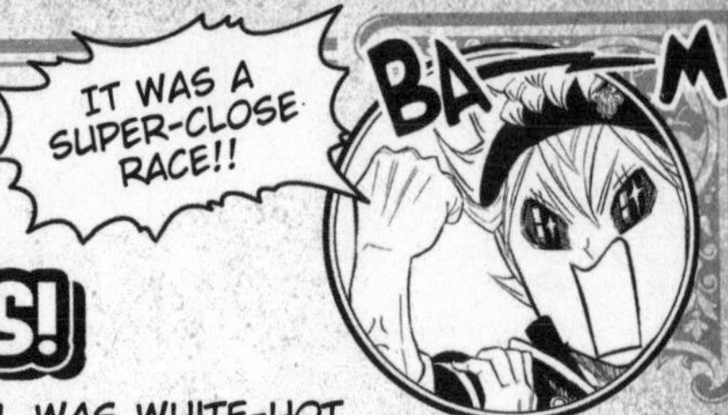
IT WAS A SUPER-CLOSE RACE!!
BA—M

THIS CHARACTER POPULARITY POLL WAS WHITE-HOT ONCE AGAIN!! ON THIS PAGE, YOU'LL FIND THE CHARACTERS WHO PLACED 11TH THROUGH 18TH, JUST BELOW THE TOP TEN!!

11th Fuegoleon Vermillion

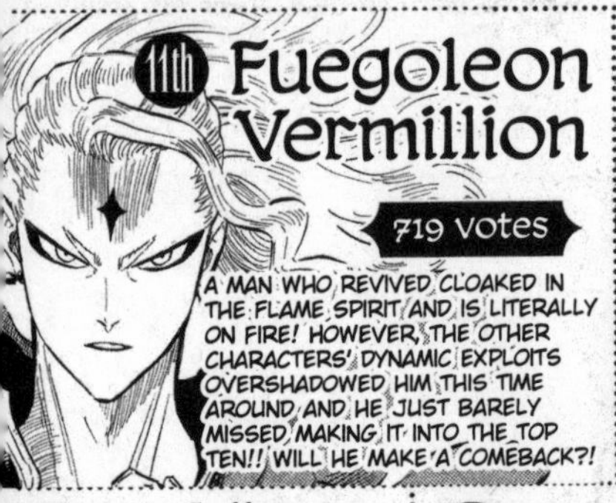

719 votes

A MAN WHO REVIVED CLOAKED IN THE FLAME SPIRIT AND IS LITERALLY ON FIRE! HOWEVER, THE OTHER CHARACTERS' DYNAMIC EXPLOITS OVERSHADOWED HIM THIS TIME AROUND AND HE JUST BARELY MISSED MAKING IT INTO THE TOP TEN!! WILL HE MAKE A COMEBACK?!

12th Magna Swing

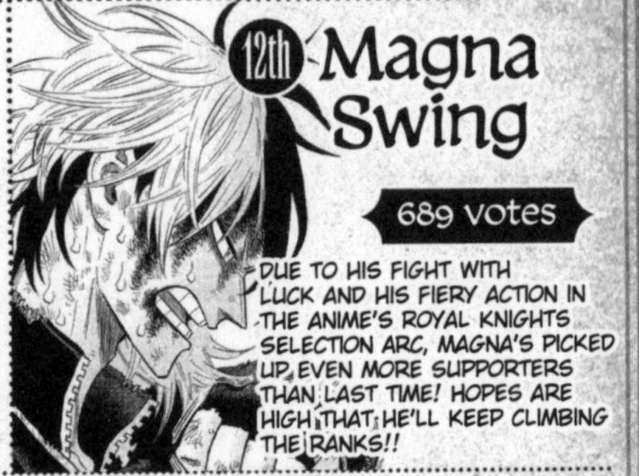

689 votes

DUE TO HIS FIGHT WITH LUCK AND HIS FIERY ACTION IN THE ANIME'S ROYAL KNIGHTS SELECTION ARC, MAGNA'S PICKED UP EVEN MORE SUPPORTERS THAN LAST TIME! HOPES ARE HIGH THAT HE'LL KEEP CLIMBING THE RANKS!!

13th Julius Novachrono

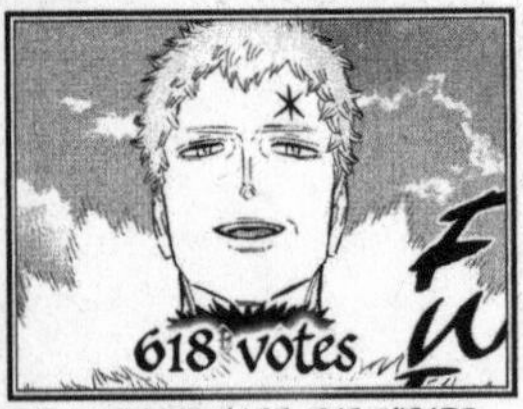
618 votes

THE ULTIMATE MAGE, THE WIZARD KING!! EVEN THOUGH IT'S BEEN A WHILE SINCE HE WAS LAST SEEN IN ACTION, HIS HUMANITY AND SKILLS WON HIM OVERWHELMING SUPPORT!!

14th Nozel Silva

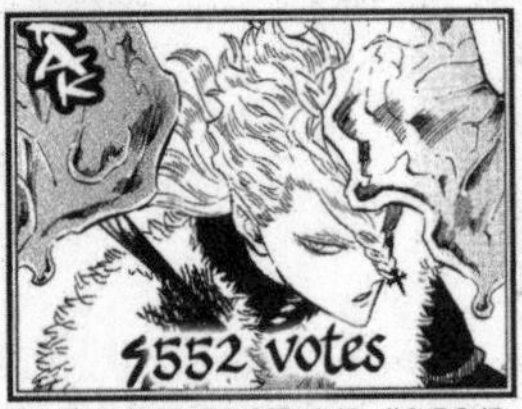
552 votes

HIS TOP-TIER POWER AND HIS BOND WITH HIS SISTER NOELLE ATTRACTED VOTES! WILL THE ALMIGHTY MAGE SHINE EVEN BRIGHTER NEXT TIME?!

15th Zora Ideale

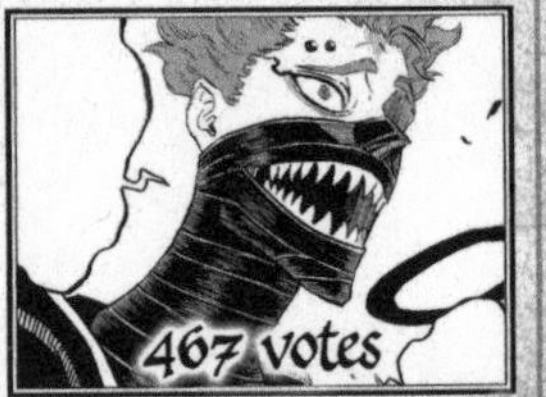
467 votes

HE MAY BE SARCASTIC, BUT THIS GUY TRIES HARDER TO BE A MAGIC KNIGHT THAN ANYONE ELSE! HIS SURPRISINGLY STRAIGHTFORWARD PERSONALITY AND HIS ENTHUSIASM MADE HIM POPULAR!

16th Nero

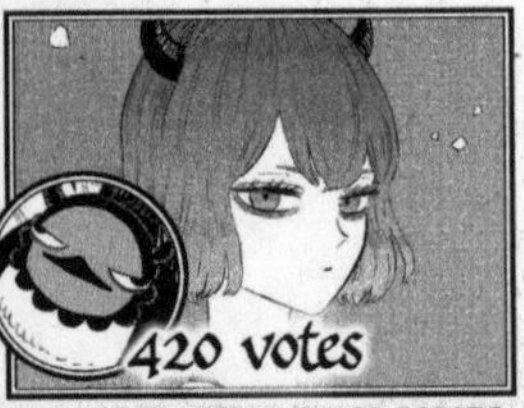
420 votes

THE VOTING PERIOD ENDED BEFORE THE FORBIDDEN MAGIC CAME UNDONE AND SHE REGAINED HER HUMAN FORM. EVEN SO, SHE PICKED UP A LOT OF VOTES!

17th Kahono

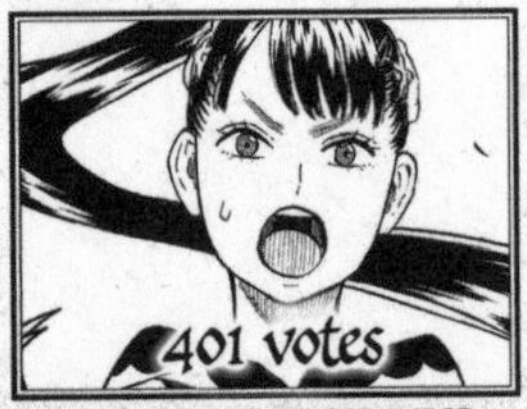
401 votes

THE SONGSTRESS OF THE UNDERWATER TEMPLE WHO BECAME CLOSE FRIENDS WITH ASTA AND NOELLE WAS TENACIOUSLY POPULAR IN THIS CONTEST TOO!!

18th Finral Roulacase

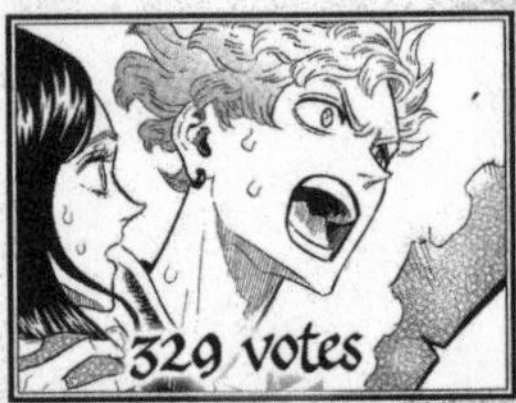
329 votes

HIS FIGHT TO SAVE HIS LITTLE BROTHER LANGRIS, WHOSE BODY HAD BEEN HIJACKED BY THE ELVES, WAS A HIT!! IS HE THE REAL MVP OF THE REINCARNATION ARC?!

Continues on page 106!!

The top ten are on pages 86~87!

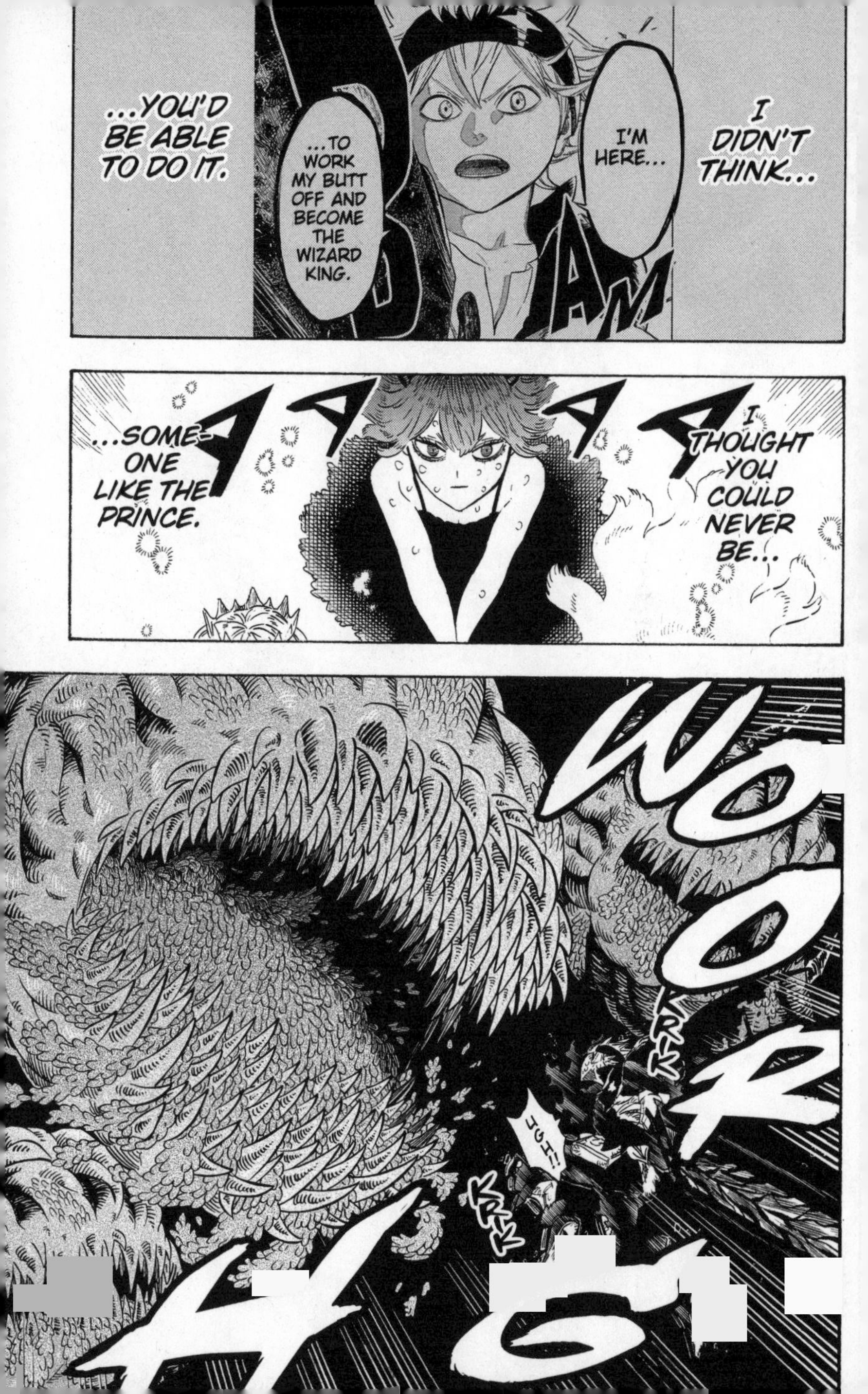
I DIDN'T THINK...
I'M HERE...
...TO WORK MY BUTT OFF AND BECOME THE WIZARD KING.
...YOU'D BE ABLE TO DO IT.
I THOUGHT YOU COULD NEVER BE...
...SOME-ONE LIKE THE PRINCE.
KRIK
UGH!!
KRIK

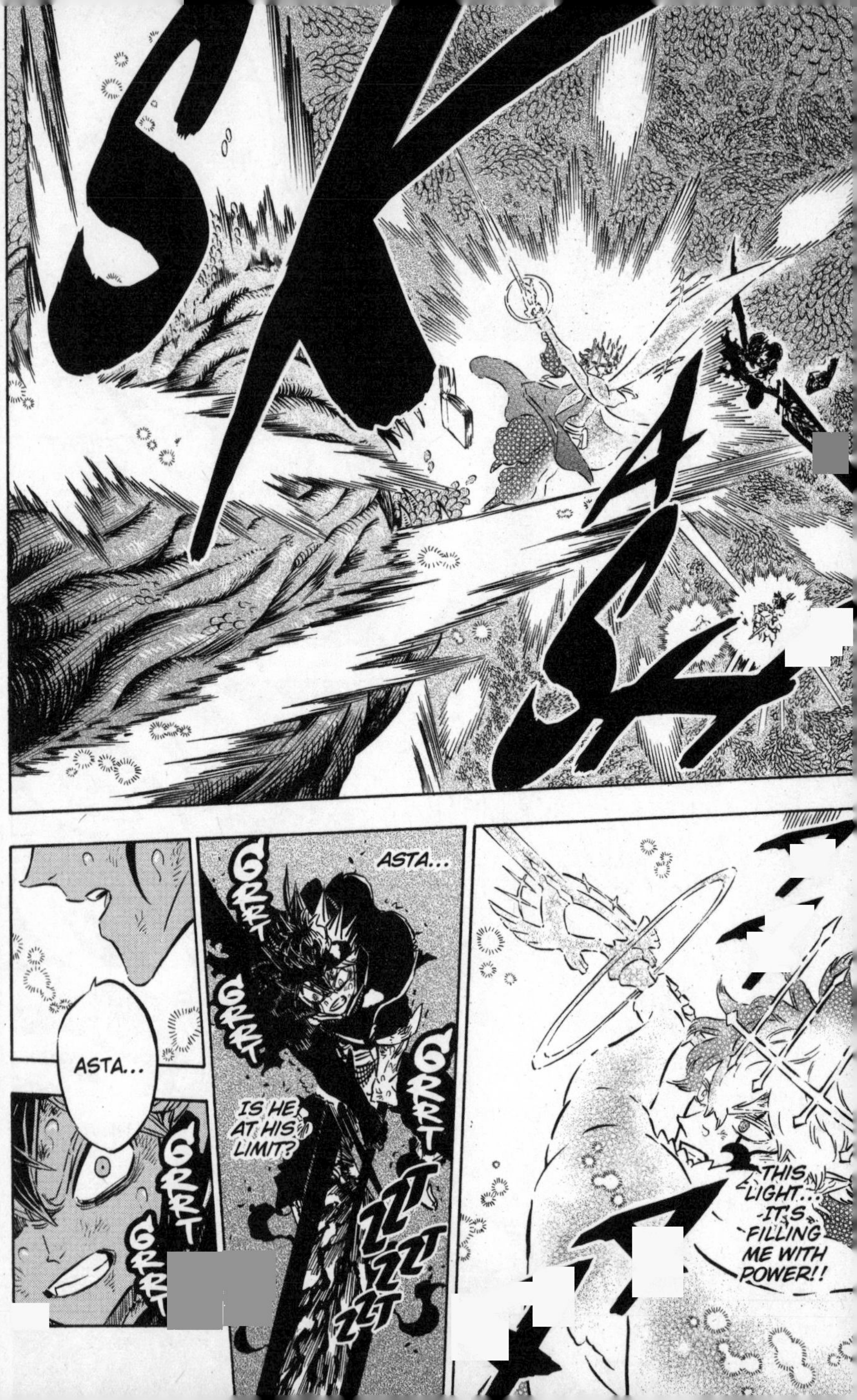
THIS LIGHT... IT'S FILLING ME WITH POWER!!
ASTA...
GRRT GRRT GRRT
IS HE AT HIS LIMIT?
ZZZT ZZZT ZZZT
ASTA...
GRRT GRRT

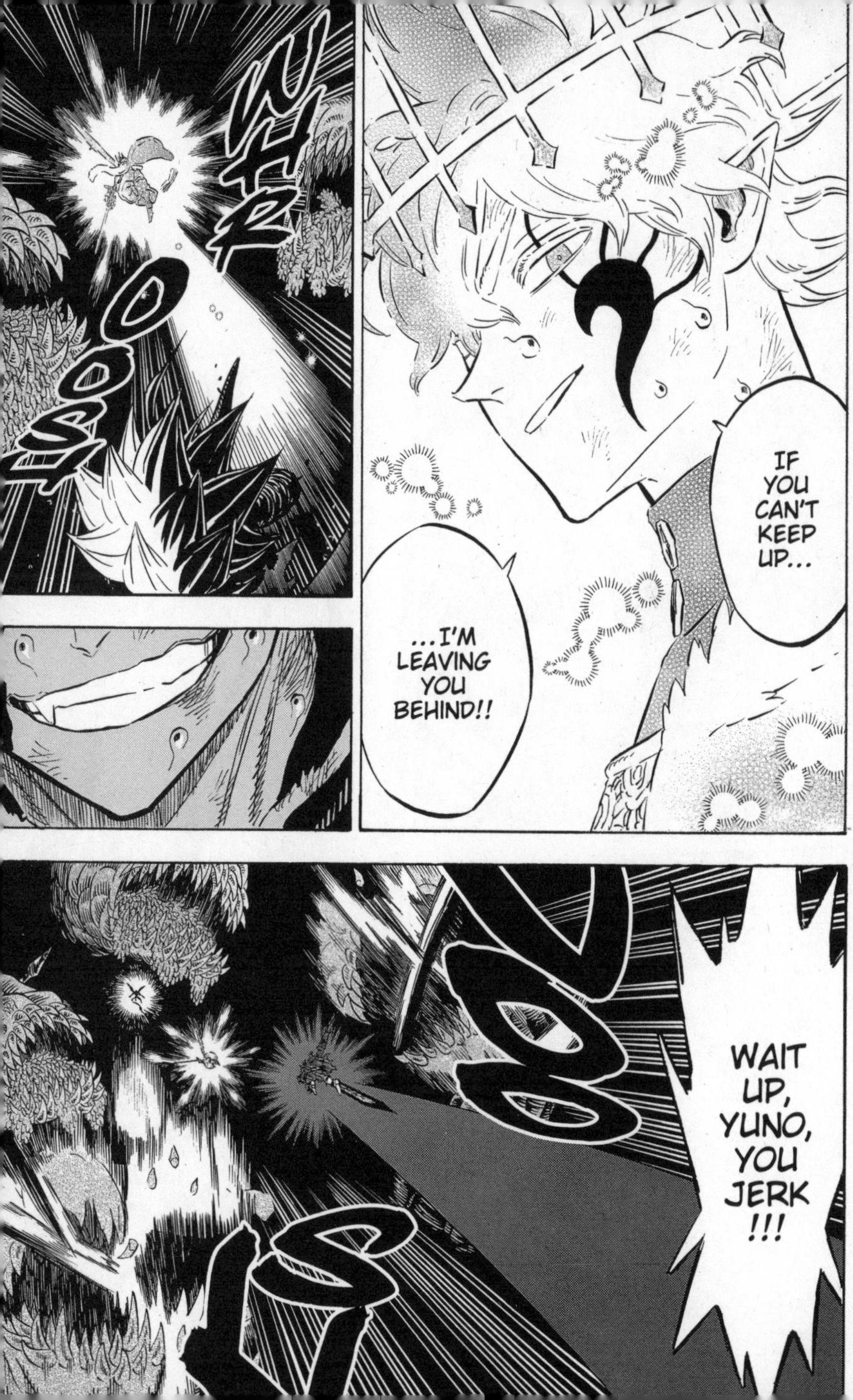
IF YOU CAN'T KEEP UP...
...I'M LEAVING YOU BEHIND!!
WAIT UP, YUNO, YOU JERK!!!

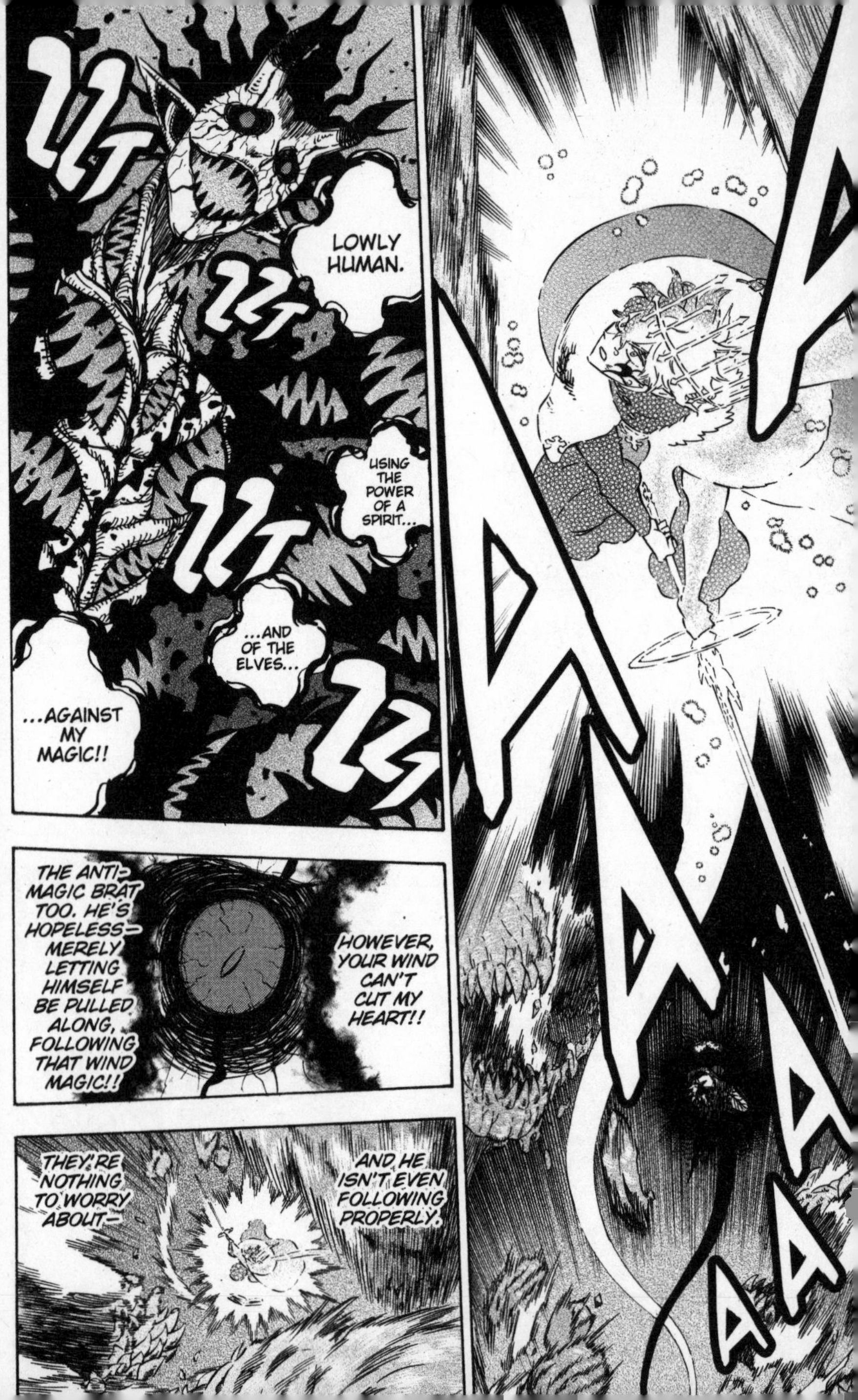
LOWLY HUMAN.
USING THE POWER OF A SPIRIT...
...AND OF THE ELVES...
...AGAINST MY MAGIC!!
HOWEVER, YOUR WIND CAN'T CUT MY HEART!!
THE ANTI-MAGIC BRAT TOO. HE'S HOPELESS—MERELY LETTING HIMSELF BE PULLED ALONG, FOLLOWING THAT WIND MAGIC!!
AND HE ISN'T EVEN FOLLOWING PROPERLY.
THEY'RE NOTHING TO WORRY ABOUT—

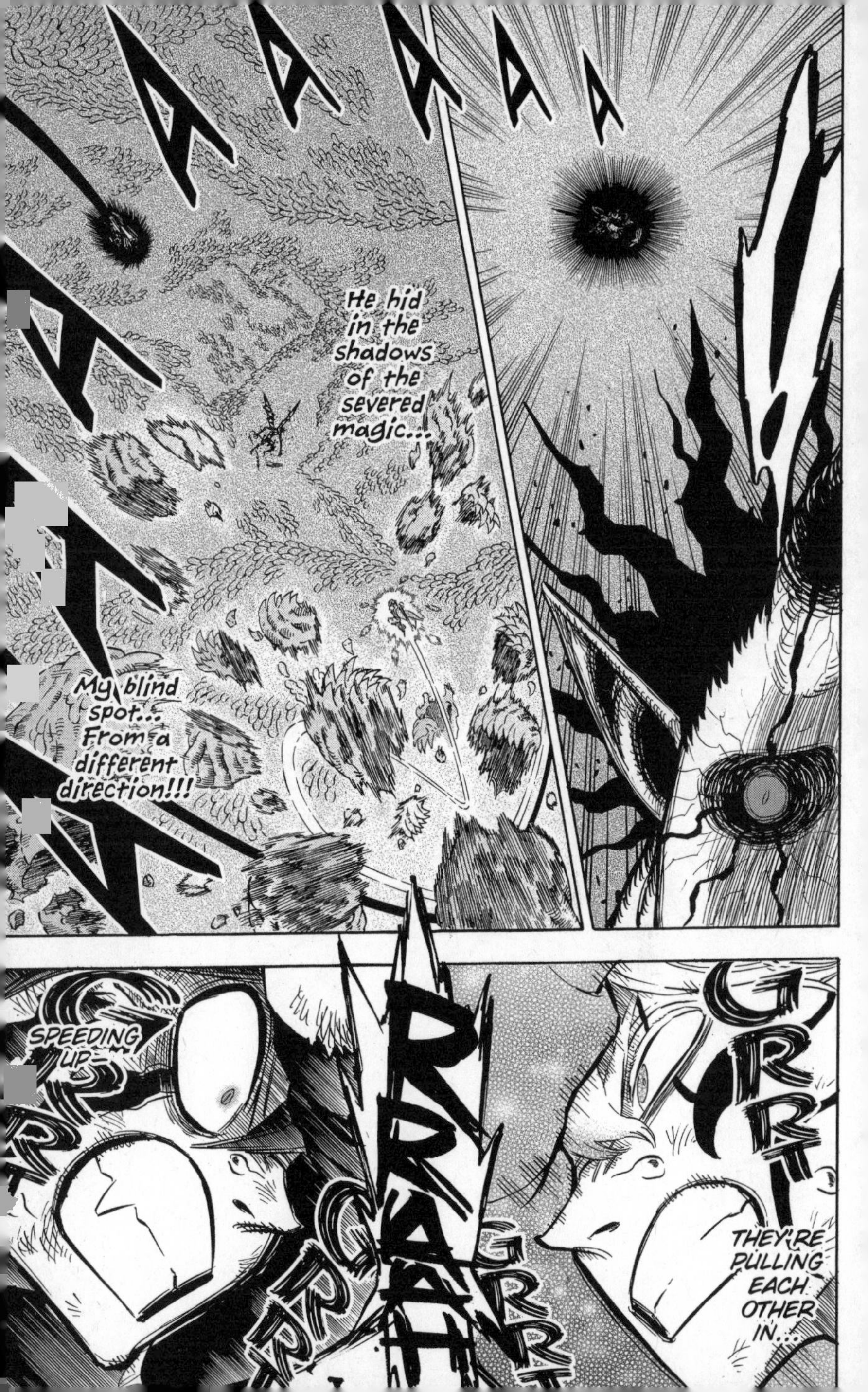
AAAAAAAA
He hid in the shadows of the severed magic...
My blind spot... From a different direction!!!
GRRR
DRAAAH
GRRR
THEY'RE PULLING EACH OTHER IN...
SPEEDING UP

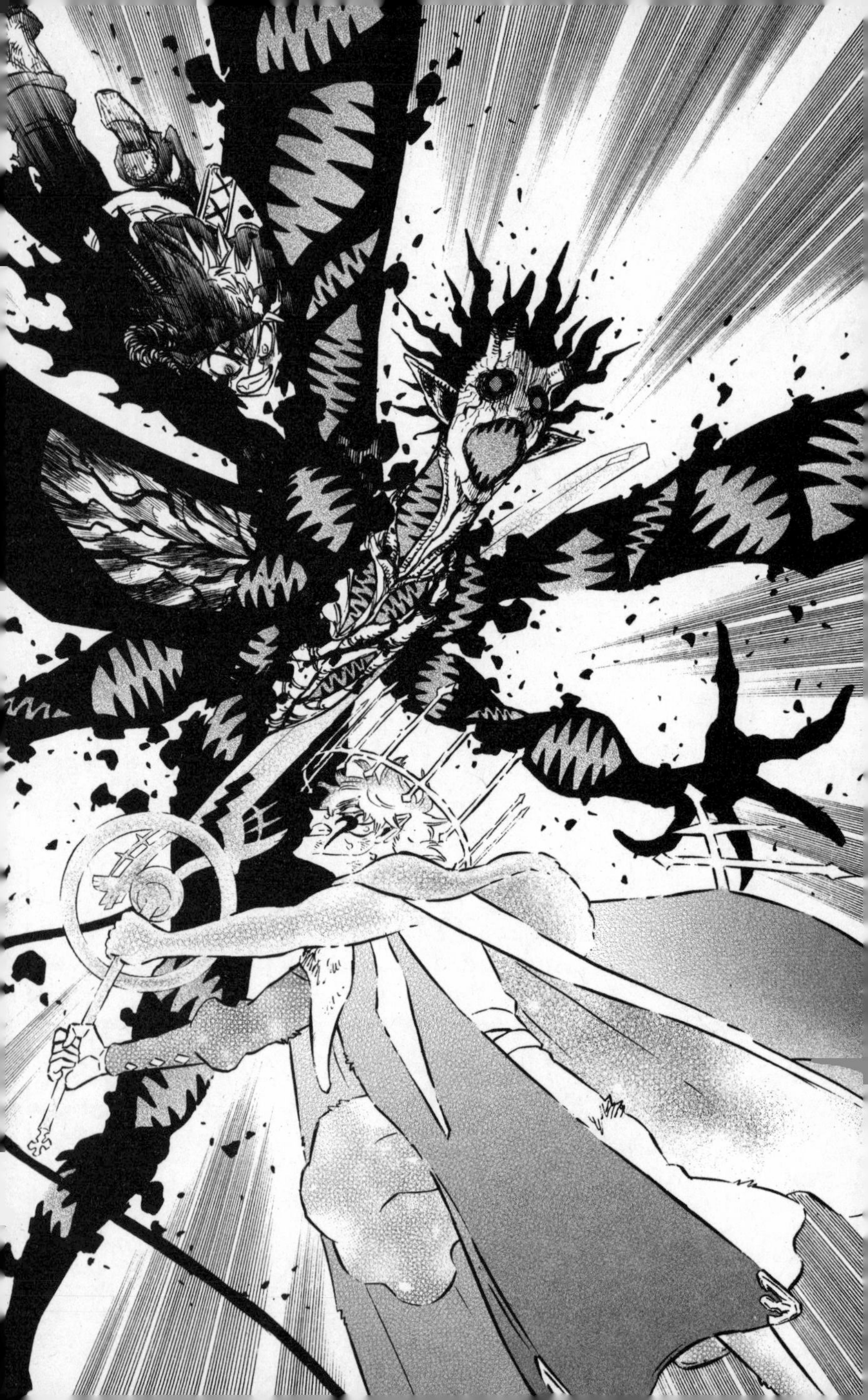

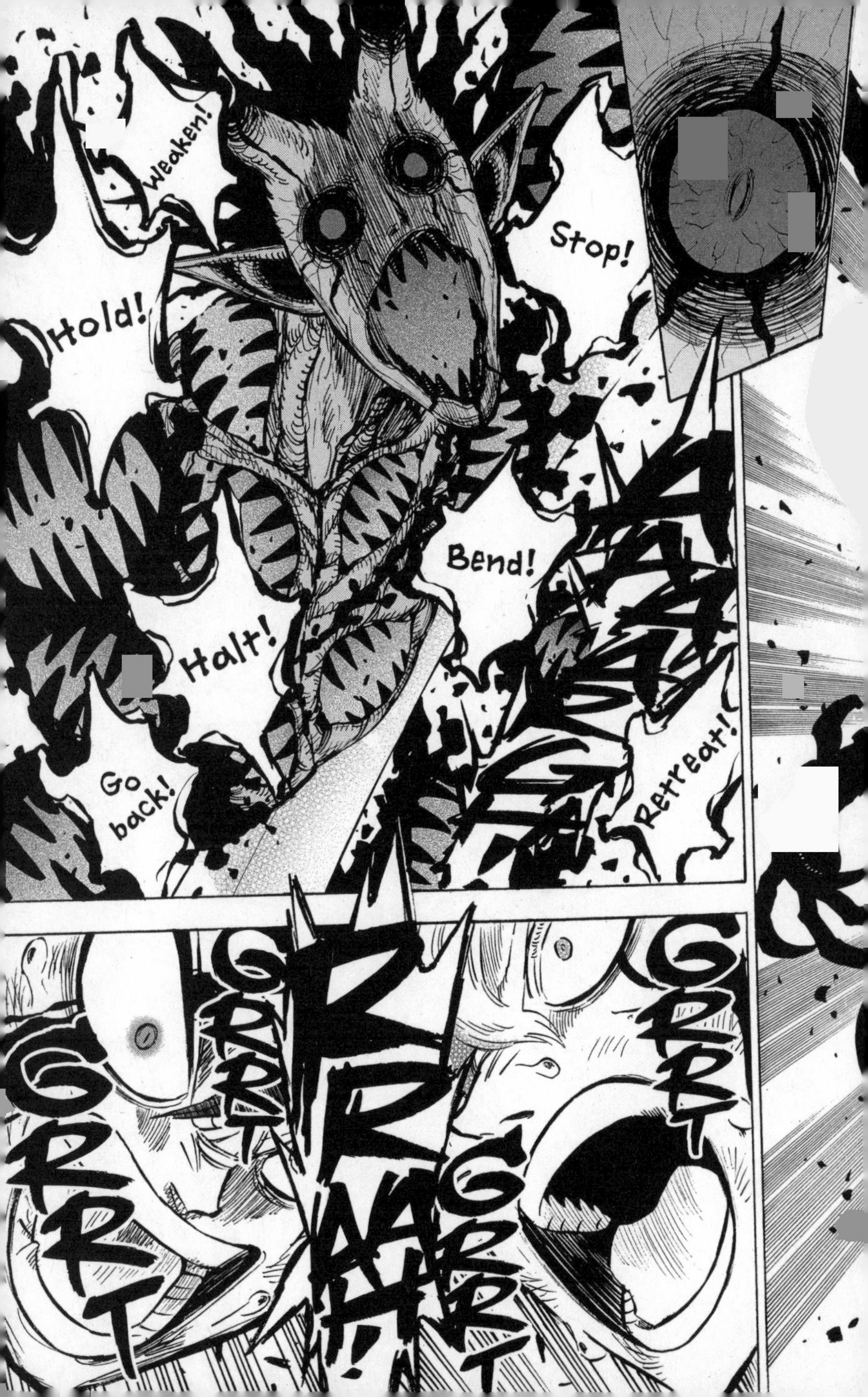
Stop!
Weaken!
Hold!
Bend!
Halt!
Retreat!
Go back!
GRRT
GRRT
GRRT

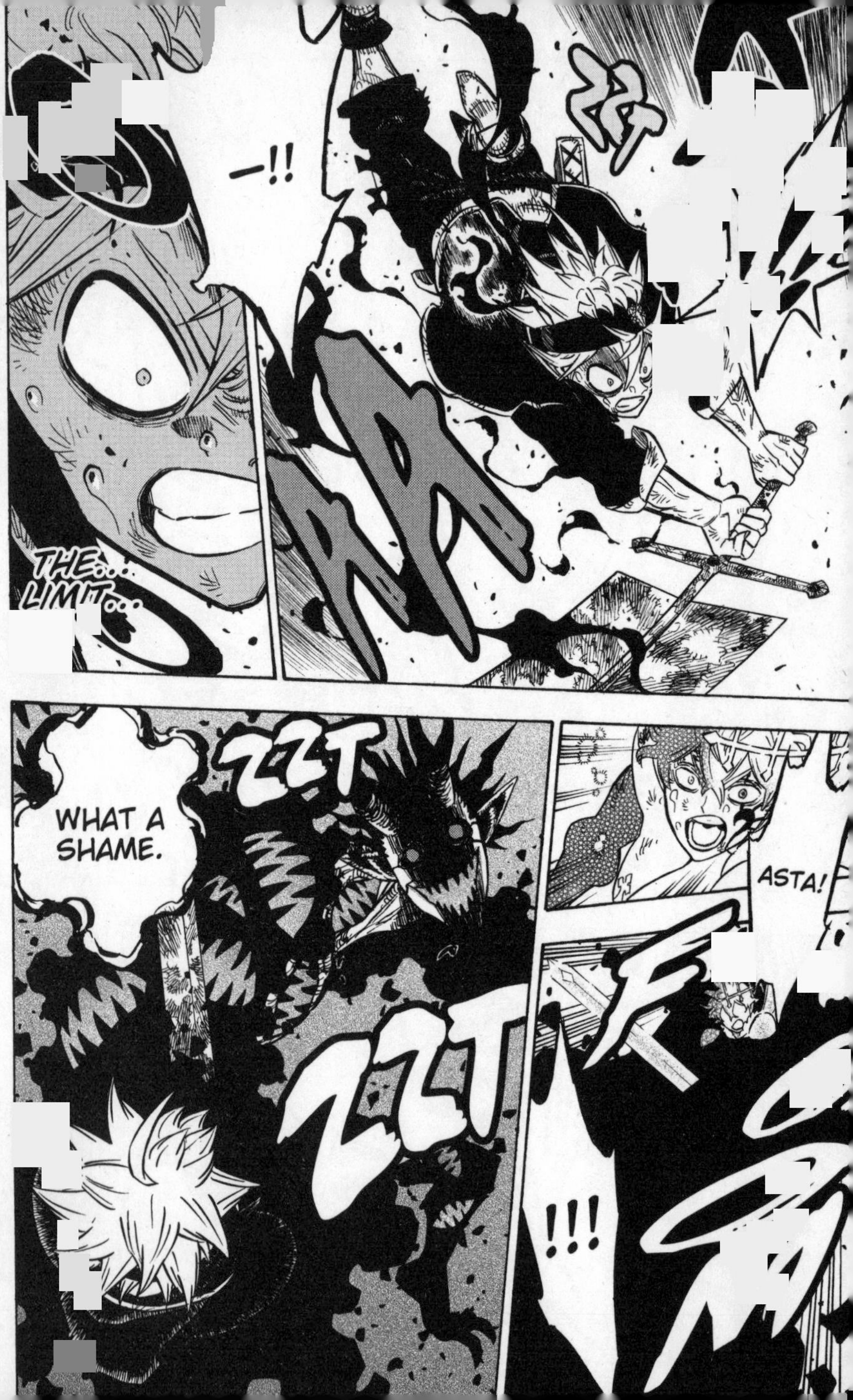
ZZT
—!!
THE... LIMIT...
ASTA!
!!!
ZZT
WHAT A SHAME.
ZZT

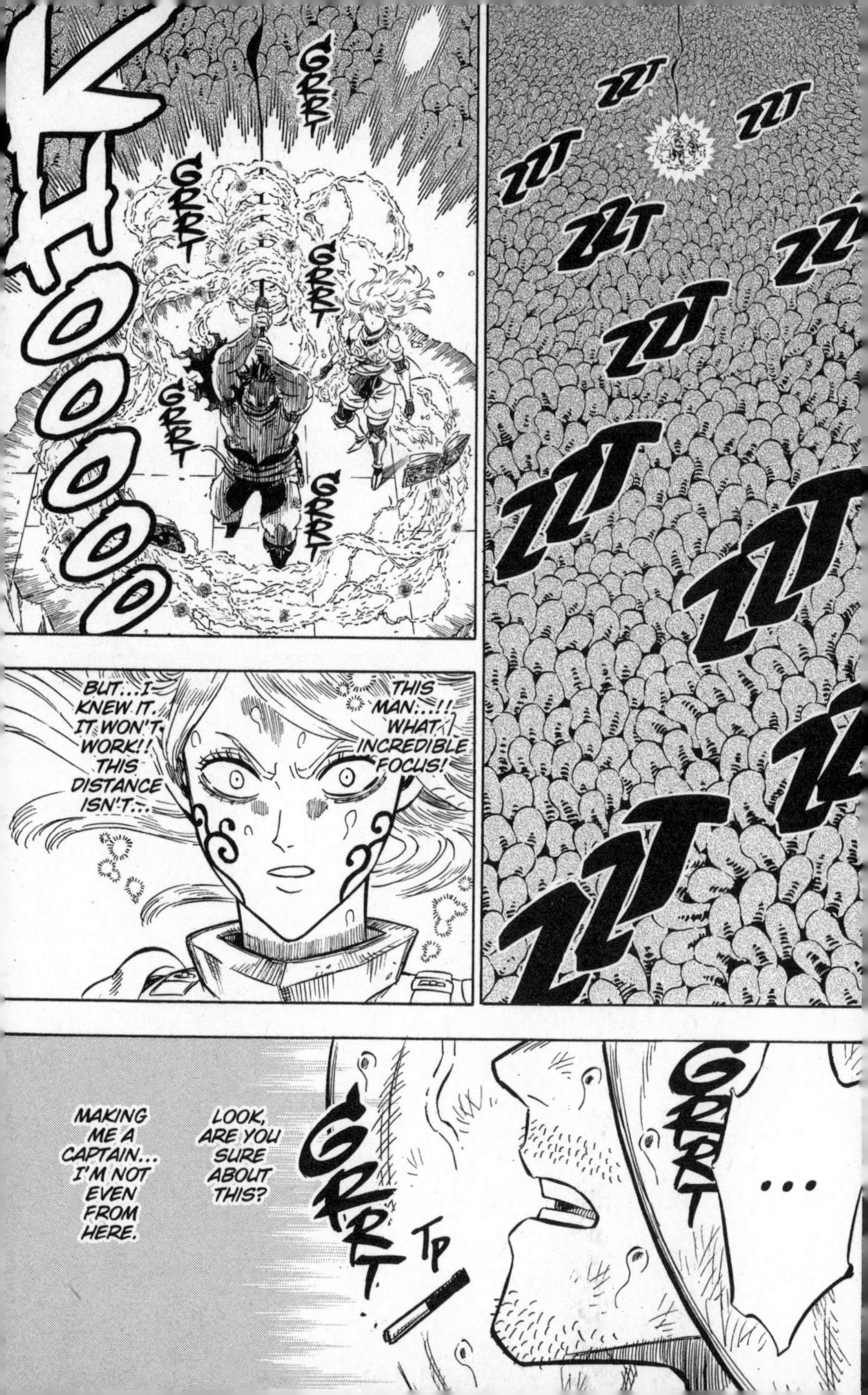
ZZZT
ZZZT
ZZZT
ZZZT
ZZZT
ZZ
ZZZT
ZZ
ZZZT
ZZ
ZZZT
KWOOOOOOO
GRRRT
GRRRT
GRRRT
GRRRT
GRRRT
THIS MAN...!! WHAT INCREDIBLE FOCUS!
BUT...I KNEW IT. IT WON'T WORK!! THIS DISTANCE ISN'T...
GRRRT
...
GRRRT
TP
LOOK, ARE YOU SURE ABOUT THIS?
MAKING ME A CAPTAIN... I'M NOT EVEN FROM HERE.

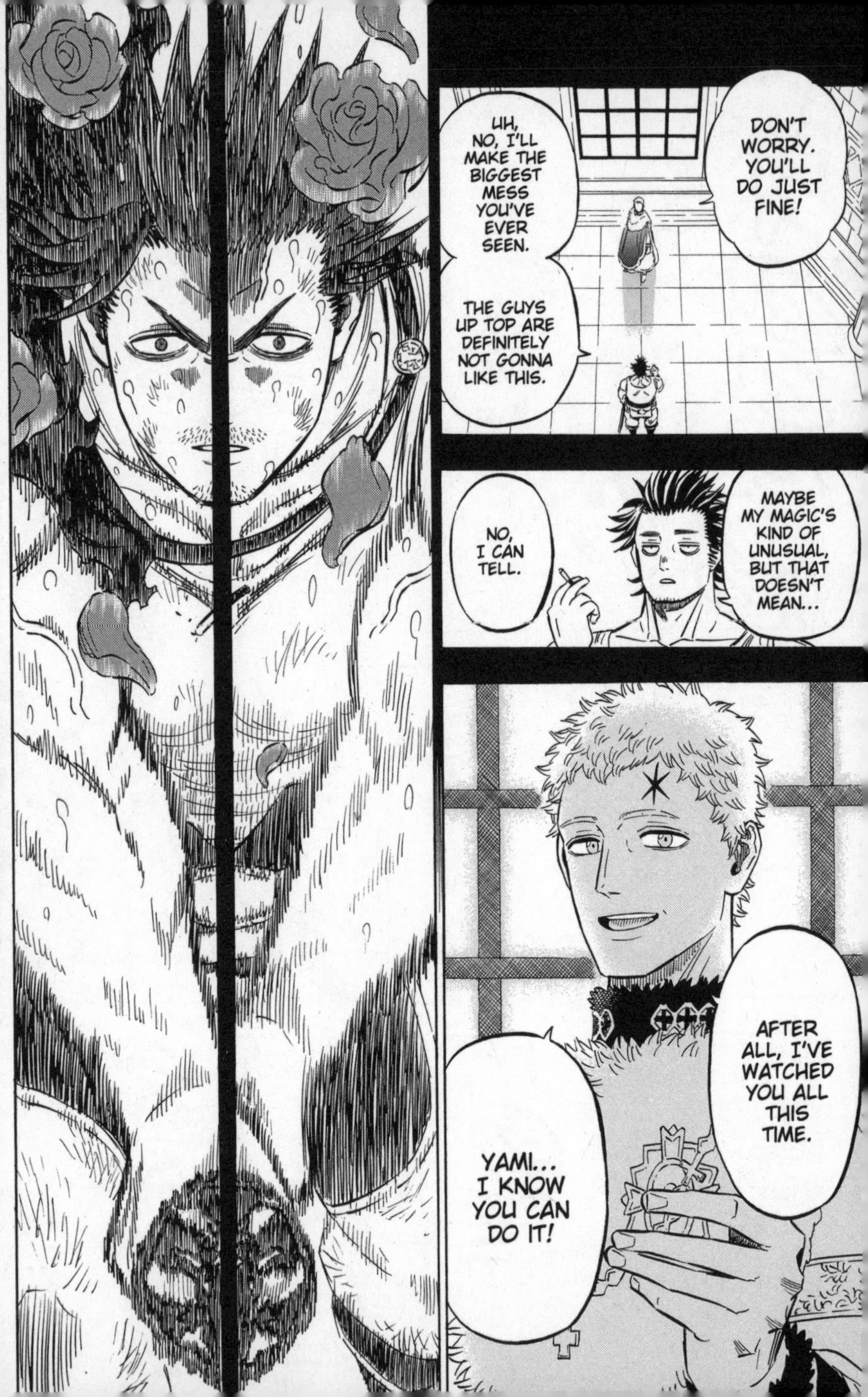
DON'T WORRY. YOU'LL DO JUST FINE!
UH, NO, I'LL MAKE THE BIGGEST MESS YOU'VE EVER SEEN.
THE GUYS UP TOP ARE DEFINITELY NOT GONNA LIKE THIS.
MAYBE MY MAGIC'S KIND OF UNUSUAL, BUT THAT DOESN'T MEAN...
NO, I CAN TELL.
AFTER ALL, I'VE WATCHED YOU ALL THIS TIME.
YAMI... I KNOW YOU CAN DO IT!

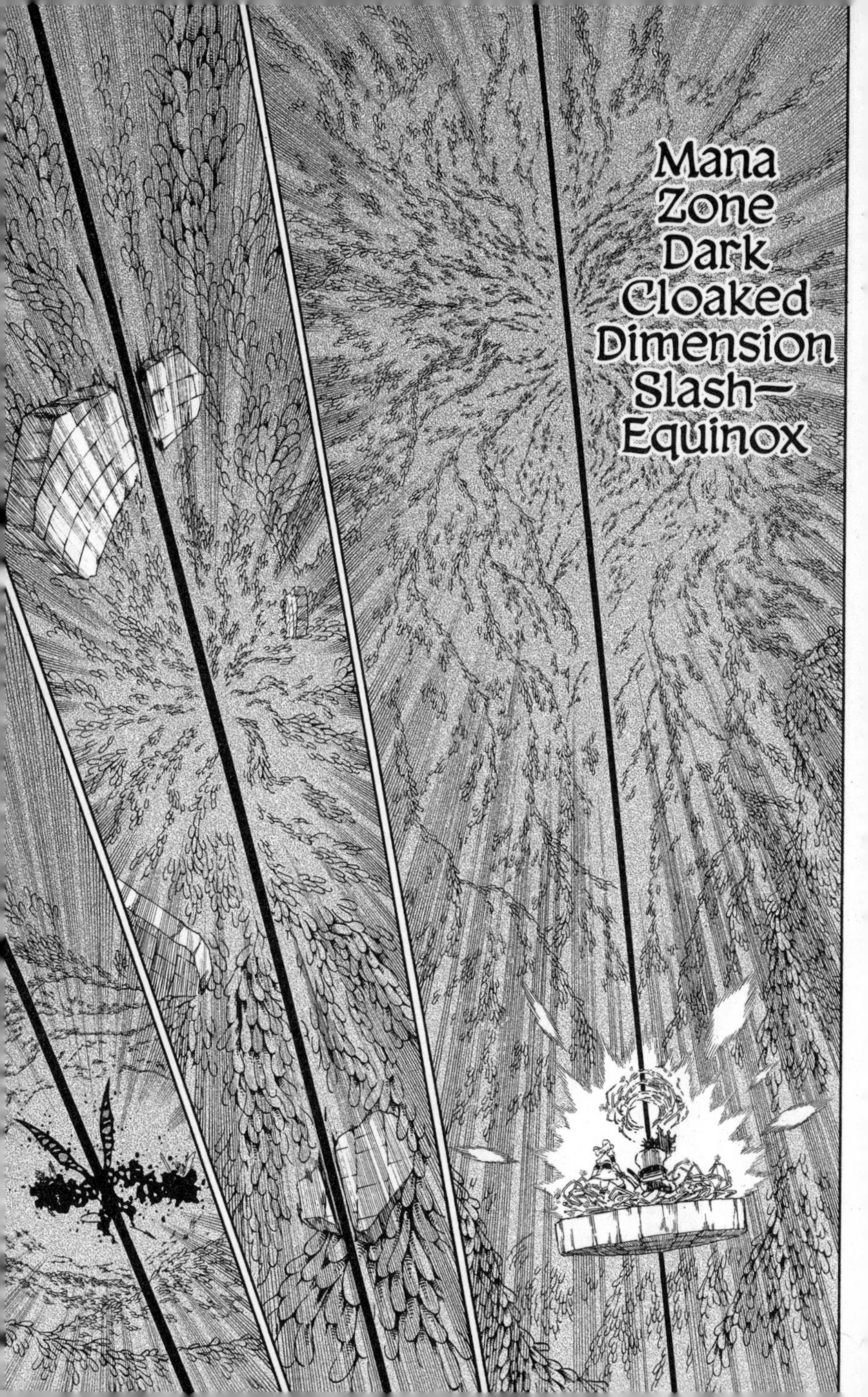
Mana Zone Dark Cloaked Dimension Slash—Equinox

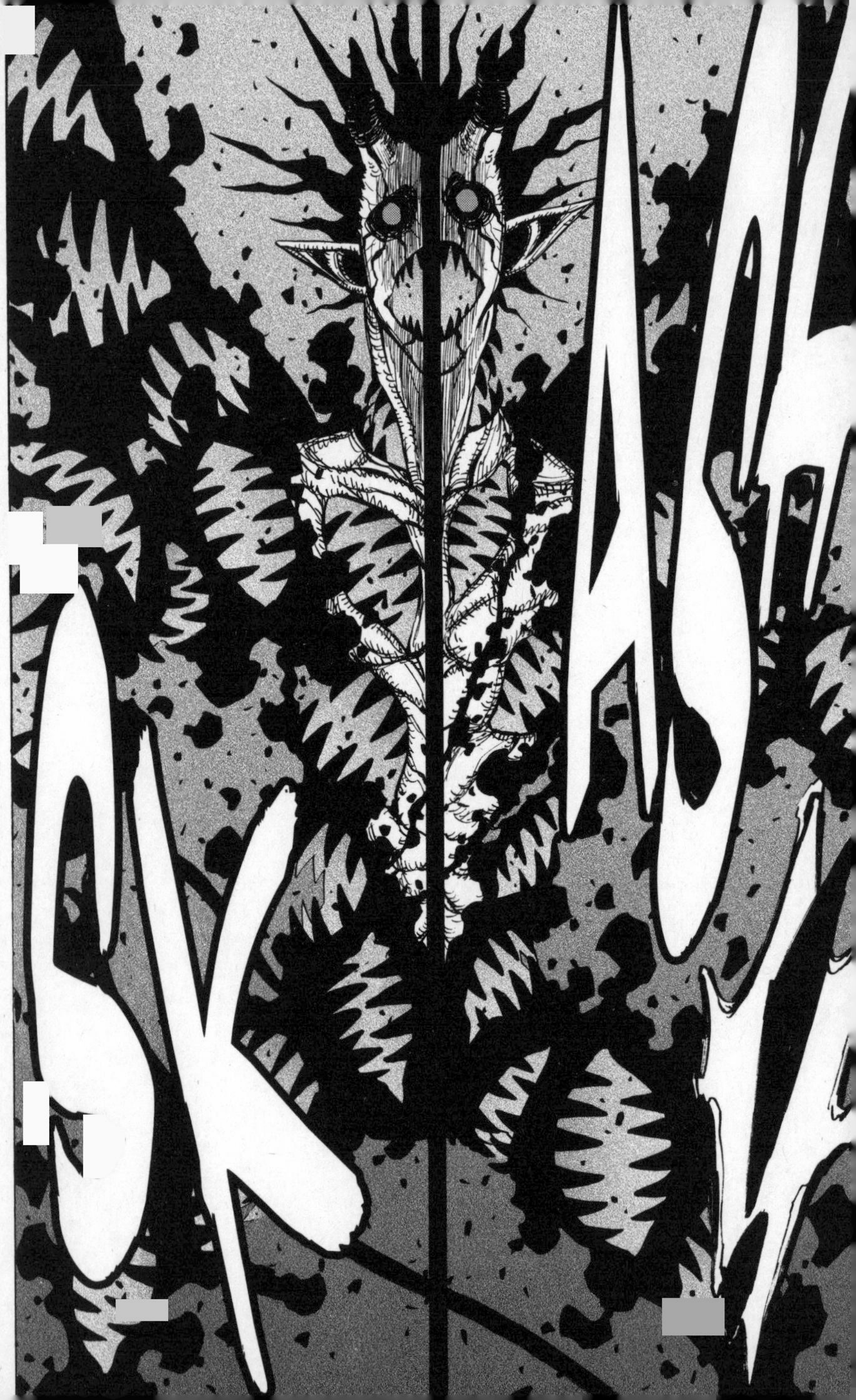

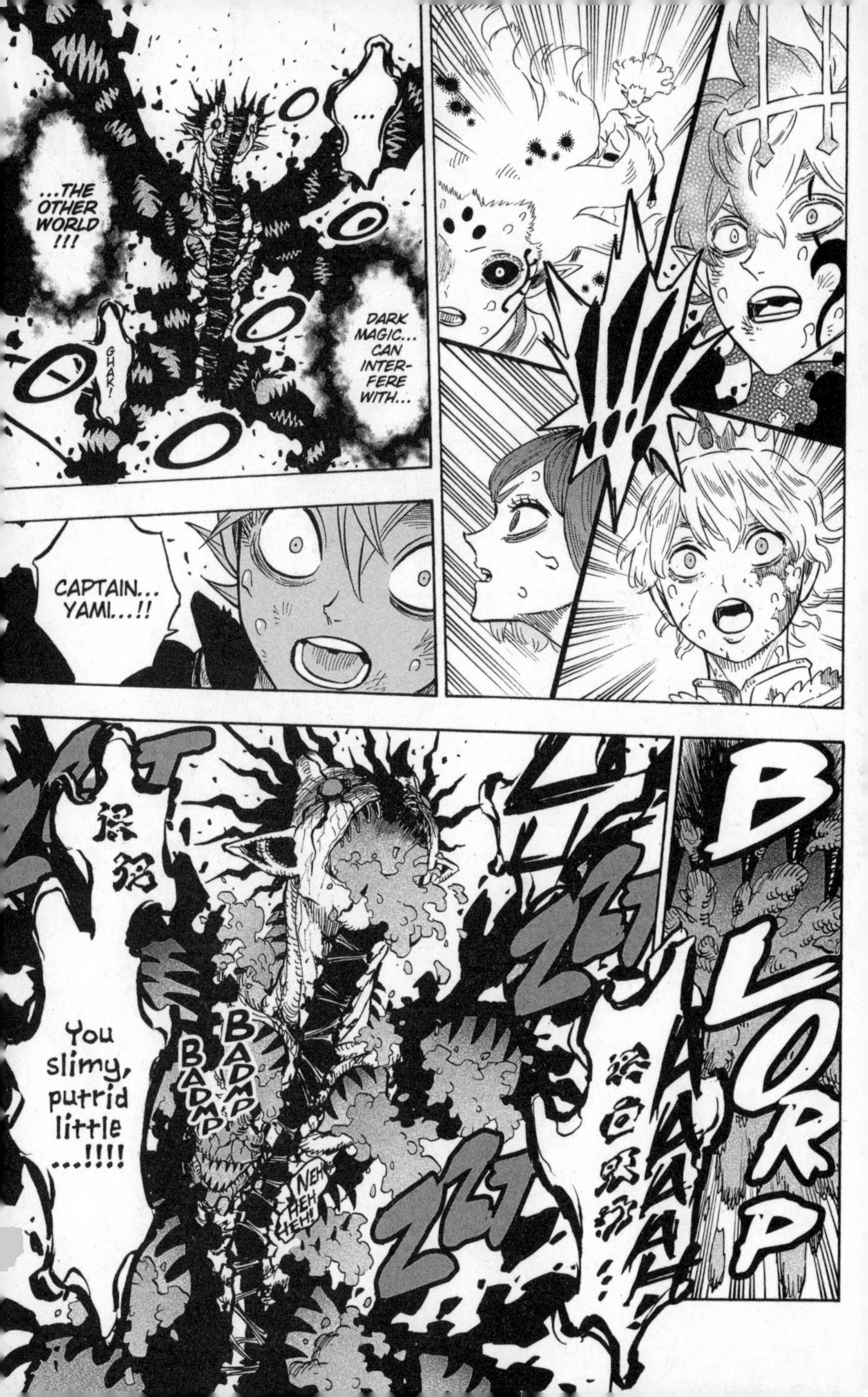
...
DARK MAGIC... CAN INTERFERE WITH...
...THE OTHER WORLD!!!
GHAK!
CAPTAIN... YAMI...!!
BLORP
You slimy, putrid little ...!!!!
BADMP
BADMP
NEH HEH HEH!

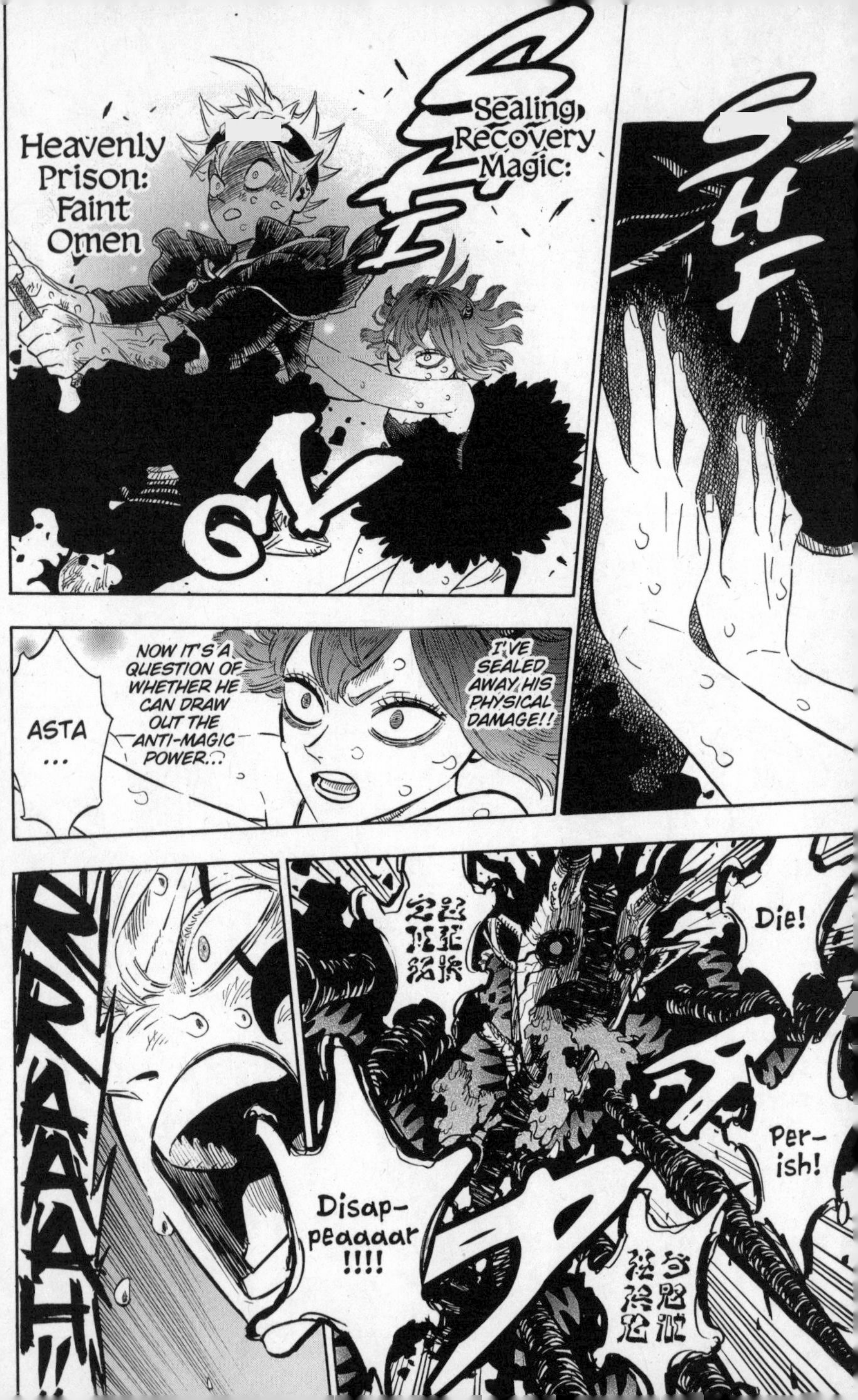
Sealing Recovery Magic:
Heavenly Prison: Faint Omen
I'VE SEALED AWAY HIS PHYSICAL DAMAGE!!
NOW IT'S A QUESTION OF WHETHER HE CAN DRAW OUT THE ANTI-MAGIC POWER...?
ASTA ...
Die!
Per-ish!
Disap-peaaaar!!!!

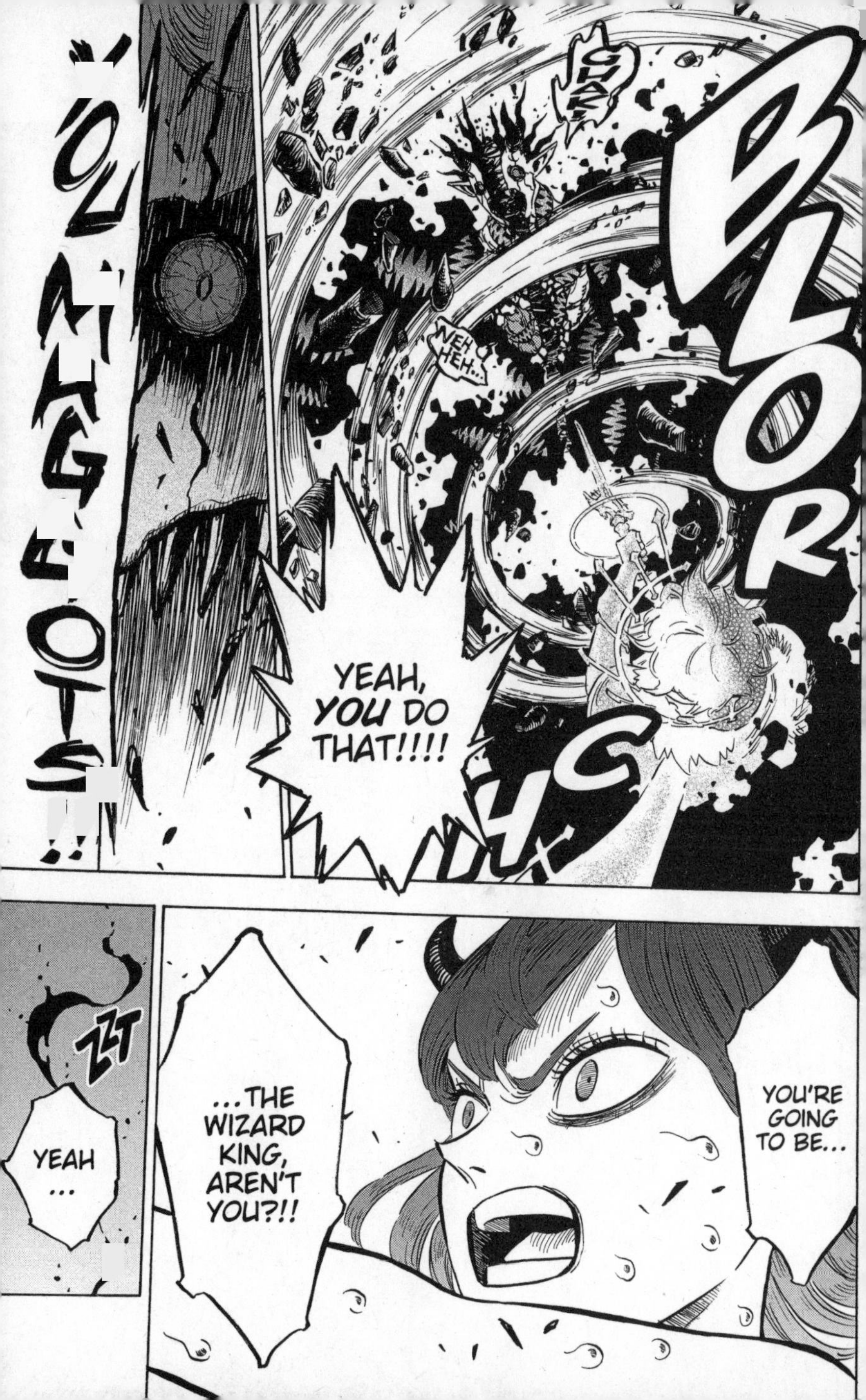
GHAK
WEH HEH...
YEAH, YOU DO THAT!!!!
YOU'RE GOING TO BE...
...THE WIZARD KING, AREN'T YOU?!!
ZZT
YEAH ...

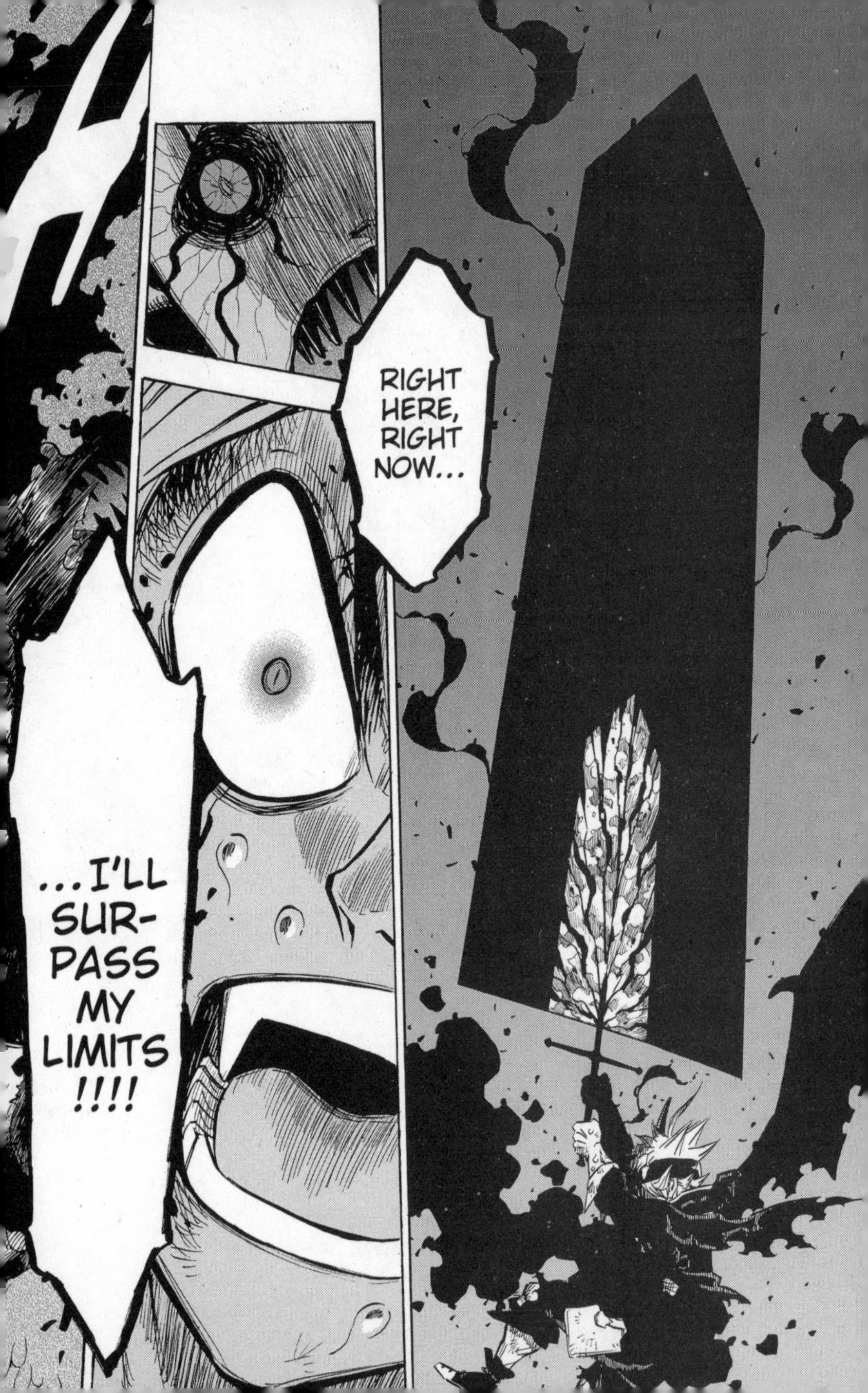
RIGHT HERE, RIGHT NOW...
...I'LL SUR-PASS MY LIMITS !!!!

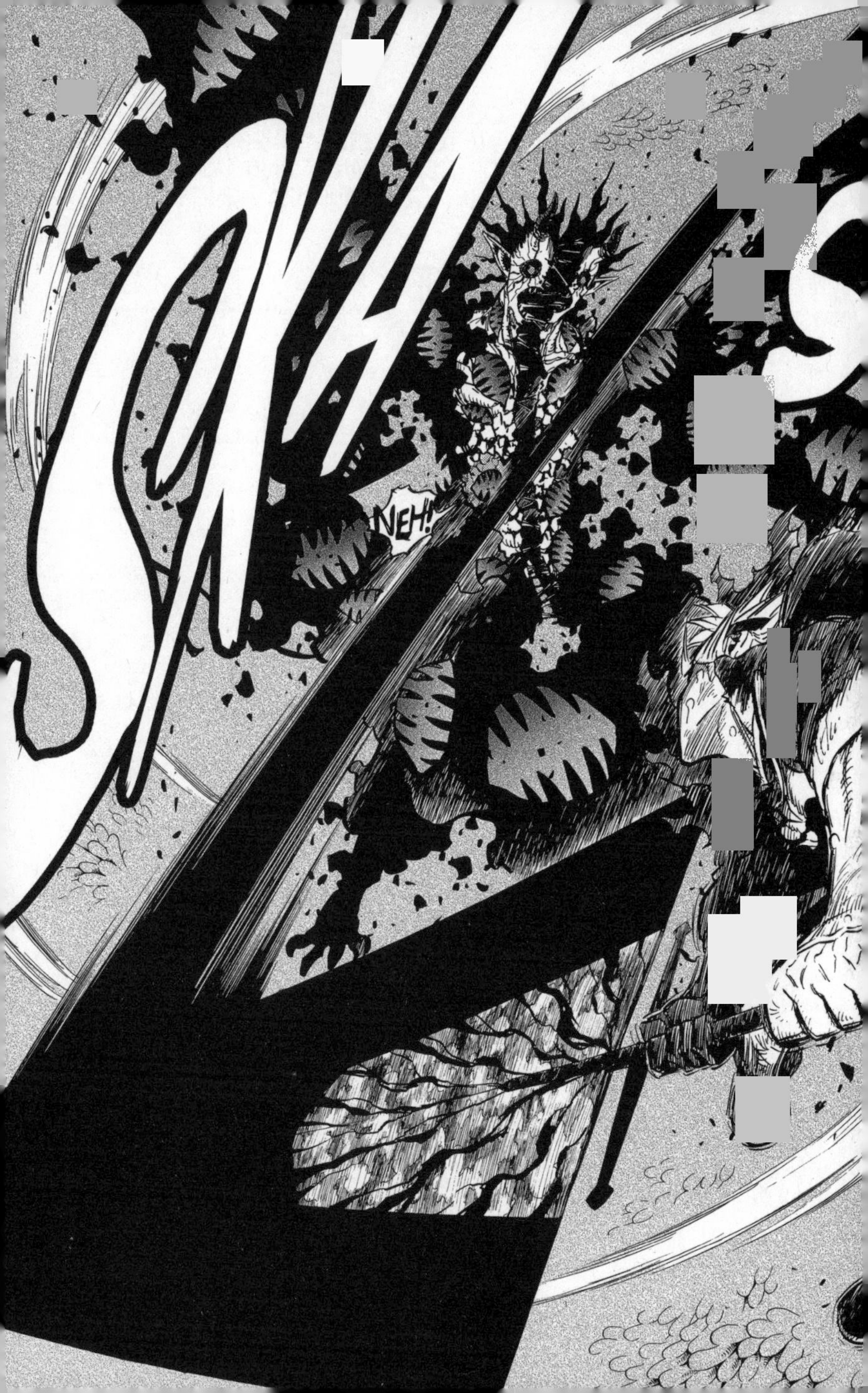
NEH!

PRESENTING PLACES 19 THROUGH 30!!

OBVIOUS OR UNEXPECTED?! WE'RE LIKELY TO GET ALL SORTS OF REACTIONS! AND DON'T MISS THE "ODDBALL RANKING"!

19th Vanessa Enoteca

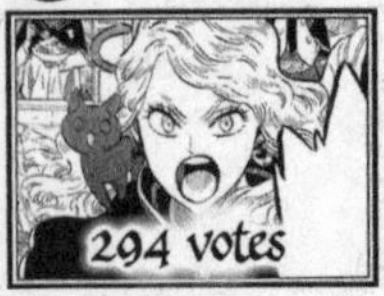
294 votes

HER ULTRA-POWERFUL, FATE-CONTROLLING SPELL AND HER RELIABLE "BIG SISTER" PERSONALITY MADE HER POPULAR!

20th Sister Lily

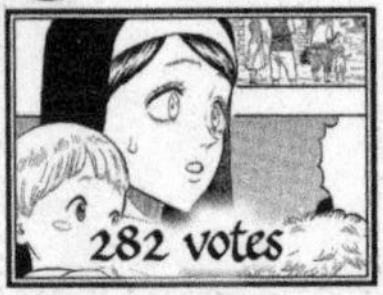
282 votes

SHE'S EVERYBODY'S FAVORITE NUN AND THE OBJECT OF ASTA'S AFFECTIONS, AND SHE WAS HUGELY POPULAR WITH READERS TOO!!

21st Raia

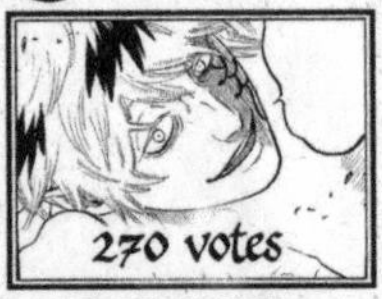
270 votes

THOSE LIES AND TRUE THOUGHTS DIRECTED AT LICHT. HIS FEELINGS FOR HIS FRIEND WON HIM SUPPORT!!

22nd Langris Vaude

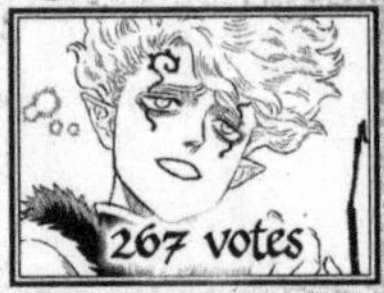
267 votes

A LITTLE BROTHER WHO'S BITTERLY CONSCIOUS OF HIS BIG BROTHER. NOW THAT THEIR FIGHT IS OVER, PEOPLE ARE WONDERING WHAT'S NEXT FOR THEM!

23rd Leopold Vermillion

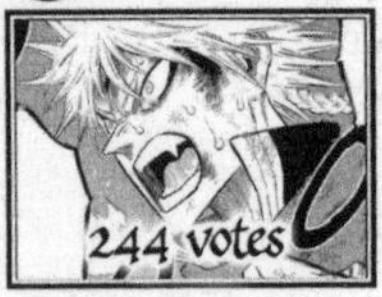
244 votes

HIS HIDDEN POTENTIAL AND GRIT WON HIM ENTHUSIASTIC SUPPORT!! HE'S WORKING TO BE LIKE HIS BIG BROTHER!!

24th Grey

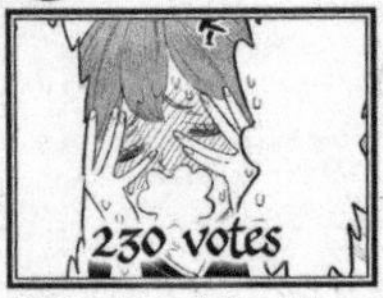
230 votes

"SHE'S CUTE WHEN SHE'S EMBARRASSED, HER MAGIC IS TOUGH, TELL US HER REAL NAME!" SHE'S HUGELY POPULAR!

25th Rill Boismortier

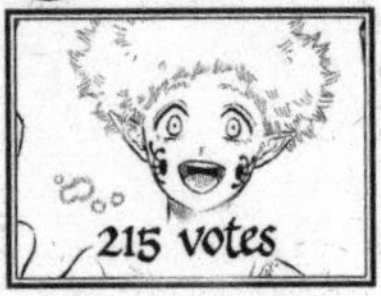
215 votes

THE YOUNGEST CAPTAIN'S INNOCENT, CHEERFUL PERSONALITY AND OVERWHELMING TALENT WON HIM POPULARITY!

26th Jack the Ripper

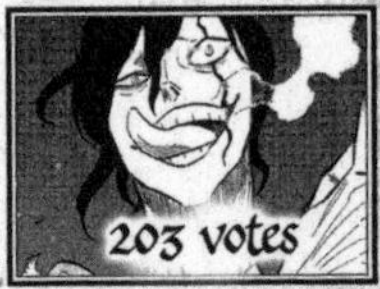
203 votes

HE'S A RECOGNIZED GENIUS, IF ONLY WHERE SLASHING SPELLS ARE CONCERNED! A COMMITTED, SINGLE-MINDED GUY!!

27th Kirsch Vermillion

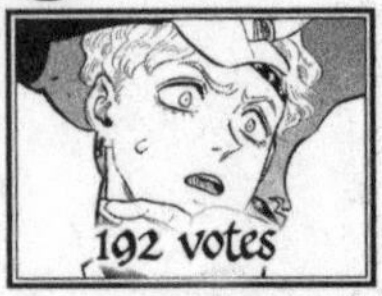
192 votes

THE HIGH-PRESSURE, PLANT-ATTRIBUTE VERMILLION. HE MADE IT INTO THE RANKINGS BEAUTIFULLY!!

28th Henry Legolant

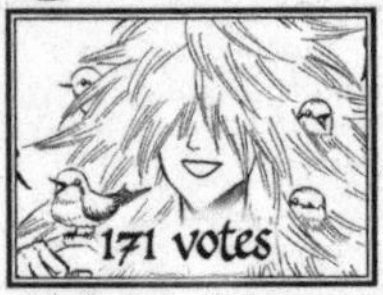
171 votes

HE WON POPULARITY FOR NOT LETTING HIS LONELY CIRCUMSTANCES CRUSH HIM, AND FOR THE WAY HE FOUGHT FOR THE FRIENDS HE BELIEVED IN!

29th William Vangeance

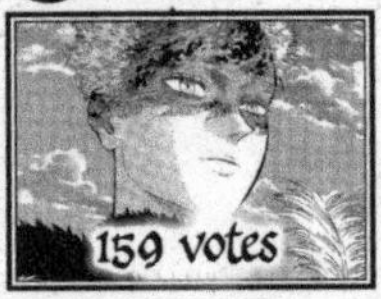
159 votes

THE MAN WHO'S VERY NEARLY THE MOST POWERFUL FIGURE AROUND. WHAT IS HE THINKING NOW, AND WHAT'S HE GOING TO DO?!

30th Gordon Agrippa

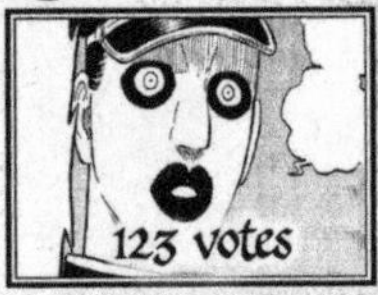
123 votes

HE'S MORE AWKWARD THAN ANYONE, BUT LOOK HOW MANY PEOPLE SUPPORTED HIM!

The Oddball Ranking

PRESENTING THE TOP SPOTS IN THE ODD RANKINGS THAT SURFACED DURING THE CURRENT POPULARITY POLL!!

Most Popular?!

GAUCHE AND CHARLOTTE

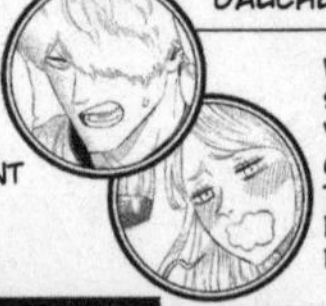

WHEN INDIVIDUALS SENT IN MULTIPLE VOTES, THESE TWO GOT MOST OF THEM! THESE GORGEOUS PEOPLE HAVE SOME DIE-HARD FANS!!

The most popular character whose name hasn't been revealed!

THE POISON PLANT MAGIC GUY FROM THE PURPLE ORCAS

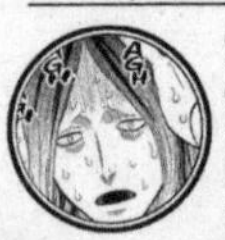
AGH

MAYBE IT WAS BECAUSE HE SEEMED LIKE A NICE PERSON, OR MAYBE IT WAS HIS GOOD LOOKS, BUT HE WAS POPULAR! HIS NAME IS ***DIGIT TALIS!*** HE'S AN AGREEABLE YOUNG GUY WHO'S WORKING STEADILY TO RECOVER HIS BRIGADE'S HONOR!!

Continues on page 122!!

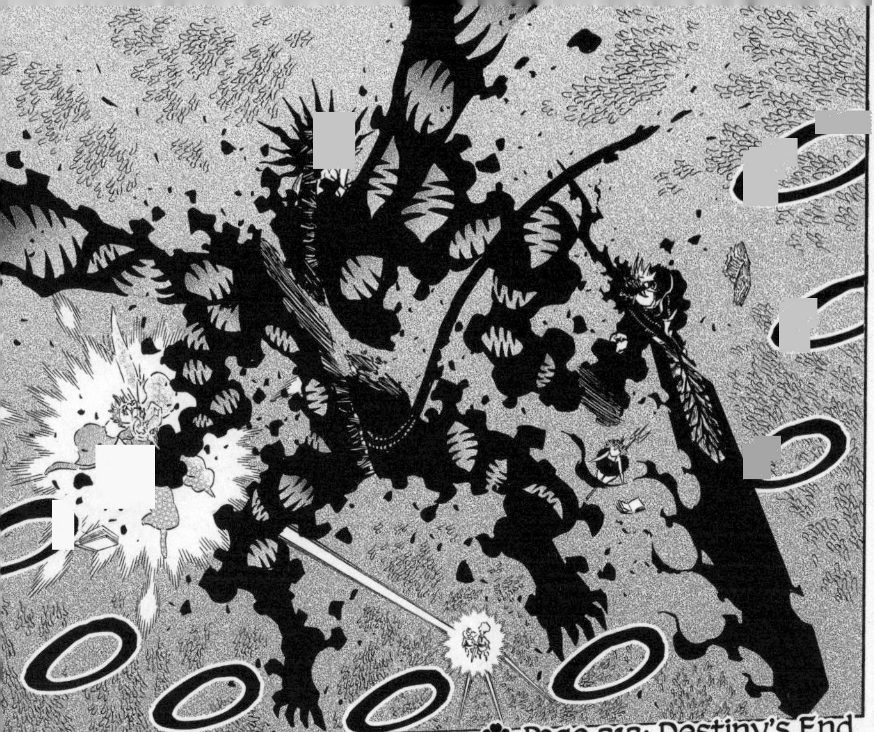

Page 212: Destiny's End

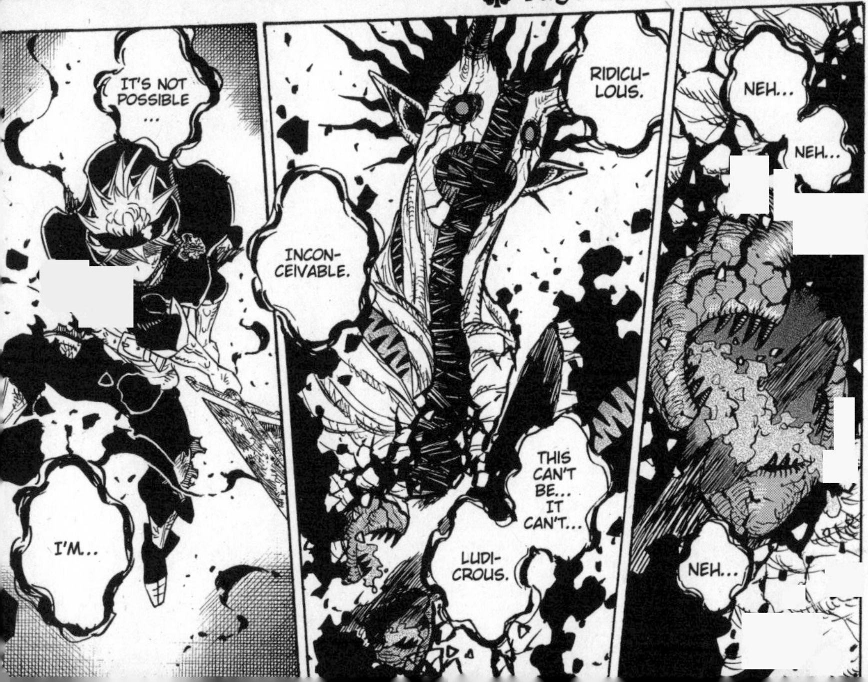
NEH...
NEH...
NEH...
RIDICULOUS.
INCONCEIVABLE.
THIS CAN'T BE... IT CAN'T...
LUDICROUS.
IT'S NOT POSSIBLE...
I'M...

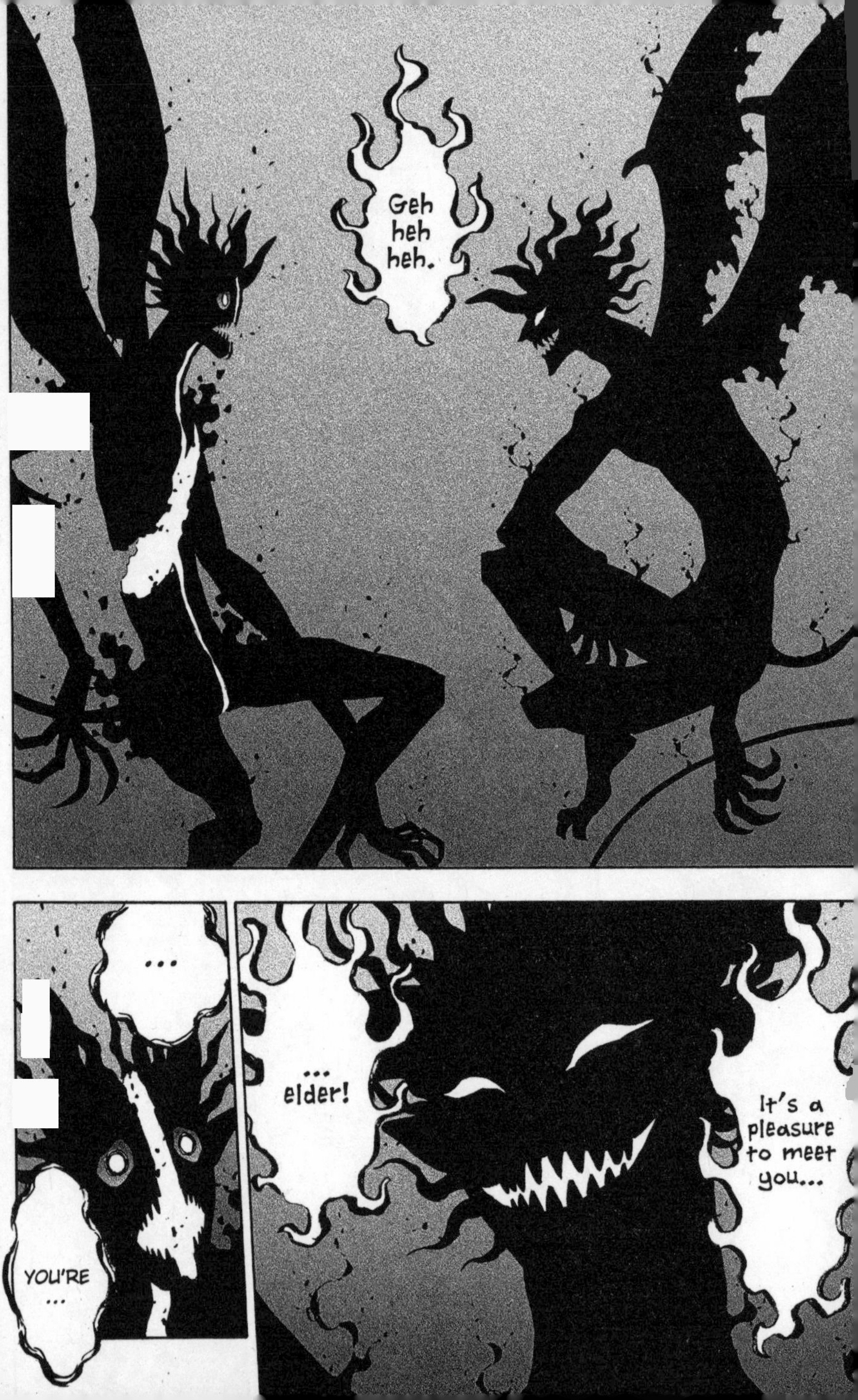
Geh heh heh.
It's a pleasure to meet you...
...elder!
...
YOU'RE ...

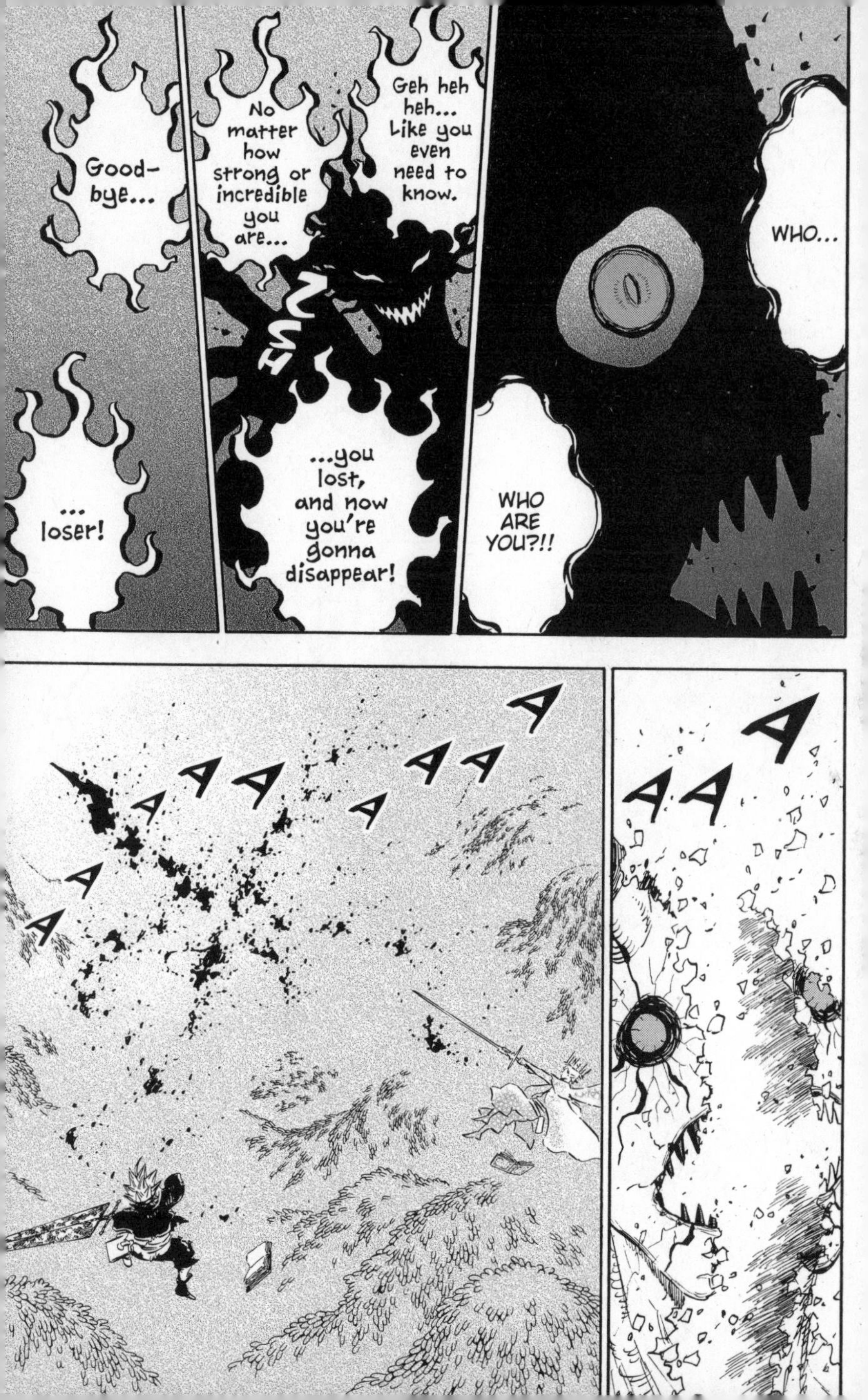

WHO...
WHO ARE YOU?!!
Geh heh heh... Like you even need to know.
No matter how strong or incredible you are...
ZSH
...you lost, and now you're gonna disappear!
Good-bye...
...loser!
AAA
AAAAAAAAAA

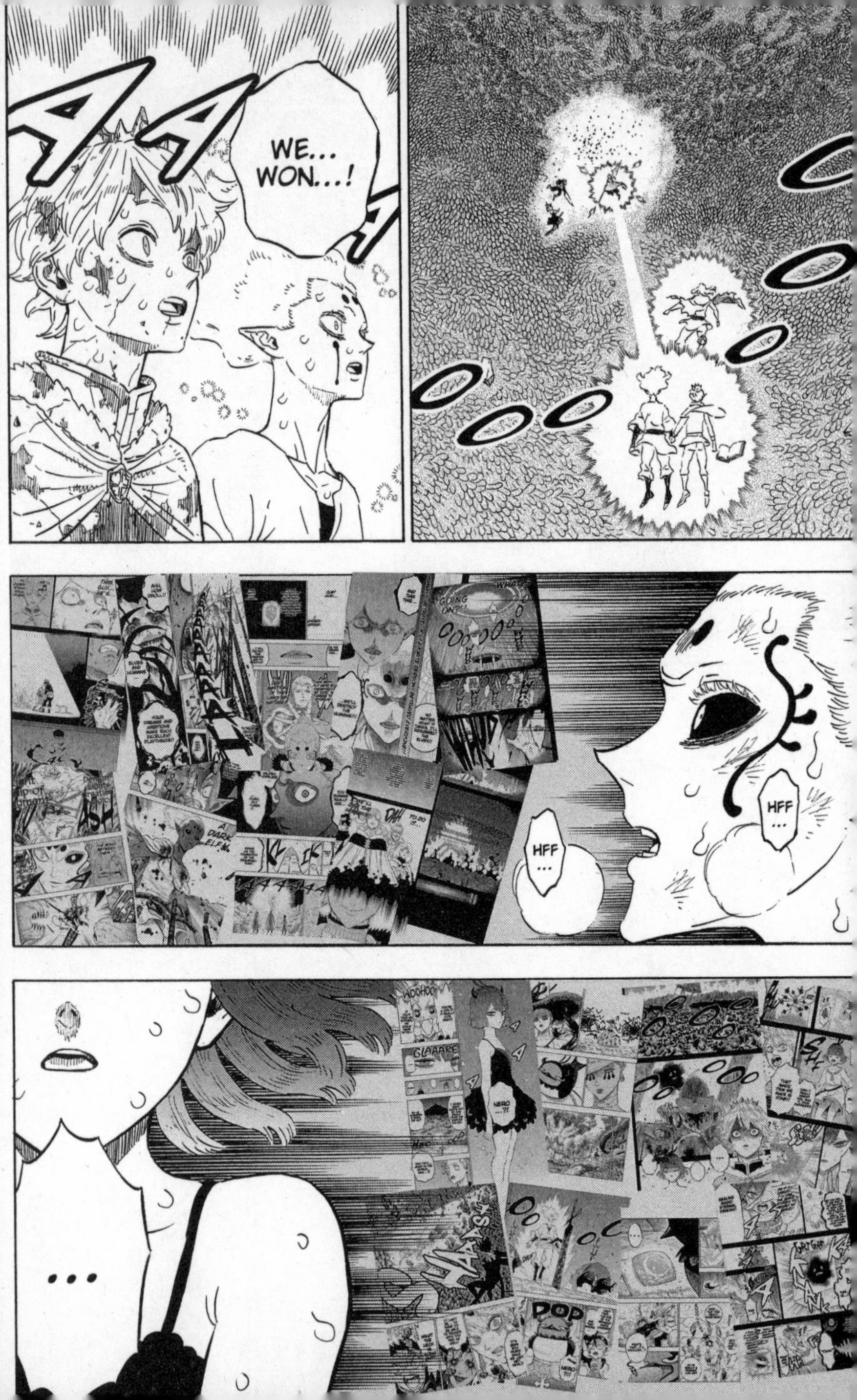
WE... WON...!
HFF ...
HFF ...
...

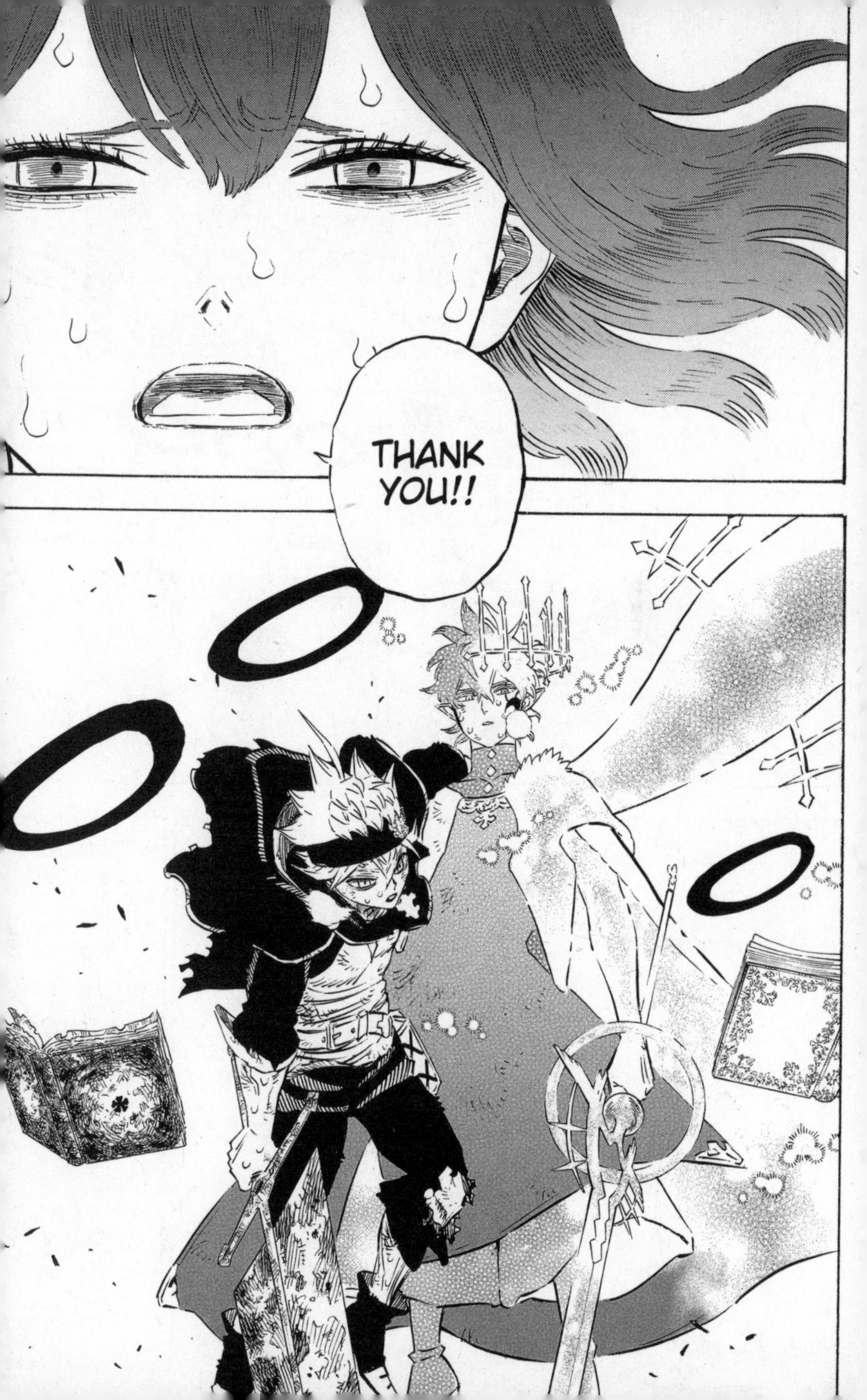
THANK YOU!!

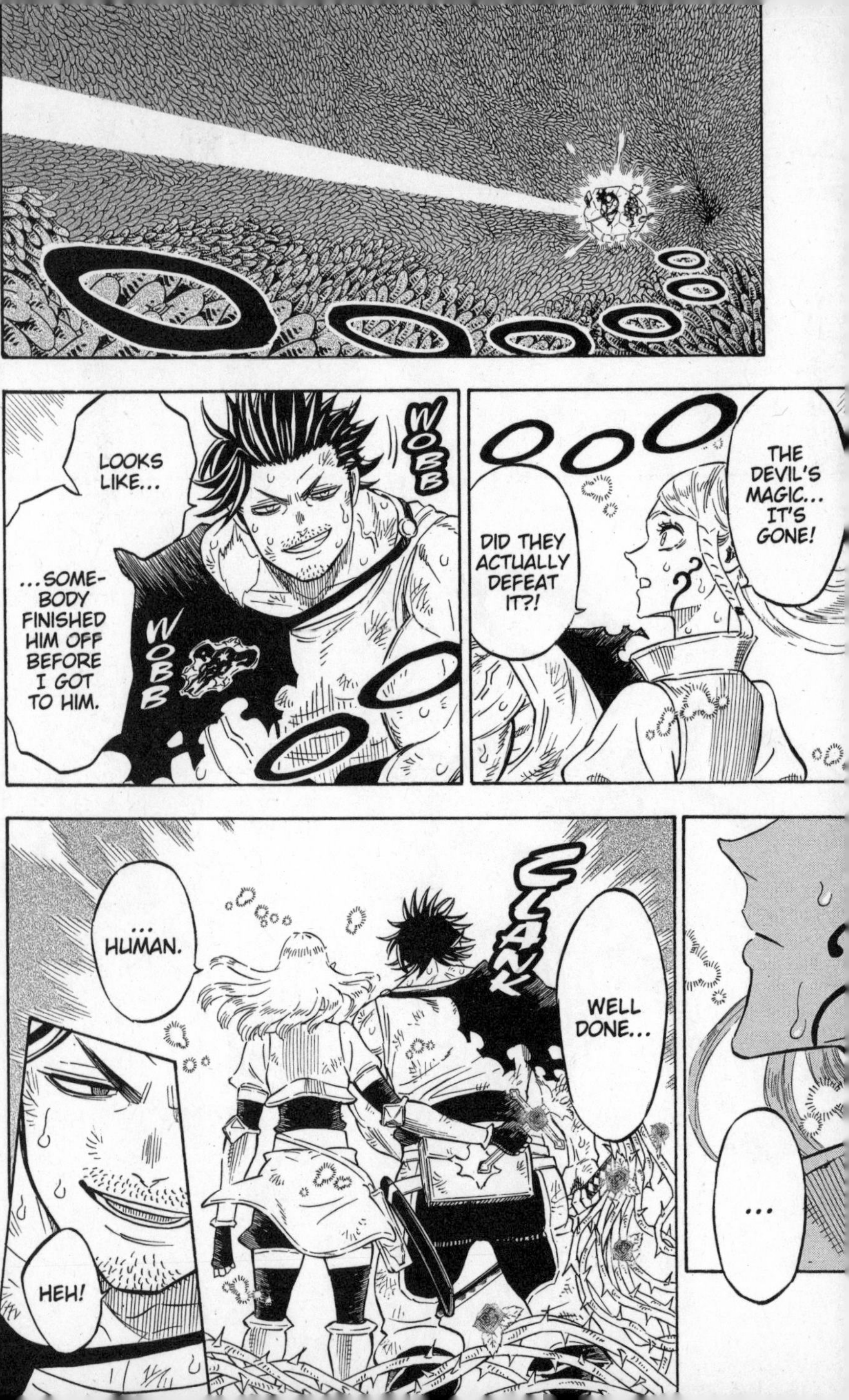
THE DEVIL'S MAGIC... IT'S GONE!
DID THEY ACTUALLY DEFEAT IT?!
WOBB
LOOKS LIKE...
WOBB
...SOME-BODY FINISHED HIM OFF BEFORE I GOT TO HIM.
...
CLANK
WELL DONE...
...HUMAN.
HEH!

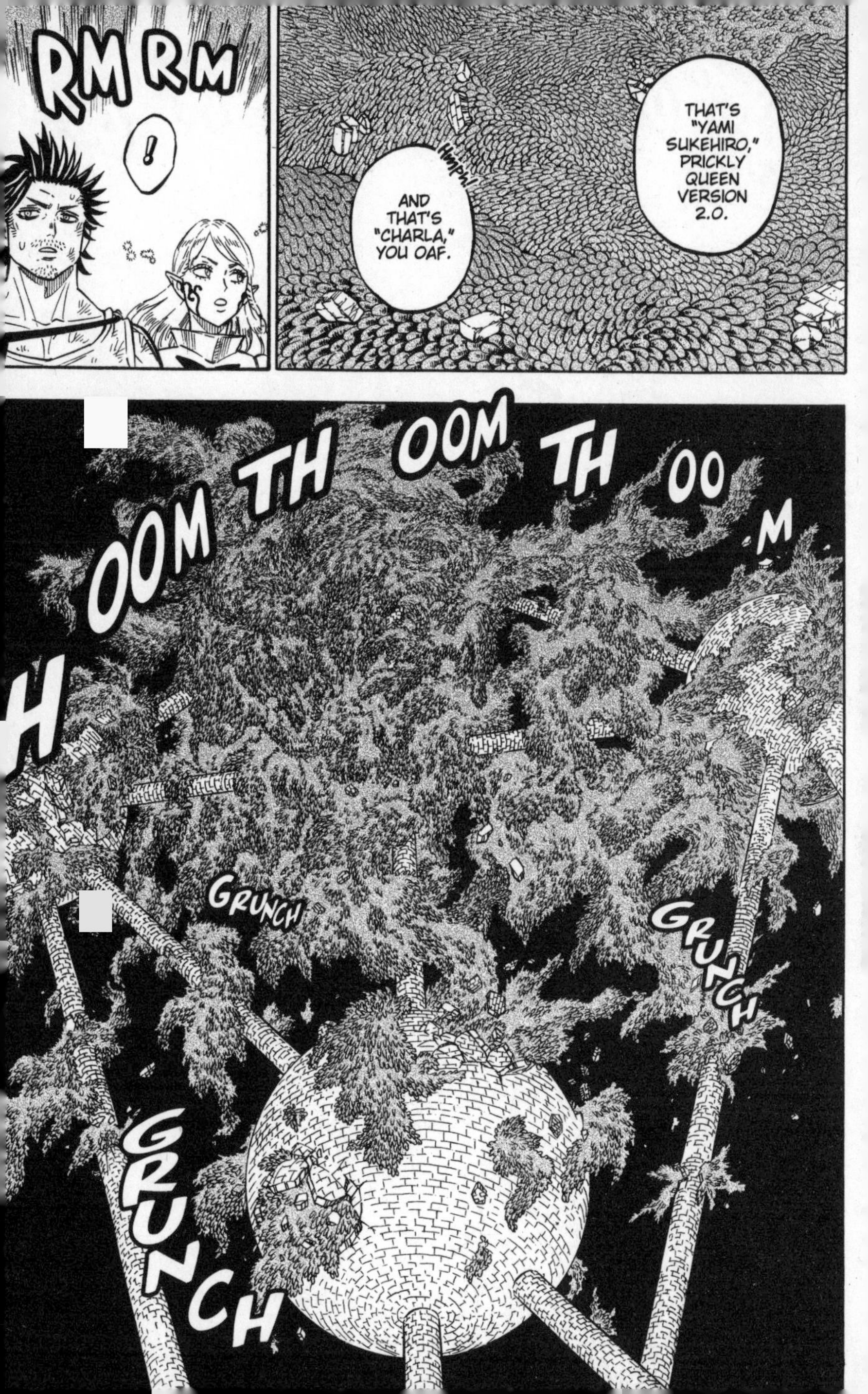
THAT'S "YAMI SUKEHIRO," PRICKLY QUEEN VERSION 2.0.
Hmph!
AND THAT'S "CHARLA," YOU OAF.
RMRM
!
THOOM THOOM THOOM
GRUNCH
GRUNCH
GRUNCH

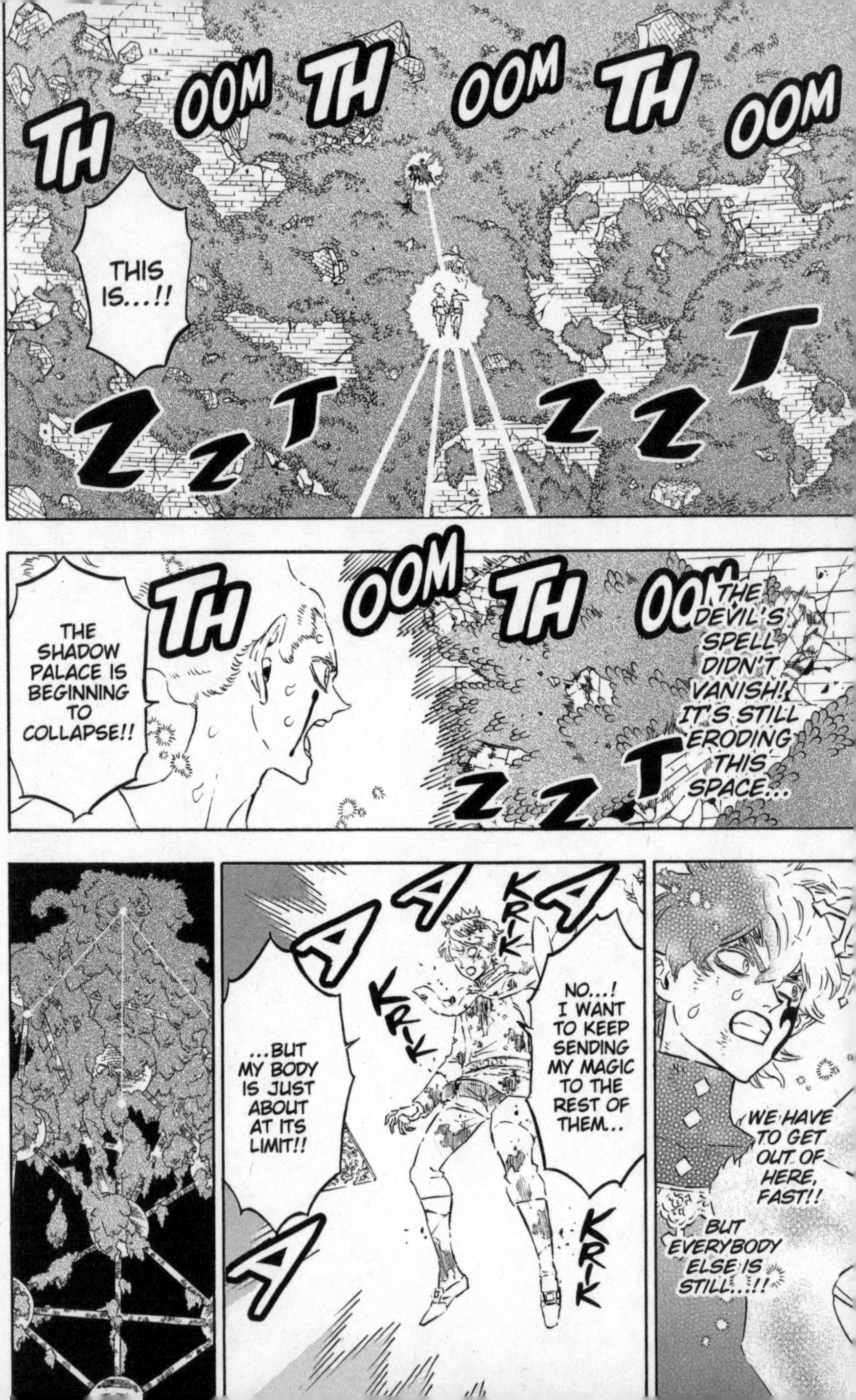
THOOM THOOM THOOM
THIS IS...!!
ZZZT ZZZT
THE DEVIL'S SPELL DIDN'T VANISH! IT'S STILL ERODING THIS SPACE...
THOOM THOOM
THE SHADOW PALACE IS BEGINNING TO COLLAPSE!!
ZZZT
WE HAVE TO GET OUT OF HERE, FAST!!
BUT EVERYBODY ELSE IS STILL...!!
AAAA
KRIK
NO...! I WANT TO KEEP SENDING MY MAGIC TO THE REST OF THEM...
KRIK
...BUT MY BODY IS JUST ABOUT AT ITS LIMIT!!
KRIK

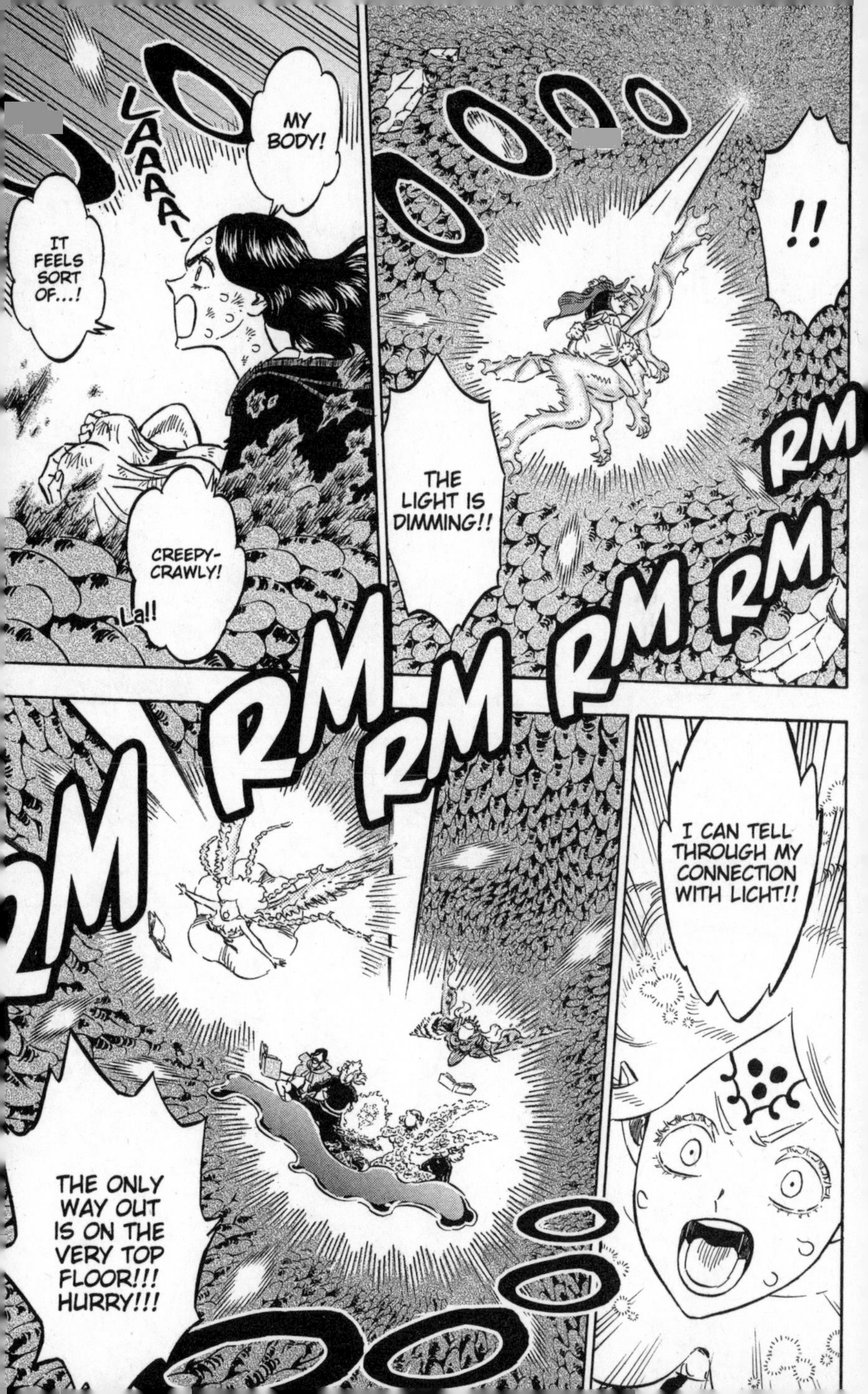
!!
THE LIGHT IS DIMMING!!
RM
RM RM RM
MY BODY!
LAAAA!
IT FEELS SORT OF...!
CREEPY-CRAWLY!
La!!
I CAN TELL THROUGH MY CONNECTION WITH LICHT!!
RM RM RM
THE ONLY WAY OUT IS ON THE VERY TOP FLOOR!!! HURRY!!!

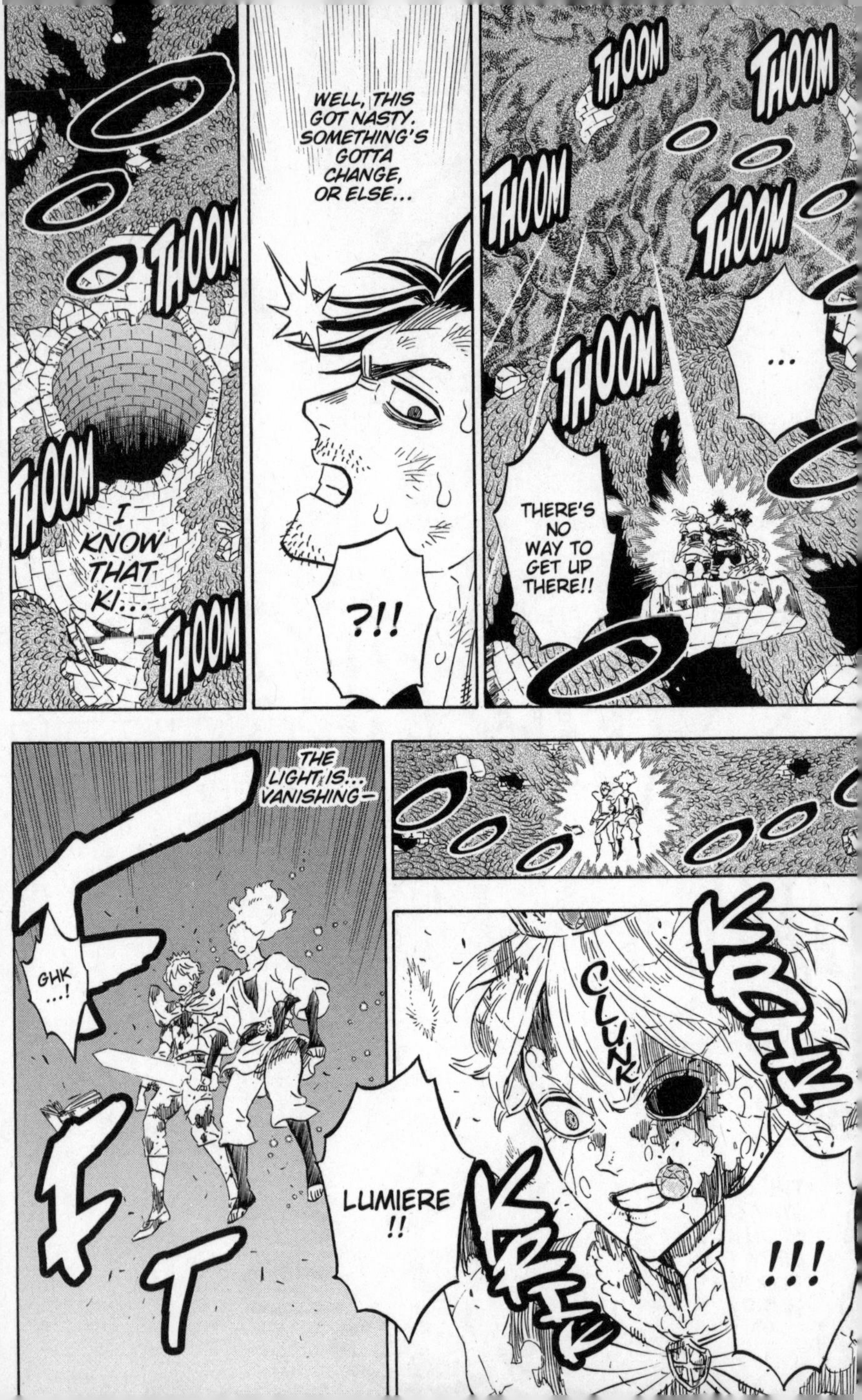

THOOM
THOOM
THOOM
THOOM
...
THOOM
THERE'S NO WAY TO GET UP THERE!!
WELL, THIS GOT NASTY. SOMETHING'S GOTTA CHANGE, OR ELSE...
?!!
THOOM
THOOM
I KNOW THAT KI...
THOOM
CLUNK
!!!
LUMIERE !!
THE LIGHT IS... VANISHING—
GHK ...!

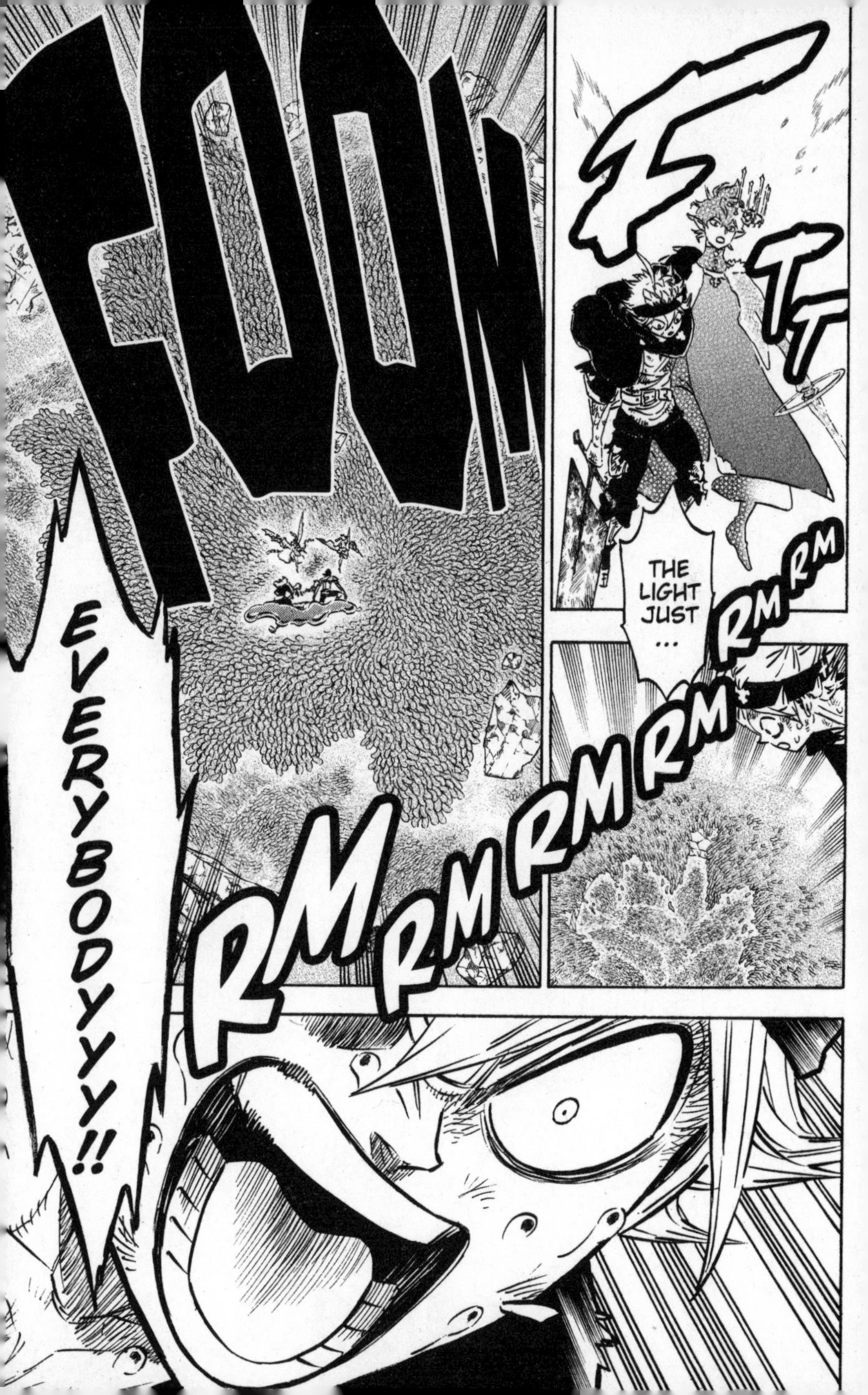
FTT
FOOM
THE LIGHT JUST ...
RM RM RM RM RM RM RM RM
EVERYBODYYYY!!

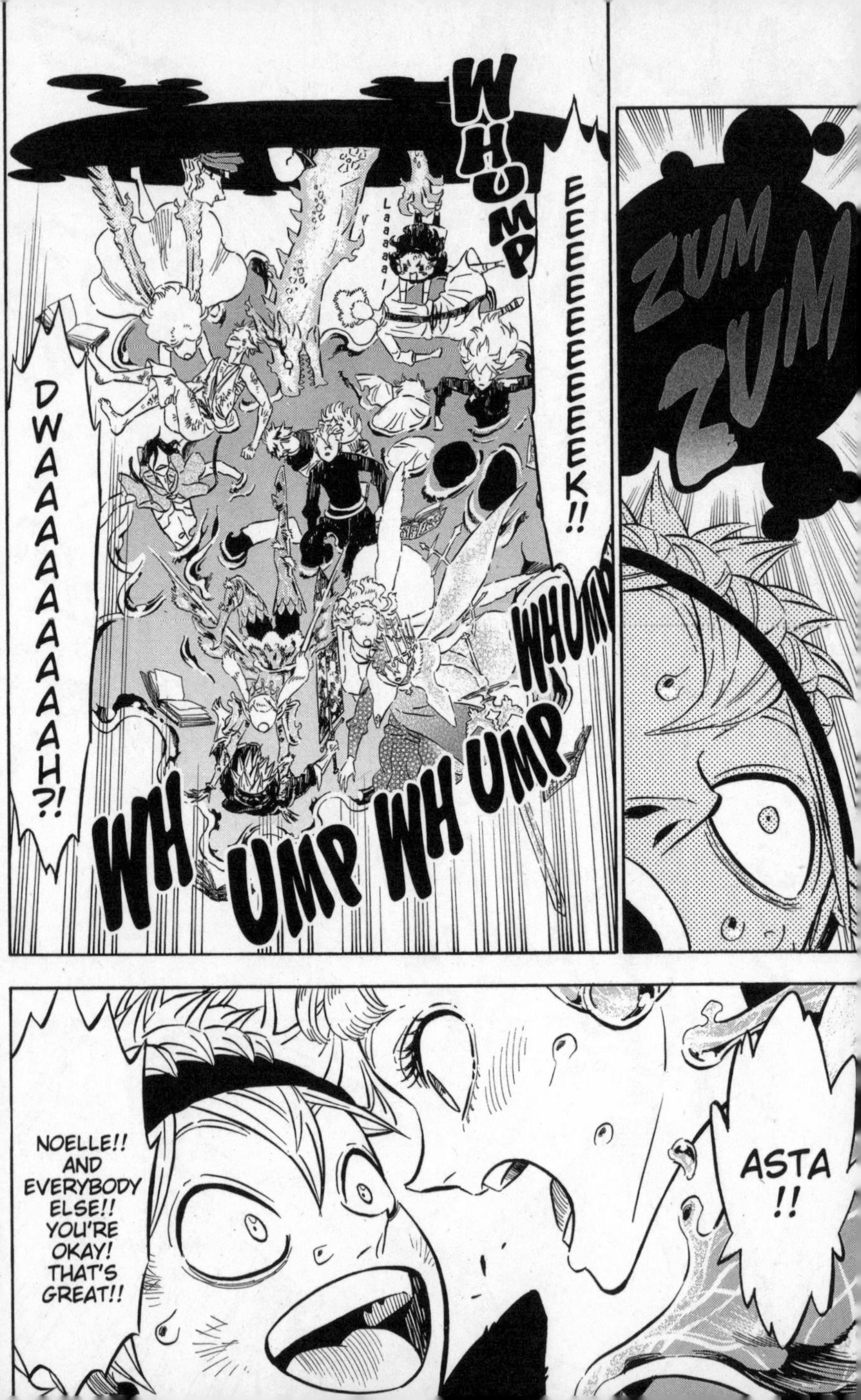
ZUM
ZUM
WHUMP
EEEEEEEEEEK!!
Laaaaa!
DWAAAAAAAAAAH?!
WH
UMP
WH
UMP
WHUMP
ASTA!!
NOELLE!! AND EVERYBODY ELSE!! YOU'RE OKAY! THAT'S GREAT!!

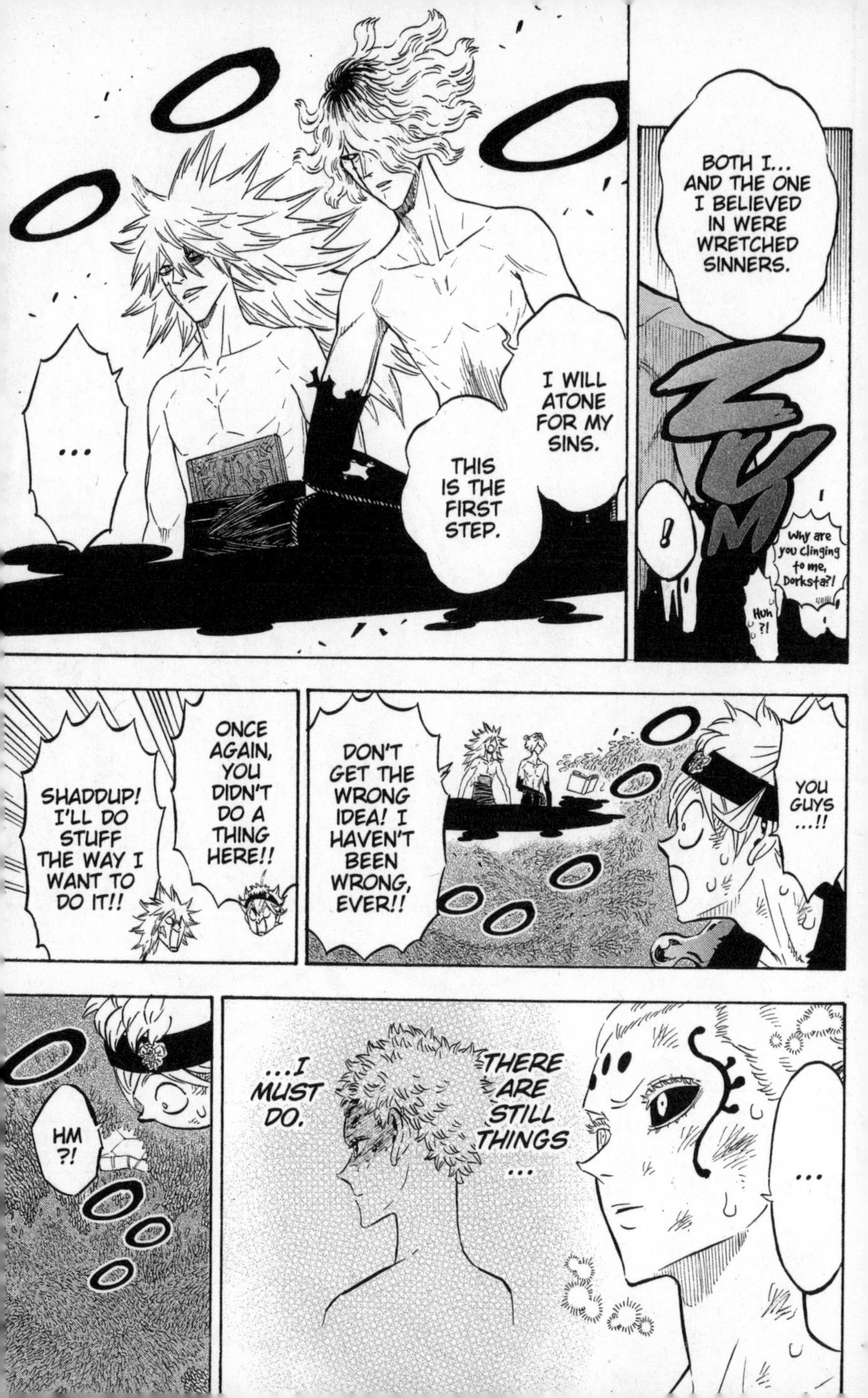
BOTH I... AND THE ONE I BELIEVED IN WERE WRETCHED SINNERS.
ZUM
!
Why are you clinging to me, Dorksta?!
Huh ?!
I WILL ATONE FOR MY SINS.
THIS IS THE FIRST STEP.
...
YOU GUYS ...!!
DON'T GET THE WRONG IDEA! I HAVEN'T BEEN WRONG, EVER!!
ONCE AGAIN, YOU DIDN'T DO A THING HERE!!
SHADDUP! I'LL DO STUFF THE WAY I WANT TO DO IT!!
...
THERE ARE STILL THINGS ...
...I MUST DO.
HM ?!

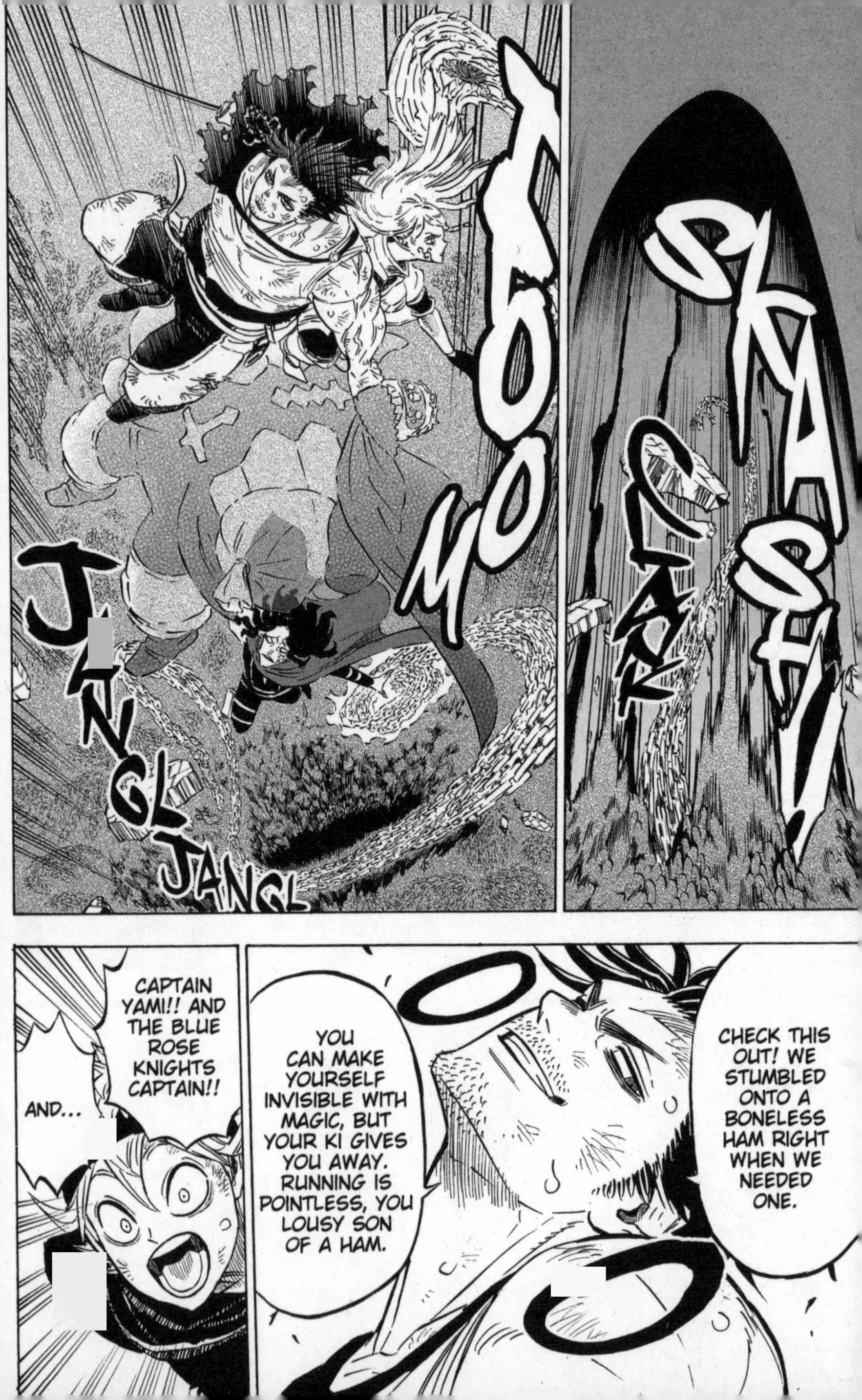
SKRASH!!
CLACK
JANGL
JANGL
CHECK THIS OUT! WE STUMBLED ONTO A BONELESS HAM RIGHT WHEN WE NEEDED ONE.
YOU CAN MAKE YOURSELF INVISIBLE WITH MAGIC, BUT YOUR KI GIVES YOU AWAY. RUNNING IS POINTLESS, YOU LOUSY SON OF A HAM.
CAPTAIN YAMI!! AND THE BLUE ROSE KNIGHTS CAPTAIN!!
AND...

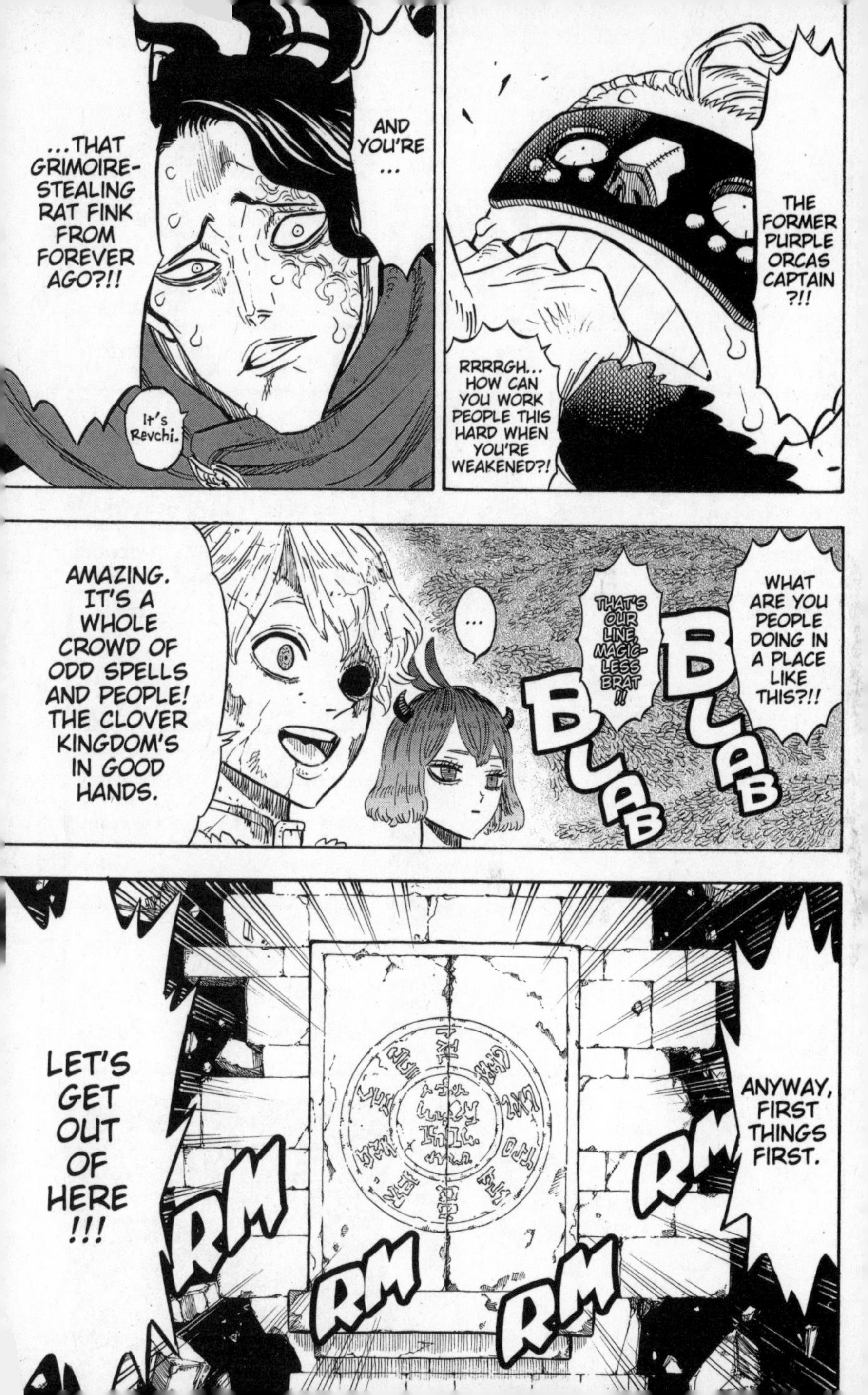
THE FORMER PURPLE ORCAS CAPTAIN?!!
RRRRGH... HOW CAN YOU WORK PEOPLE THIS HARD WHEN YOU'RE WEAKENED?!
AND YOU'RE ...
...THAT GRIMOIRE-STEALING RAT FINK FROM FOREVER AGO?!!
It's Revchi.
WHAT ARE YOU PEOPLE DOING IN A PLACE LIKE THIS?!!
BLAB
BLAB
THAT'S OUR LINE, MAGIC-LESS BRAT!!
...
AMAZING. IT'S A WHOLE CROWD OF ODD SPELLS AND PEOPLE! THE CLOVER KINGDOM'S IN GOOD HANDS.
ANYWAY, FIRST THINGS FIRST.
RM
RM
RM
RM
LET'S GET OUT OF HERE!!!

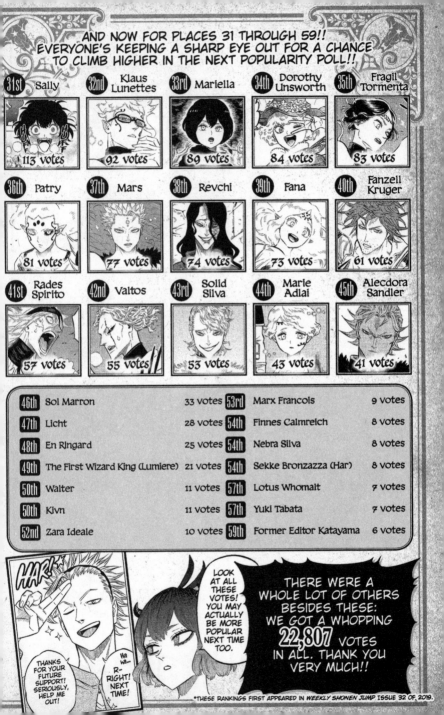

AND NOW FOR PLACES 31 THROUGH 59!! EVERYONE'S KEEPING A SHARP EYE OUT FOR A CHANCE TO CLIMB HIGHER IN THE NEXT POPULARITY POLL!!

31st Sally
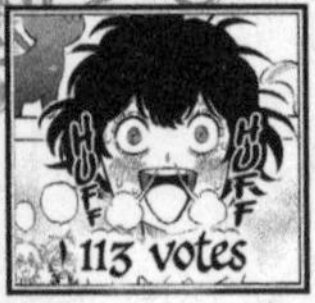
113 votes

32nd Klaus Lunettes
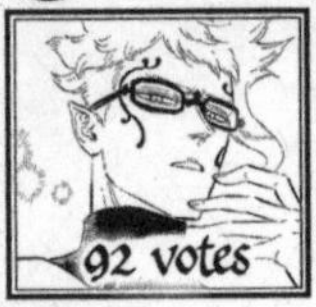
92 votes

33rd Mariella
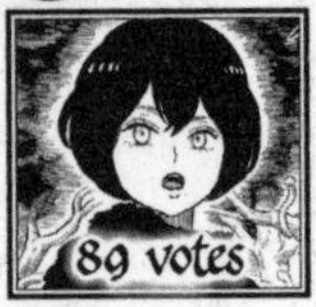
89 votes

34th Dorothy Unsworth
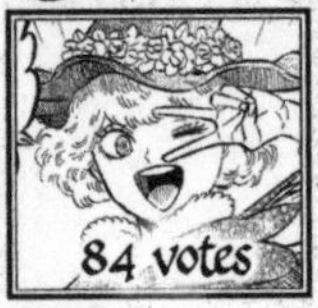
84 votes

35th Fragil Tormenta
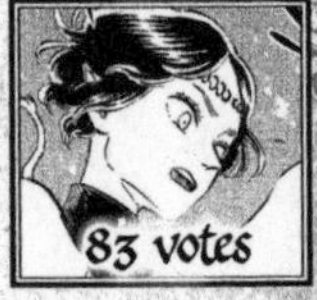
83 votes

36th Patry
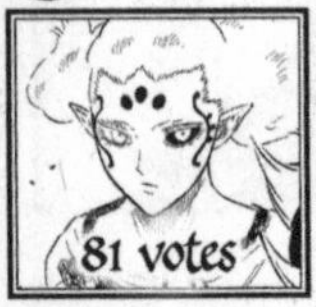
81 votes

37th Mars
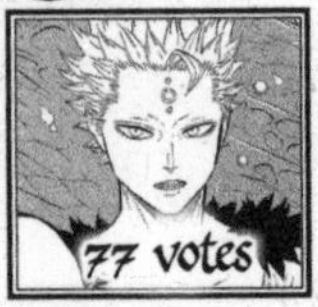
77 votes

38th Revchi
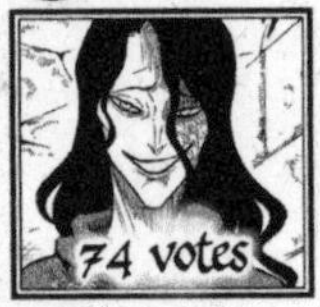
74 votes

39th Fana
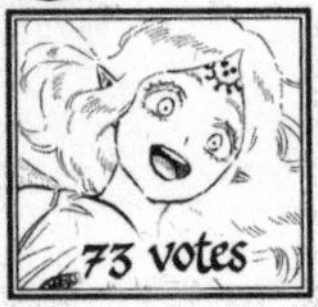
73 votes

40th Fanzell Kruger
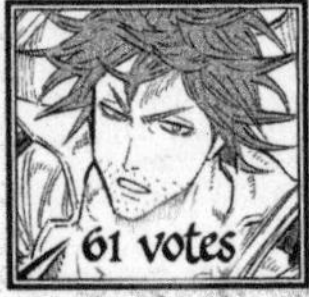
61 votes

41st Rades Spirito
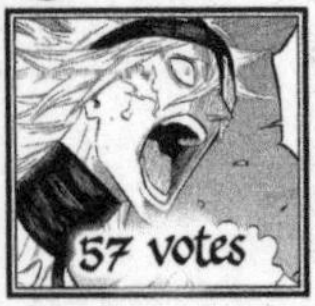
57 votes

42nd Valtos
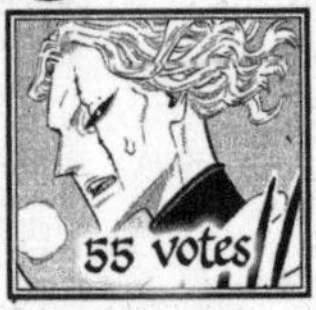
55 votes

43rd Solid Silva
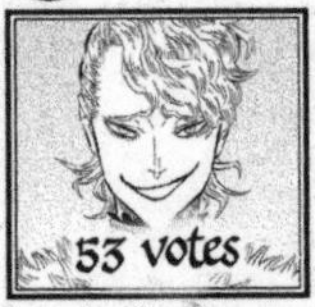
53 votes

44th Marie Adlai
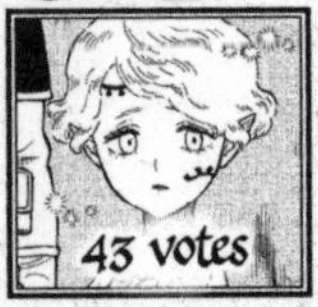
43 votes

45th Alecdora Sandler
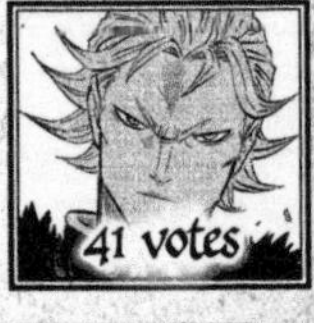
41 votes

46th	Sol Marron	33 votes	53rd	Marx Francois	9 votes
47th	Licht	28 votes	54th	Finnes Calmreich	8 votes
48th	En Ringard	25 votes	54th	Nebra Silva	8 votes
49th	The First Wizard King (Lumiere)	21 votes	54th	Sekke Bronzazza (Har)	8 votes
50th	Walter	11 votes	57th	Lotus Whomalt	7 votes
50th	Kivn	11 votes	57th	Yuki Tabata	7 votes
52nd	Zara Ideale	10 votes	59th	Former Editor Katayama	6 votes

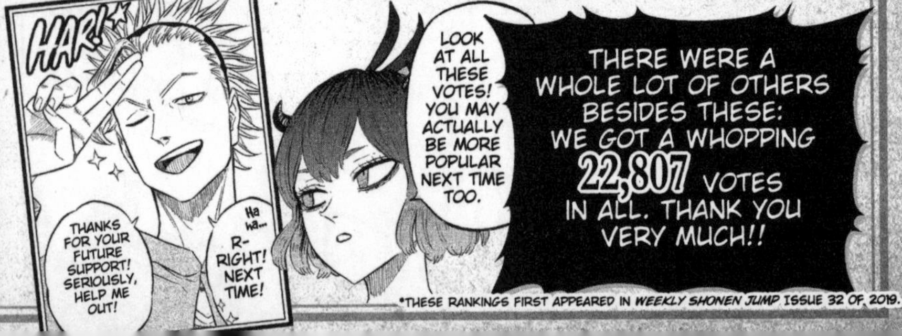
THERE WERE A WHOLE LOT OF OTHERS BESIDES THESE: WE GOT A WHOPPING 22,807 VOTES IN ALL. THANK YOU VERY MUCH!!
LOOK AT ALL THESE VOTES! YOU MAY ACTUALLY BE MORE POPULAR NEXT TIME TOO.
HAR!
THANKS FOR YOUR FUTURE SUPPORT! SERIOUSLY, HELP ME OUT!
Ha ha... R-RIGHT! NEXT TIME!

*THESE RANKINGS FIRST APPEARED IN *WEEKLY SHONEN JUMP* ISSUE 32 OF 2019.

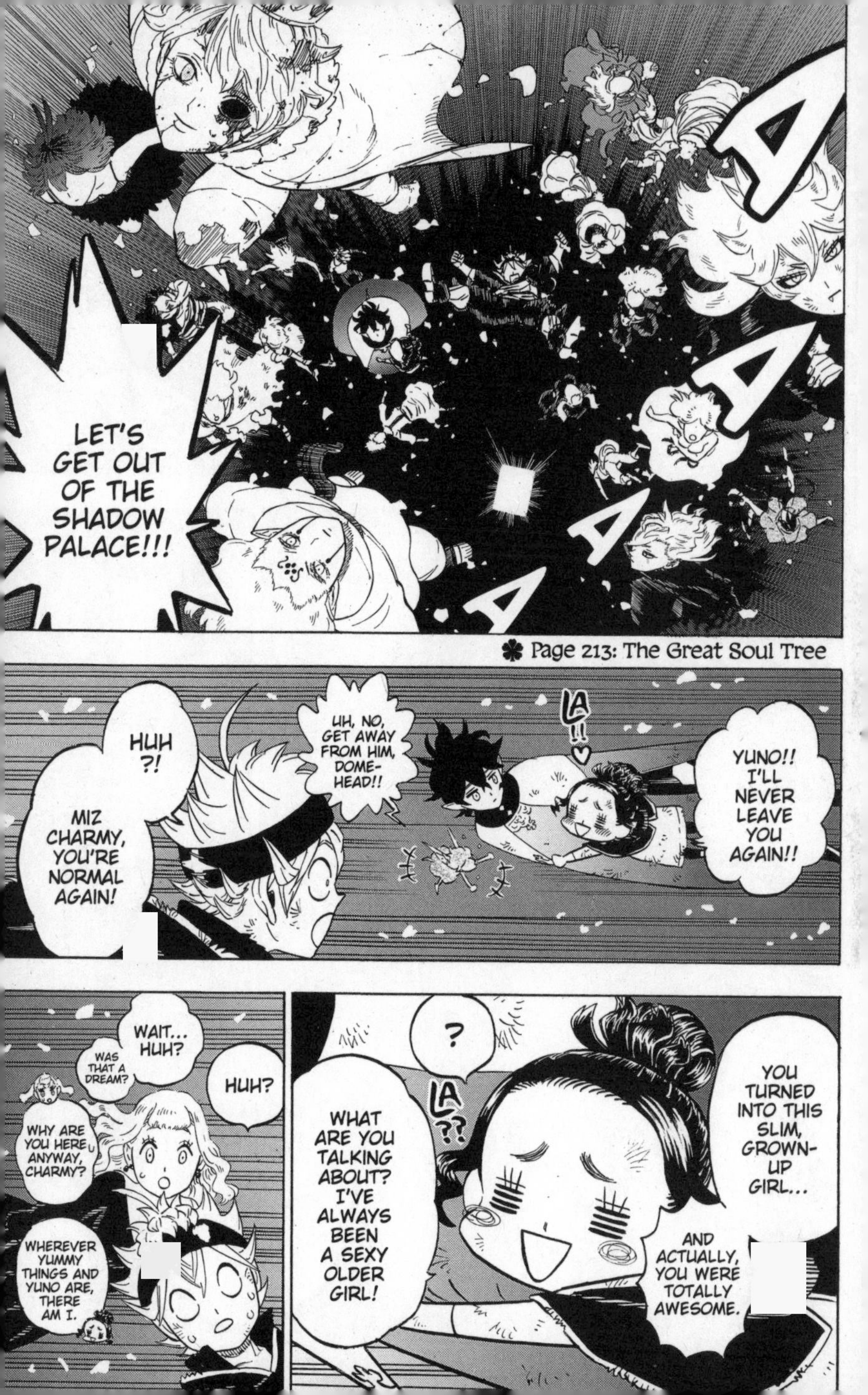
AAAA
LET'S GET OUT OF THE SHADOW PALACE!!!
Page 213: The Great Soul Tree
YUNO!! I'LL NEVER LEAVE YOU AGAIN!!
LA!! ♥
UH, NO, GET AWAY FROM HIM, DOME-HEAD!!
HUH?!
MIZ CHARMY, YOU'RE NORMAL AGAIN!
YOU TURNED INTO THIS SLIM, GROWN-UP GIRL...
AND ACTUALLY, YOU WERE TOTALLY AWESOME.
?
LA??
WHAT ARE YOU TALKING ABOUT? I'VE ALWAYS BEEN A SEXY OLDER GIRL!
HUH?
WAIT... HUH?
WAS THAT A DREAM?
WHY ARE YOU HERE ANYWAY, CHARMY?
WHEREVER YUMMY THINGS AND YUNO ARE, THERE AM I.

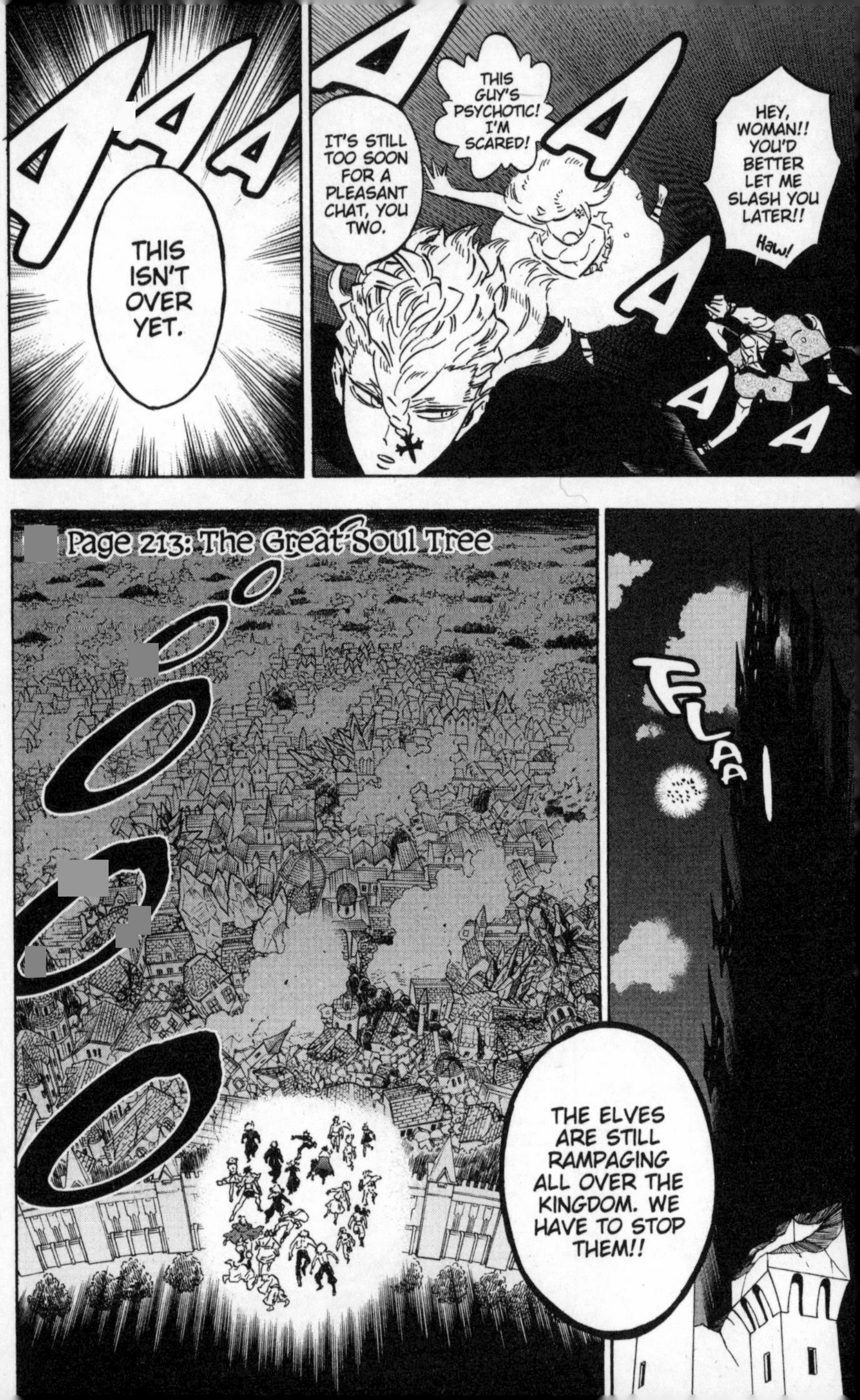
HEY, WOMAN!! YOU'D BETTER LET ME SLASH YOU LATER!!
Haw!
THIS GUY'S PSYCHOTIC! I'M SCARED!
IT'S STILL TOO SOON FOR A PLEASANT CHAT, YOU TWO.
AAAAAA
THIS ISN'T OVER YET.
FLAAA
THE ELVES ARE STILL RAMPAGING ALL OVER THE KINGDOM. WE HAVE TO STOP THEM!!
Page 213: The Great Soul Tree

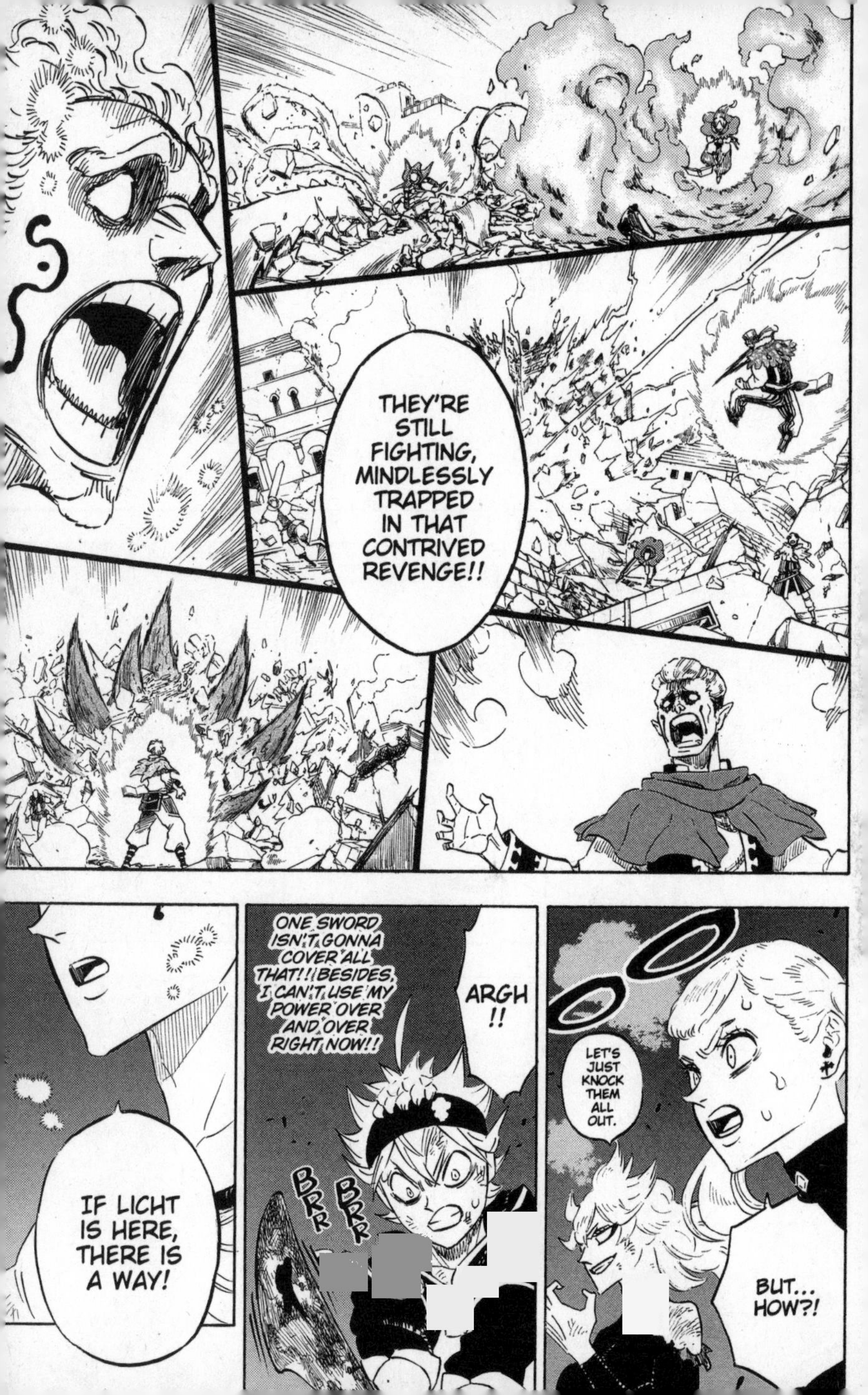
THEY'RE STILL FIGHTING, MINDLESSLY TRAPPED IN THAT CONTRIVED REVENGE!!
LET'S JUST KNOCK THEM ALL OUT.
BUT... HOW?!
ARGH!!
ONE SWORD ISN'T GONNA COVER ALL THAT!! BESIDES, I CAN'T USE MY POWER OVER AND OVER RIGHT NOW!!
BRR BRR
IF LICHT IS HERE, THERE IS A WAY!

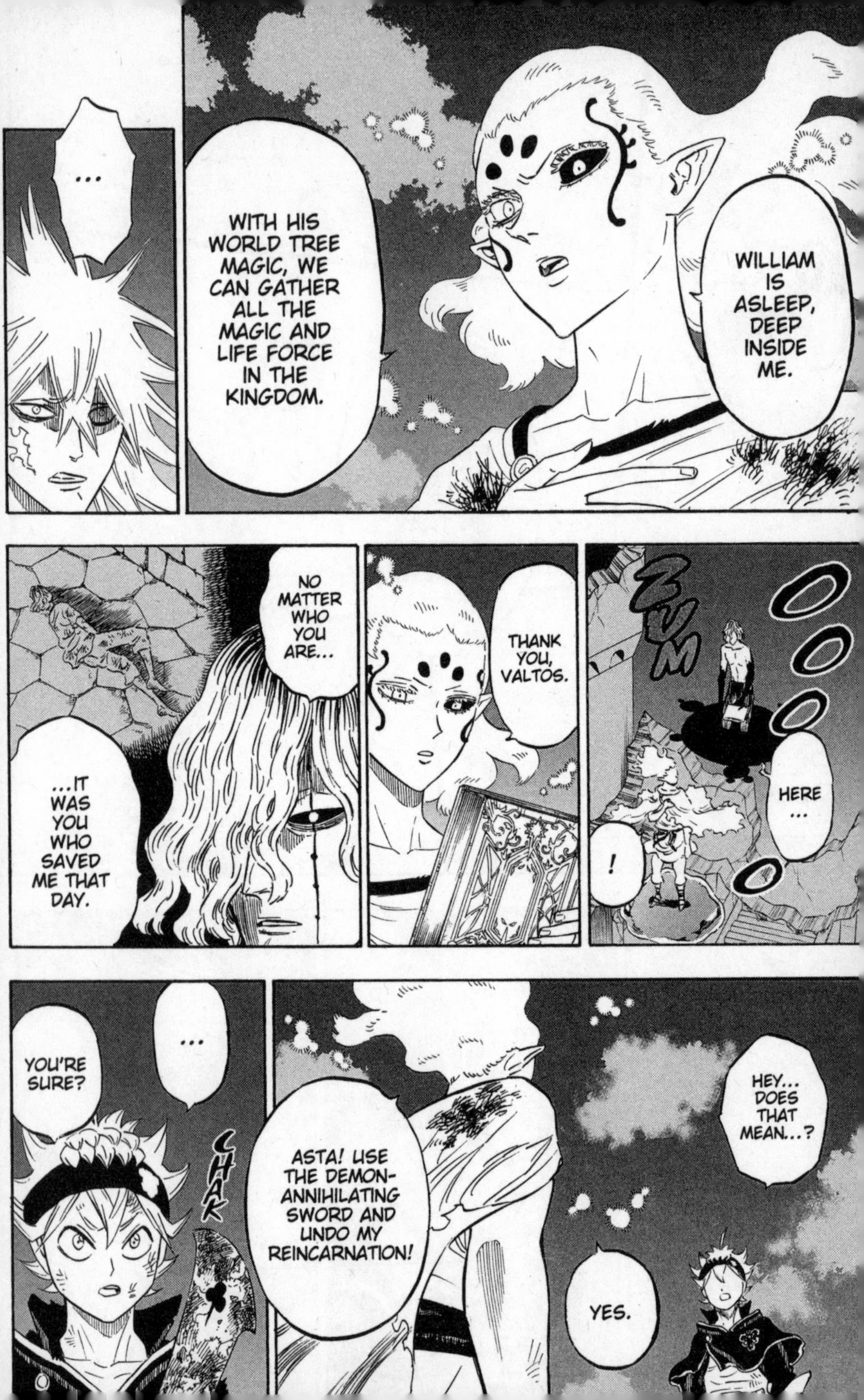
WILLIAM IS ASLEEP, DEEP INSIDE ME.
WITH HIS WORLD TREE MAGIC, WE CAN GATHER ALL THE MAGIC AND LIFE FORCE IN THE KINGDOM.
...
ZUMOOOOO
HERE...
!
THANK YOU, VALTOS.
NO MATTER WHO YOU ARE...
...IT WAS YOU WHO SAVED ME THAT DAY.
HEY... DOES THAT MEAN...?
YES.
ASTA! USE THE DEMON-ANNIHILATING SWORD AND UNDO MY REINCARNATION!
...
YOU'RE SURE?
CHAK

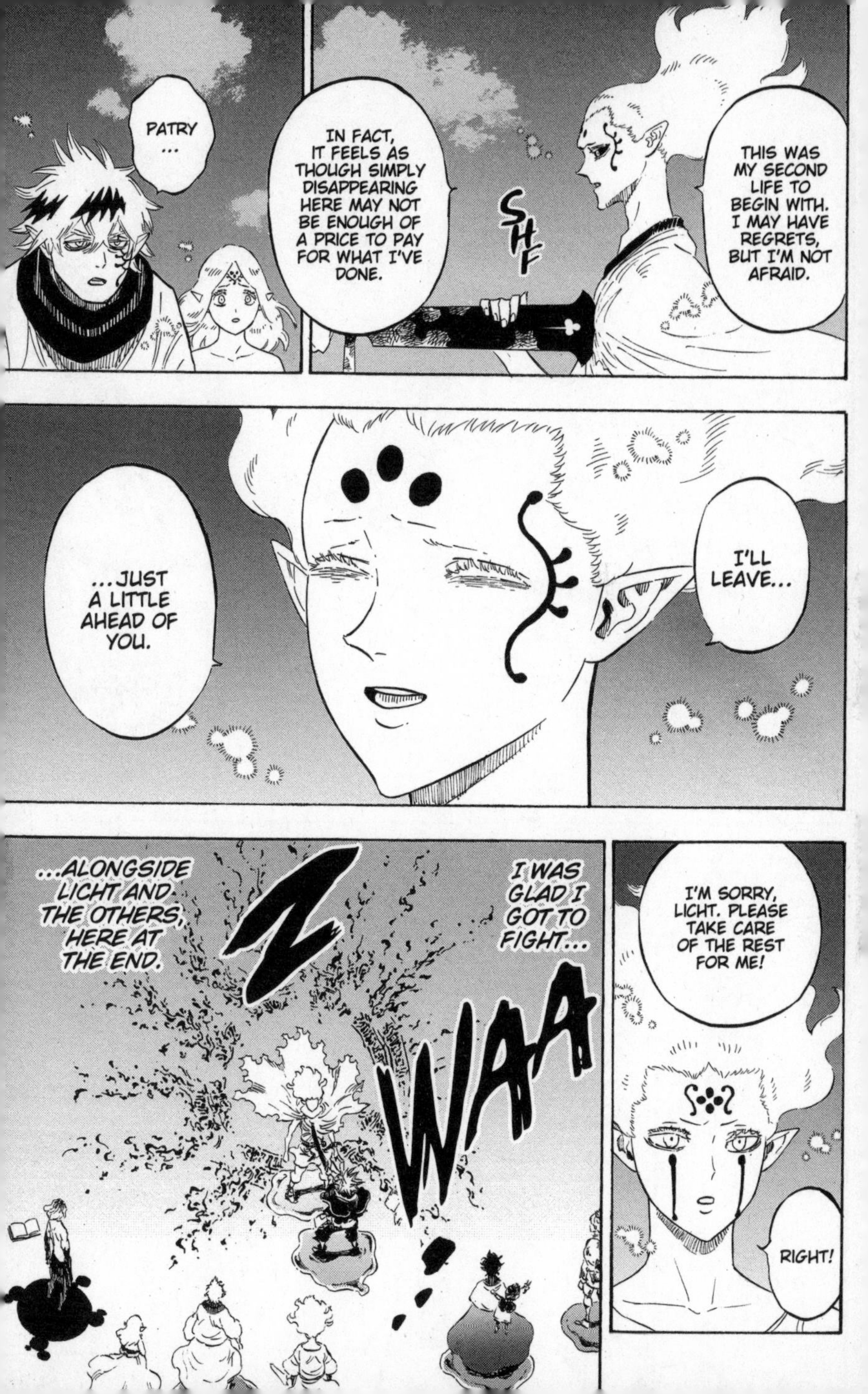
THIS WAS MY SECOND LIFE TO BEGIN WITH. I MAY HAVE REGRETS, BUT I'M NOT AFRAID.
IN FACT, IT FEELS AS THOUGH SIMPLY DISAPPEARING HERE MAY NOT BE ENOUGH OF A PRICE TO PAY FOR WHAT I'VE DONE.
SHF
PATRY...
I'LL LEAVE...
...JUST A LITTLE AHEAD OF YOU.
I'M SORRY, LICHT. PLEASE TAKE CARE OF THE REST FOR ME!
RIGHT!
I WAS GLAD I GOT TO FIGHT...
...ALONGSIDE LICHT AND THE OTHERS, HERE AT THE END.
ZWAA

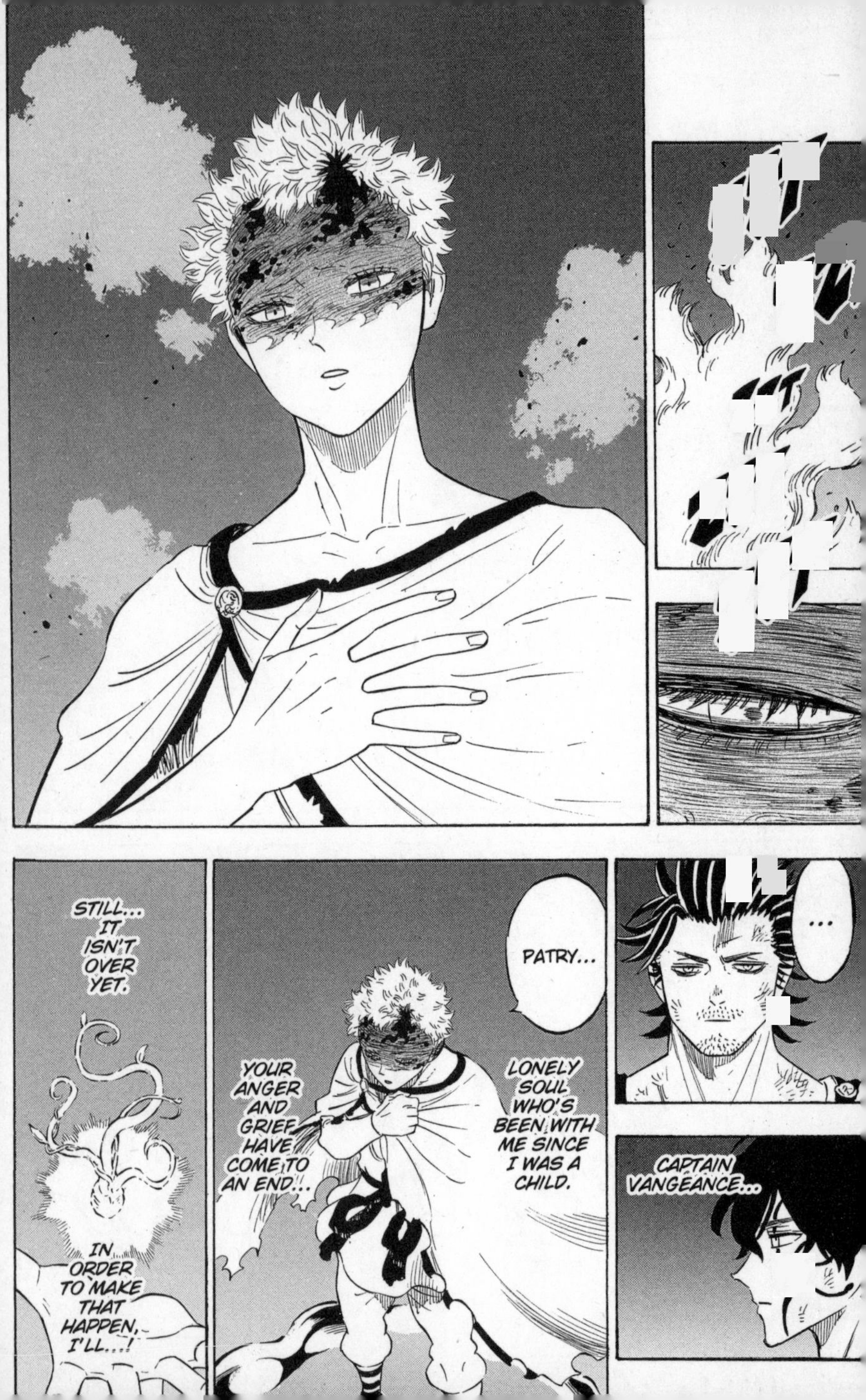
...
CAPTAIN VANGEANCE...
PATRY...
LONELY SOUL WHO'S BEEN WITH ME SINCE I WAS A CHILD.
YOUR ANGER AND GRIEF HAVE COME TO AN END...
STILL... IT ISN'T OVER YET.
IN ORDER TO MAKE THAT HAPPEN, I'LL...!

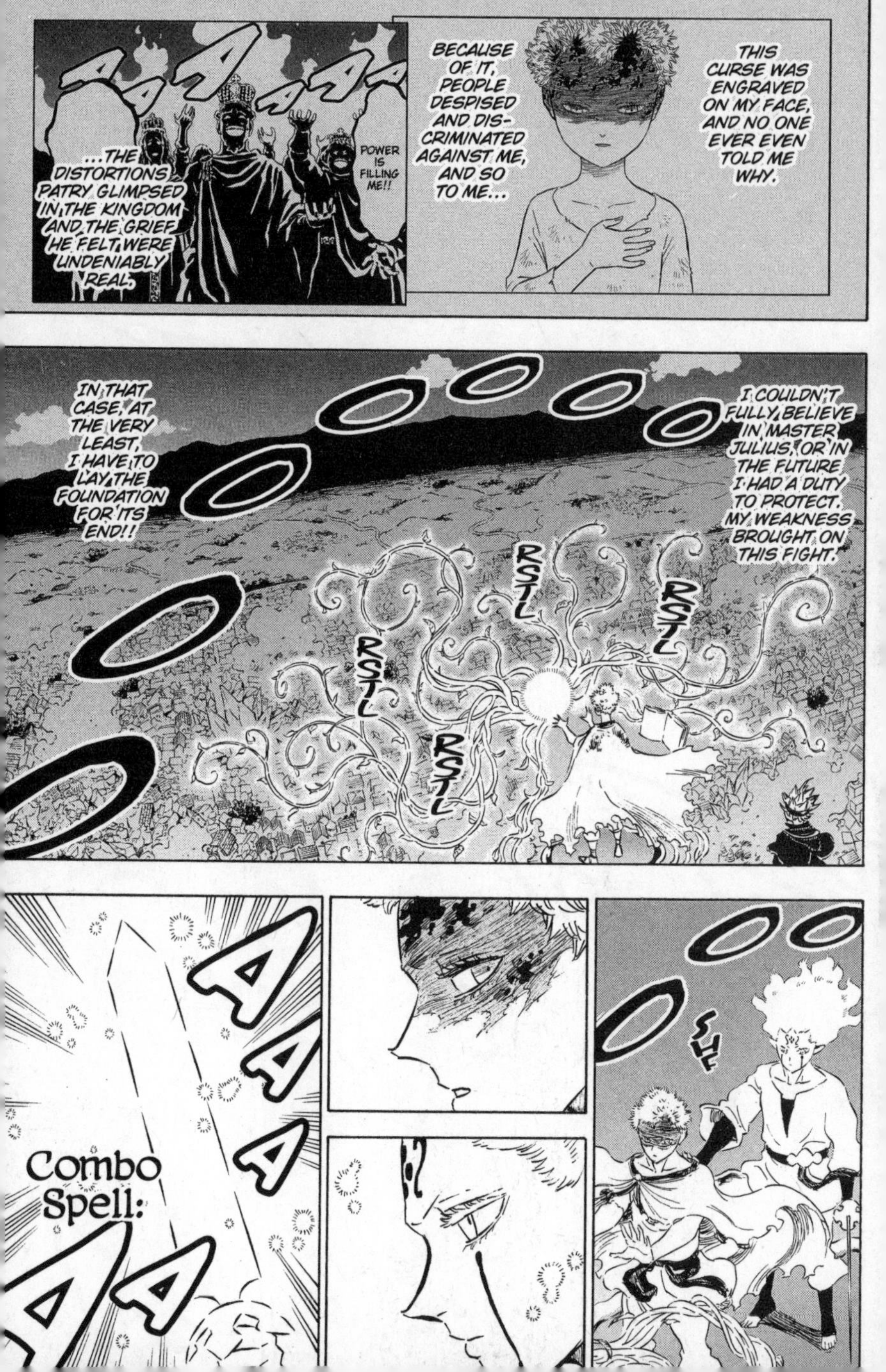
THIS CURSE WAS ENGRAVED ON MY FACE, AND NO ONE EVER EVEN TOLD ME WHY.
BECAUSE OF IT, PEOPLE DESPISED AND DIS-CRIMINATED AGAINST ME, AND SO TO ME...
AAAAAA
POWER IS FILLING ME!!
...THE DISTORTIONS PATRY GLIMPSED IN THE KINGDOM AND THE GRIEF HE FELT WERE UNDENIABLY REAL.
I COULDN'T FULLY BELIEVE IN MASTER JULIUS, OR IN THE FUTURE I HAD A DUTY TO PROTECT. MY WEAKNESS BROUGHT ON THIS FIGHT.
OOOOOOOO
RSTL
RSTL
RSTL
RSTL
IN THAT CASE, AT THE VERY LEAST, I HAVE TO LAY THE FOUNDATION FOR ITS END!!
OOO
SHF
AAAAAAA
Combo Spell:

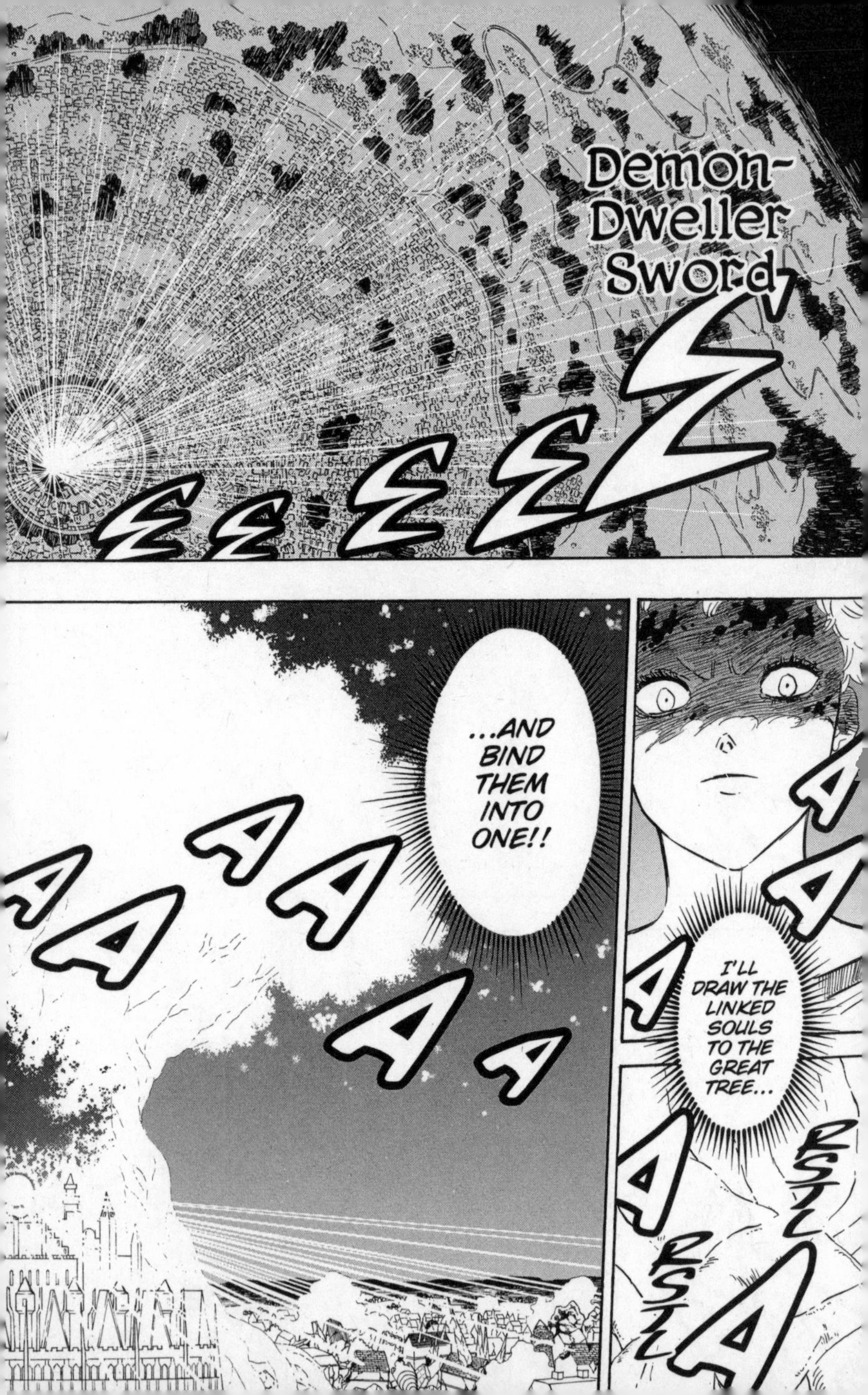
Demon-Dweller Sword
EEEEE
I'LL DRAW THE LINKED SOULS TO THE GREAT TREE...
RSTL
RSTL
AAAAA
...AND BIND THEM INTO ONE!!
AAAAAA

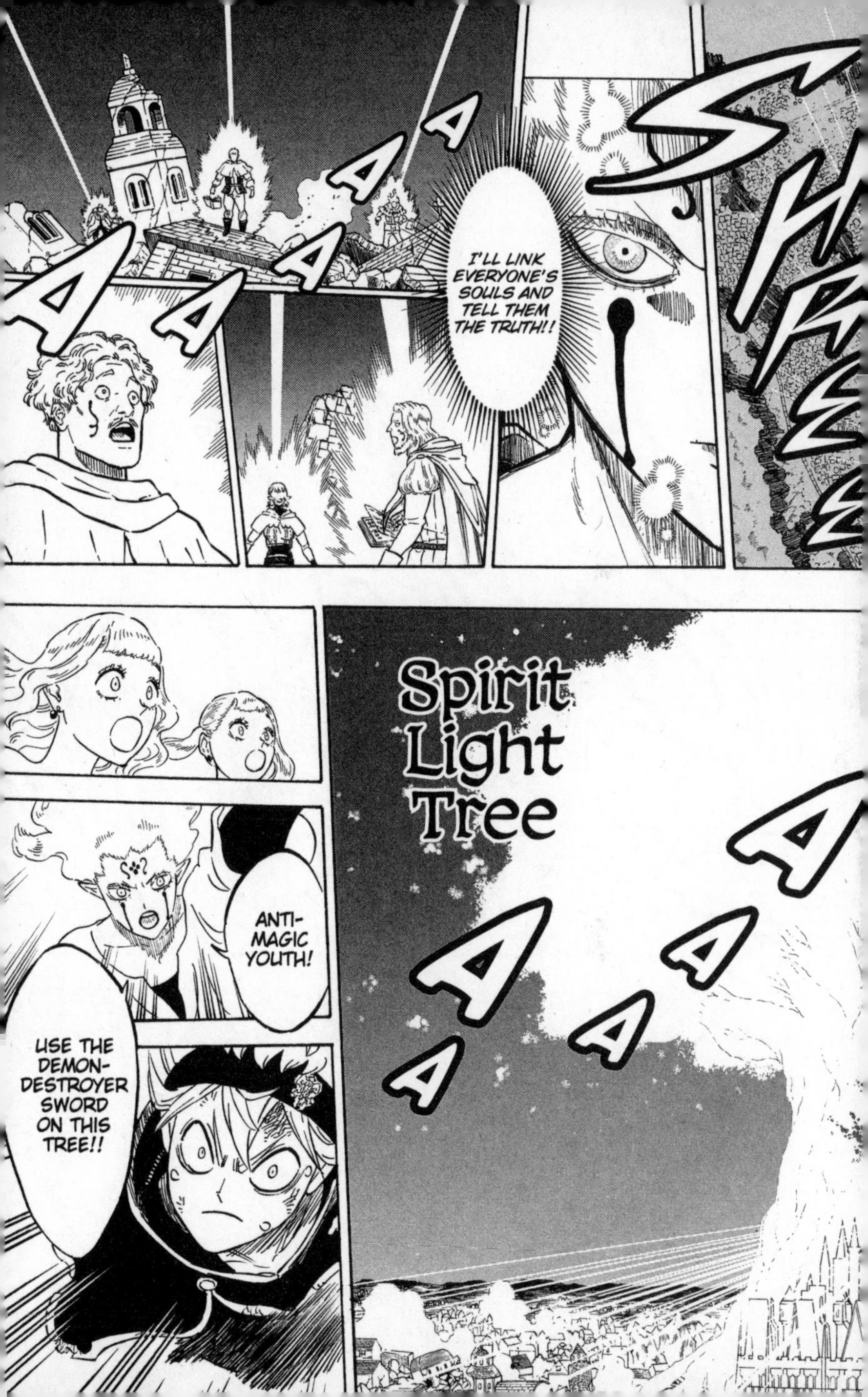
SHAAA
I'LL LINK EVERYONE'S SOULS AND TELL THEM THE TRUTH!!
AAAAAA
Spirit Light Tree
AAAAA
ANTI-MAGIC YOUTH!
USE THE DEMON-DESTROYER SWORD ON THIS TREE!!

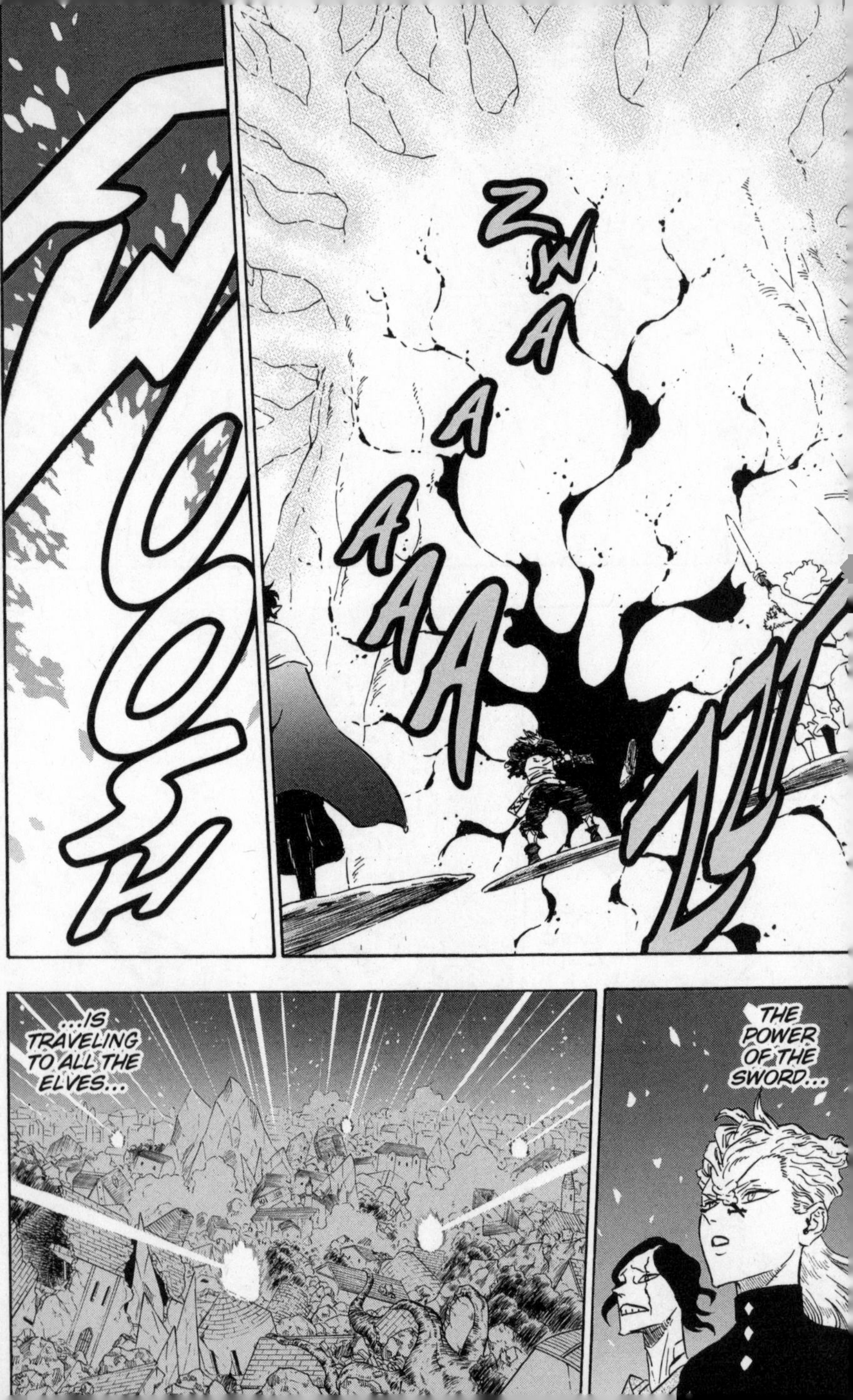
ZWAAAAAA
THE POWER OF THE SWORD...
...IS TRAVELING TO ALL THE ELVES...

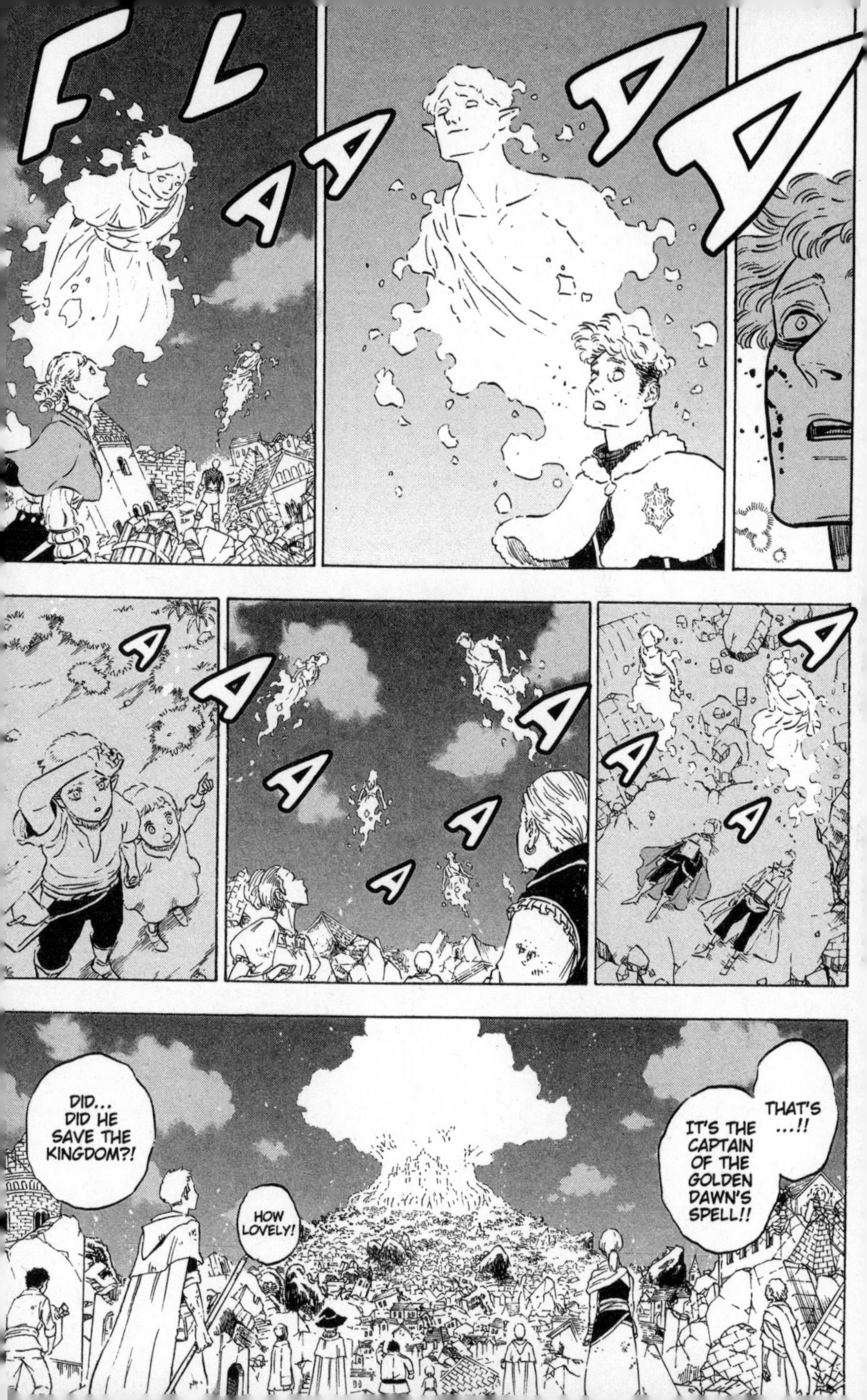
FLAAAAA
AAAAAAAAAAA
THAT'S ...!!
IT'S THE CAPTAIN OF THE GOLDEN DAWN'S SPELL!!
HOW LOVELY!
DID... DID HE SAVE THE KINGDOM?!

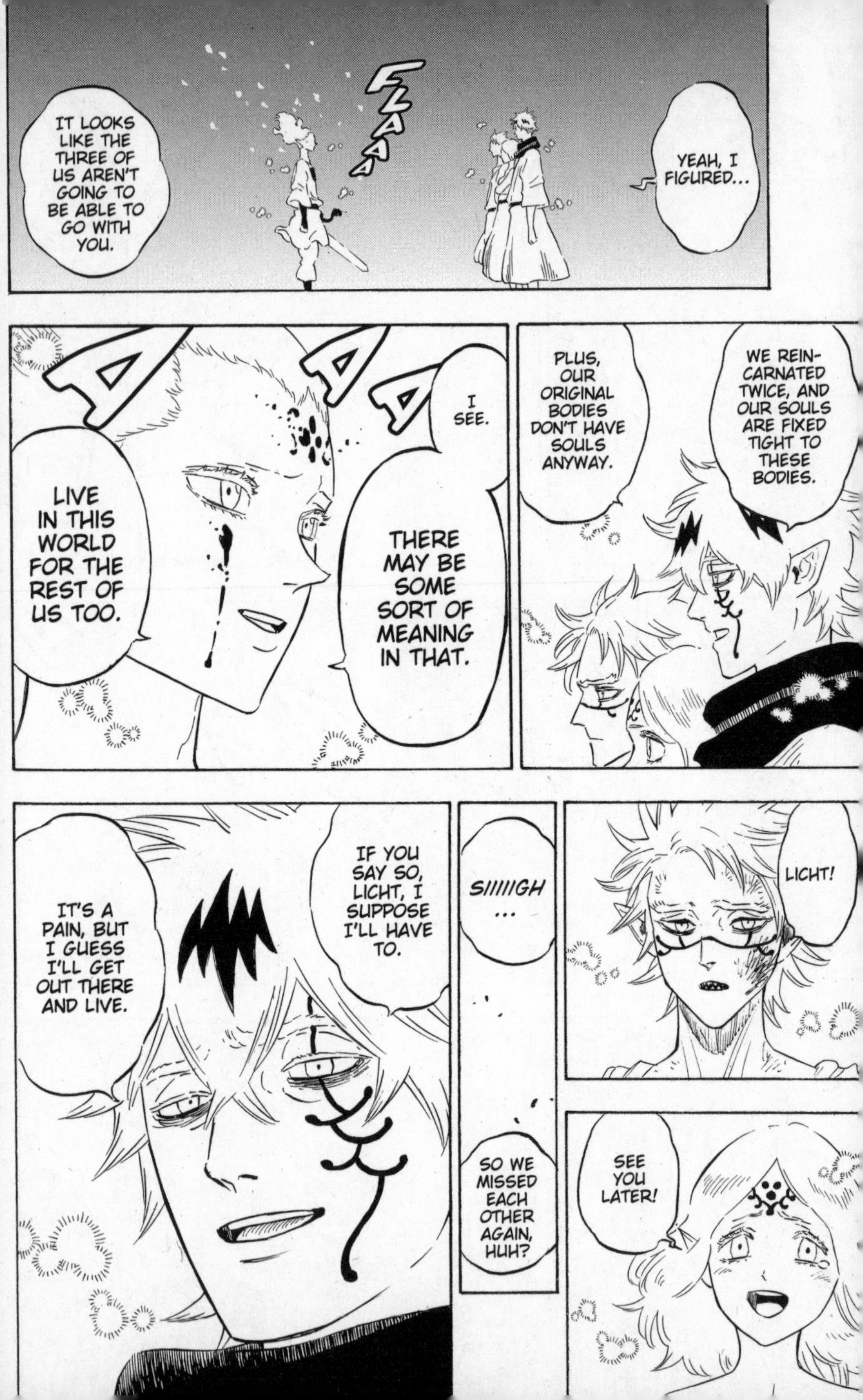
YEAH, I FIGURED...
FLAAAA
IT LOOKS LIKE THE THREE OF US AREN'T GOING TO BE ABLE TO GO WITH YOU.
WE REIN-CARNATED TWICE, AND OUR SOULS ARE FIXED TIGHT TO THESE BODIES.
PLUS, OUR ORIGINAL BODIES DON'T HAVE SOULS ANYWAY.
AAA
I SEE.
THERE MAY BE SOME SORT OF MEANING IN THAT.
LIVE IN THIS WORLD FOR THE REST OF US TOO.
LICHT!
SEE YOU LATER!
SIIIIGH ...
SO WE MISSED EACH OTHER AGAIN, HUH?
IF YOU SAY SO, LICHT, I SUPPOSE I'LL HAVE TO.
IT'S A PAIN, BUT I GUESS I'LL GET OUT THERE AND LIVE.

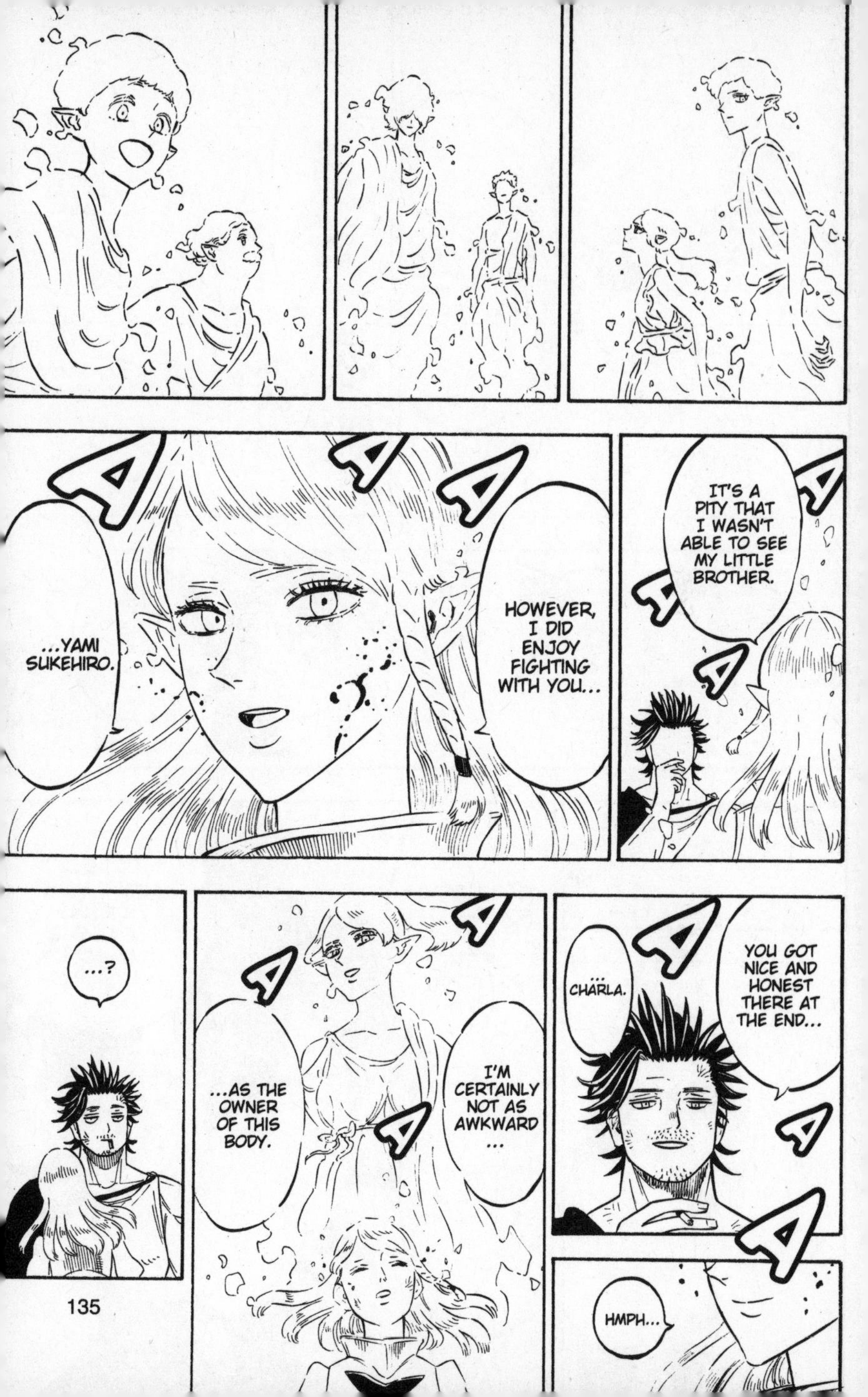
IT'S A PITY THAT I WASN'T ABLE TO SEE MY LITTLE BROTHER.
A
A
A
A
A
A
HOWEVER, I DID ENJOY FIGHTING WITH YOU...
...YAMI SUKEHIRO.
A
A
YOU GOT NICE AND HONEST THERE AT THE END...
...CHARLA.
A
HMPH...
A
A
I'M CERTAINLY NOT AS AWKWARD...
...AS THE OWNER OF THIS BODY.
A
...?

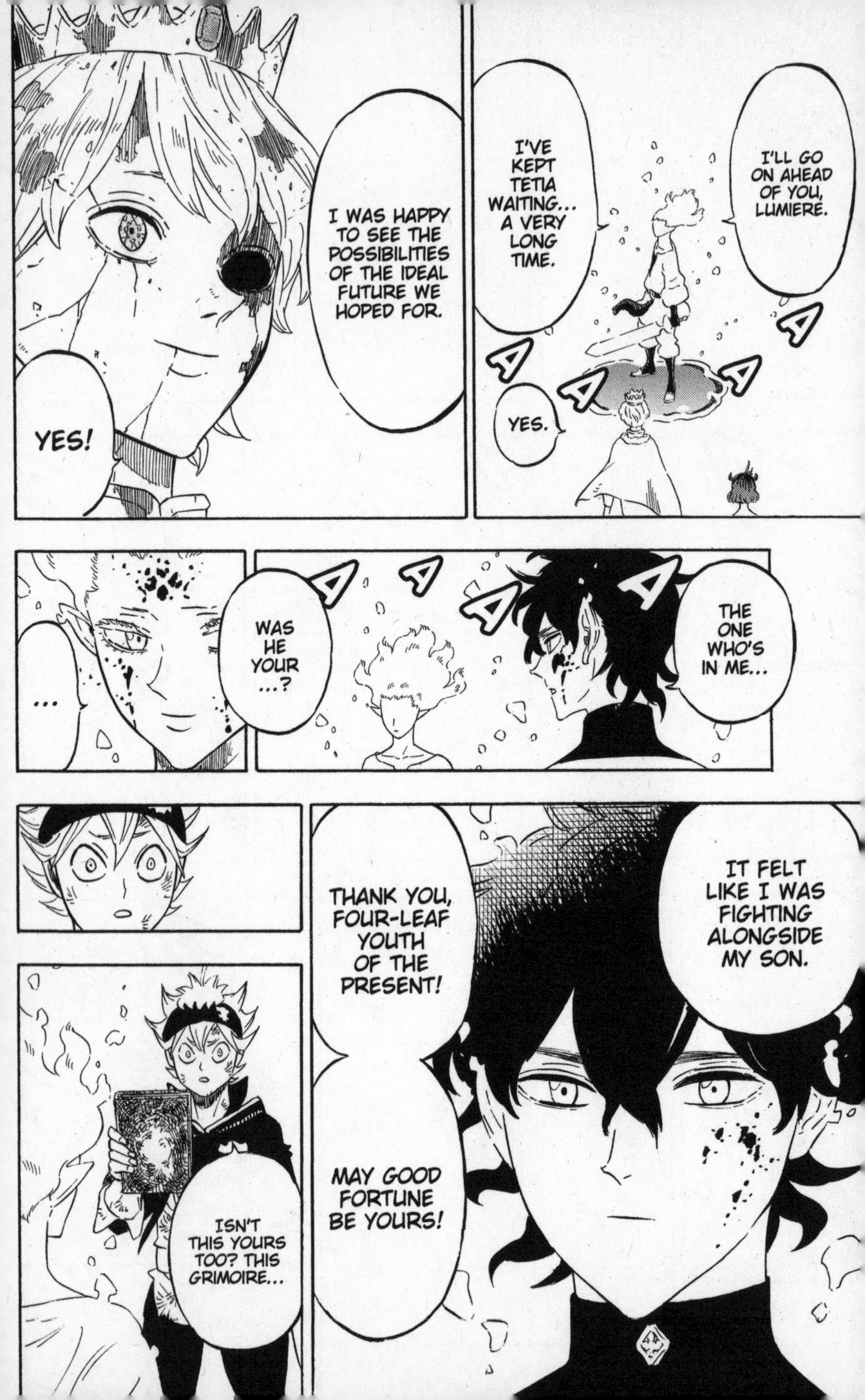
I'LL GO ON AHEAD OF YOU, LUMIERE.
I'VE KEPT TETIA WAITING... A VERY LONG TIME.
A A A A A
YES.
I WAS HAPPY TO SEE THE POSSIBILITIES OF THE IDEAL FUTURE WE HOPED FOR.
YES!
THE ONE WHO'S IN ME...
A A A A
WAS HE YOUR ...?
...
IT FELT LIKE I WAS FIGHTING ALONGSIDE MY SON.
THANK YOU, FOUR-LEAF YOUTH OF THE PRESENT!
MAY GOOD FORTUNE BE YOURS!
ISN'T THIS YOURS TOO? THIS GRIMOIRE...

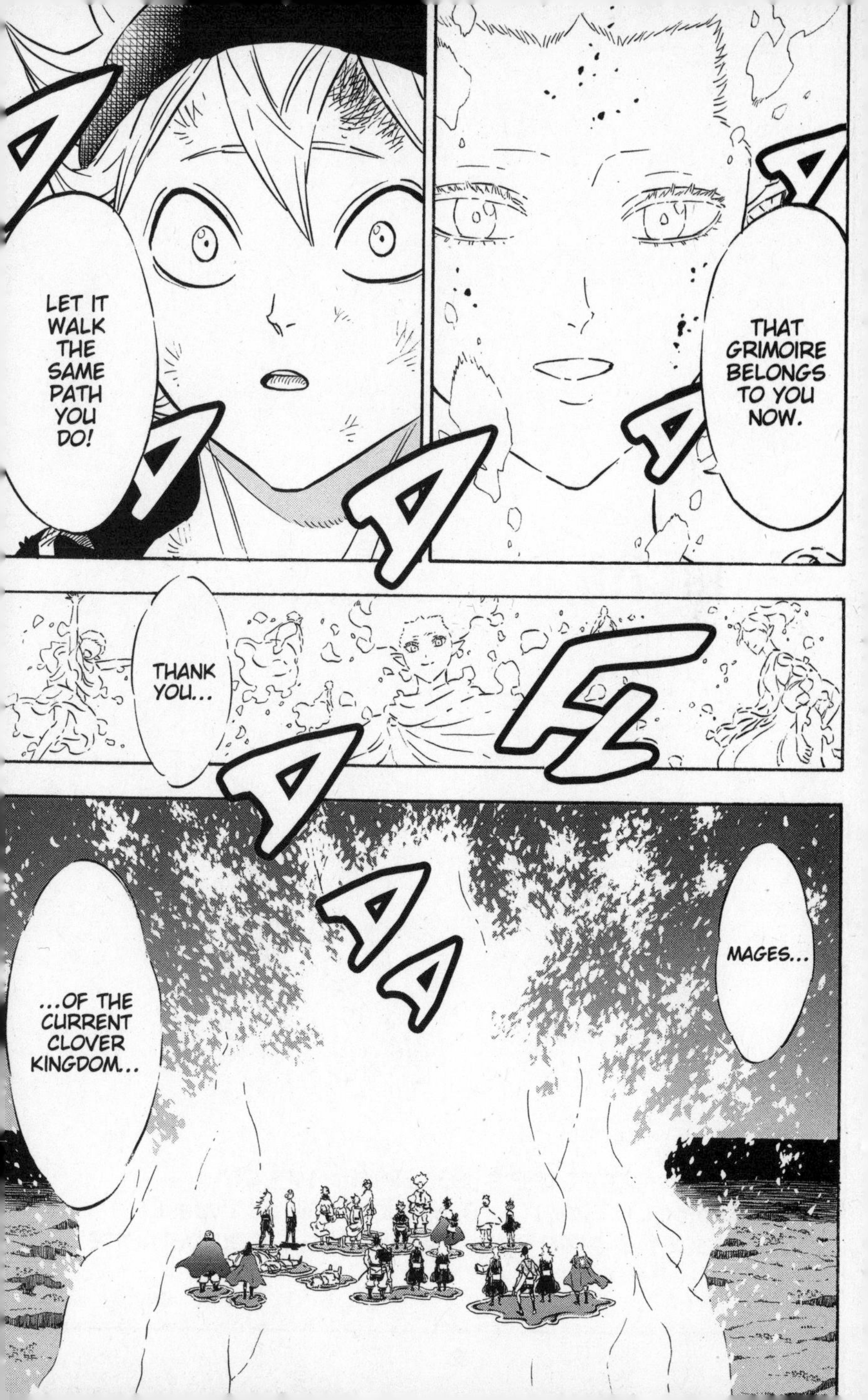
THAT GRIMOIRE BELONGS TO YOU NOW.
LET IT WALK THE SAME PATH YOU DO!
THANK YOU...
MAGES...
...OF THE CURRENT CLOVER KINGDOM...

Licht

Age: 25 at the time   Height: 173 cm
Birthday: October 1   Sign: Libra   Blood Type: O
Likes: Peaceful time spent with all his companions

Character   Profile

✤

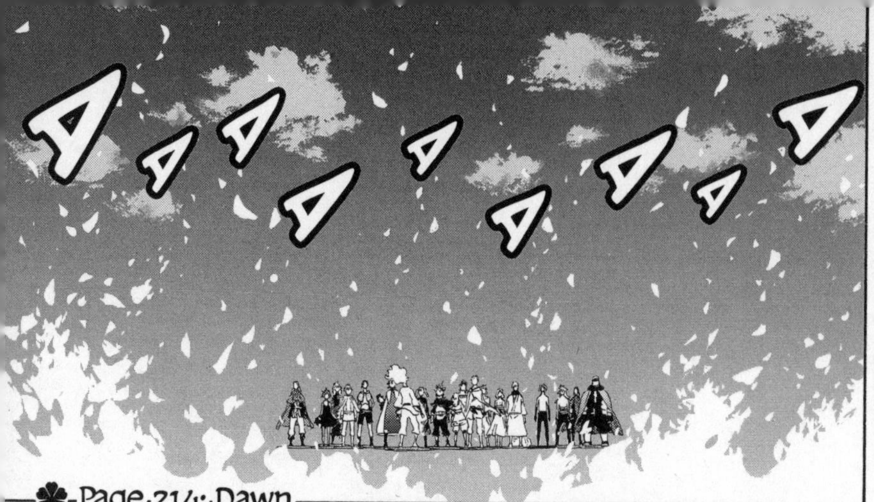
AAAAAAAAA

Page 214: Dawn

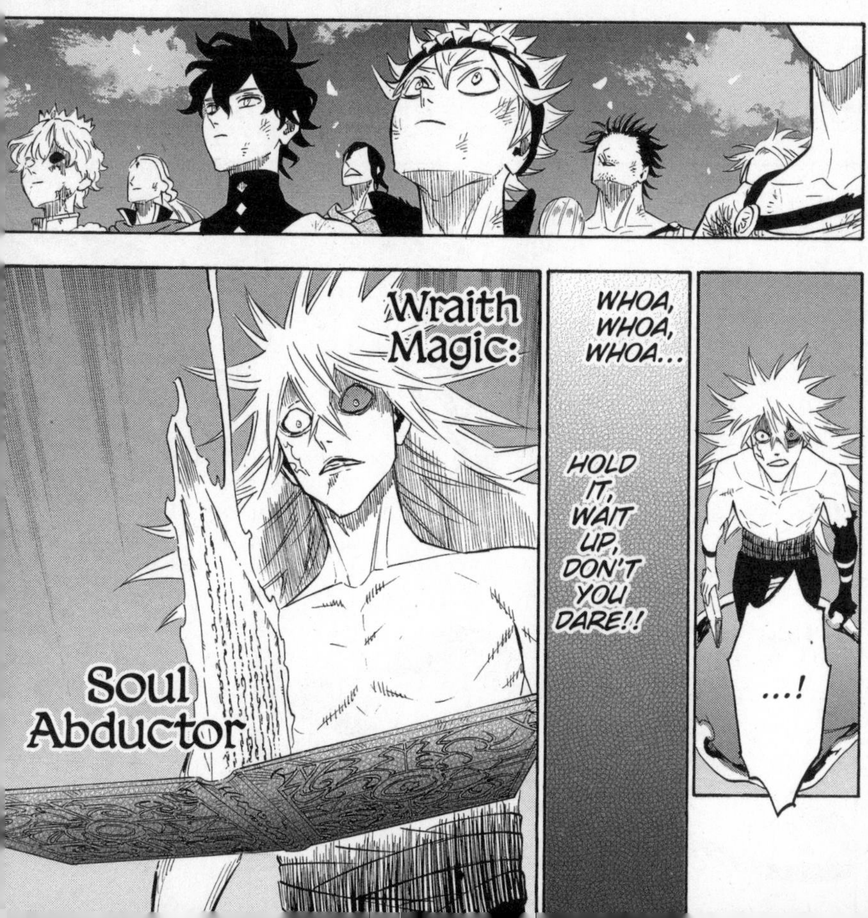
...!
WHOA, WHOA, WHOA...
HOLD IT, WAIT UP, DON'T YOU DARE!!
Wraith Magic:
Soul Abductor

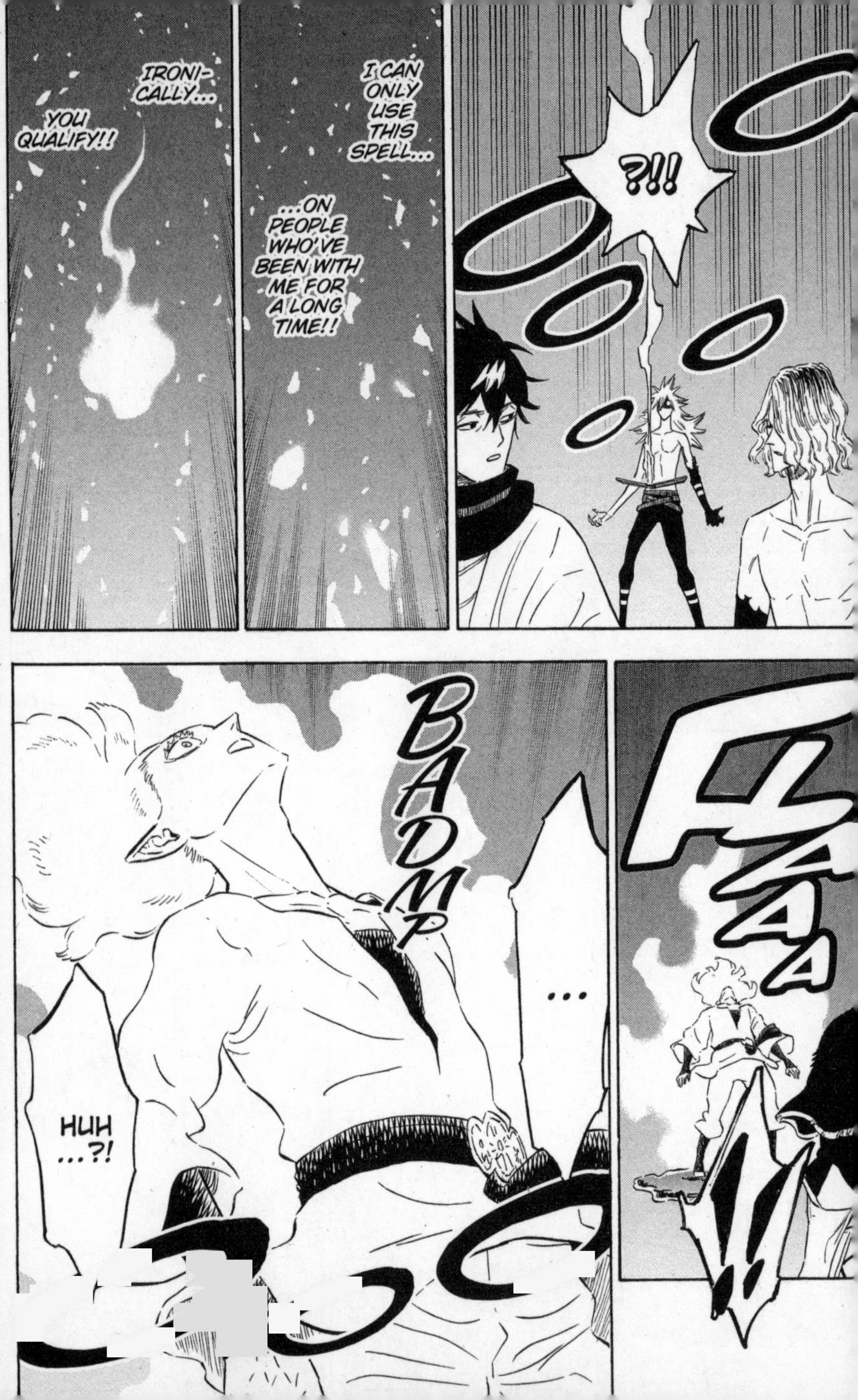
?!!
I CAN ONLY USE THIS SPELL...
...ON PEOPLE WHO'VE BEEN WITH ME FOR A LONG TIME!!
IRONI-CALLY...
YOU QUALIFY!!
HAAA
BADMP
...
HUH ...?!

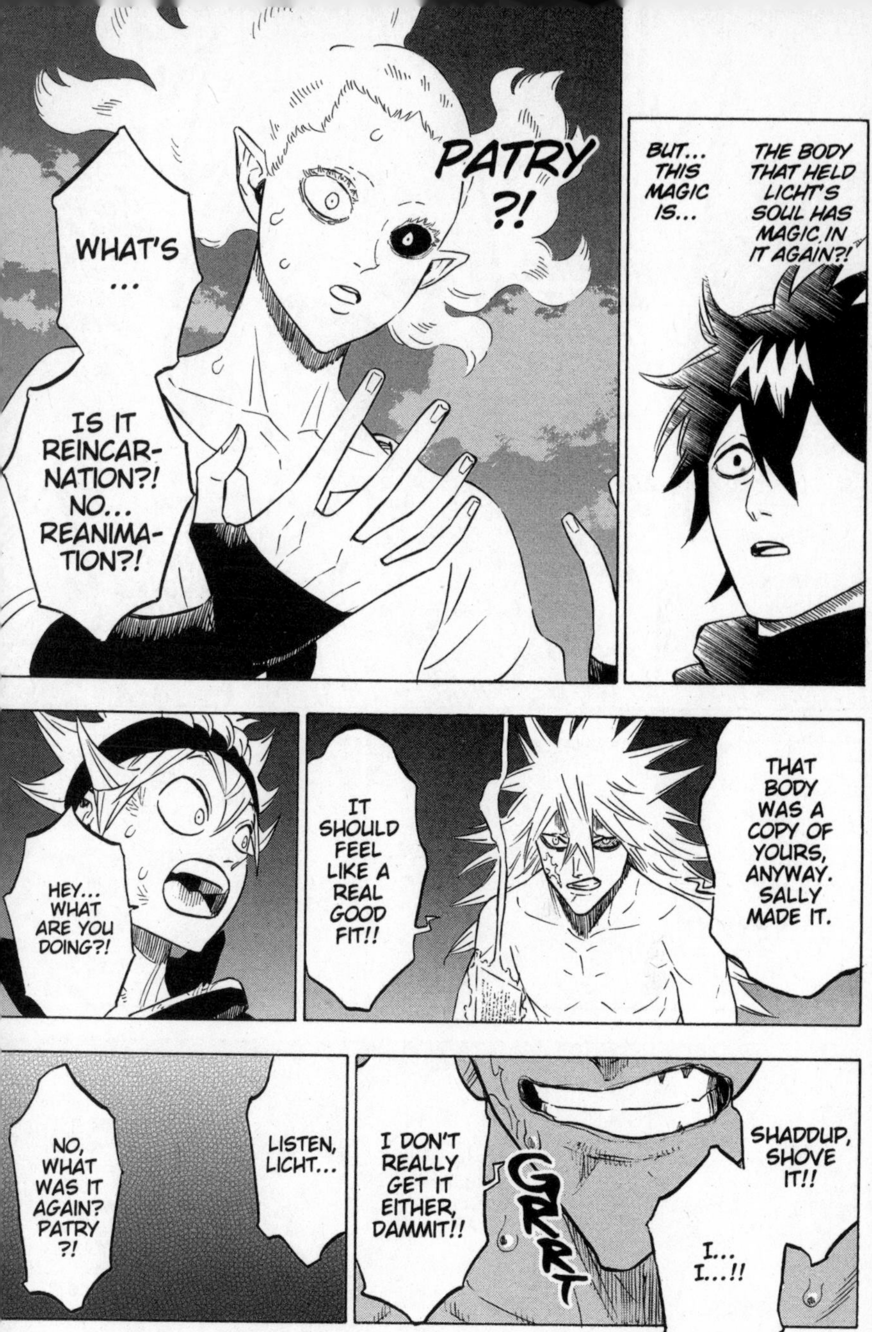
THE BODY THAT HELD LICHT'S SOUL HAS MAGIC IN IT AGAIN?!
BUT... THIS MAGIC IS...
PATRY ?!
WHAT'S ...
IS IT REINCARNATION?! NO... REANIMATION?!
THAT BODY WAS A COPY OF YOURS, ANYWAY. SALLY MADE IT.
IT SHOULD FEEL LIKE A REAL GOOD FIT!!
HEY... WHAT ARE YOU DOING?!
SHADDUP, SHOVE IT!!
GRRT
I... I...!!
I DON'T REALLY GET IT EITHER, DAMMIT!!
LISTEN, LICHT...
NO, WHAT WAS IT AGAIN? PATRY ?!

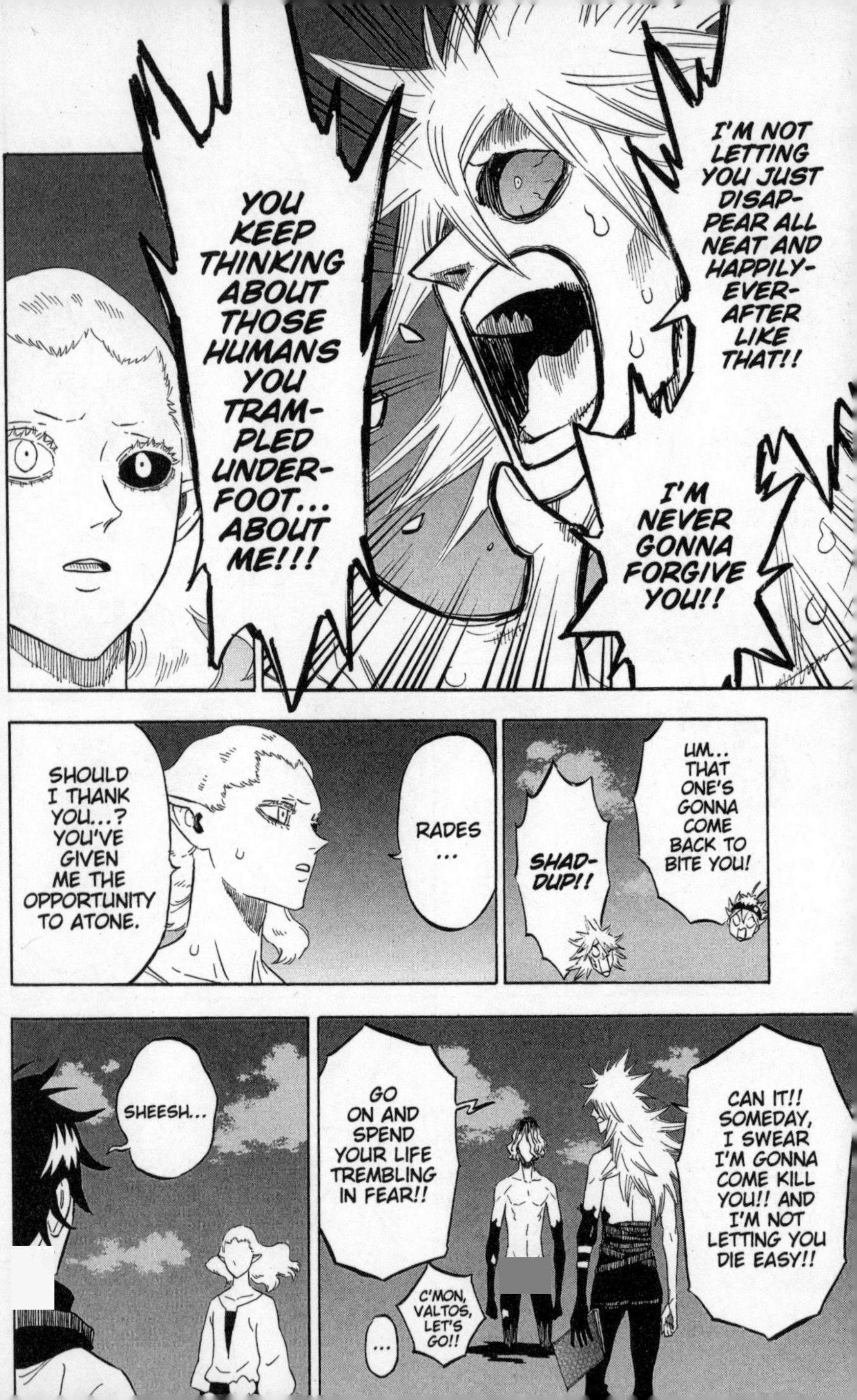
I'M NOT LETTING YOU JUST DISAPPEAR ALL NEAT AND HAPPILY-EVER-AFTER LIKE THAT!!
YOU KEEP THINKING ABOUT THOSE HUMANS YOU TRAMPLED UNDERFOOT... ABOUT ME!!!
I'M NEVER GONNA FORGIVE YOU!!
UM... THAT ONE'S GONNA COME BACK TO BITE YOU!
SHADDUP!!
RADES...
SHOULD I THANK YOU...? YOU'VE GIVEN ME THE OPPORTUNITY TO ATONE.
CAN IT!! SOMEDAY, I SWEAR I'M GONNA COME KILL YOU!! AND I'M NOT LETTING YOU DIE EASY!!
GO ON AND SPEND YOUR LIFE TREMBLING IN FEAR!!
C'MON, VALTOS, LET'S GO!!
...
SHEESH...

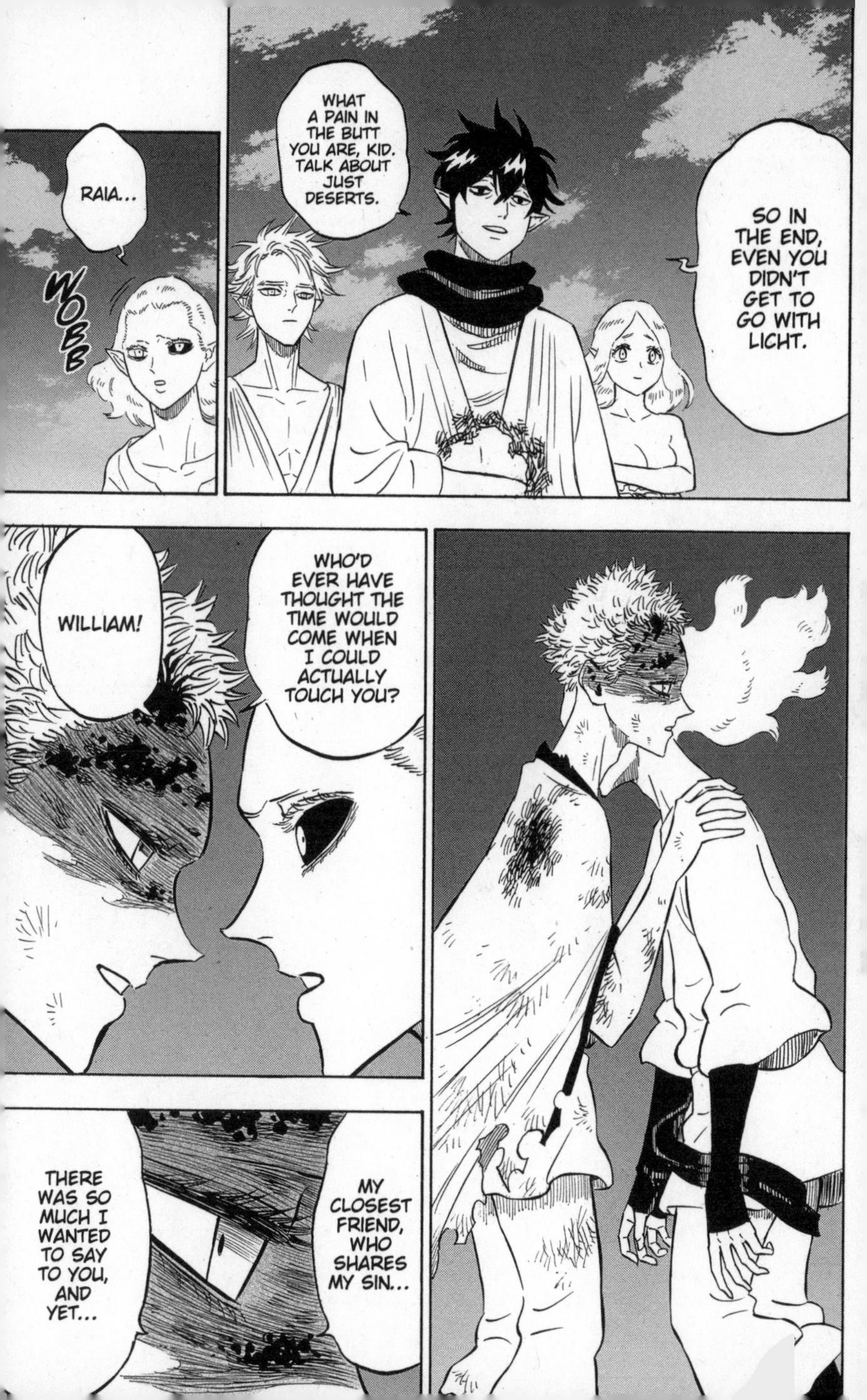
SO IN THE END, EVEN YOU DIDN'T GET TO GO WITH LICHT.
WHAT A PAIN IN THE BUTT YOU ARE, KID. TALK ABOUT JUST DESERTS.
RAIA...
WOBB
WHO'D EVER HAVE THOUGHT THE TIME WOULD COME WHEN I COULD ACTUALLY TOUCH YOU?
WILLIAM!
MY CLOSEST FRIEND, WHO SHARES MY SIN...
THERE WAS SO MUCH I WANTED TO SAY TO YOU, AND YET...

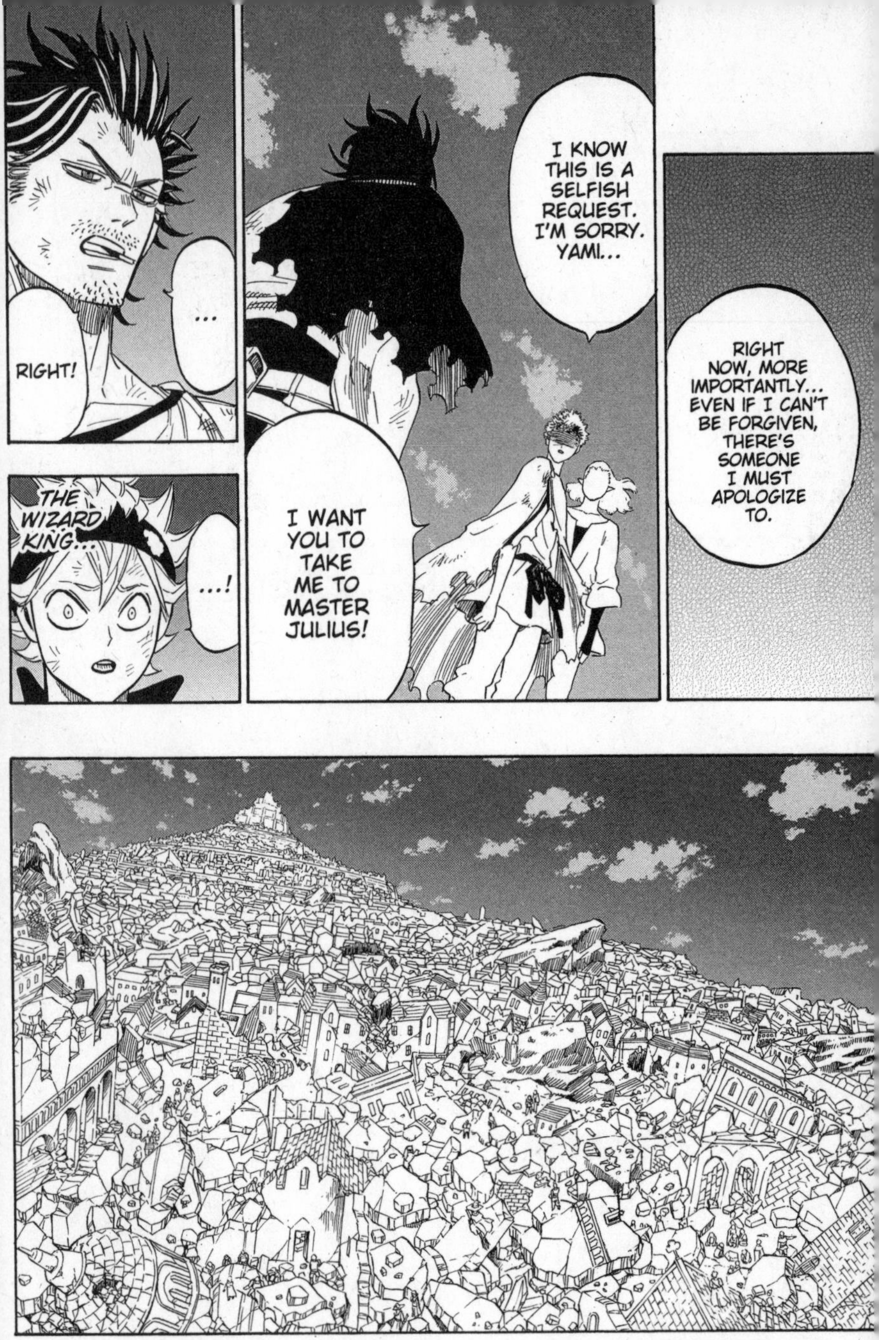
RIGHT NOW, MORE IMPORTANTLY... EVEN IF I CAN'T BE FORGIVEN, THERE'S SOMEONE I MUST APOLOGIZE TO.
I KNOW THIS IS A SELFISH REQUEST. I'M SORRY. YAMI...
I WANT YOU TO TAKE ME TO MASTER JULIUS!
...
RIGHT!
...!
THE WIZARD KING...

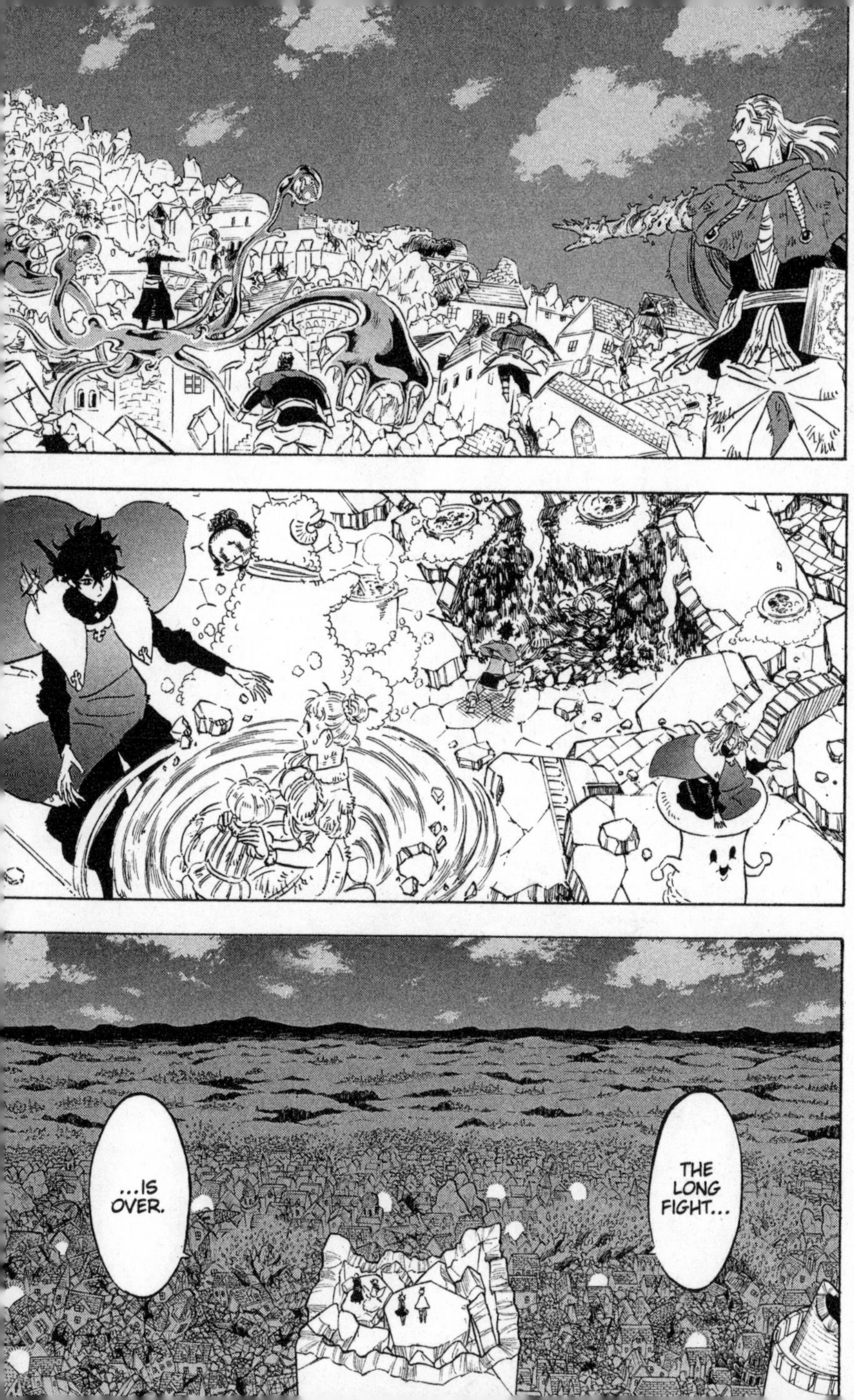
THE LONG FIGHT...
...IS OVER.

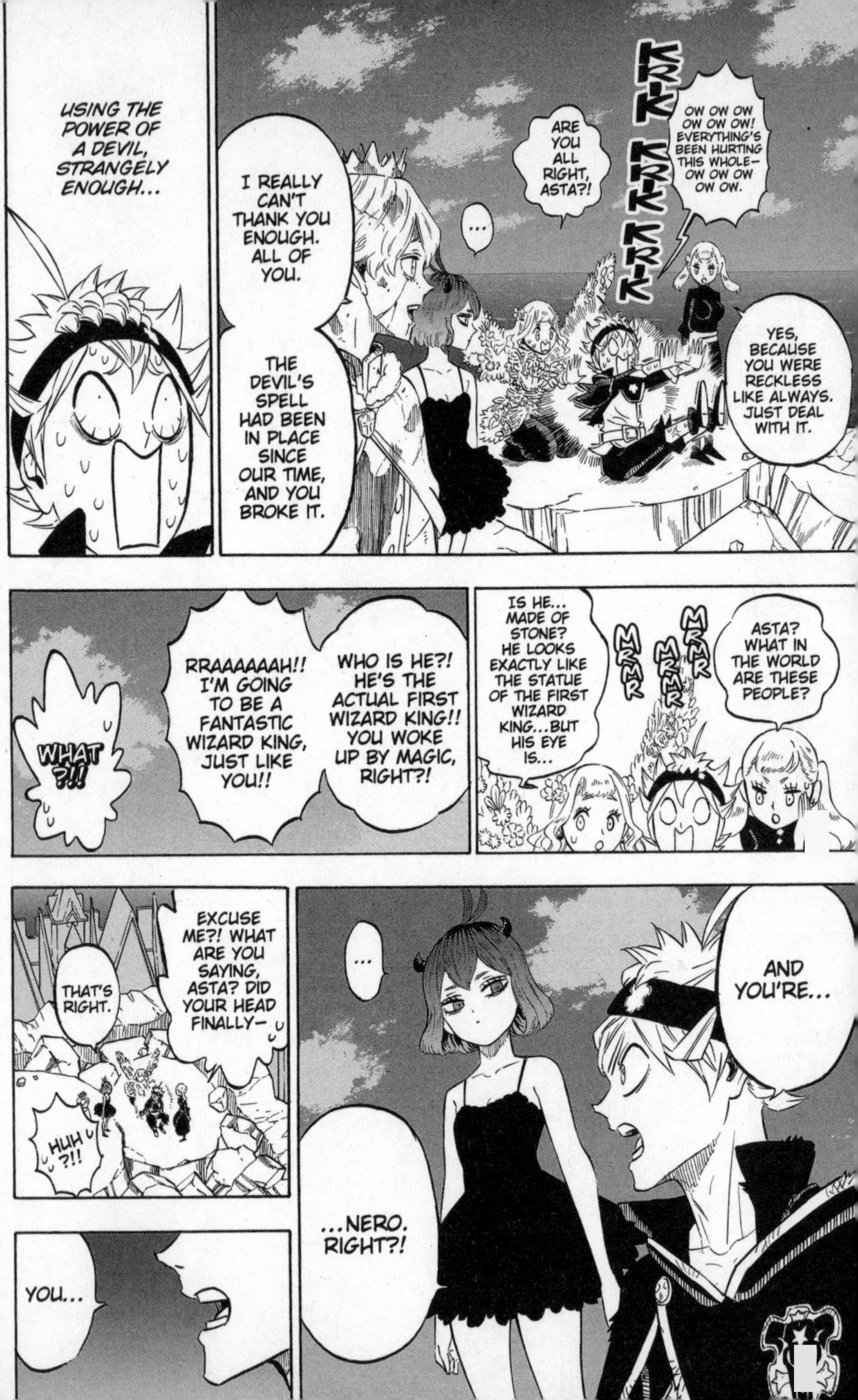
OW OW OW OW OW OW! EVERYTHING'S BEEN HURTING THIS WHOLE— OW OW OW OW OW.
KRIK KRIK KRIK KRIK
ARE YOU ALL RIGHT, ASTA?!
...
YES, BECAUSE YOU WERE RECKLESS LIKE ALWAYS. JUST DEAL WITH IT.
I REALLY CAN'T THANK YOU ENOUGH. ALL OF YOU.
THE DEVIL'S SPELL HAD BEEN IN PLACE SINCE OUR TIME, AND YOU BROKE IT.
USING THE POWER OF A DEVIL, STRANGELY ENOUGH...
ASTA? WHAT IN THE WORLD ARE THESE PEOPLE?
MRMR MRMR MRMR
IS HE... MADE OF STONE? HE LOOKS EXACTLY LIKE THE STATUE OF THE FIRST WIZARD KING...BUT HIS EYE IS...
WHO IS HE?! HE'S THE ACTUAL FIRST WIZARD KING!! YOU WOKE UP BY MAGIC, RIGHT?!
RRAAAAAAH!! I'M GOING TO BE A FANTASTIC WIZARD KING, JUST LIKE YOU!!
WHAT ?!!
AND YOU'RE...
...
...NERO. RIGHT?!
EXCUSE ME?! WHAT ARE YOU SAYING, ASTA? DID YOUR HEAD FINALLY—
THAT'S RIGHT.
HUH ?!!
YOU...

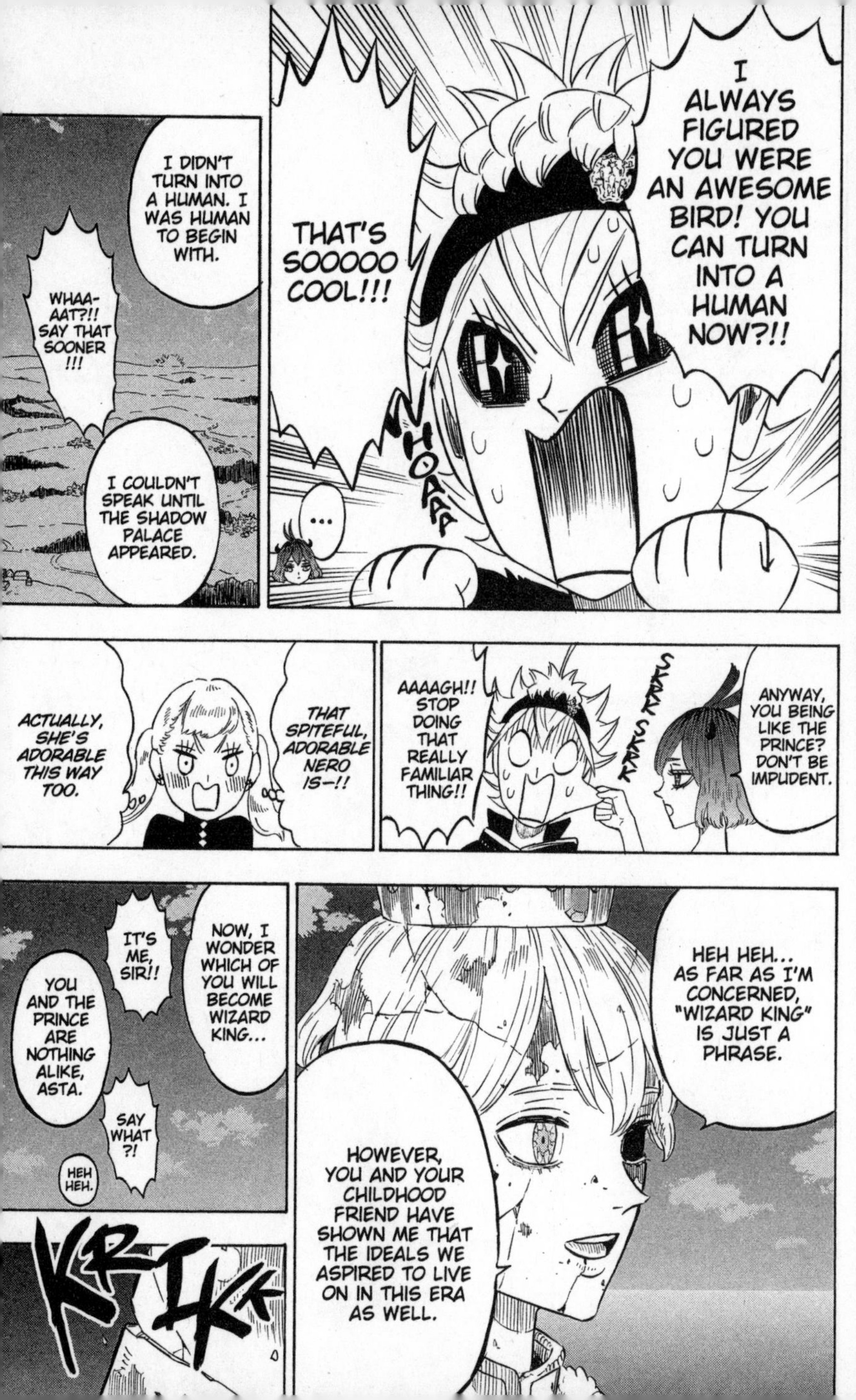
I ALWAYS FIGURED YOU WERE AN AWESOME BIRD! YOU CAN TURN INTO A HUMAN NOW?!!
THAT'S SOOOOO COOL!!!
WHOAAA
...
I DIDN'T TURN INTO A HUMAN. I WAS HUMAN TO BEGIN WITH.
WHAA-AAT?!! SAY THAT SOONER !!!
I COULDN'T SPEAK UNTIL THE SHADOW PALACE APPEARED.
ANYWAY, YOU BEING LIKE THE PRINCE? DON'T BE IMPUDENT.
SKRK SKRK
AAAAGH!! STOP DOING THAT REALLY FAMILIAR THING!!
THAT SPITEFUL, ADORABLE NERO IS—!!
ACTUALLY, SHE'S ADORABLE THIS WAY TOO.
HEH HEH... AS FAR AS I'M CONCERNED, "WIZARD KING" IS JUST A PHRASE.
HOWEVER, YOU AND YOUR CHILDHOOD FRIEND HAVE SHOWN ME THAT THE IDEALS WE ASPIRED TO LIVE ON IN THIS ERA AS WELL.
NOW, I WONDER WHICH OF YOU WILL BECOME WIZARD KING...
IT'S ME, SIR!!
YOU AND THE PRINCE ARE NOTHING ALIKE, ASTA.
SAY WHAT?!
HEH HEH.
KRIKK

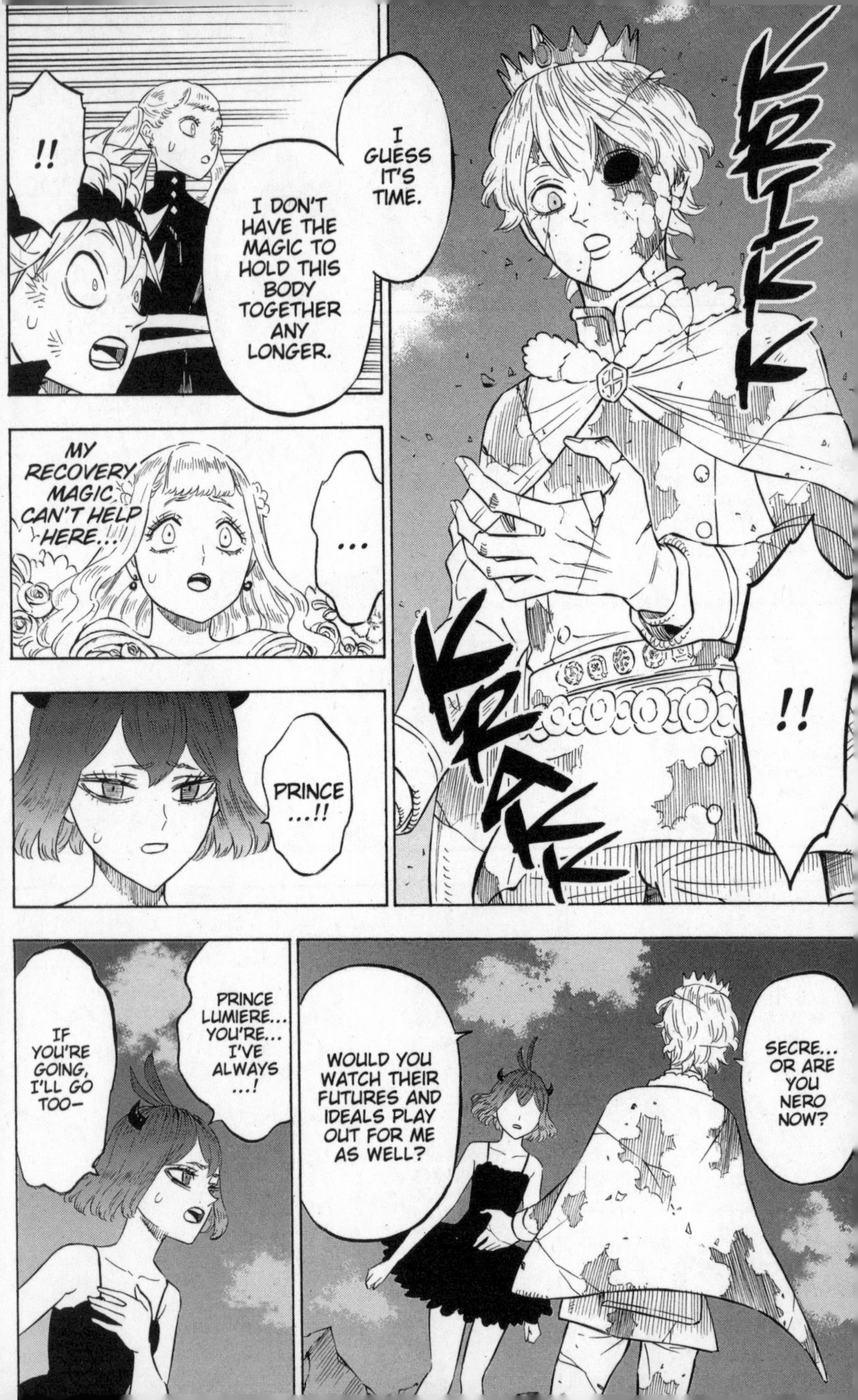
!!
I GUESS IT'S TIME.
I DON'T HAVE THE MAGIC TO HOLD THIS BODY TOGETHER ANY LONGER.
!!
MY RECOVERY MAGIC CAN'T HELP HERE...
...
PRINCE ...!!
SECRE... OR ARE YOU NERO NOW?
WOULD YOU WATCH THEIR FUTURES AND IDEALS PLAY OUT FOR ME AS WELL?
PRINCE LUMIERE... YOU'RE... I'VE ALWAYS ...!
IF YOU'RE GOING, I'LL GO TOO—

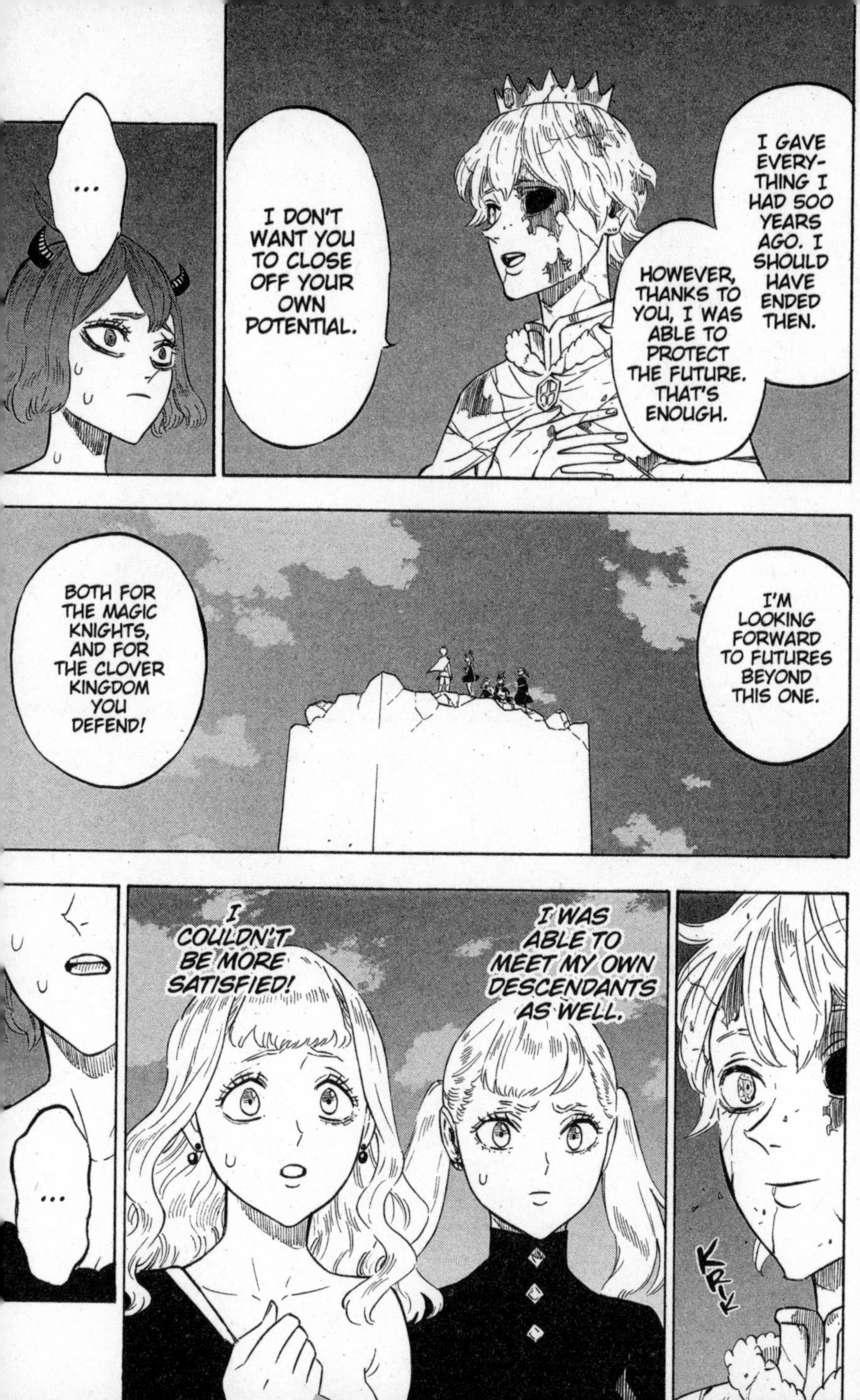
I GAVE EVERYTHING I HAD 500 YEARS AGO. I SHOULD HAVE ENDED THEN.
HOWEVER, THANKS TO YOU, I WAS ABLE TO PROTECT THE FUTURE. THAT'S ENOUGH.
I DON'T WANT YOU TO CLOSE OFF YOUR OWN POTENTIAL.
...
I'M LOOKING FORWARD TO FUTURES BEYOND THIS ONE.
BOTH FOR THE MAGIC KNIGHTS, AND FOR THE CLOVER KINGDOM YOU DEFEND!
KRIK
I WAS ABLE TO MEET MY OWN DESCENDANTS AS WELL.
I COULDN'T BE MORE SATISFIED!
...

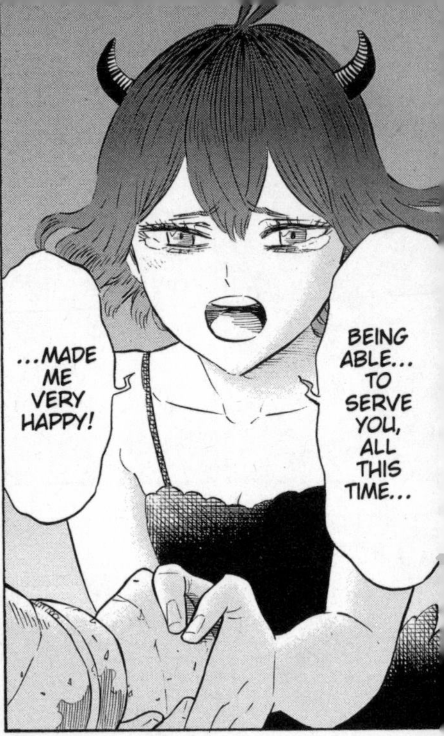
BEING ABLE... TO SERVE YOU, ALL THIS TIME...
...MADE ME VERY HAPPY!
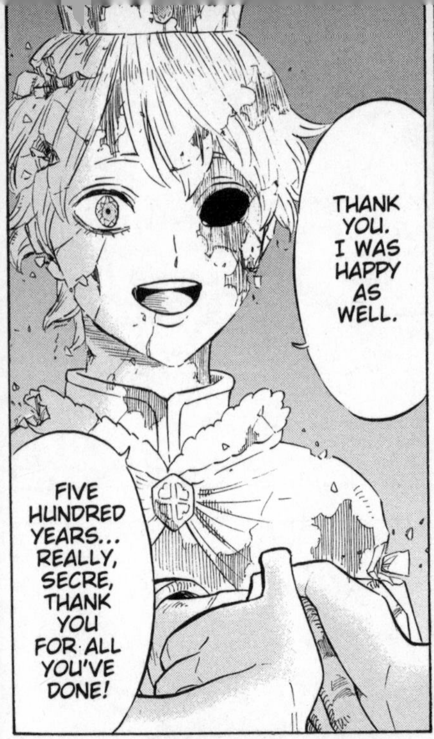
THANK YOU. I WAS HAPPY AS WELL.
FIVE HUNDRED YEARS... REALLY, SECRE, THANK YOU FOR ALL YOU'VE DONE!
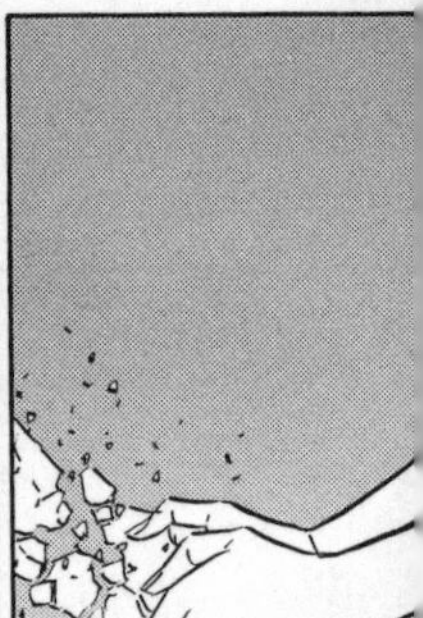
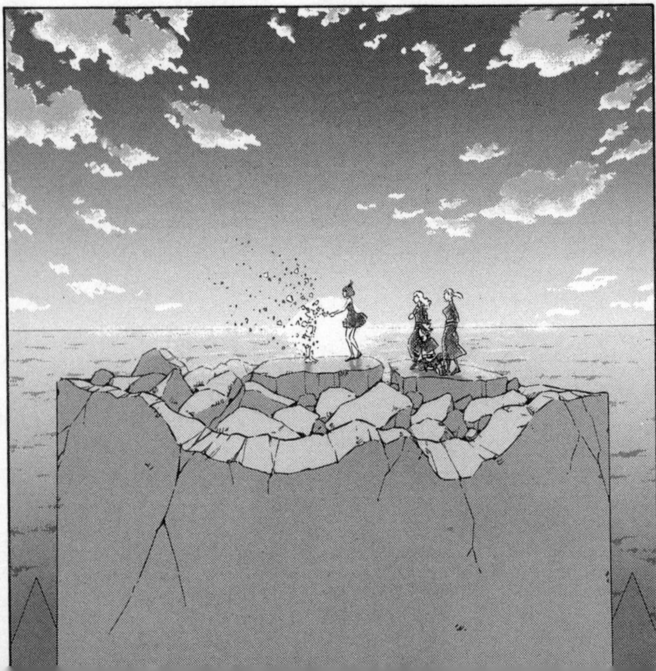

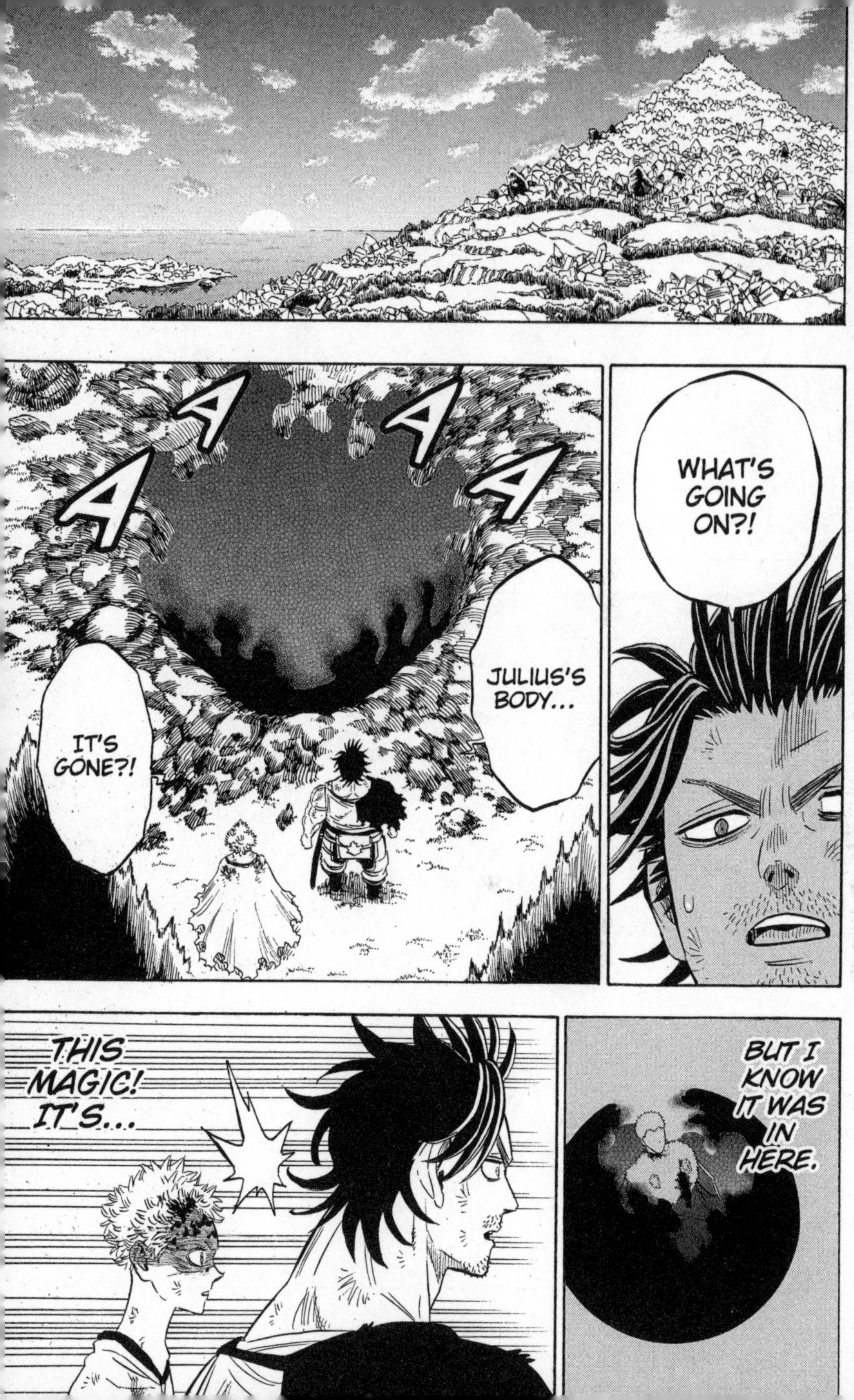
AAAA
WHAT'S GOING ON?!
JULIUS'S BODY...
IT'S GONE?!
BUT I KNOW IT WAS IN HERE.
THIS MAGIC! IT'S...

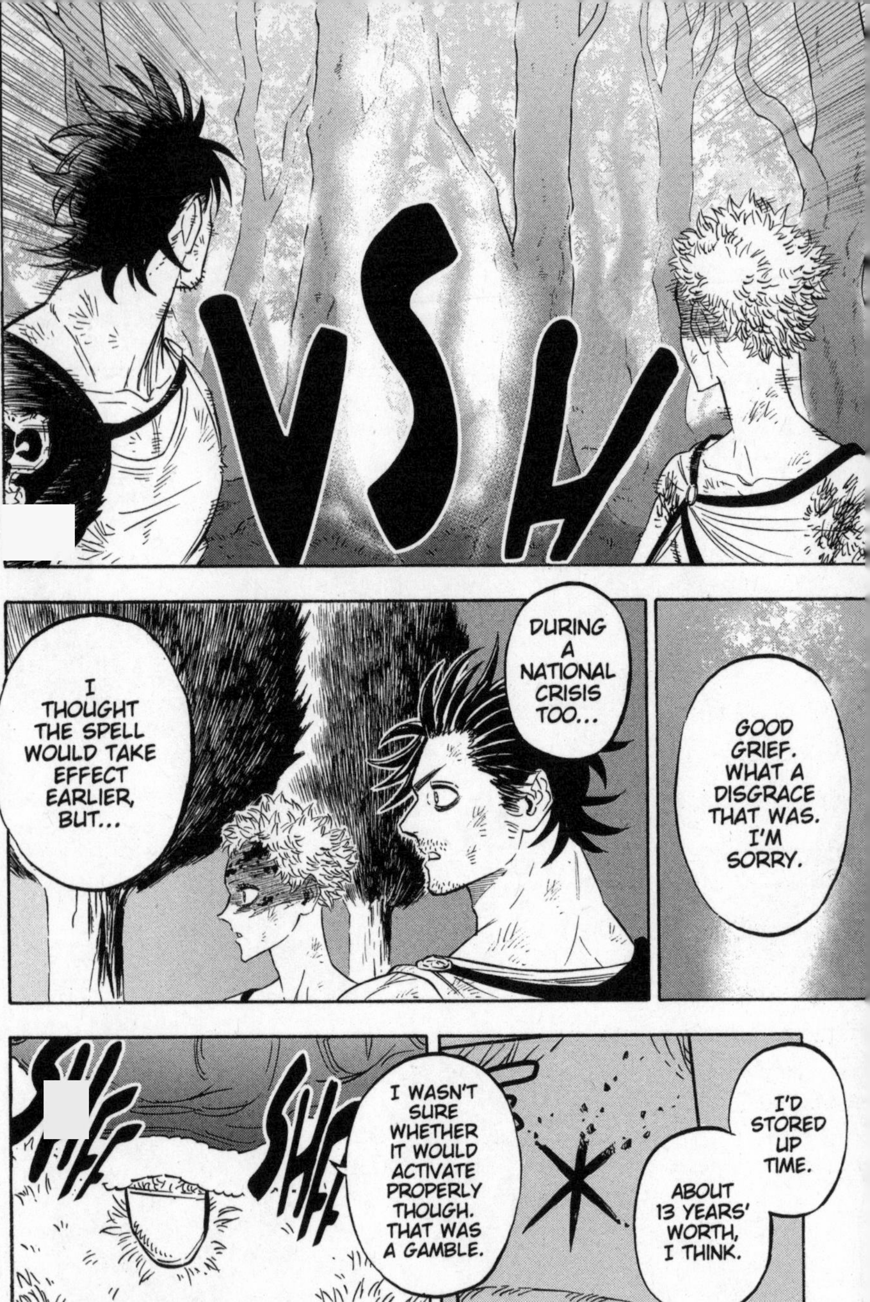
VSH
GOOD GRIEF. WHAT A DISGRACE THAT WAS. I'M SORRY.
DURING A NATIONAL CRISIS TOO...
I THOUGHT THE SPELL WOULD TAKE EFFECT EARLIER, BUT...
I'D STORED UP TIME.
ABOUT 13 YEARS' WORTH, I THINK.
I WASN'T SURE WHETHER IT WOULD ACTIVATE PROPERLY THOUGH. THAT WAS A GAMBLE.

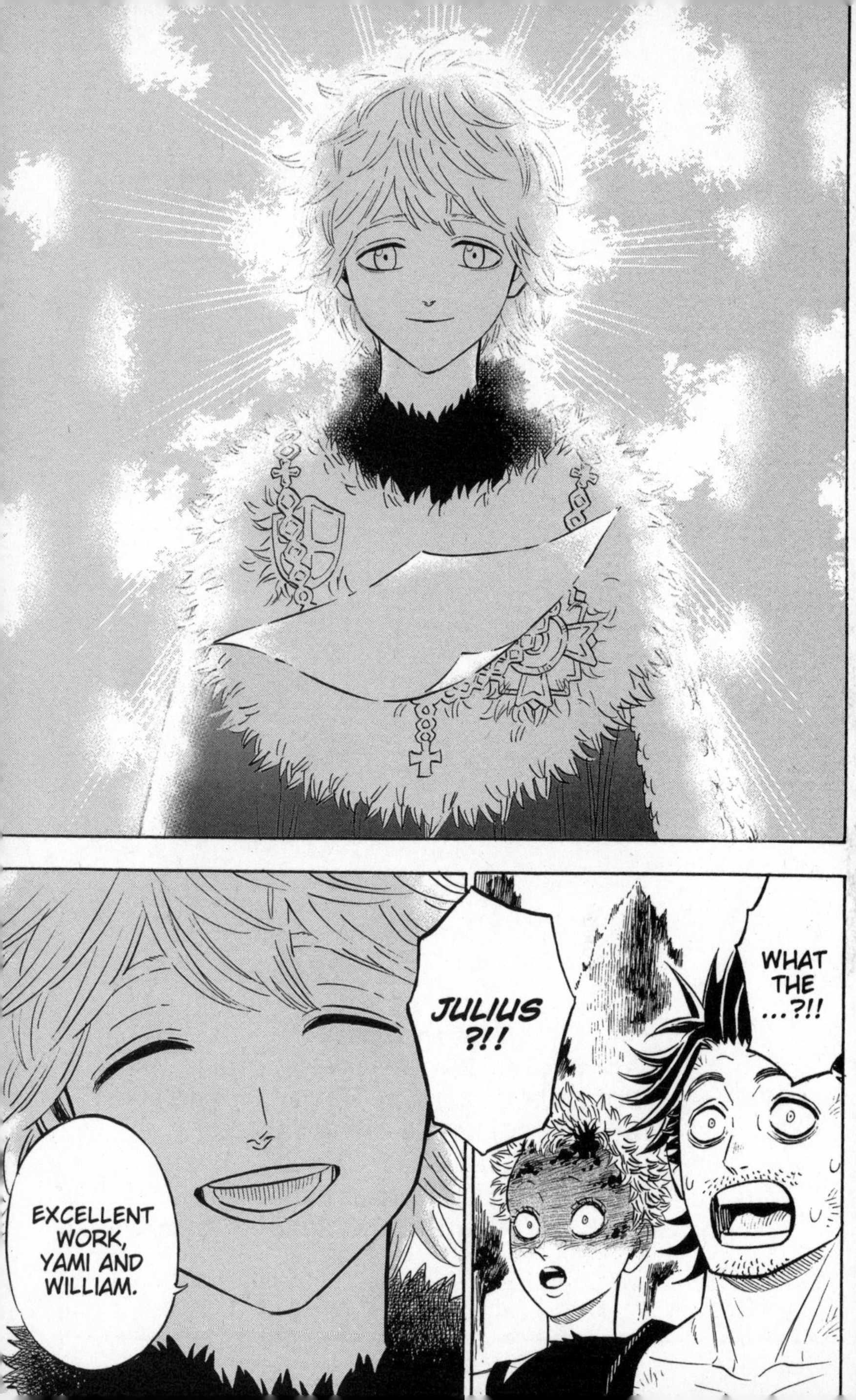
WHAT THE ...?!!
JULIUS ?!!
EXCELLENT WORK, YAMI AND WILLIAM.

Vetto

⟨Elf (at the time)⟩
Age of Soul: 25   Height: 195 cm
Birthday: September 12   Sign: Virgo Blood Type: O
Likes: Exercise, his elf comrades

⟨Human Clone (current)⟩
Age of body: 15 Height: 166 cm Blood Type: O

C h a r a c t e r   P r o f i l e

✽

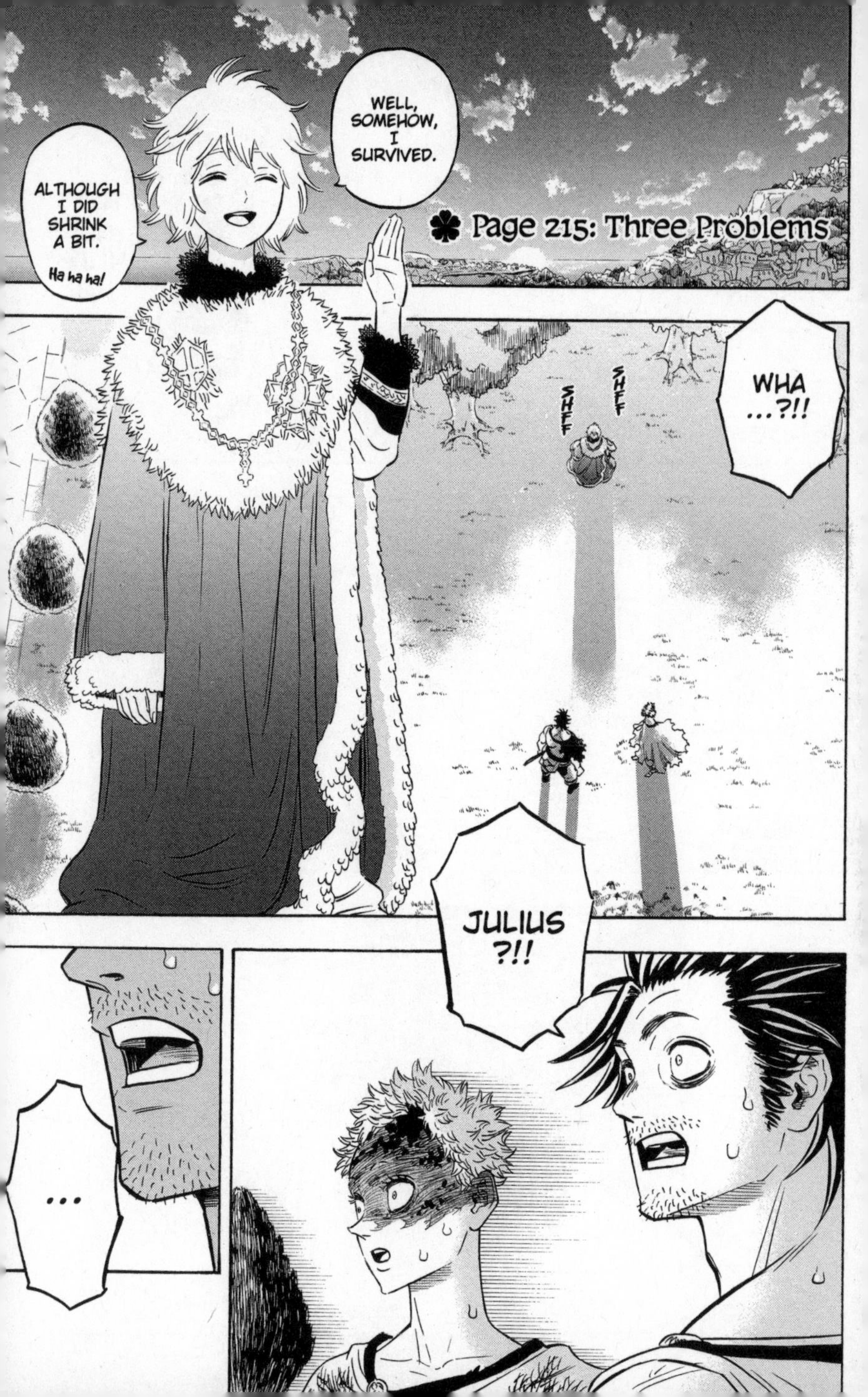
WELL, SOMEHOW, I SURVIVED.
ALTHOUGH I DID SHRINK A BIT.
Ha ha ha!
Page 215: Three Problems
WHA ...?!!
SHFF
SHFF
JULIUS ?!!
...

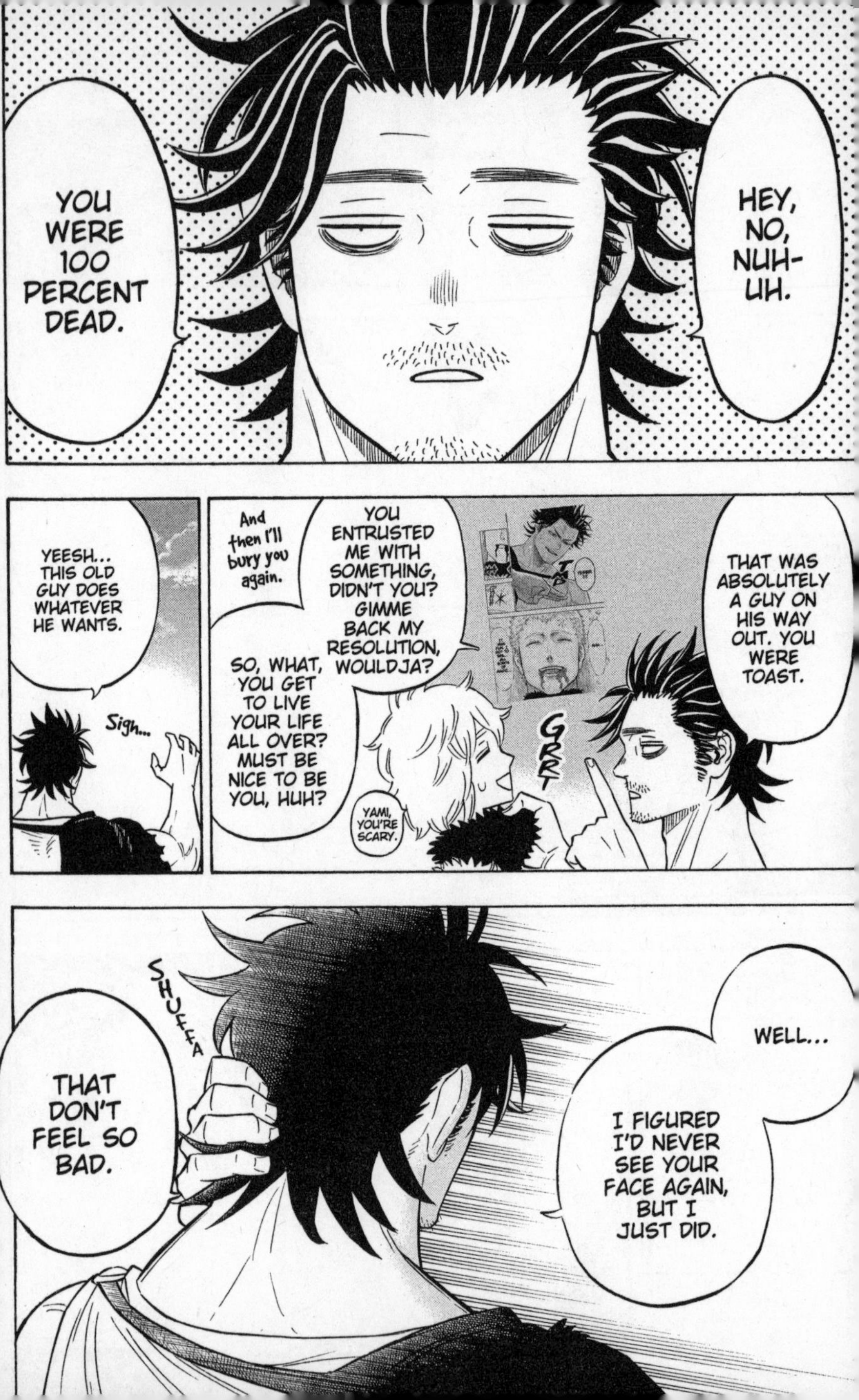
HEY, NO, NUH-UH.
YOU WERE 100 PERCENT DEAD.
THAT WAS ABSOLUTELY A GUY ON HIS WAY OUT. YOU WERE TOAST.
YOU ENTRUSTED ME WITH SOMETHING, DIDN'T YOU? GIMME BACK MY RESOLUTION, WOULDJA?
And then I'll bury you again.
GRRT
SO, WHAT, YOU GET TO LIVE YOUR LIFE ALL OVER? MUST BE NICE TO BE YOU, HUH?
YAMI, YOU'RE SCARY.
YEESH... THIS OLD GUY DOES WHATEVER HE WANTS.
Sigh...
WELL...
I FIGURED I'D NEVER SEE YOUR FACE AGAIN, BUT I JUST DID.
SHUFFA
THAT DON'T FEEL SO BAD.

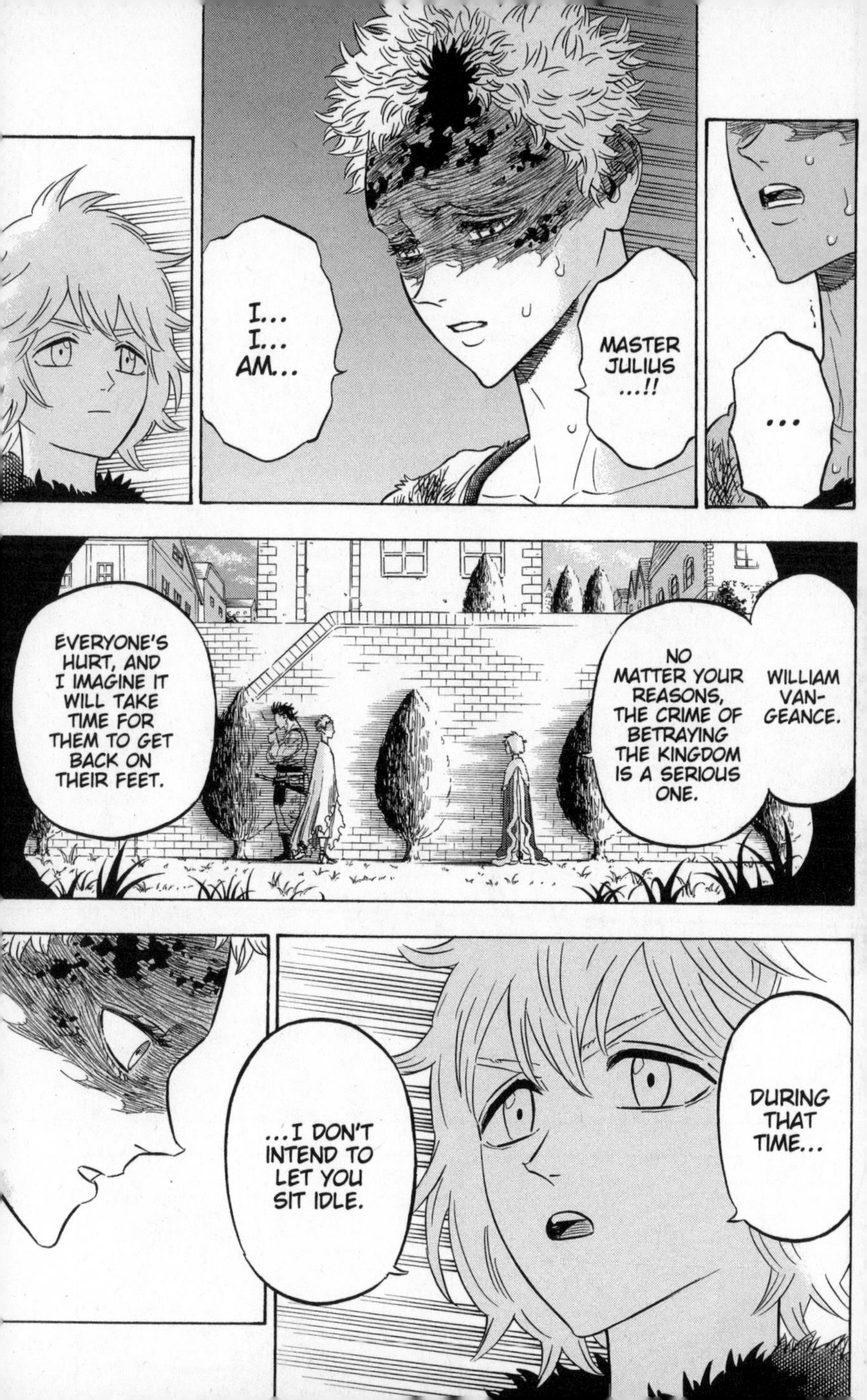
...
MASTER JULIUS ...!!
I... I... AM...
WILLIAM VAN-GEANCE.
NO MATTER YOUR REASONS, THE CRIME OF BETRAYING THE KINGDOM IS A SERIOUS ONE.
EVERYONE'S HURT, AND I IMAGINE IT WILL TAKE TIME FOR THEM TO GET BACK ON THEIR FEET.
DURING THAT TIME...
...I DON'T INTEND TO LET YOU SIT IDLE.

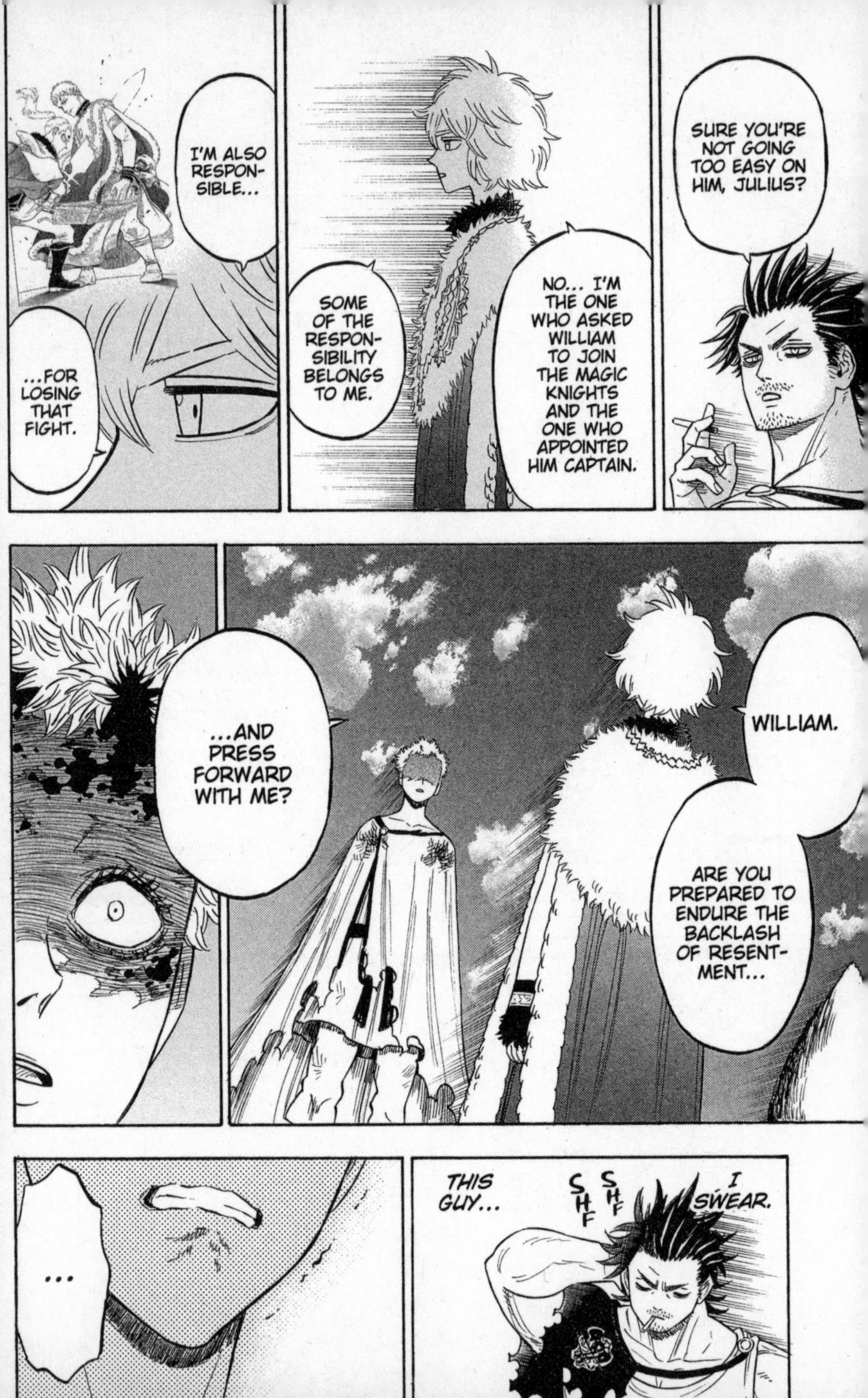
SURE YOU'RE NOT GOING TOO EASY ON HIM, JULIUS?
NO... I'M THE ONE WHO ASKED WILLIAM TO JOIN THE MAGIC KNIGHTS AND THE ONE WHO APPOINTED HIM CAPTAIN.
SOME OF THE RESPONSIBILITY BELONGS TO ME.
I'M ALSO RESPONSIBLE...
...FOR LOSING THAT FIGHT.
WILLIAM.
ARE YOU PREPARED TO ENDURE THE BACKLASH OF RESENTMENT...
...AND PRESS FORWARD WITH ME?
THIS GUY...
SHF SHF
I SWEAR.
...

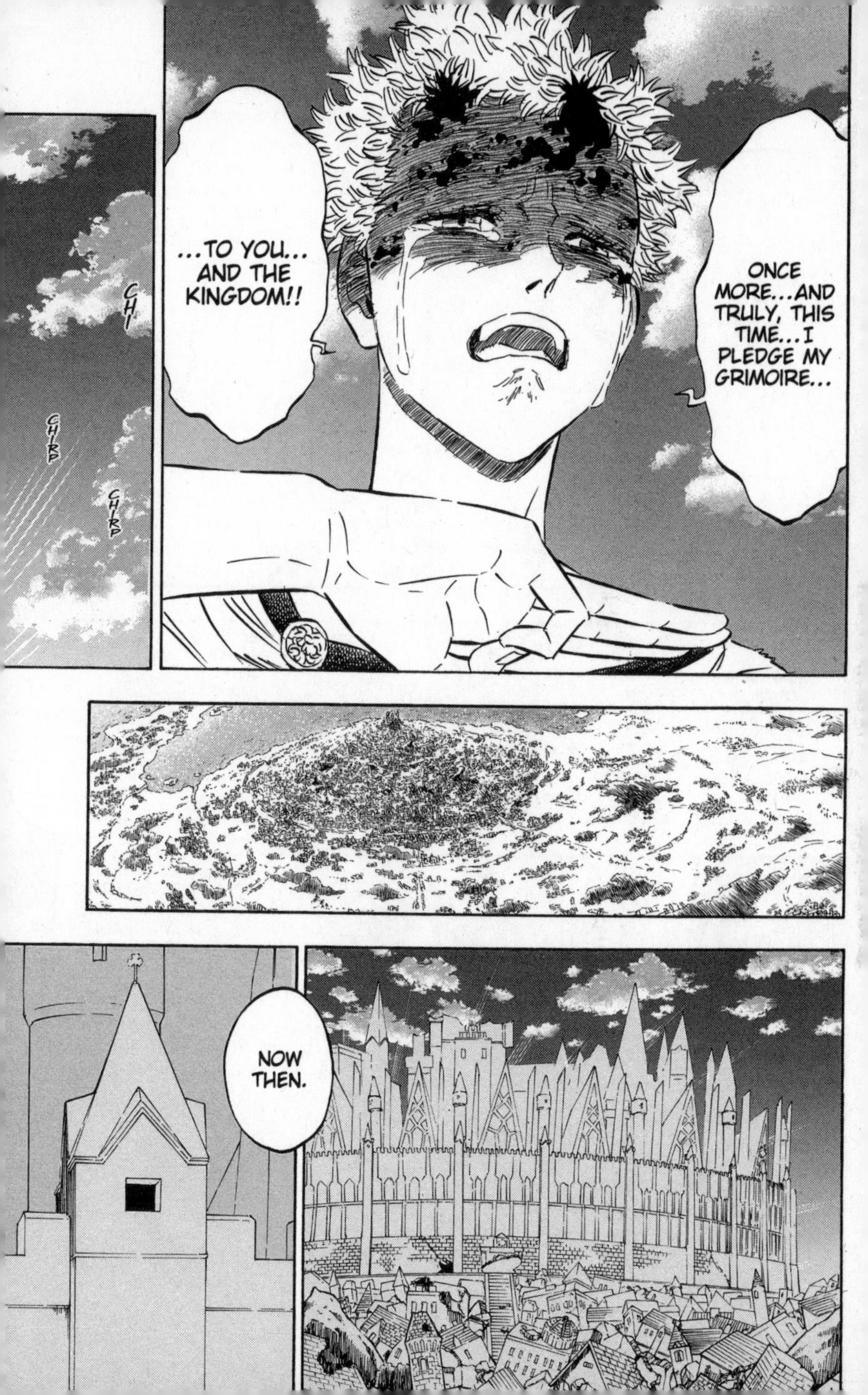
ONCE MORE...AND TRULY, THIS TIME...I PLEDGE MY GRIMOIRE...
...TO YOU... AND THE KINGDOM!!
CHI
CHIRP
CHIRP
NOW THEN.

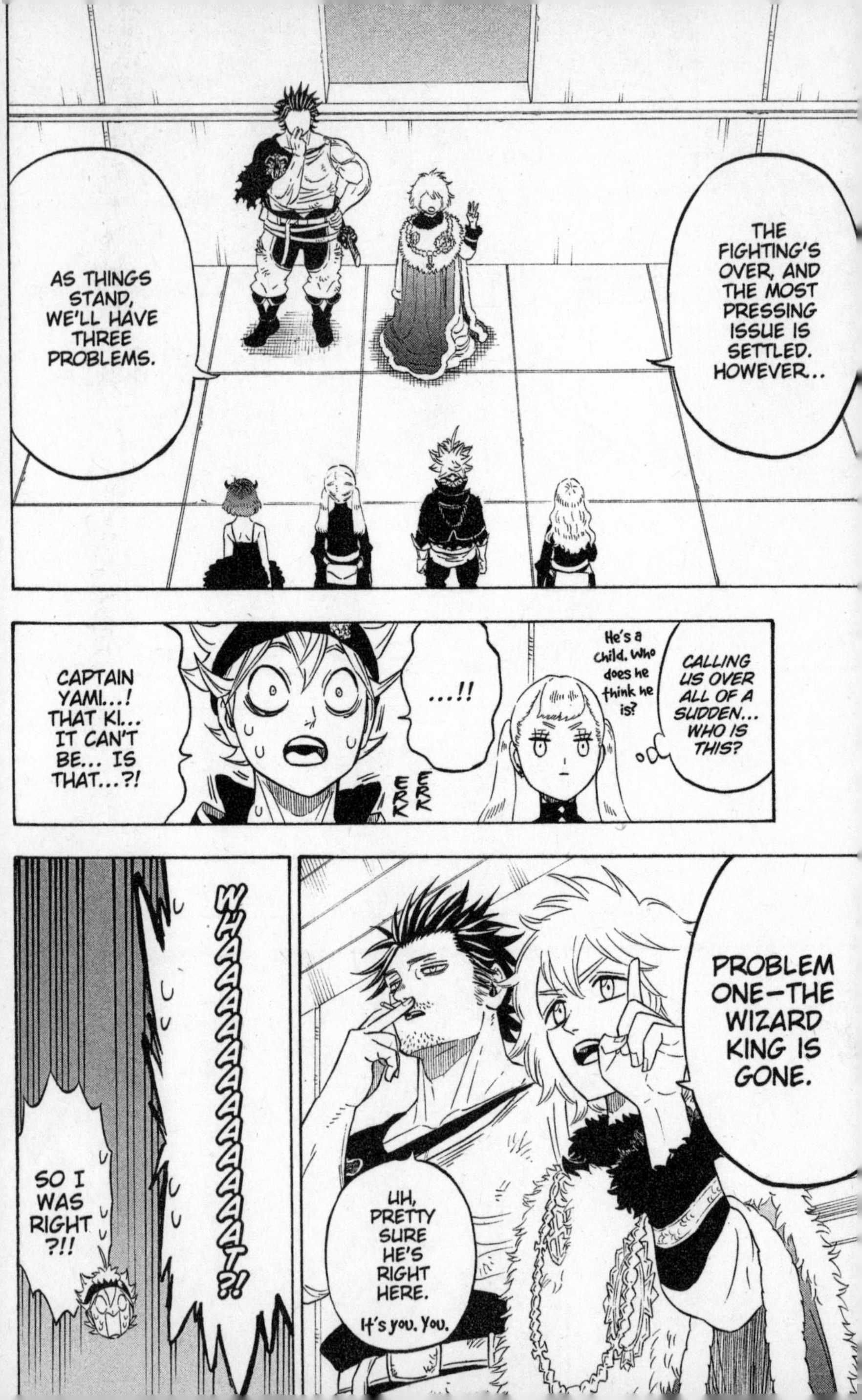
THE FIGHTING'S OVER, AND THE MOST PRESSING ISSUE IS SETTLED. HOWEVER..
AS THINGS STAND, WE'LL HAVE THREE PROBLEMS.
CALLING US OVER ALL OF A SUDDEN... WHO IS THIS?
He's a child. Who does he think he is?
...!!
ERK ERK
CAPTAIN YAMI...! THAT KI... IT CAN'T BE... IS THAT...?!
PROBLEM ONE—THE WIZARD KING IS GONE.
UH, PRETTY SURE HE'S RIGHT HERE.
It's you. You.
WHAAAAAAAAAAAAAAT?!
SO I WAS RIGHT ?!!

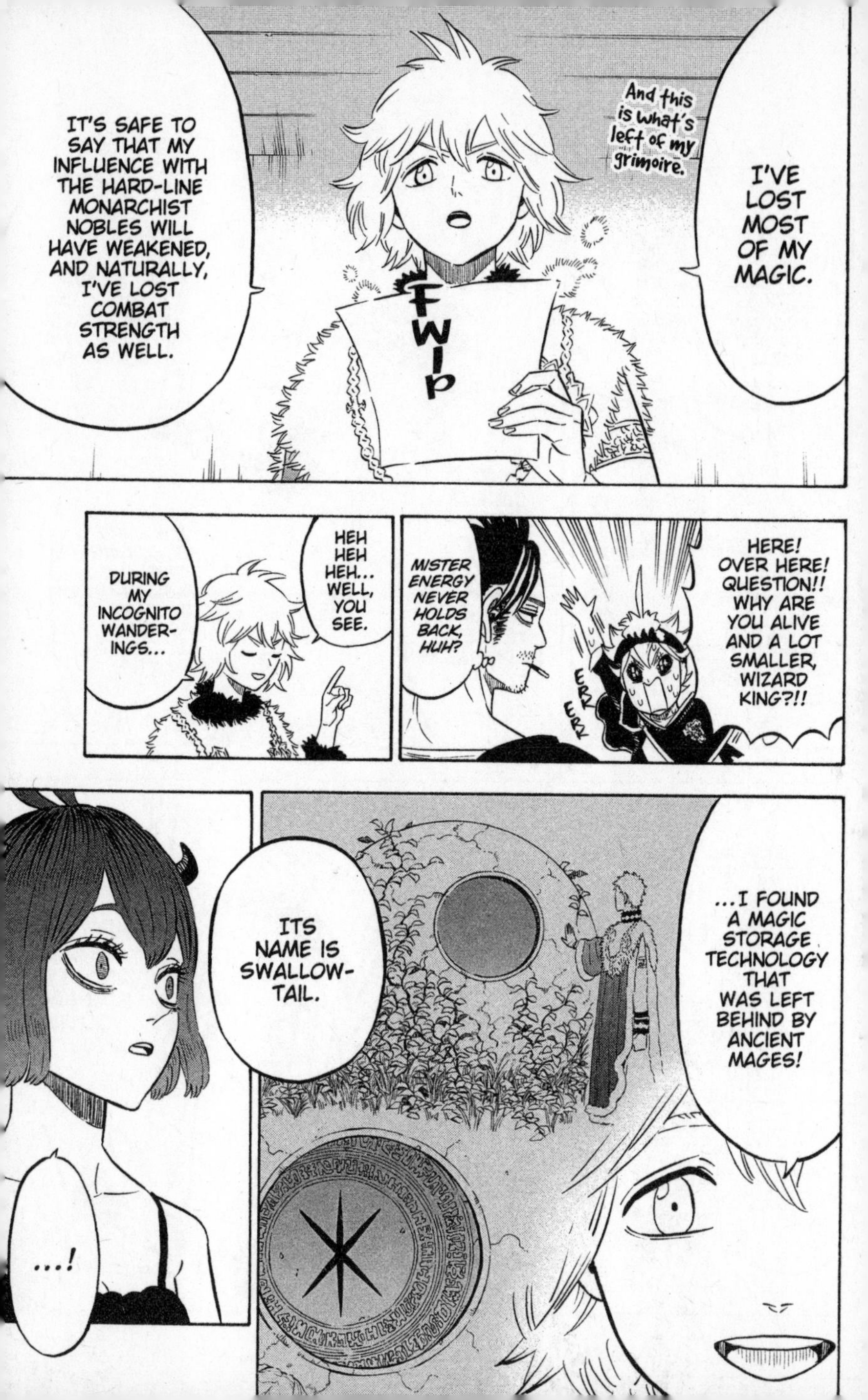
I'VE LOST MOST OF MY MAGIC.
And this is what's left of my grimoire.
FWIP
IT'S SAFE TO SAY THAT MY INFLUENCE WITH THE HARD-LINE MONARCHIST NOBLES WILL HAVE WEAKENED, AND NATURALLY, I'VE LOST COMBAT STRENGTH AS WELL.
HERE! OVER HERE! QUESTION!! WHY ARE YOU ALIVE AND A LOT SMALLER, WIZARD KING?!!
ERR ERR ERR
MISTER ENERGY NEVER HOLDS BACK, HUH?
HEH HEH HEH... WELL, YOU SEE.
DURING MY INCOGNITO WANDER-INGS...
...I FOUND A MAGIC STORAGE TECHNOLOGY THAT WAS LEFT BEHIND BY ANCIENT MAGES!
ITS NAME IS SWALLOW-TAIL.
...!

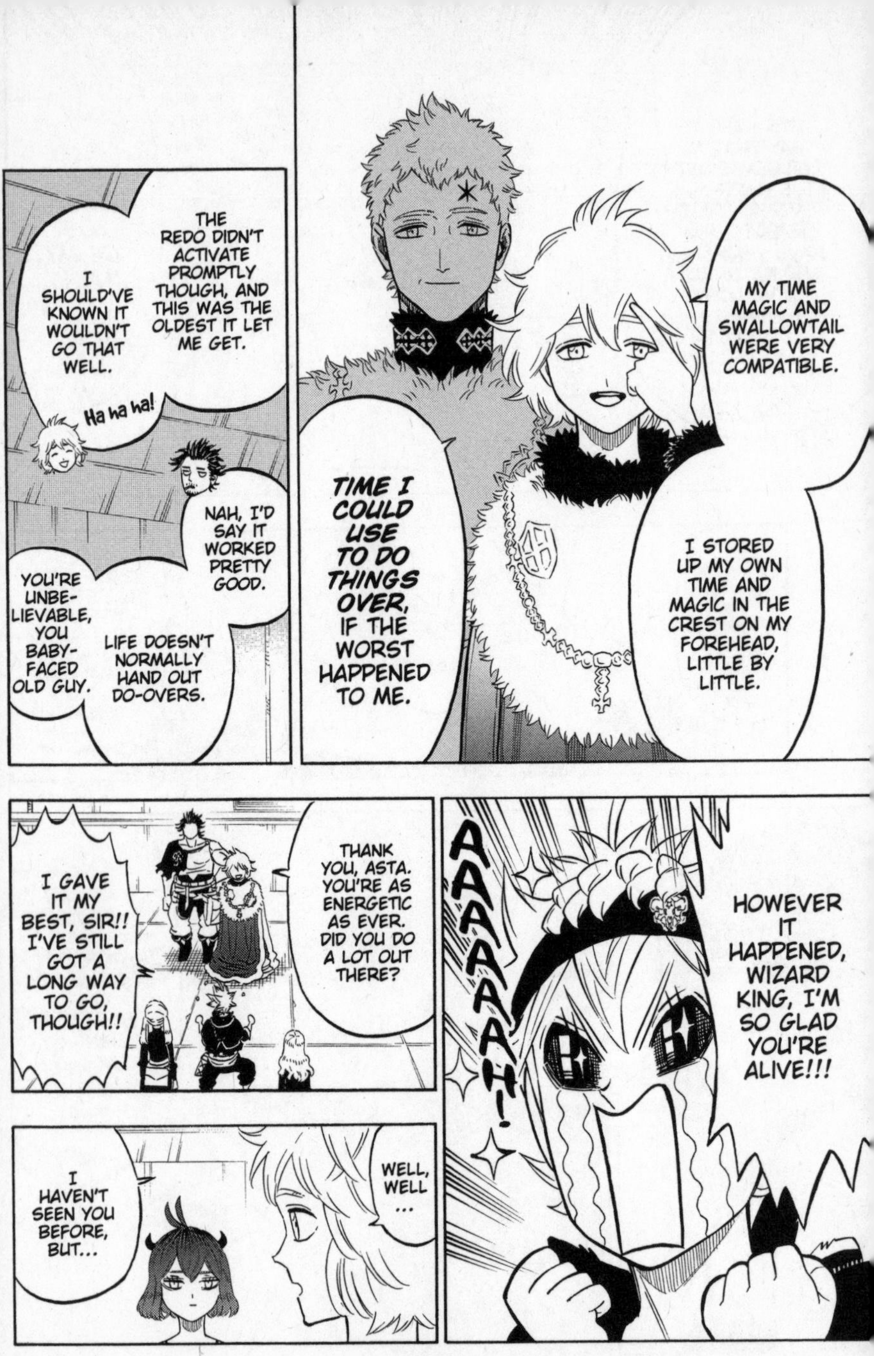
MY TIME MAGIC AND SWALLOWTAIL WERE VERY COMPATIBLE.
I STORED UP MY OWN TIME AND MAGIC IN THE CREST ON MY FOREHEAD, LITTLE BY LITTLE.
TIME I COULD USE TO DO THINGS OVER, IF THE WORST HAPPENED TO ME.
THE REDO DIDN'T ACTIVATE PROMPTLY THOUGH, AND THIS WAS THE OLDEST IT LET ME GET.
I SHOULD'VE KNOWN IT WOULDN'T GO THAT WELL.
Ha ha ha!
NAH, I'D SAY IT WORKED PRETTY GOOD.
LIFE DOESN'T NORMALLY HAND OUT DO-OVERS.
YOU'RE UNBE-LIEVABLE, YOU BABY-FACED OLD GUY.
HOWEVER IT HAPPENED, WIZARD KING, I'M SO GLAD YOU'RE ALIVE!!!
AAAAAAH!
THANK YOU, ASTA. YOU'RE AS ENERGETIC AS EVER. DID YOU DO A LOT OUT THERE?
I GAVE IT MY BEST, SIR!! I'VE STILL GOT A LONG WAY TO GO, THOUGH!!
WELL, WELL...
I HAVEN'T SEEN YOU BEFORE, BUT...

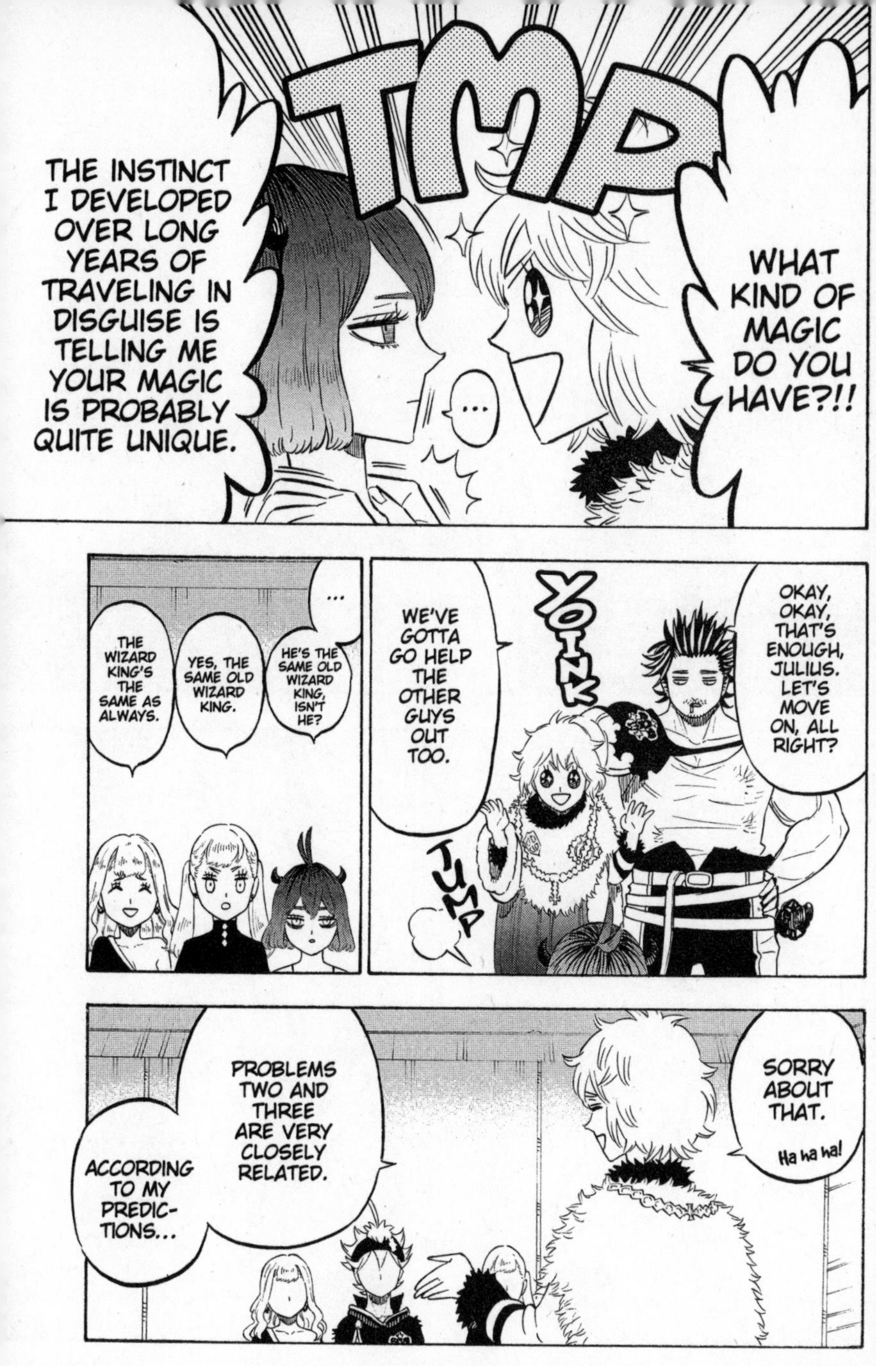
TMP
WHAT KIND OF MAGIC DO YOU HAVE?!!
...
THE INSTINCT I DEVELOPED OVER LONG YEARS OF TRAVELING IN DISGUISE IS TELLING ME YOUR MAGIC IS PROBABLY QUITE UNIQUE.
OKAY, OKAY, THAT'S ENOUGH, JULIUS. LET'S MOVE ON, ALL RIGHT?
YOINK
WE'VE GOTTA GO HELP THE OTHER GUYS OUT TOO.
JUMP
...
HE'S THE SAME OLD WIZARD KING, ISN'T HE?
YES, THE SAME OLD WIZARD KING.
THE WIZARD KING'S THE SAME AS ALWAYS.
SORRY ABOUT THAT.
Ha ha ha!
PROBLEMS TWO AND THREE ARE VERY CLOSELY RELATED.
ACCORDING TO MY PREDICTIONS...

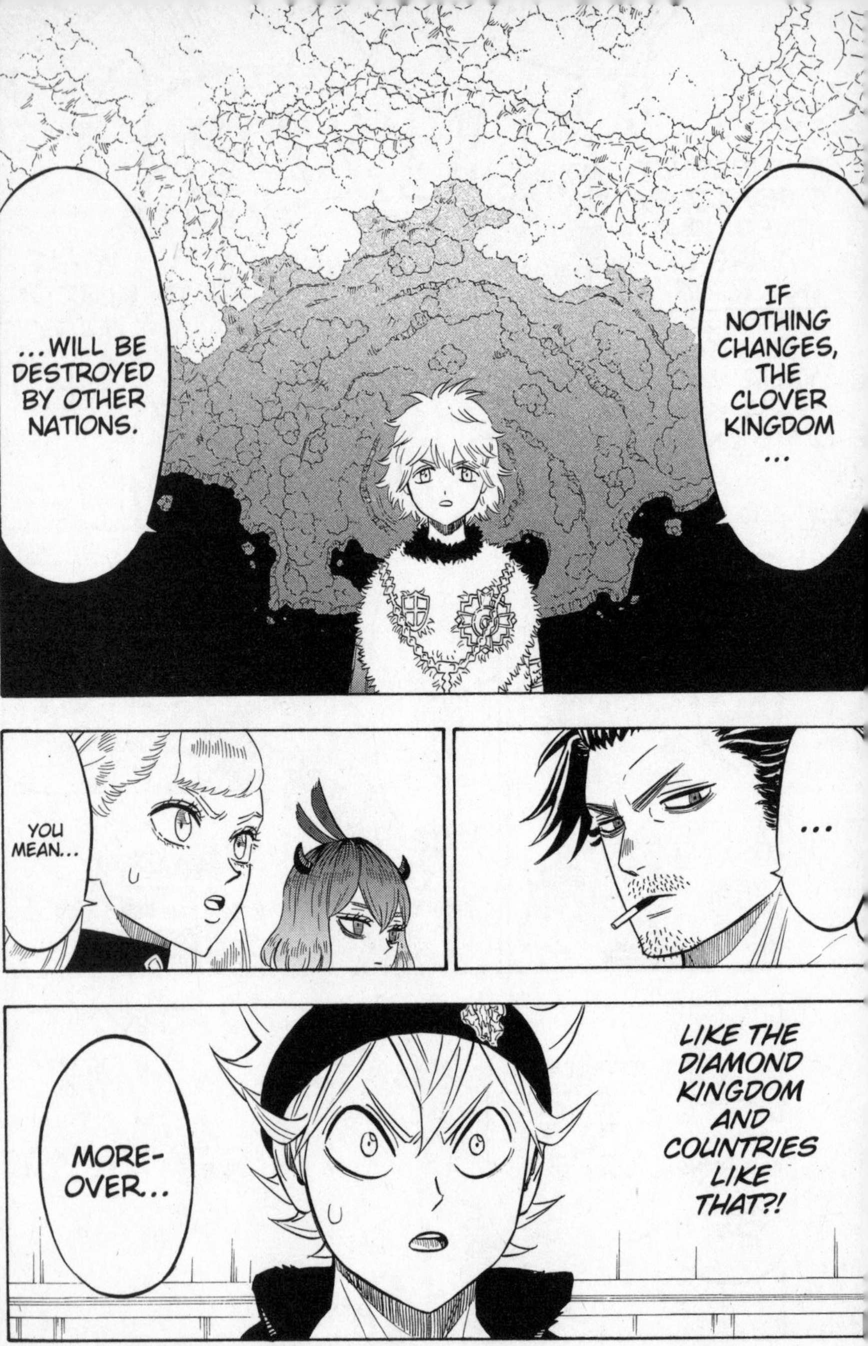
IF NOTHING CHANGES, THE CLOVER KINGDOM...
...WILL BE DESTROYED BY OTHER NATIONS.
...
YOU MEAN...
LIKE THE DIAMOND KINGDOM AND COUNTRIES LIKE THAT?!
MORE-OVER...

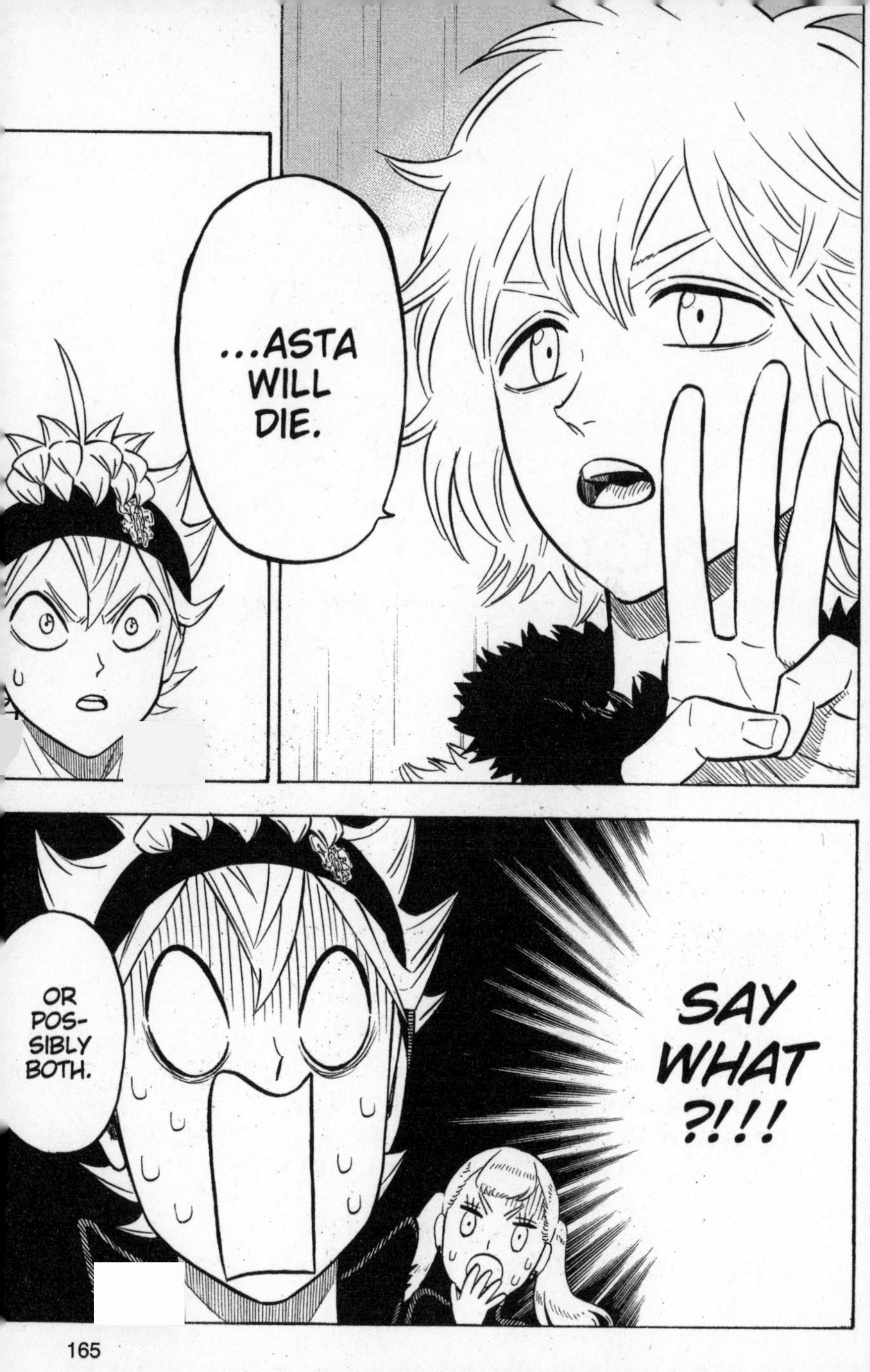
...ASTA WILL DIE.
OR POS-SIBLY BOTH.
SAY WHAT ?!!!

Fana (Elf)

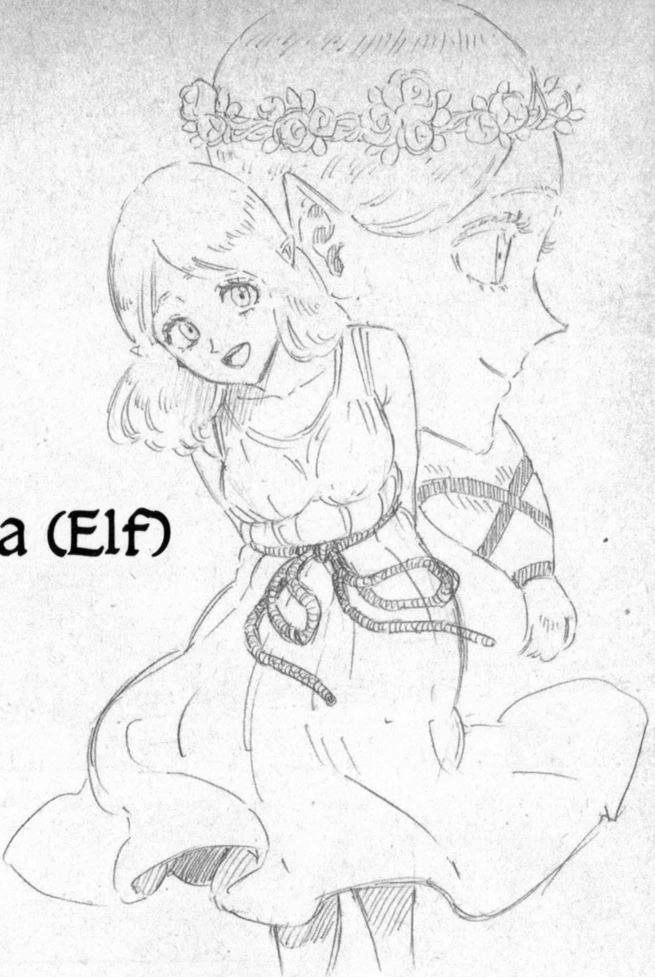

‹Elf (at the time)›
Age of Soul: 24 Height: 160 cm
Birthday: March 24 Sign: Aries Blood Type: A
Likes: Chatting, his elf comrades

‹Human Clone (current)›
Age of body: 15 Height: 158 cm Blood Type: A

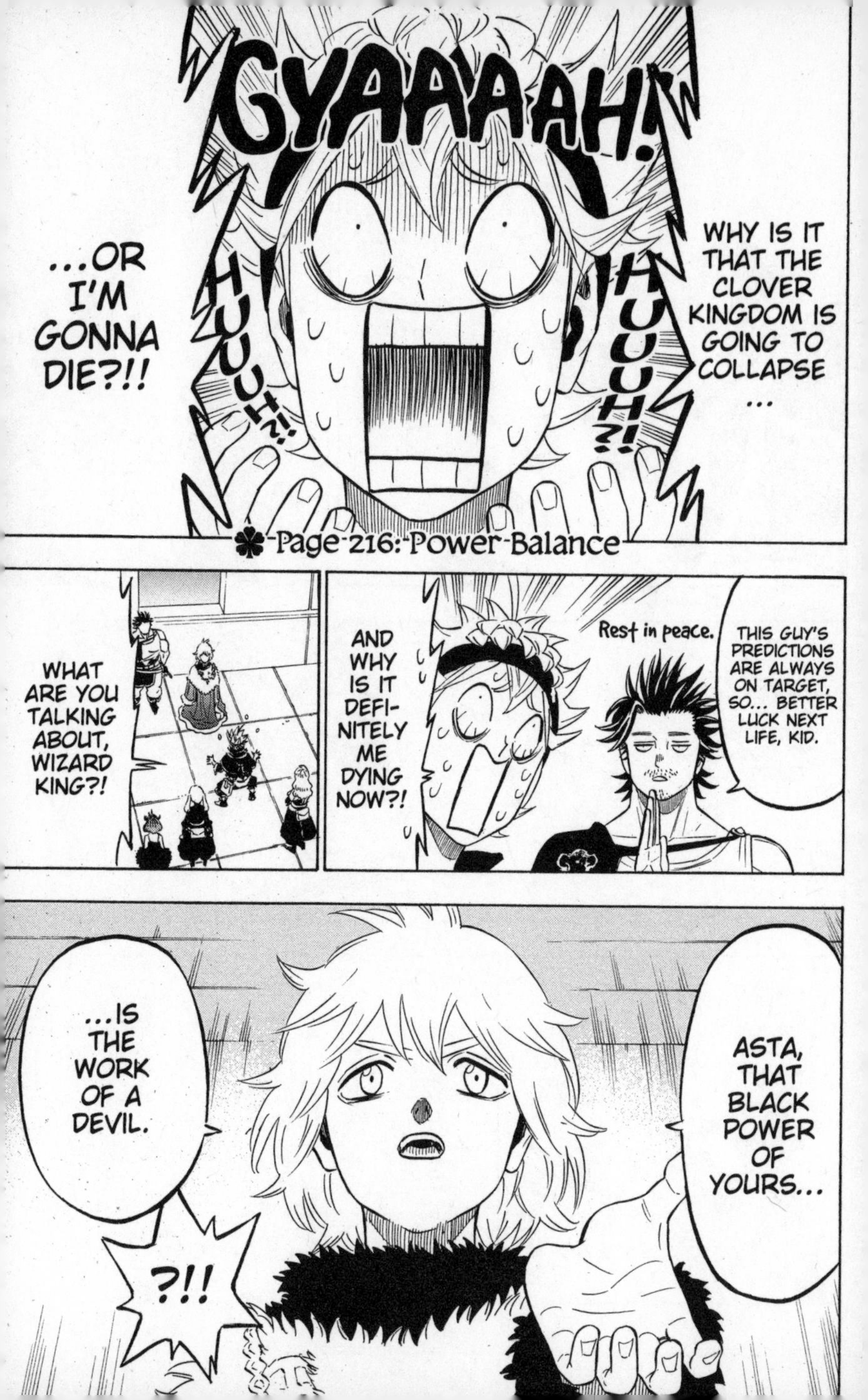
GYAAAAH!
WHY IS IT THAT THE CLOVER KINGDOM IS GOING TO COLLAPSE...
HUUUH?!!
HUUUH?!!
...OR I'M GONNA DIE?!!
Page 216: Power Balance
THIS GUY'S PREDICTIONS ARE ALWAYS ON TARGET, SO... BETTER LUCK NEXT LIFE, KID.
Rest in peace.
AND WHY IS IT DEFINITELY ME DYING NOW?!
WHAT ARE YOU TALKING ABOUT, WIZARD KING?!
ASTA, THAT BLACK POWER OF YOURS...
...IS THE WORK OF A DEVIL.
?!!

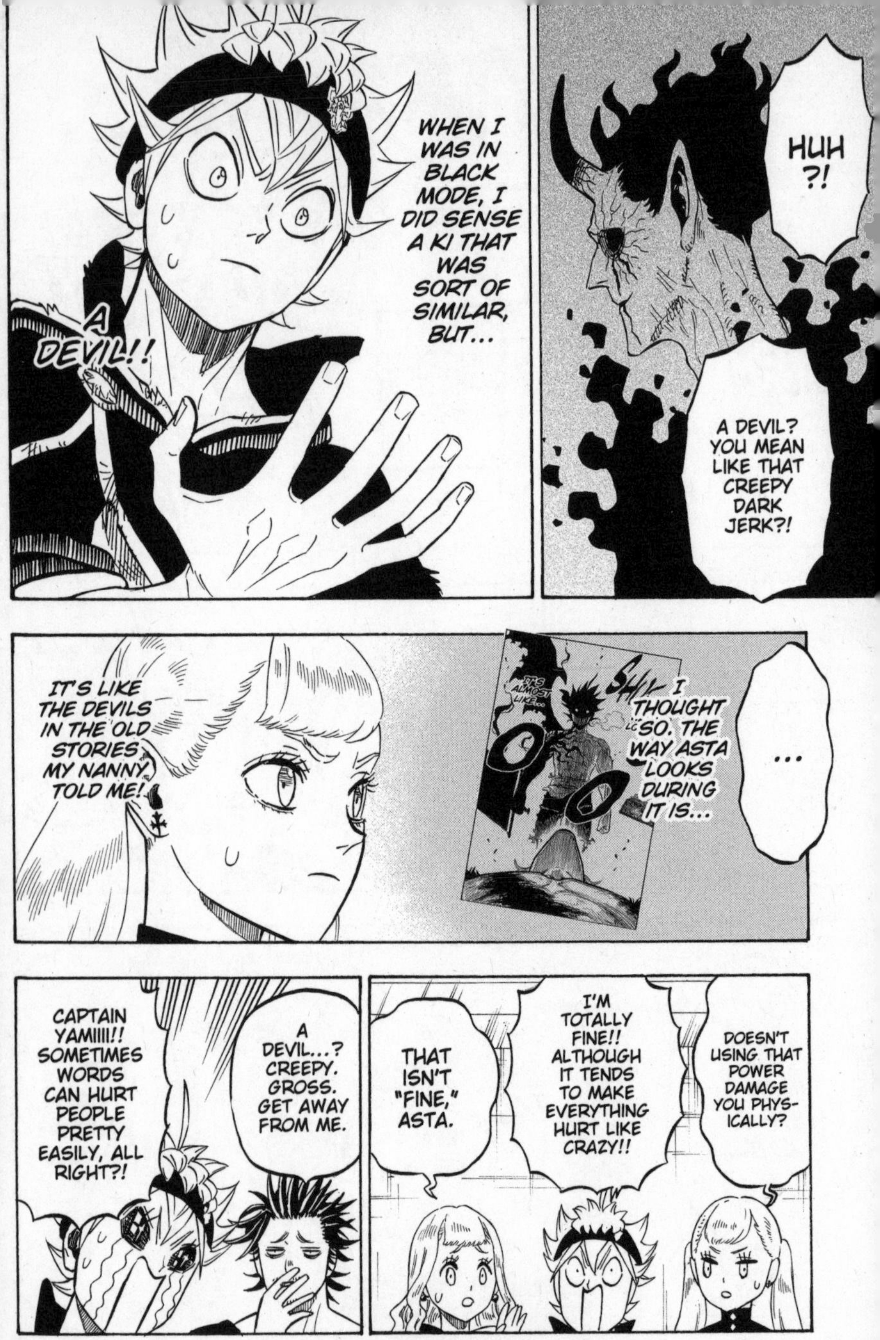
HUH ?!
A DEVIL? YOU MEAN LIKE THAT CREEPY DARK JERK?!
WHEN I WAS IN BLACK MODE, I DID SENSE A KI THAT WAS SORT OF SIMILAR, BUT...
A DEVIL!!
...
I THOUGHT SO. THE WAY ASTA LOOKS DURING IT IS...
IT'S ALMOST LIKE...
IT'S LIKE THE DEVILS IN THE OLD STORIES MY NANNY TOLD ME!
DOESN'T USING THAT POWER DAMAGE YOU PHYS-ICALLY?
I'M TOTALLY FINE!! ALTHOUGH IT TENDS TO MAKE EVERYTHING HURT LIKE CRAZY!!
THAT ISN'T "FINE," ASTA.
A DEVIL...? CREEPY. GROSS. GET AWAY FROM ME.
CAPTAIN YAMIIII!! SOMETIMES WORDS CAN HURT PEOPLE PRETTY EASILY, ALL RIGHT?!

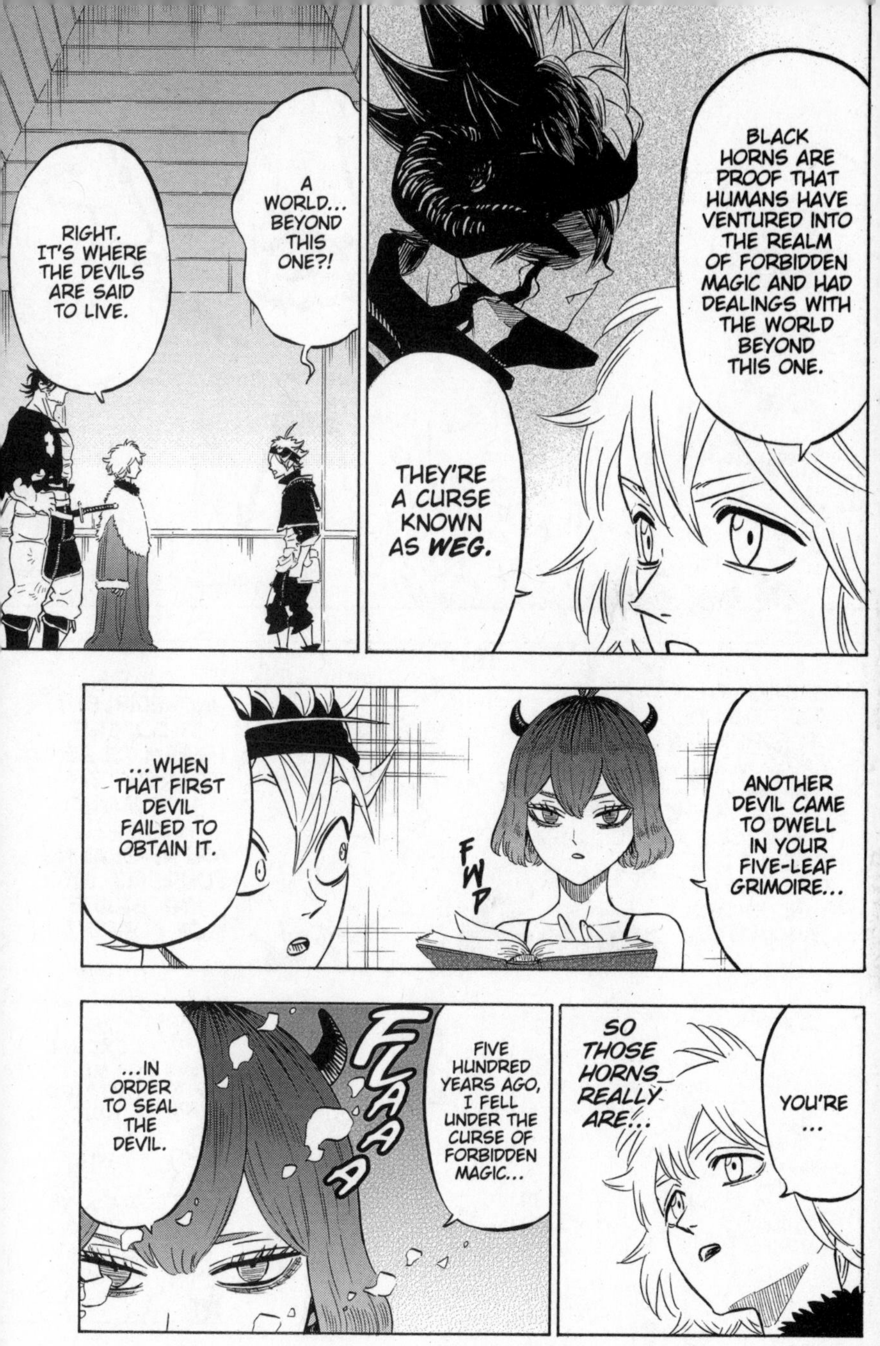
BLACK HORNS ARE PROOF THAT HUMANS HAVE VENTURED INTO THE REALM OF FORBIDDEN MAGIC AND HAD DEALINGS WITH THE WORLD BEYOND THIS ONE.
THEY'RE A CURSE KNOWN AS *WEG.*
A WORLD... BEYOND THIS ONE?!
RIGHT. IT'S WHERE THE DEVILS ARE SAID TO LIVE.
ANOTHER DEVIL CAME TO DWELL IN YOUR FIVE-LEAF GRIMOIRE...
FWP
...WHEN THAT FIRST DEVIL FAILED TO OBTAIN IT.
YOU'RE ...
SO THOSE HORNS REALLY ARE...
FIVE HUNDRED YEARS AGO, I FELL UNDER THE CURSE OF FORBIDDEN MAGIC...
FLAAAA
...IN ORDER TO SEAL THE DEVIL.

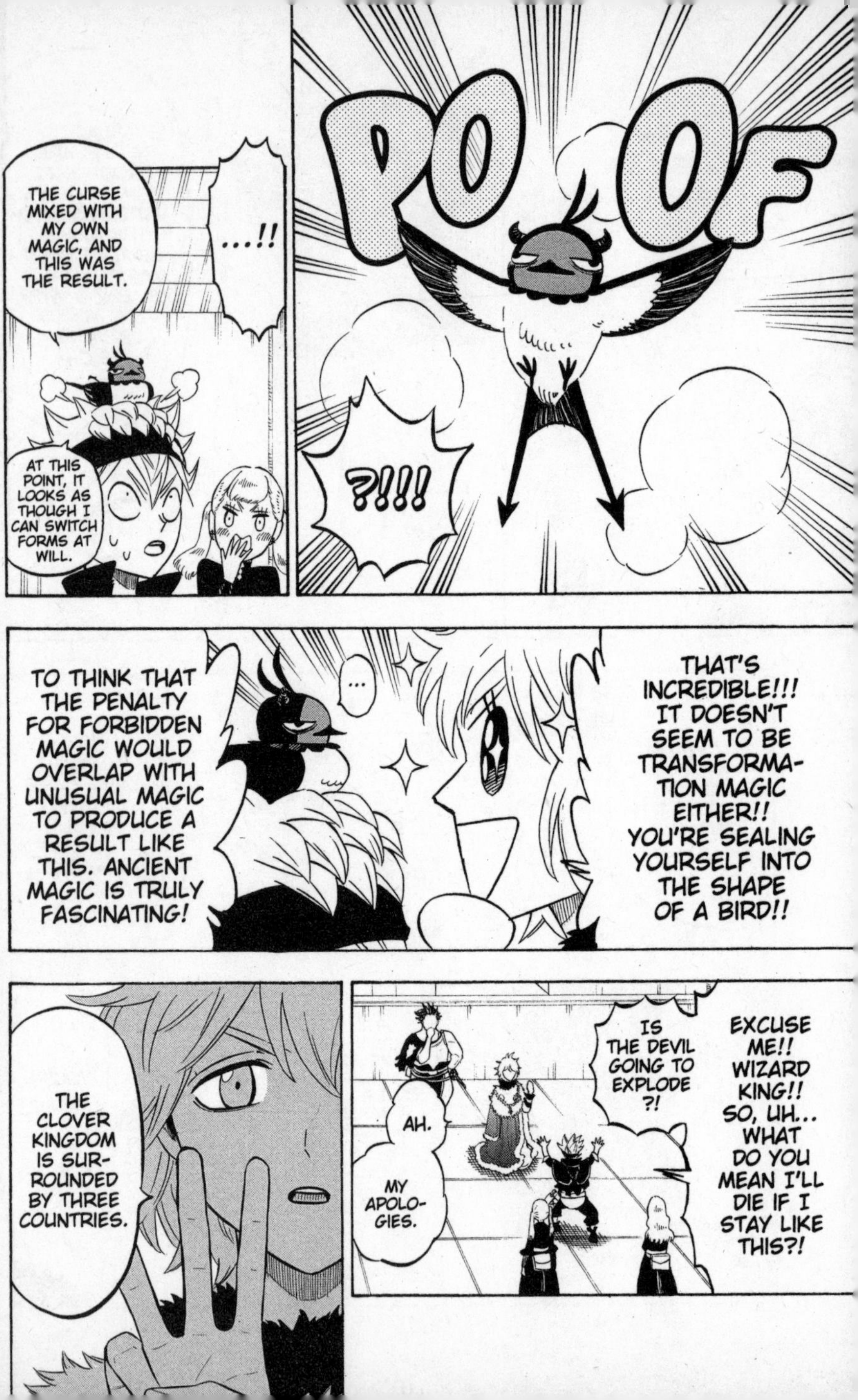
POOF
?!!!
...!!
THE CURSE MIXED WITH MY OWN MAGIC, AND THIS WAS THE RESULT.
AT THIS POINT, IT LOOKS AS THOUGH I CAN SWITCH FORMS AT WILL.
THAT'S INCREDIBLE!!! IT DOESN'T SEEM TO BE TRANSFORMATION MAGIC EITHER!! YOU'RE SEALING YOURSELF INTO THE SHAPE OF A BIRD!!
...
TO THINK THAT THE PENALTY FOR FORBIDDEN MAGIC WOULD OVERLAP WITH UNUSUAL MAGIC TO PRODUCE A RESULT LIKE THIS. ANCIENT MAGIC IS TRULY FASCINATING!
EXCUSE ME!! WIZARD KING!! SO, UH... WHAT DO YOU MEAN I'LL DIE IF I STAY LIKE THIS?!
IS THE DEVIL GOING TO EXPLODE?!
AH.
MY APOLOGIES.
THE CLOVER KINGDOM IS SURROUNDED BY THREE COUNTRIES.

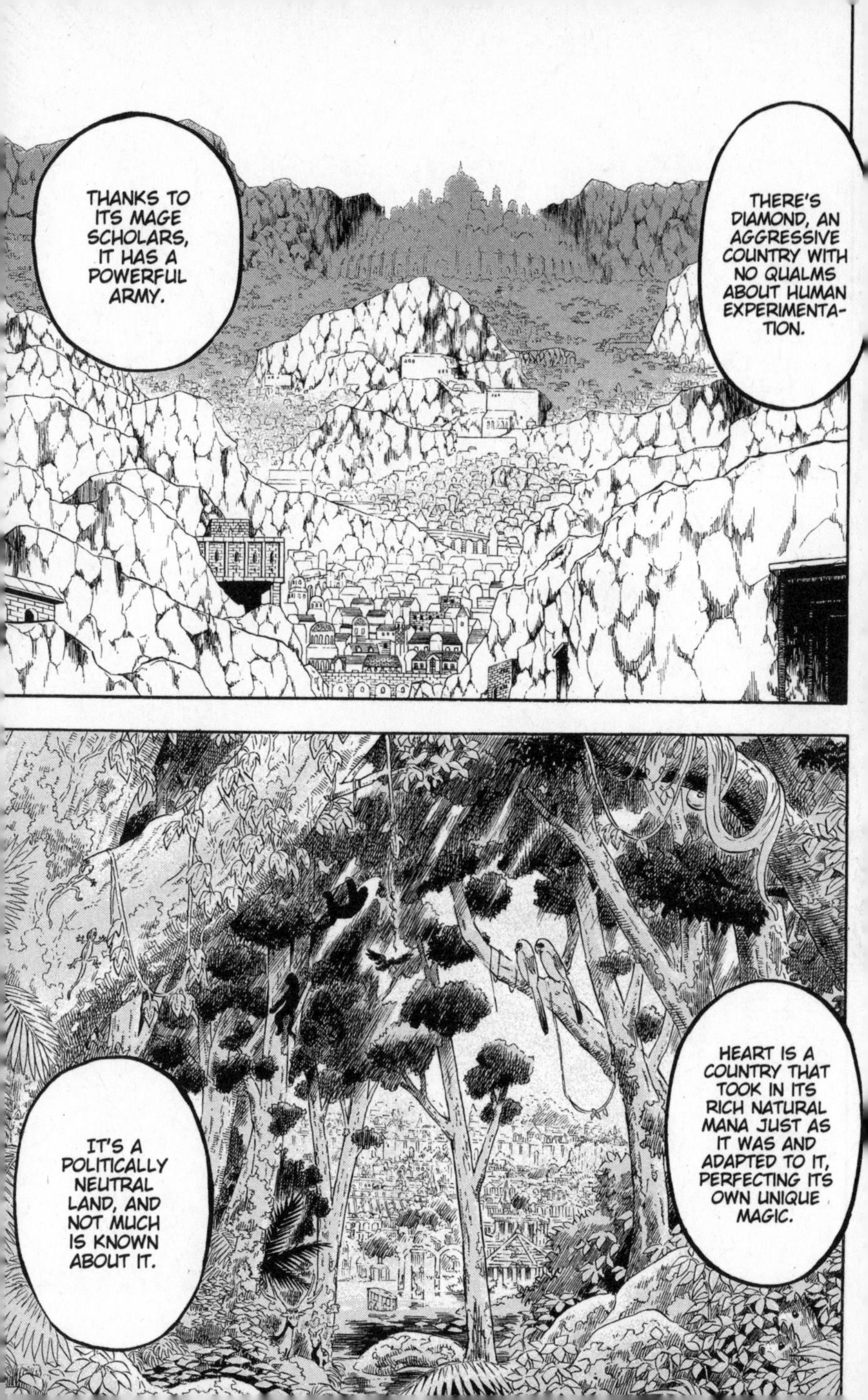
THERE'S DIAMOND, AN AGGRESSIVE COUNTRY WITH NO QUALMS ABOUT HUMAN EXPERIMENTATION.
THANKS TO ITS MAGE SCHOLARS, IT HAS A POWERFUL ARMY.
HEART IS A COUNTRY THAT TOOK IN ITS RICH NATURAL MANA JUST AS IT WAS AND ADAPTED TO IT, PERFECTING ITS OWN UNIQUE MAGIC.
IT'S A POLITICALLY NEUTRAL LAND, AND NOT MUCH IS KNOWN ABOUT IT.

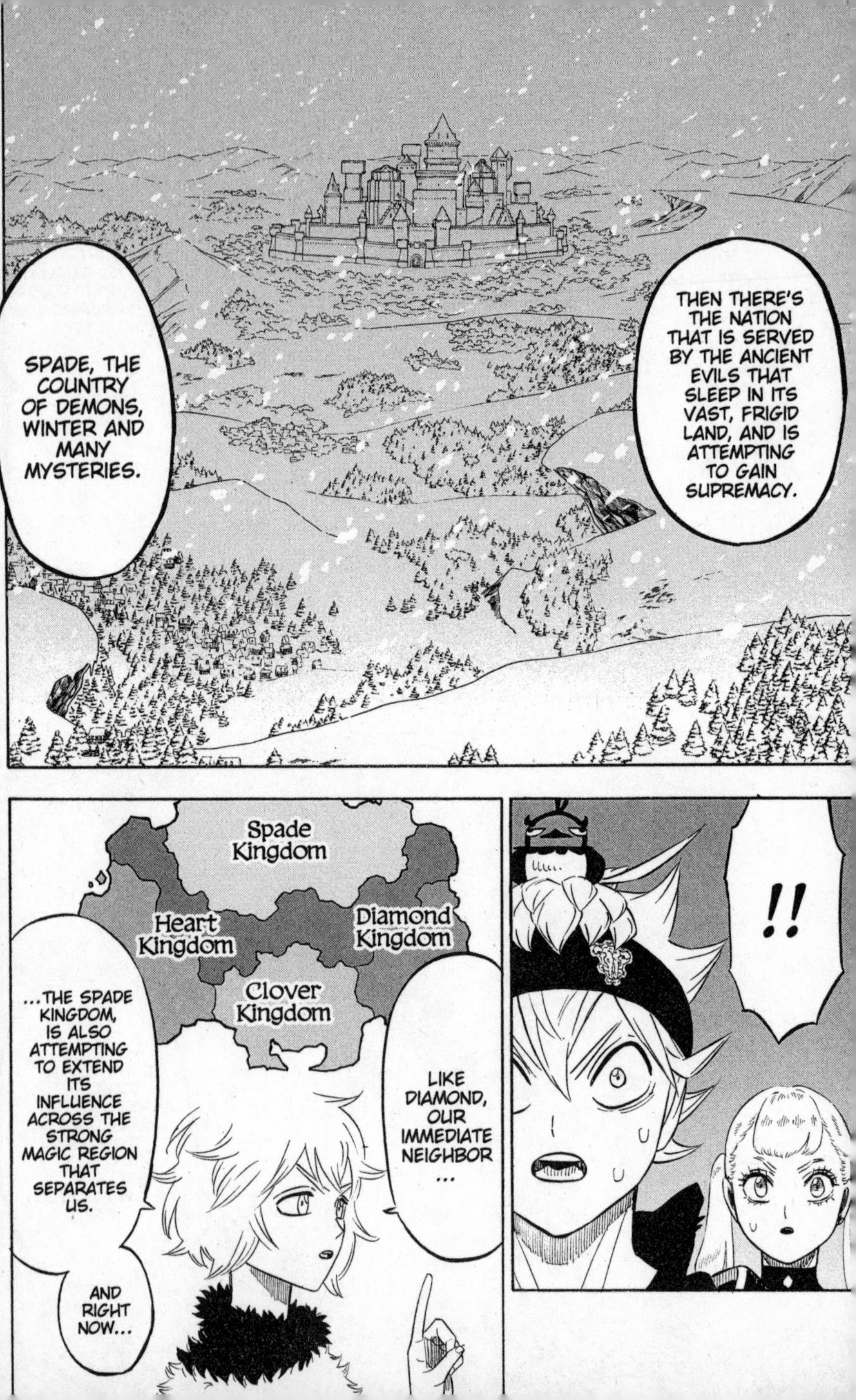
THEN THERE'S THE NATION THAT IS SERVED BY THE ANCIENT EVILS THAT SLEEP IN ITS VAST, FRIGID LAND, AND IS ATTEMPTING TO GAIN SUPREMACY.
SPADE, THE COUNTRY OF DEMONS, WINTER AND MANY MYSTERIES.
!!
Spade Kingdom
Diamond Kingdom
Heart Kingdom
Clover Kingdom
LIKE DIAMOND, OUR IMMEDIATE NEIGHBOR...
...THE SPADE KINGDOM, IS ALSO ATTEMPTING TO EXTEND ITS INFLUENCE ACROSS THE STRONG MAGIC REGION THAT SEPARATES US.
AND RIGHT NOW...

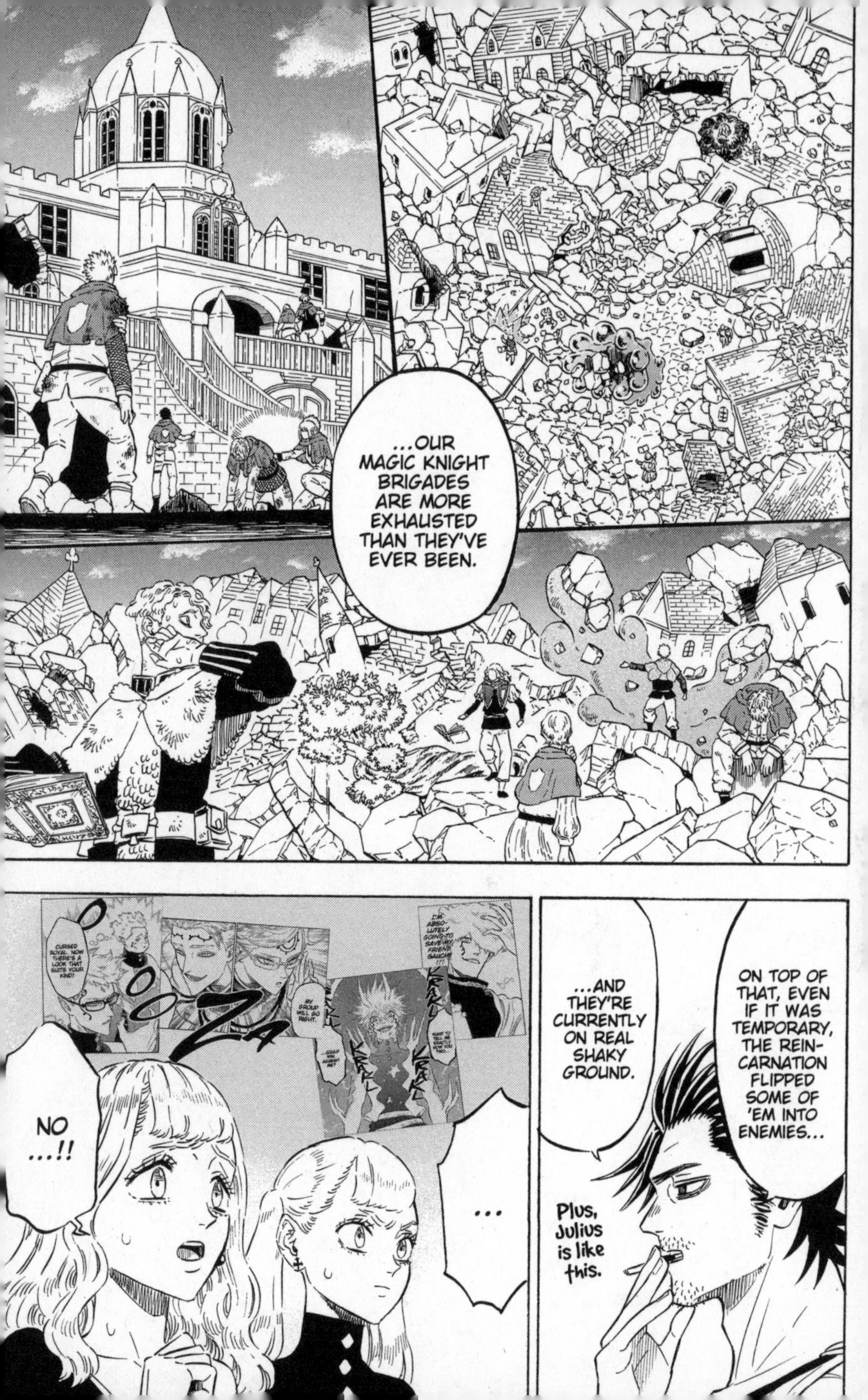
...OUR MAGIC KNIGHT BRIGADES ARE MORE EXHAUSTED THAN THEY'VE EVER BEEN.
ON TOP OF THAT, EVEN IF IT WAS TEMPORARY, THE REIN-CARNATION FLIPPED SOME OF 'EM INTO ENEMIES...
...AND THEY'RE CURRENTLY ON REAL SHAKY GROUND.
Plus, Julius is like this.
...
I'M ABSOLUTELY GOING TO SAVE MY FRIEND GAUCHE!!!
KRAKL
WANT TO TELL ME EXACTLY HOW YOU TWO...
KRAKL
KRAKL
KRAKL
MY GROUP WILL GO RIGHT.
CURSED ROYAL. NOW THERE'S A LOOK THAT SUITS YOUR KIND!
OOOOZA
NO ...!!

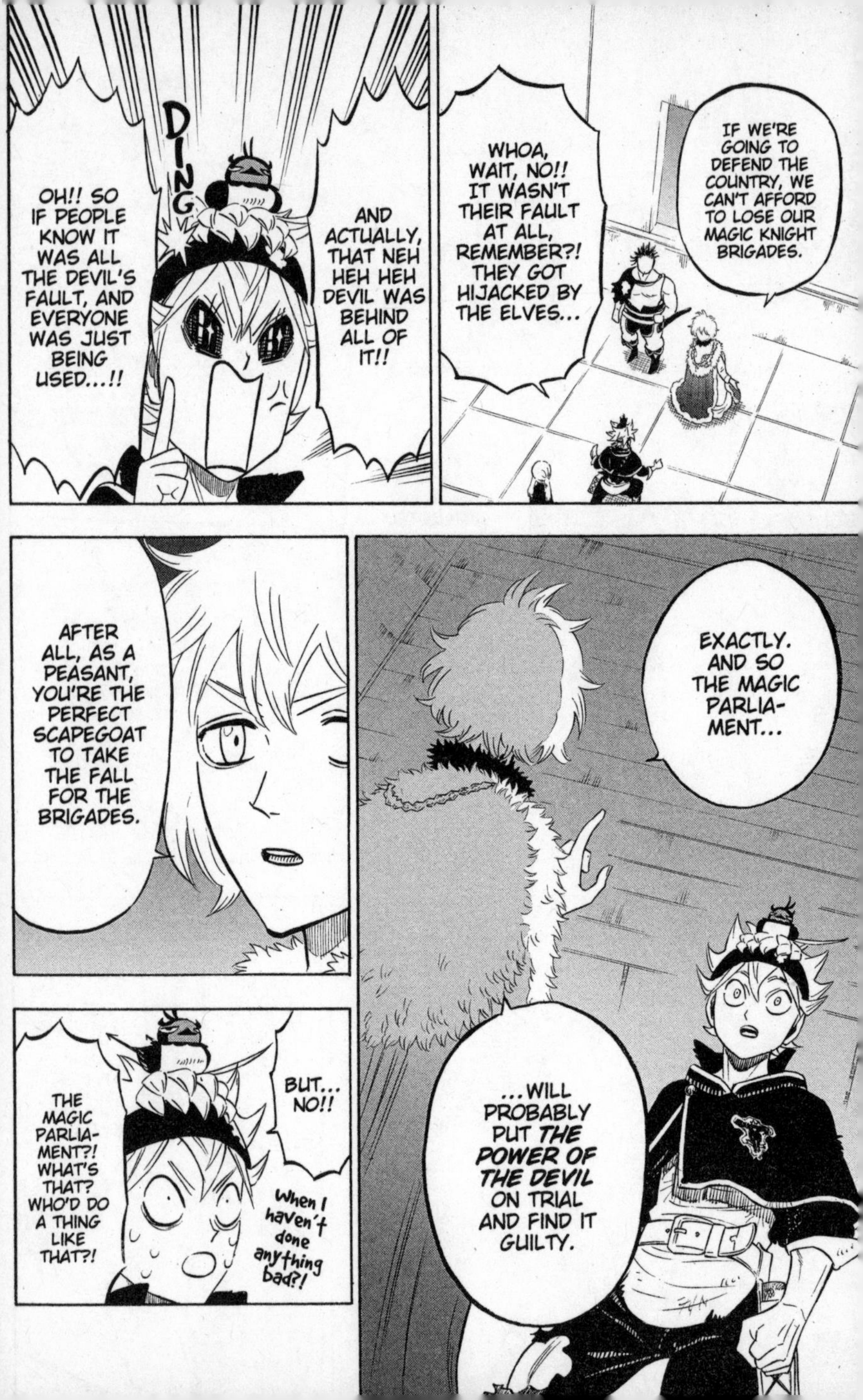

IF WE'RE GOING TO DEFEND THE COUNTRY, WE CAN'T AFFORD TO LOSE OUR MAGIC KNIGHT BRIGADES.
WHOA, WAIT, NO!! IT WASN'T THEIR FAULT AT ALL, REMEMBER?! THEY GOT HIJACKED BY THE ELVES...
DING
AND ACTUALLY, THAT NEH HEH HEH DEVIL WAS BEHIND ALL OF IT!!
OH!! SO IF PEOPLE KNOW IT WAS ALL THE DEVIL'S FAULT, AND EVERYONE WAS JUST BEING USED...!!
EXACTLY. AND SO THE MAGIC PARLIA-MENT...
...WILL PROBABLY PUT *THE POWER OF THE DEVIL* ON TRIAL AND FIND IT GUILTY.
AFTER ALL, AS A PEASANT, YOU'RE THE PERFECT SCAPEGOAT TO TAKE THE FALL FOR THE BRIGADES.
BUT... NO!!
When I haven't done anything bad?!
THE MAGIC PARLIA-MENT?! WHAT'S THAT? WHO'D DO A THING LIKE THAT?!

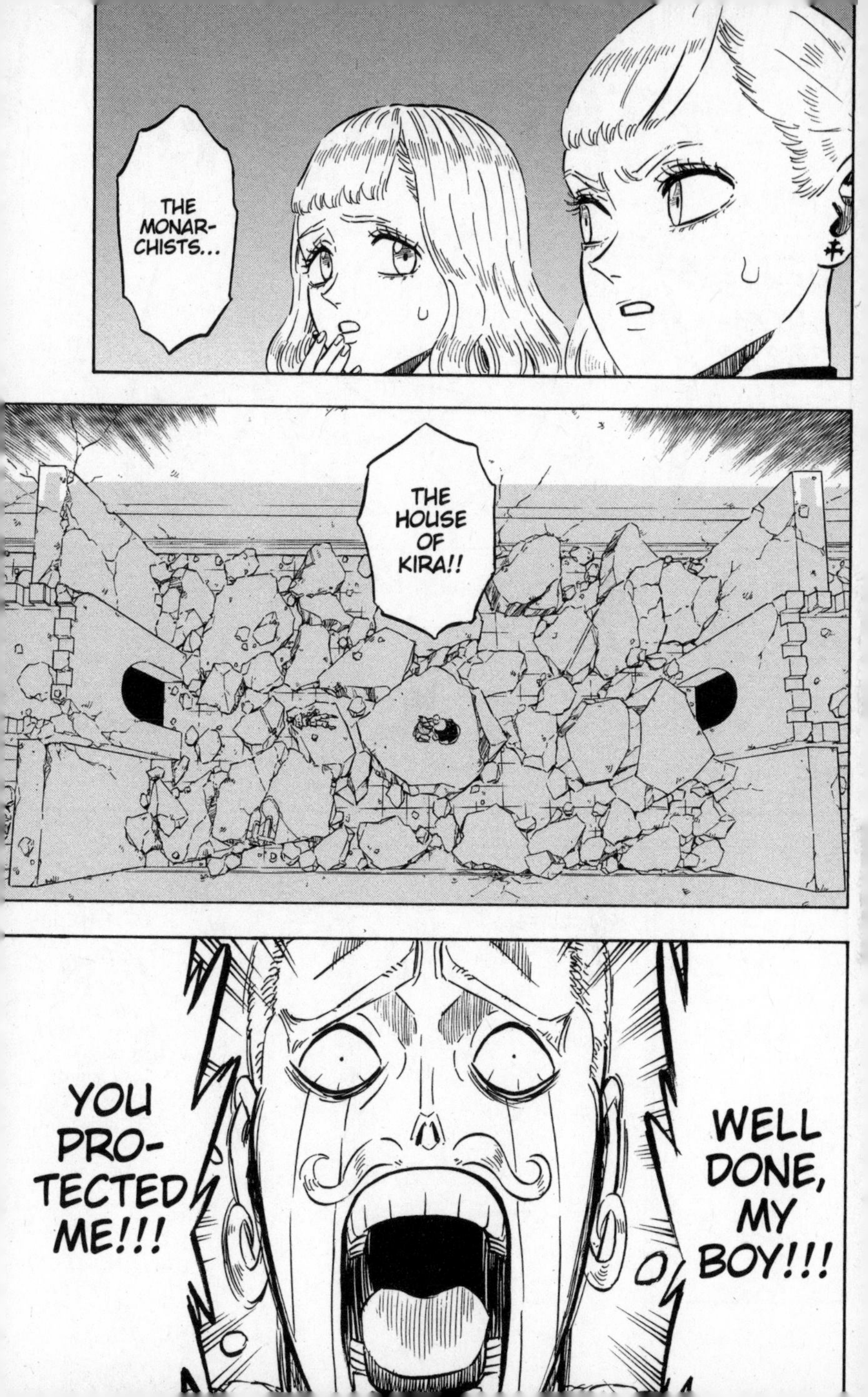
THE MONARCHISTS...
THE HOUSE OF KIRA!!
WELL DONE, MY BOY!!!
YOU PROTECTED ME!!!

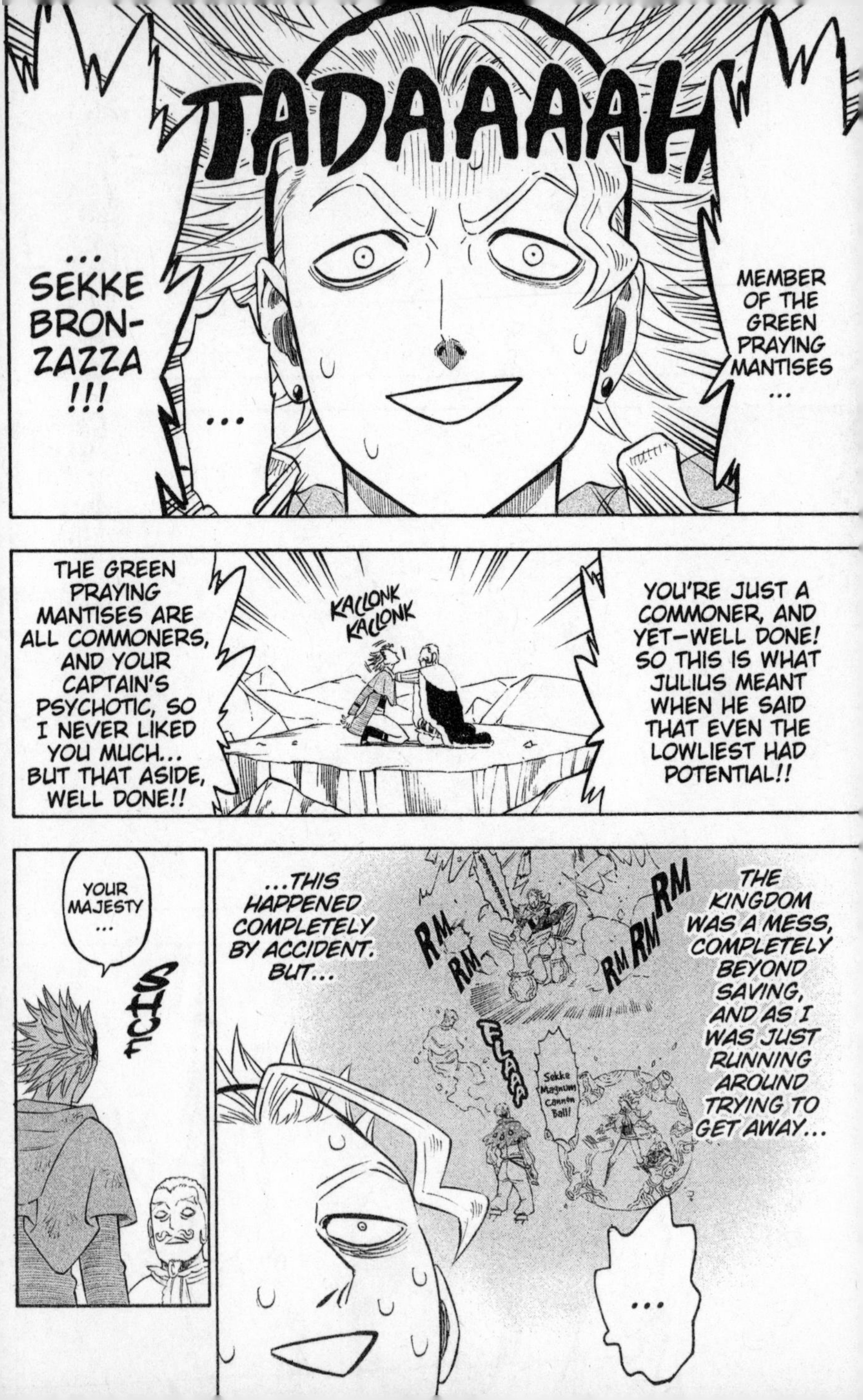
TADAAAAH
MEMBER OF THE GREEN PRAYING MANTISES ...
...
... SEKKE BRON-ZAZZA !!!
YOU'RE JUST A COMMONER, AND YET—WELL DONE! SO THIS IS WHAT JULIUS MEANT WHEN HE SAID THAT EVEN THE LOWLIEST HAD POTENTIAL!!
KALLONK KALLONK
THE GREEN PRAYING MANTISES ARE ALL COMMONERS, AND YOUR CAPTAIN'S PSYCHOTIC, SO I NEVER LIKED YOU MUCH... BUT THAT ASIDE, WELL DONE!!
THE KINGDOM WAS A MESS, COMPLETELY BEYOND SAVING, AND AS I WAS JUST RUNNING AROUND TRYING TO GET AWAY...
RM RM RM RM
...THIS HAPPENED COMPLETELY BY ACCIDENT. BUT...
RM RM
FLAAP
Sekke Magnum Cannon Ball!
...
YOUR MAJESTY ...
SHUF

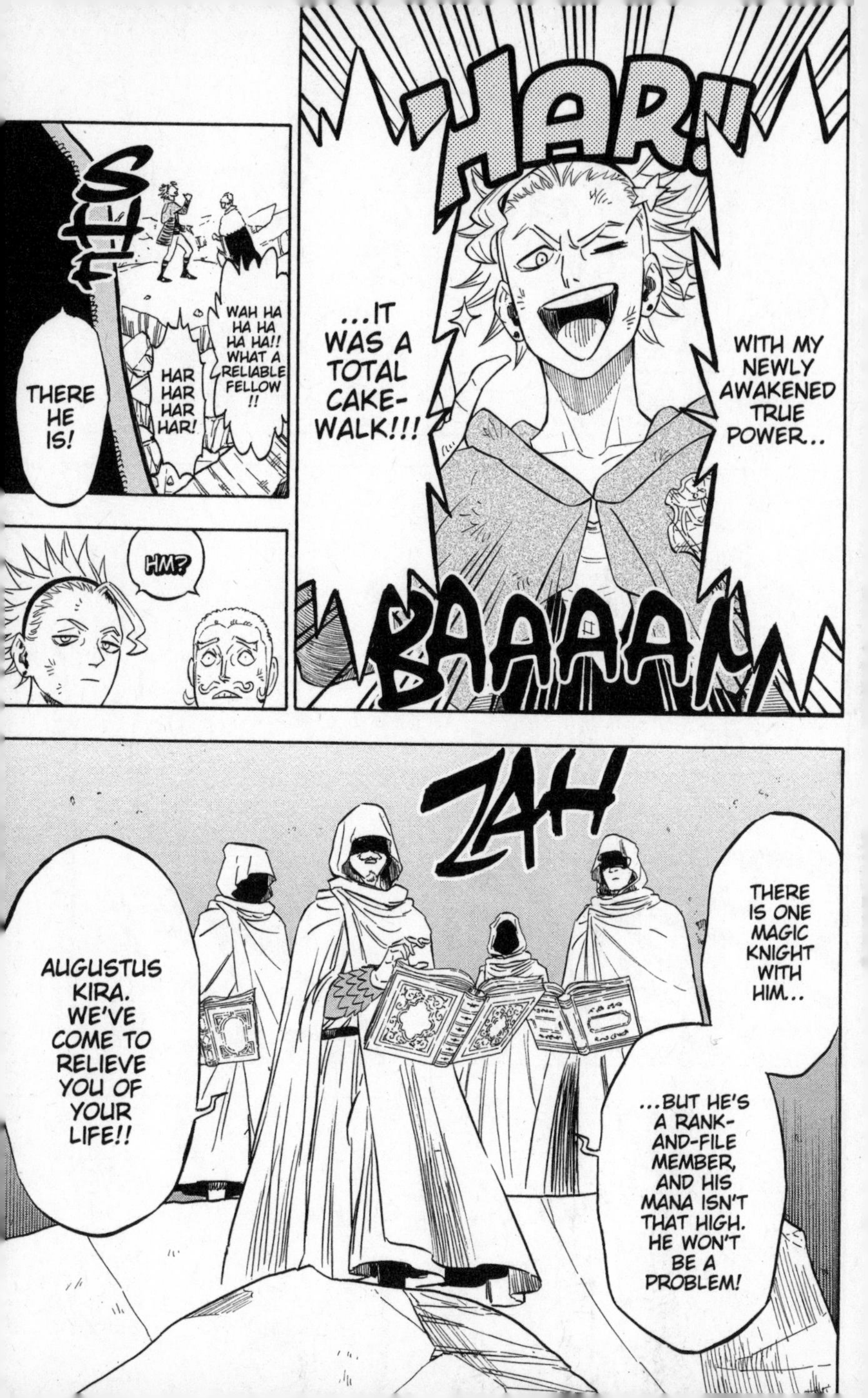
HAR!!
WITH MY NEWLY AWAKENED TRUE POWER...
...IT WAS A TOTAL CAKE-WALK!!!
BAAAAM
WAH HA HA HA HA HA!! WHAT A RELIABLE FELLOW!!
HAR HAR HAR HAR!
THERE HE IS!
HM?
ZAH
THERE IS ONE MAGIC KNIGHT WITH HIM...
...BUT HE'S A RANK-AND-FILE MEMBER, AND HIS MANA ISN'T THAT HIGH. HE WON'T BE A PROBLEM!
AUGUSTUS KIRA. WE'VE COME TO RELIEVE YOU OF YOUR LIFE!!

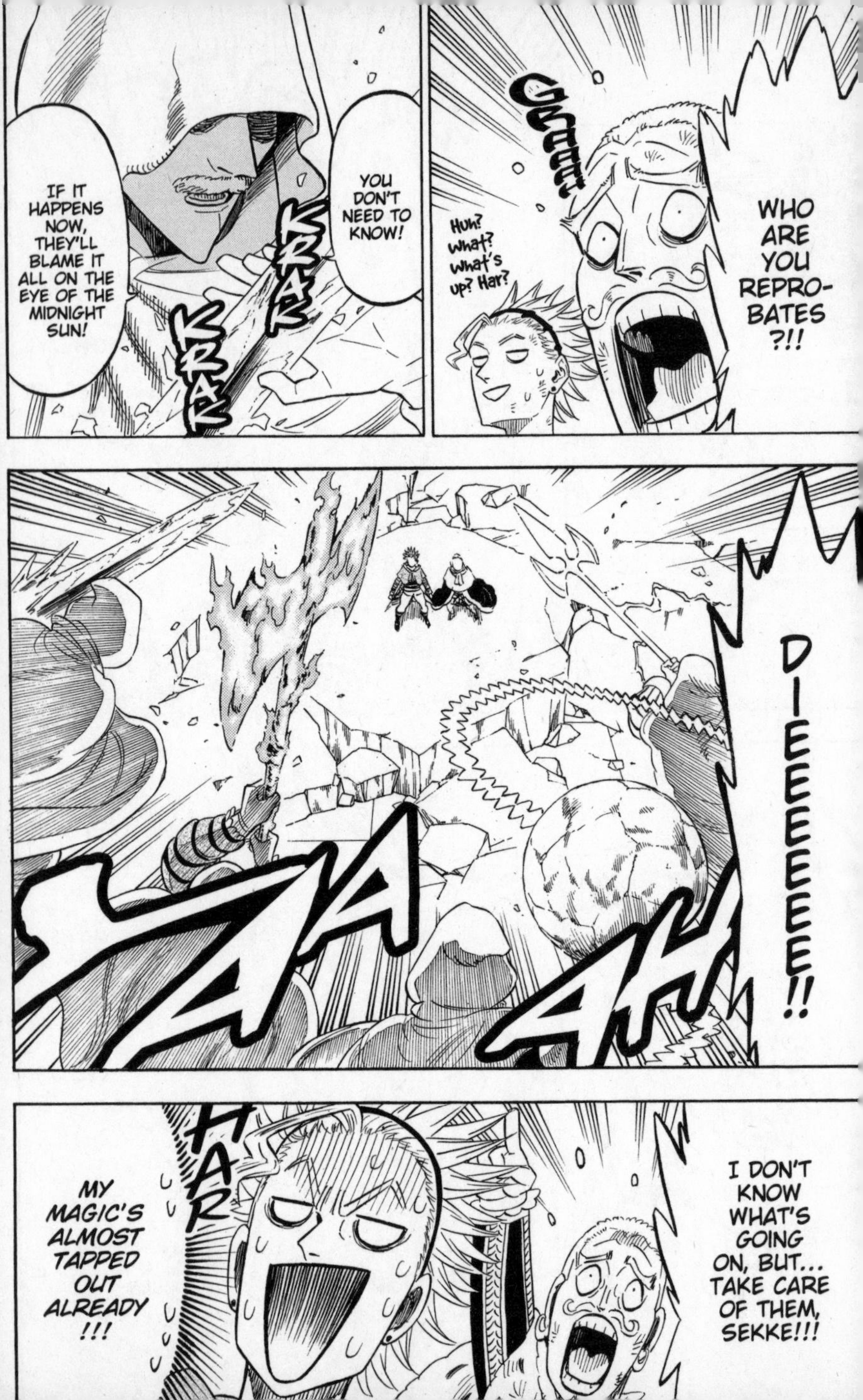
WHO ARE YOU REPROBATES?!!
Huh? what? what's up? Har?
YOU DON'T NEED TO KNOW!
KRAK
KRAK
IF IT HAPPENS NOW, THEY'LL BLAME IT ALL ON THE EYE OF THE MIDNIGHT SUN!
DIEEEEEEEE!!
I DON'T KNOW WHAT'S GOING ON, BUT... TAKE CARE OF THEM, SEKKE!!!
HAR
MY MAGIC'S ALMOST TAPPED OUT ALREADY!!!

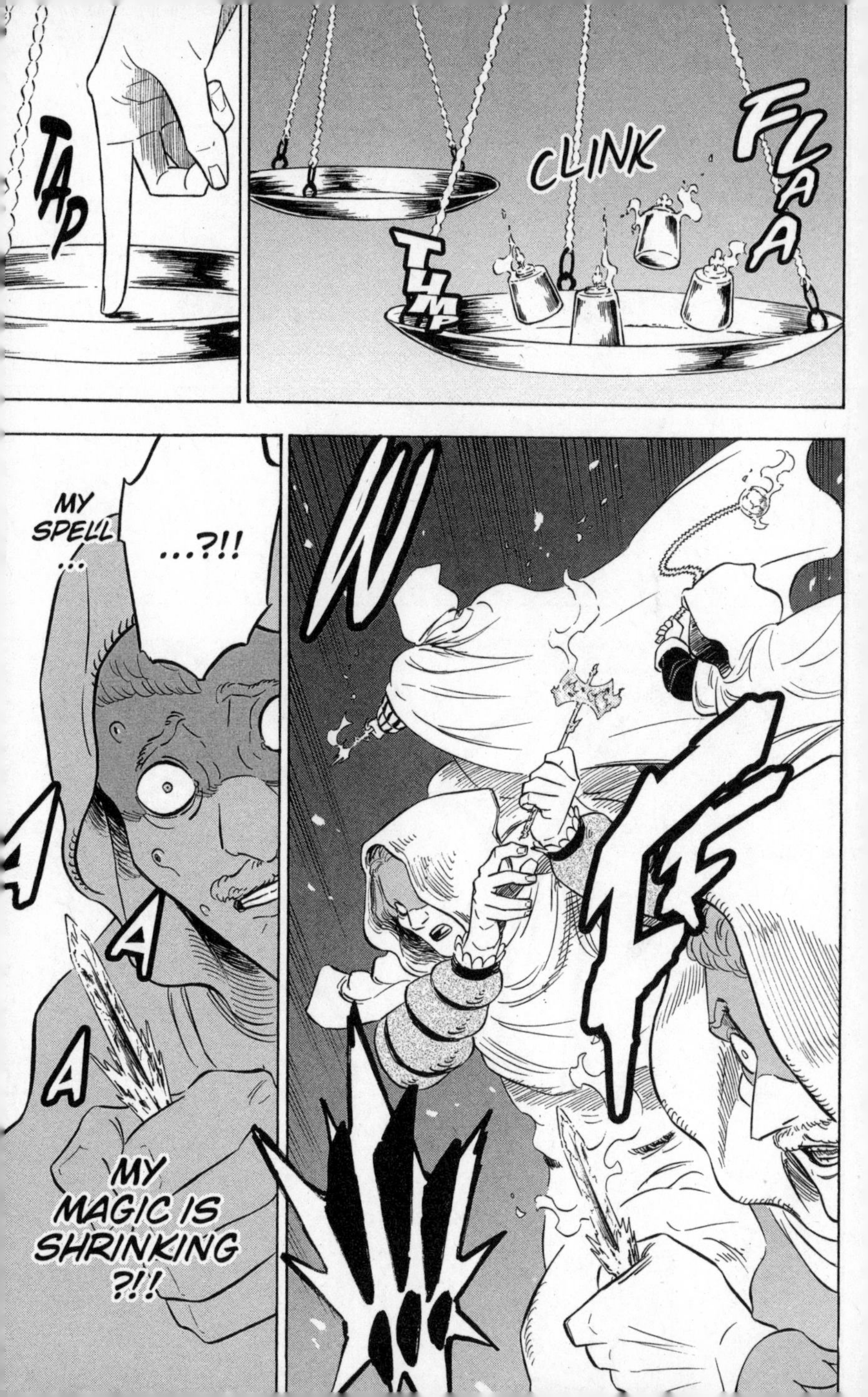
FLAA
CLINK
TUMP
TAP
...?!!
MY SPELL...
AAA
MY MAGIC IS SHRINKING?!!

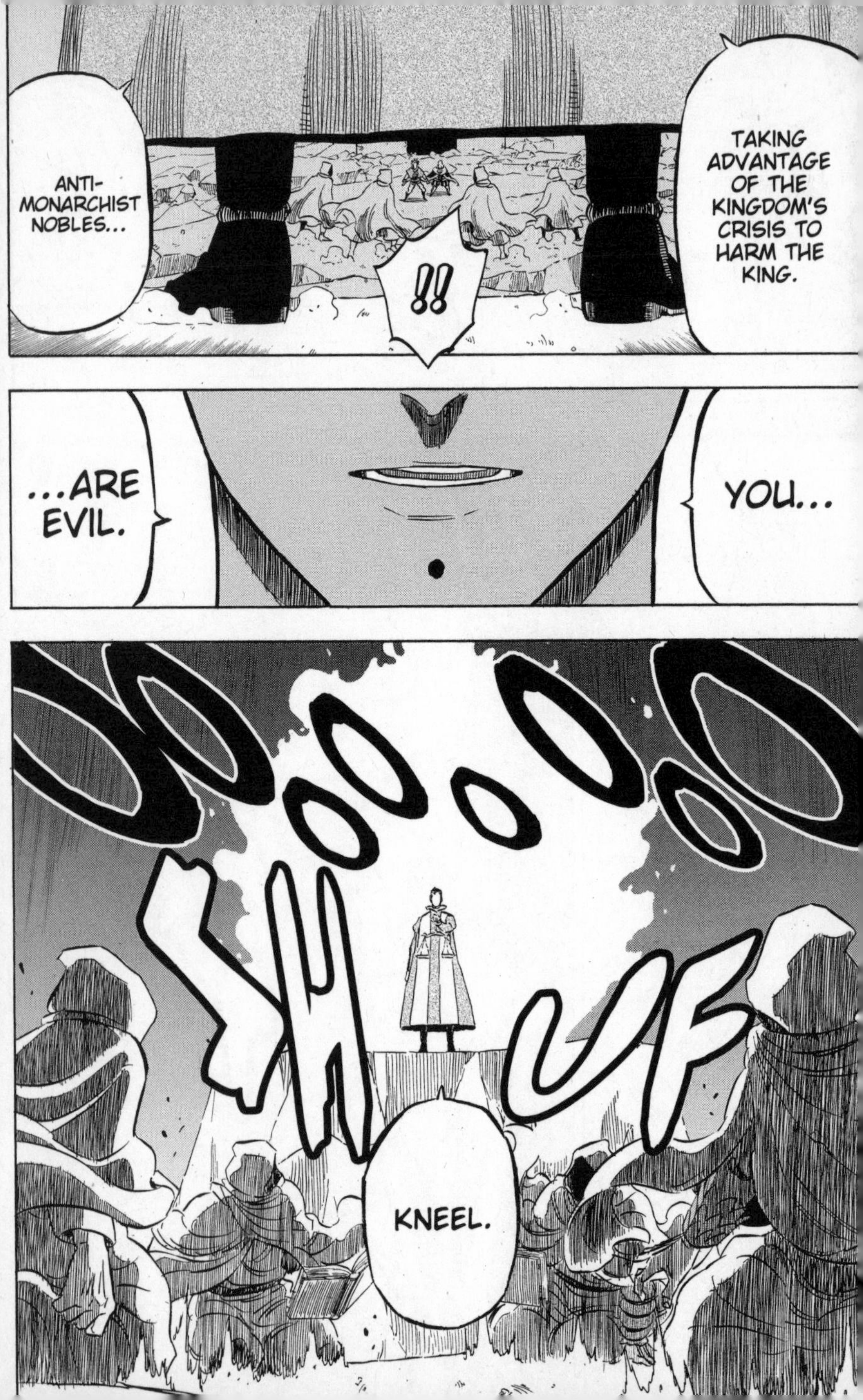
TAKING ADVANTAGE OF THE KINGDOM'S CRISIS TO HARM THE KING.
!!
ANTI-MONARCHIST NOBLES...
YOU...
...ARE EVIL.
KNEEL.

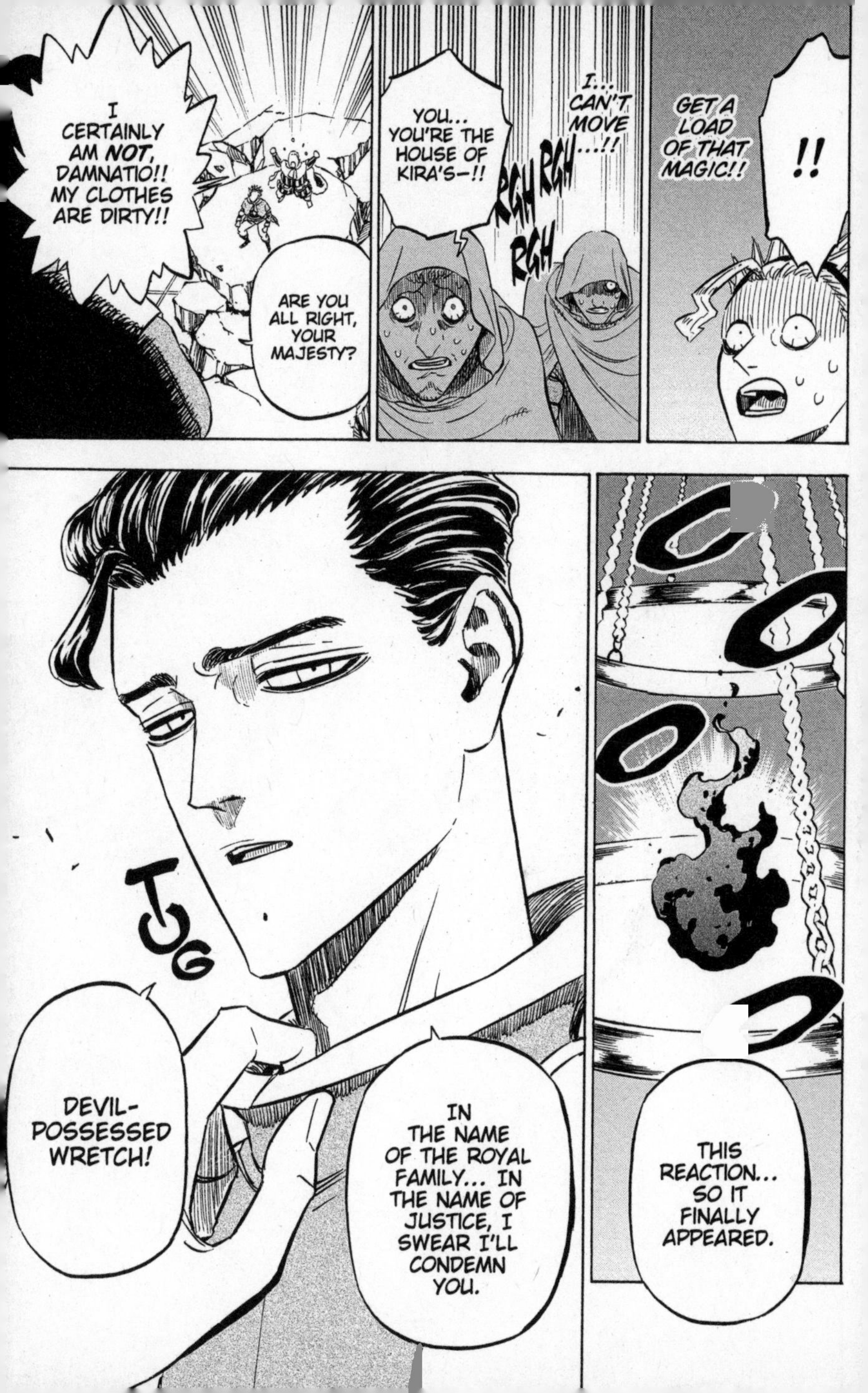
!!
GET A LOAD OF THAT MAGIC!!
I... CAN'T MOVE...!!
YOU... YOU'RE THE HOUSE OF KIRA'S—!!
RGH RGH RGH RGH
ARE YOU ALL RIGHT, YOUR MAJESTY?
I CERTAINLY AM NOT, DAMNATIO!! MY CLOTHES ARE DIRTY!!
THIS REACTION... SO IT FINALLY APPEARED.
TUG
IN THE NAME OF THE ROYAL FAMILY... IN THE NAME OF JUSTICE, I SWEAR I'LL CONDEMN YOU.
DEVIL-POSSESSED WRETCH!

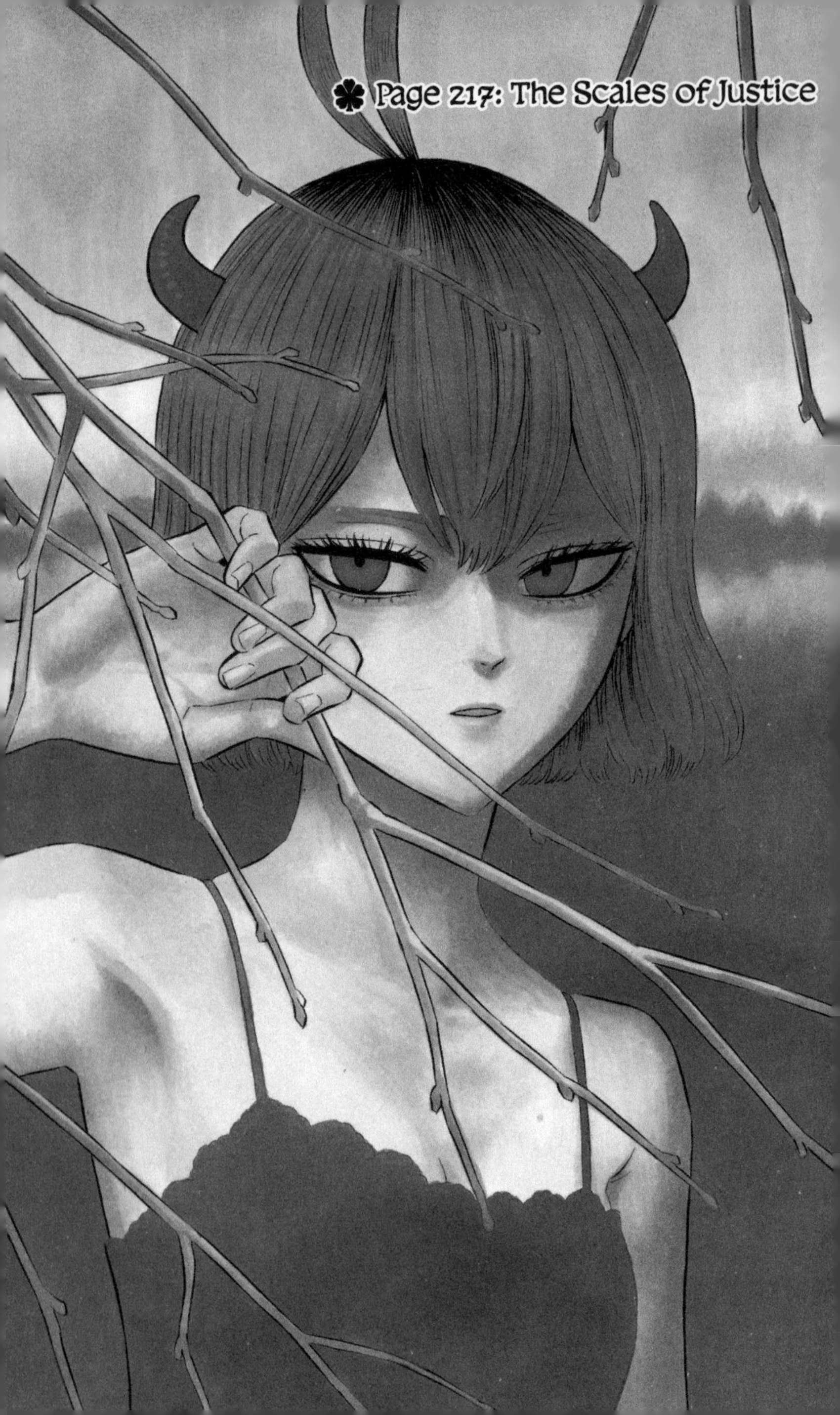
Page 217: The Scales of Justice

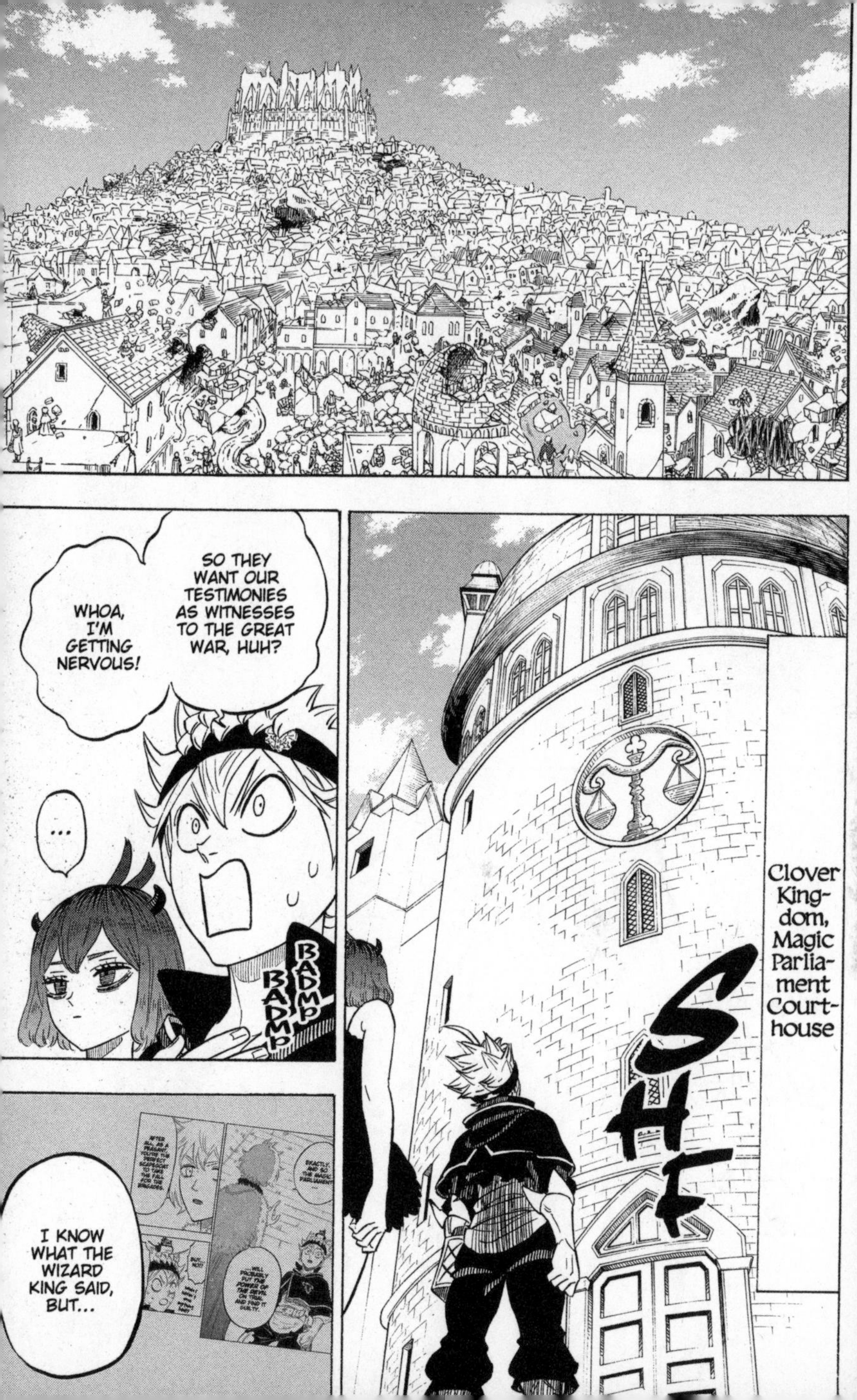
Clover Kingdom, Magic Parliament Courthouse
SHF
SO THEY WANT OUR TESTIMONIES AS WITNESSES TO THE GREAT WAR, HUH?
WHOA, I'M GETTING NERVOUS!
...
BADMP BADMP
I KNOW WHAT THE WIZARD KING SAID, BUT...
EXACTLY. AND SO THE MAGIC PARLIAMENT...
AFTER ALL, AS A PEASANT, YOU'RE THE PERFECT SCAPEGOAT TO TAKE THE FALL FOR THE BRIGADES.
...WILL PROBABLY PUT THE POWER OF THE DEVIL ON TRIAL AND FIND IT GUILTY.

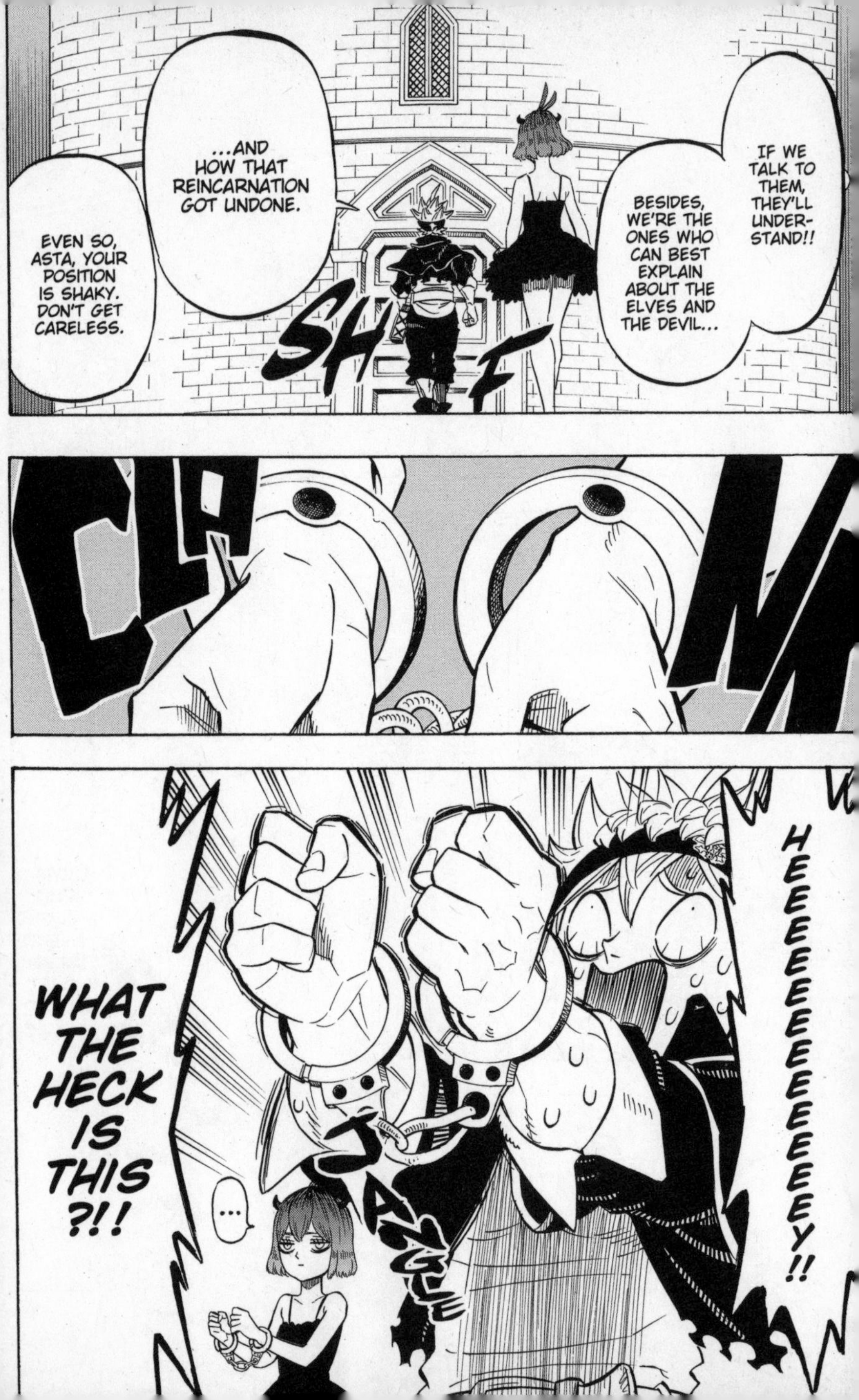
IF WE TALK TO THEM, THEY'LL UNDER-STAND!!
BESIDES, WE'RE THE ONES WHO CAN BEST EXPLAIN ABOUT THE ELVES AND THE DEVIL...
...AND HOW THAT REINCARNATION GOT UNDONE.
EVEN SO, ASTA, YOUR POSITION IS SHAKY. DON'T GET CARELESS.
SHF
HEEEEEEEEEEEEEEEY!!
WHAT THE HECK IS THIS?!!
JANGLE
...

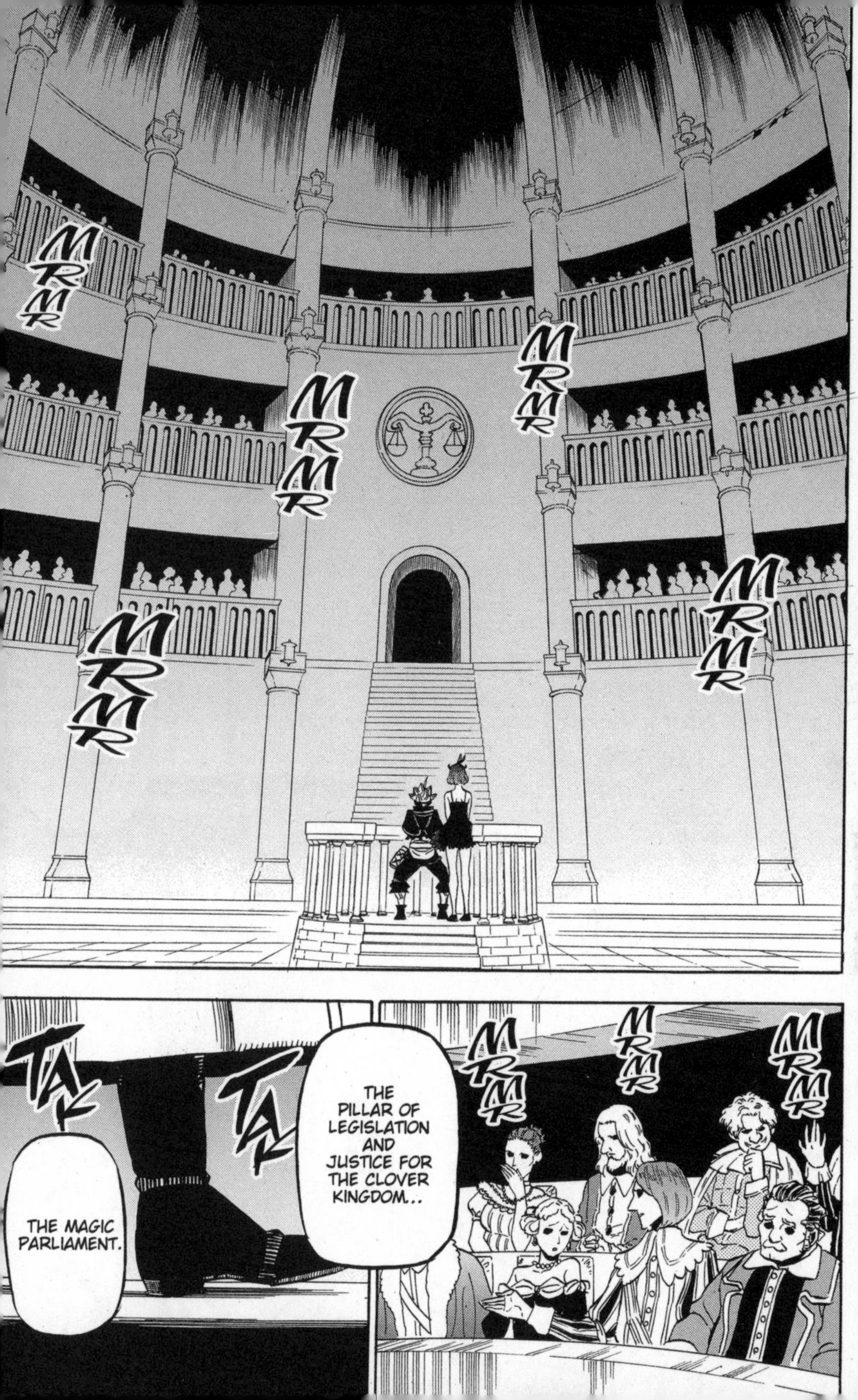
MRMR
MRMR
MRMR
MRMR
MRMR
MRMR
MRMR
MRMR
THE PILLAR OF LEGISLATION AND JUSTICE FOR THE CLOVER KINGDOM...
TAK
TAK
THE MAGIC PARLIAMENT.

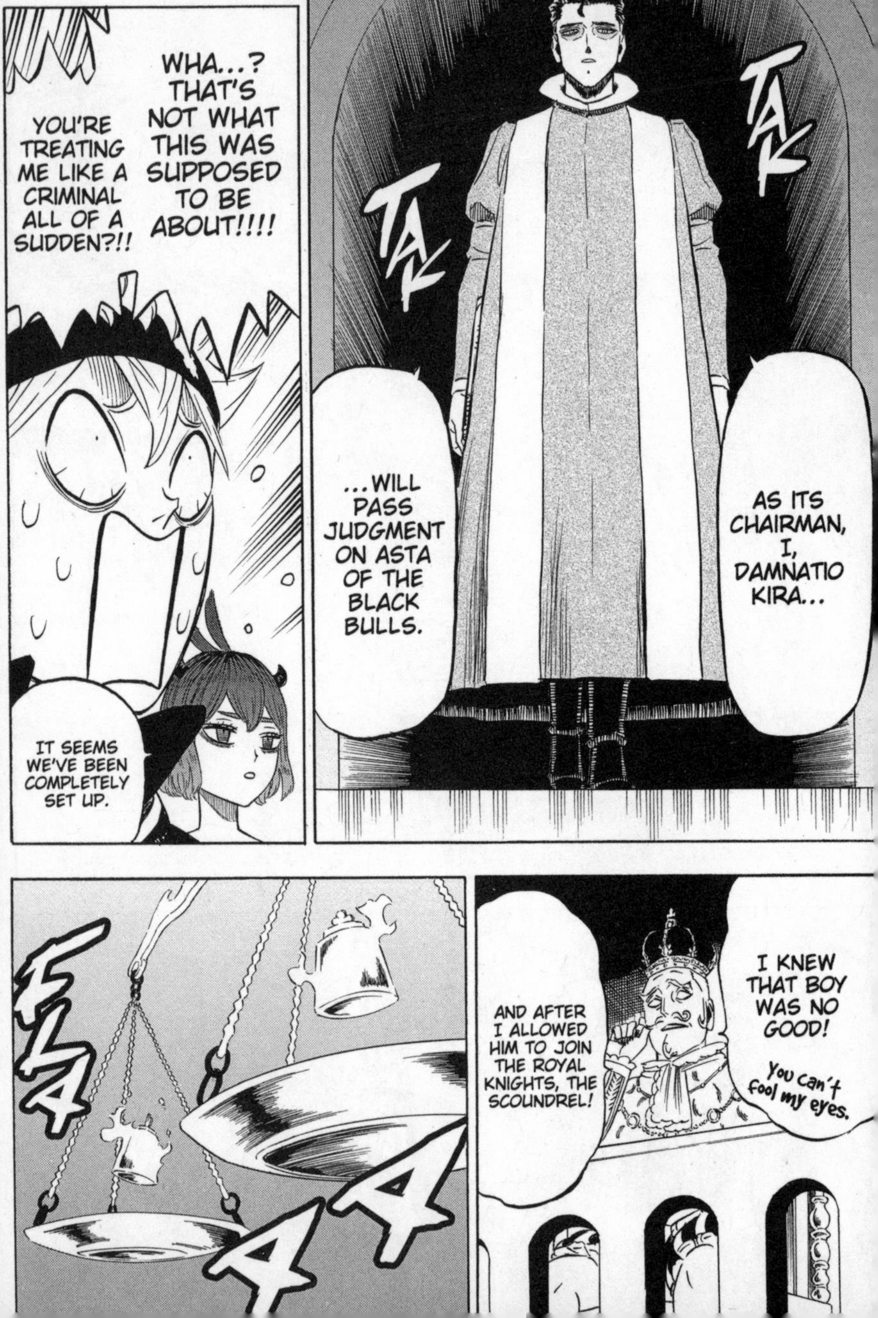
TAK
TAK
AS ITS CHAIRMAN, I, DAMNATIO KIRA...
...WILL PASS JUDGMENT ON ASTA OF THE BLACK BULLS.
WHA...? THAT'S NOT WHAT THIS WAS SUPPOSED TO BE ABOUT!!!!
YOU'RE TREATING ME LIKE A CRIMINAL ALL OF A SUDDEN?!!
IT SEEMS WE'VE BEEN COMPLETELY SET UP.
I KNEW THAT BOY WAS NO GOOD!
You can't fool my eyes.
AND AFTER I ALLOWED HIM TO JOIN THE ROYAL KNIGHTS, THE SCOUNDREL!
FLAAA

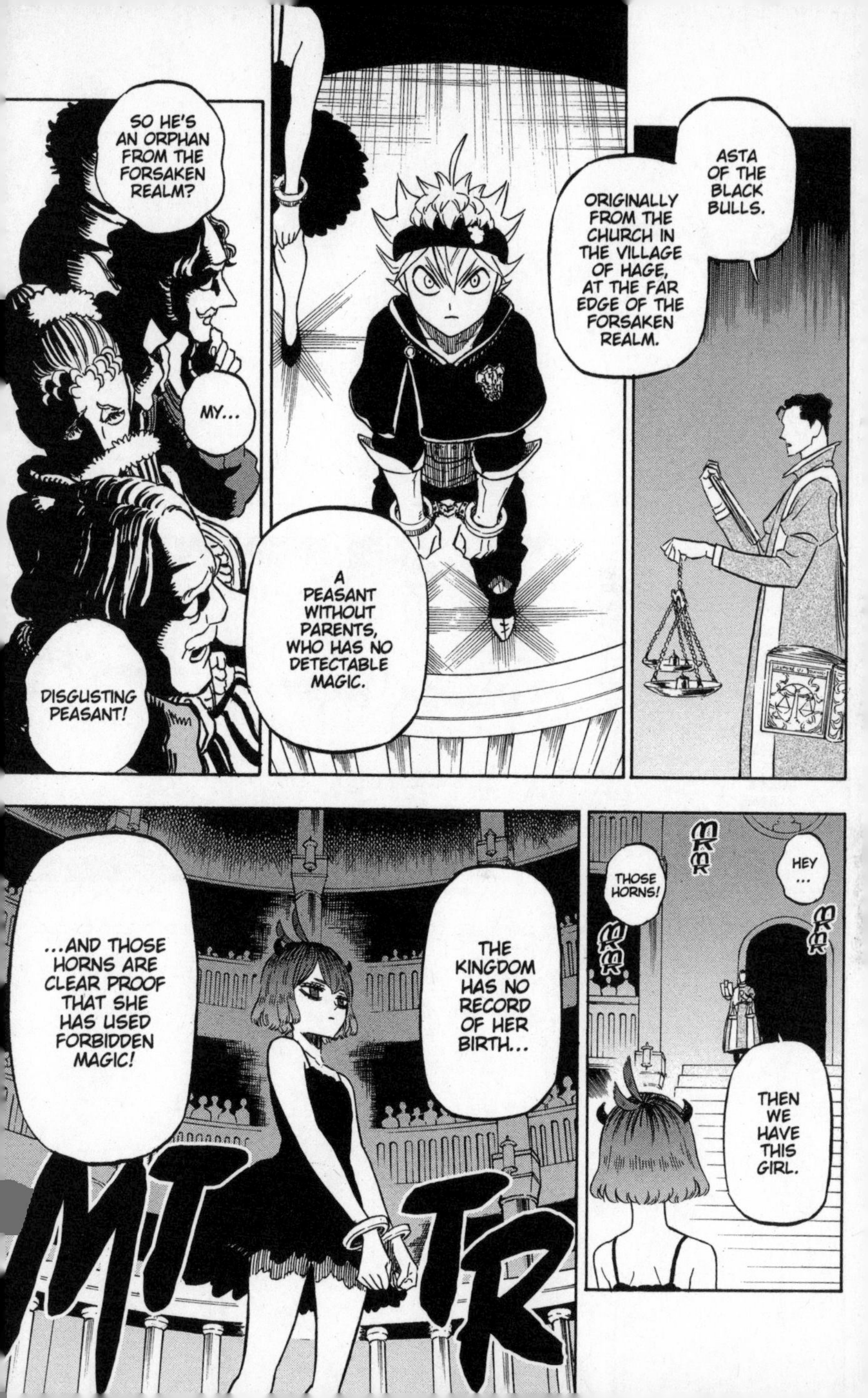
ASTA OF THE BLACK BULLS.
ORIGINALLY FROM THE CHURCH IN THE VILLAGE OF HAGE, AT THE FAR EDGE OF THE FORSAKEN REALM.
A PEASANT WITHOUT PARENTS, WHO HAS NO DETECTABLE MAGIC.
SO HE'S AN ORPHAN FROM THE FORSAKEN REALM?
MY...
DISGUSTING PEASANT!
MRMR
HEY ...
MRMR
THOSE HORNS!
MRMR
THEN WE HAVE THIS GIRL.
THE KINGDOM HAS NO RECORD OF HER BIRTH...
...AND THOSE HORNS ARE CLEAR PROOF THAT SHE HAS USED FORBIDDEN MAGIC!
TR
MT

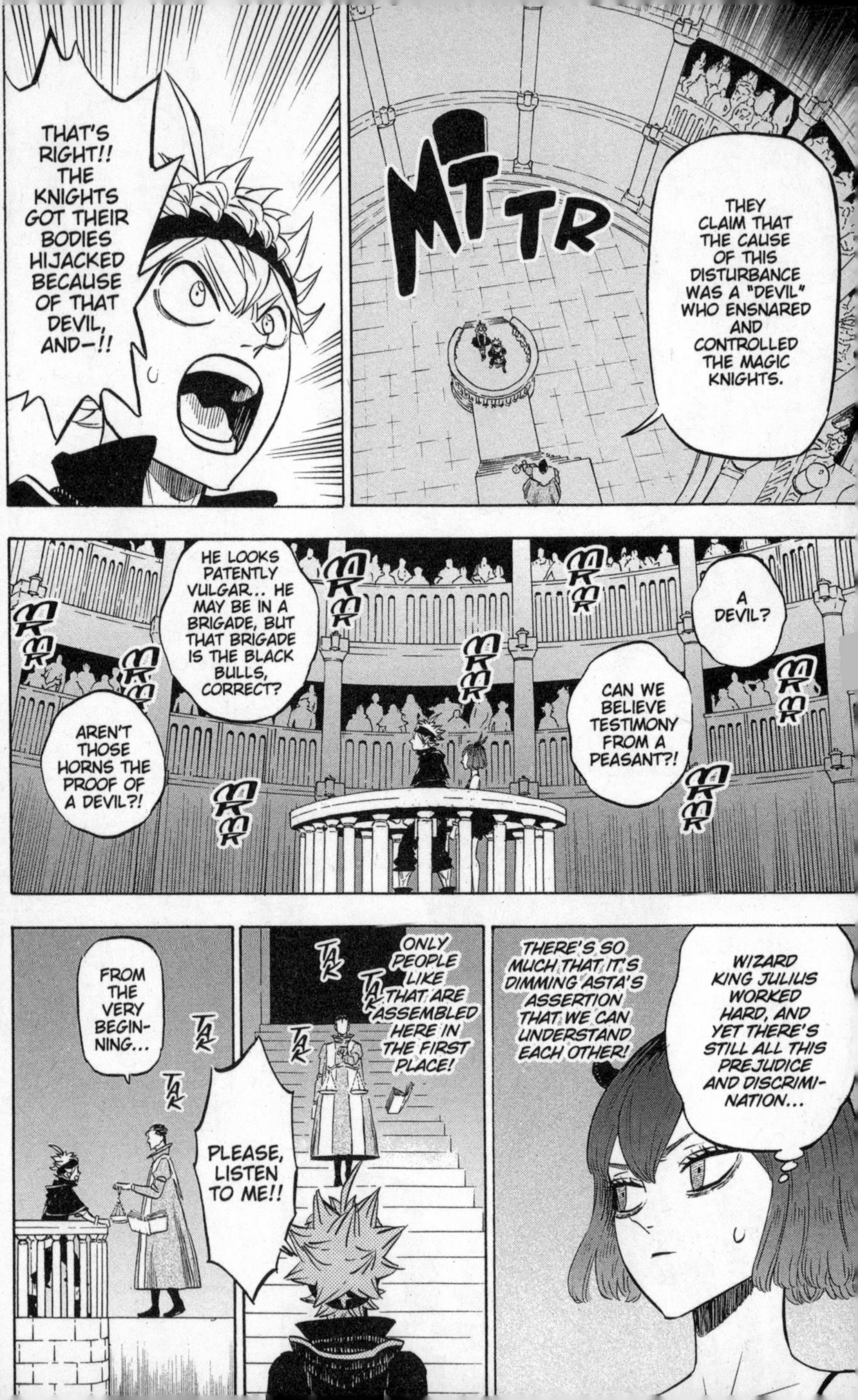
THEY CLAIM THAT THE CAUSE OF THIS DISTURBANCE WAS A "DEVIL" WHO ENSNARED AND CONTROLLED THE MAGIC KNIGHTS.
MTTR
THAT'S RIGHT!! THE KNIGHTS GOT THEIR BODIES HIJACKED BECAUSE OF THAT DEVIL, AND–!!
A DEVIL?
MRMR
CAN WE BELIEVE TESTIMONY FROM A PEASANT?!
MRMR
HE LOOKS PATENTLY VULGAR... HE MAY BE IN A BRIGADE, BUT THAT BRIGADE IS THE BLACK BULLS, CORRECT?
MRMR
AREN'T THOSE HORNS THE PROOF OF A DEVIL?!
MRMR
WIZARD KING JULIUS WORKED HARD, AND YET THERE'S STILL ALL THIS PREJUDICE AND DISCRIMINATION...
THERE'S SO MUCH THAT IT'S DIMMING ASTA'S ASSERTION THAT WE CAN UNDERSTAND EACH OTHER!
ONLY PEOPLE LIKE THAT ARE ASSEMBLED HERE IN THE FIRST PLACE!
TAK
TAK
TAK
FROM THE VERY BEGINNING...
TAK
TAK
PLEASE, LISTEN TO ME!!

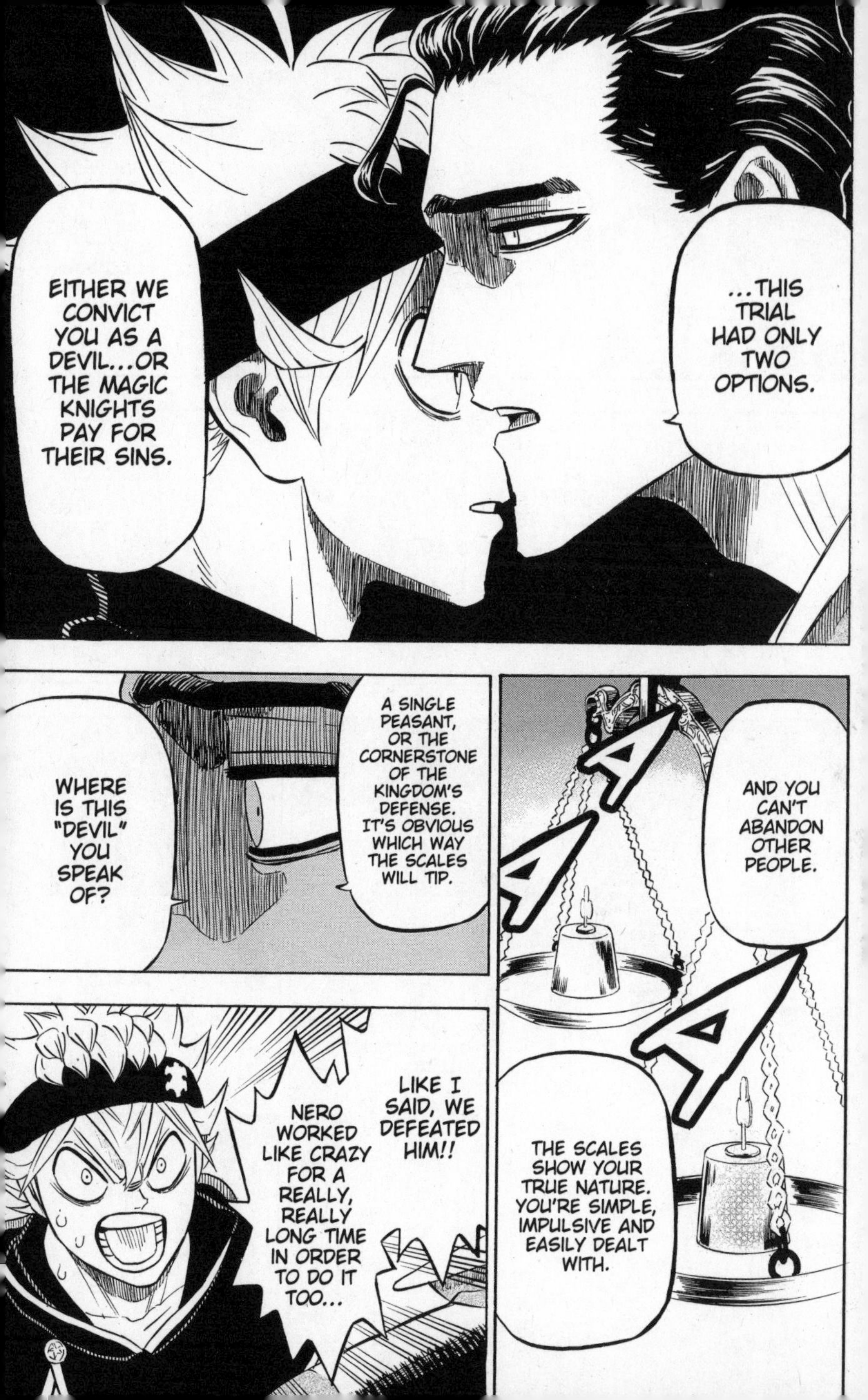
...THIS TRIAL HAD ONLY TWO OPTIONS.
EITHER WE CONVICT YOU AS A DEVIL...OR THE MAGIC KNIGHTS PAY FOR THEIR SINS.
AND YOU CAN'T ABANDON OTHER PEOPLE.
THE SCALES SHOW YOUR TRUE NATURE. YOU'RE SIMPLE, IMPULSIVE AND EASILY DEALT WITH.
A SINGLE PEASANT, OR THE CORNERSTONE OF THE KINGDOM'S DEFENSE. IT'S OBVIOUS WHICH WAY THE SCALES WILL TIP.
WHERE IS THIS "DEVIL" YOU SPEAK OF?
LIKE I SAID, WE DEFEATED HIM!!
NERO WORKED LIKE CRAZY FOR A REALLY, REALLY LONG TIME IN ORDER TO DO IT TOO...

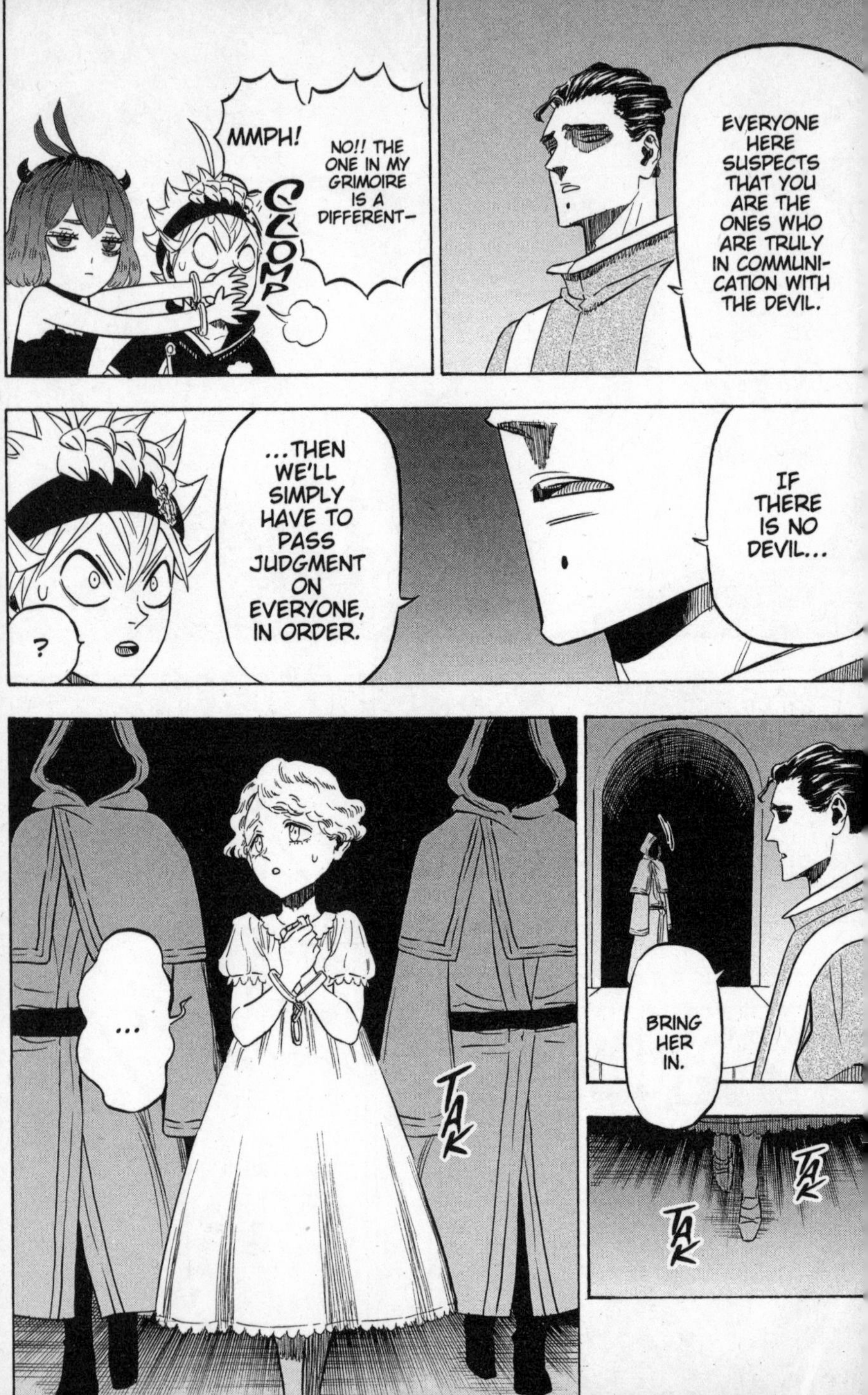
EVERYONE HERE SUSPECTS THAT YOU ARE THE ONES WHO ARE TRULY IN COMMUNICATION WITH THE DEVIL.
NO!! THE ONE IN MY GRIMOIRE IS A DIFFERENT—
MMPH!
CLOMP
IF THERE IS NO DEVIL...
...THEN WE'LL SIMPLY HAVE TO PASS JUDGMENT ON EVERYONE, IN ORDER.
?
BRING HER IN.
TAK
TAK
TAK
...

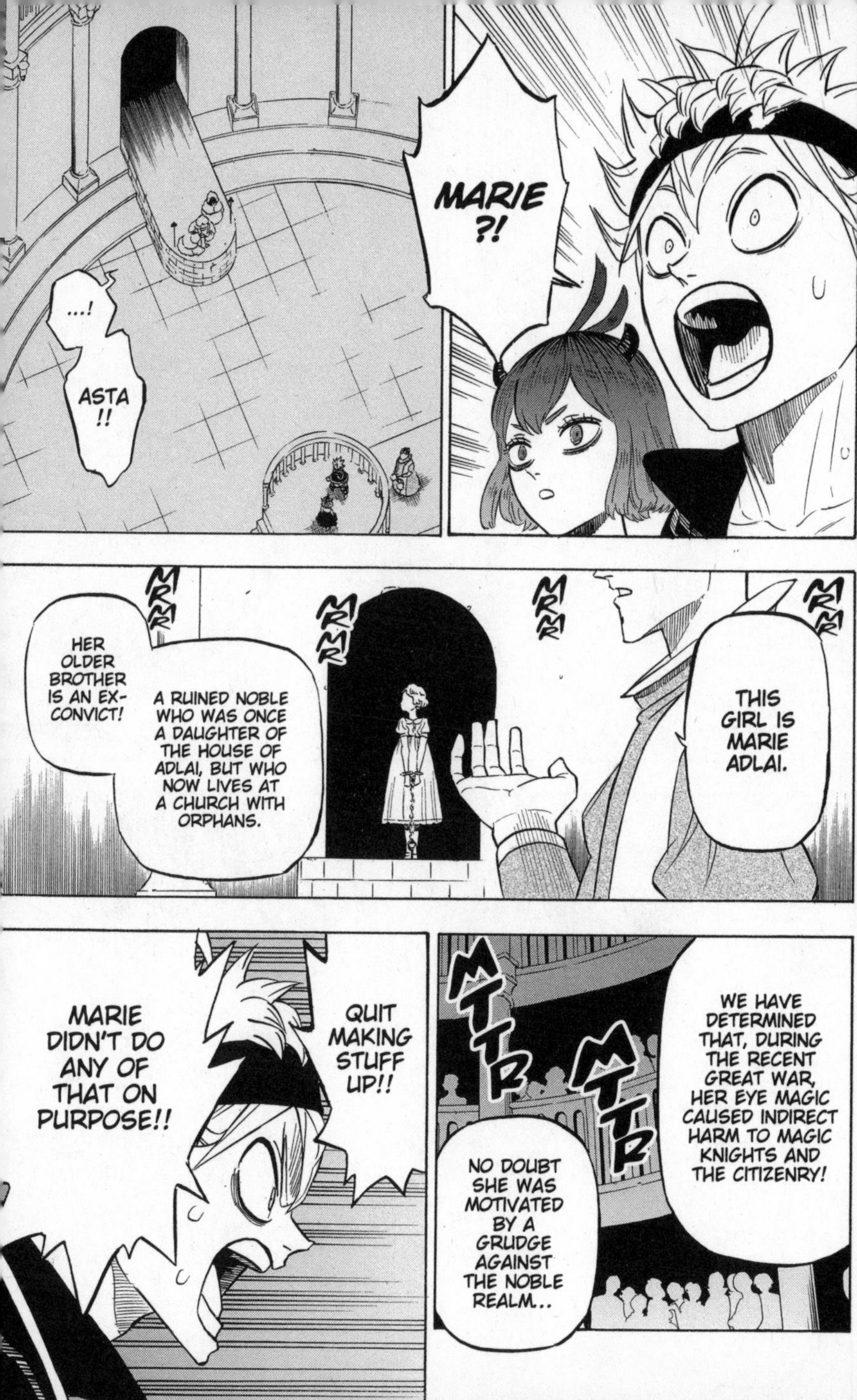
MARIE ?!
...! ASTA !!
MRMR
THIS GIRL IS MARIE ADLAI.
MRMR
A RUINED NOBLE WHO WAS ONCE A DAUGHTER OF THE HOUSE OF ADLAI, BUT WHO NOW LIVES AT A CHURCH WITH ORPHANS.
MRMR
HER OLDER BROTHER IS AN EX-CONVICT!
MRMR
WE HAVE DETERMINED THAT, DURING THE RECENT GREAT WAR, HER EYE MAGIC CAUSED INDIRECT HARM TO MAGIC KNIGHTS AND THE CITIZENRY!
MTTR MTTR
NO DOUBT SHE WAS MOTIVATED BY A GRUDGE AGAINST THE NOBLE REALM...
QUIT MAKING STUFF UP!!
MARIE DIDN'T DO ANY OF THAT ON PURPOSE!!

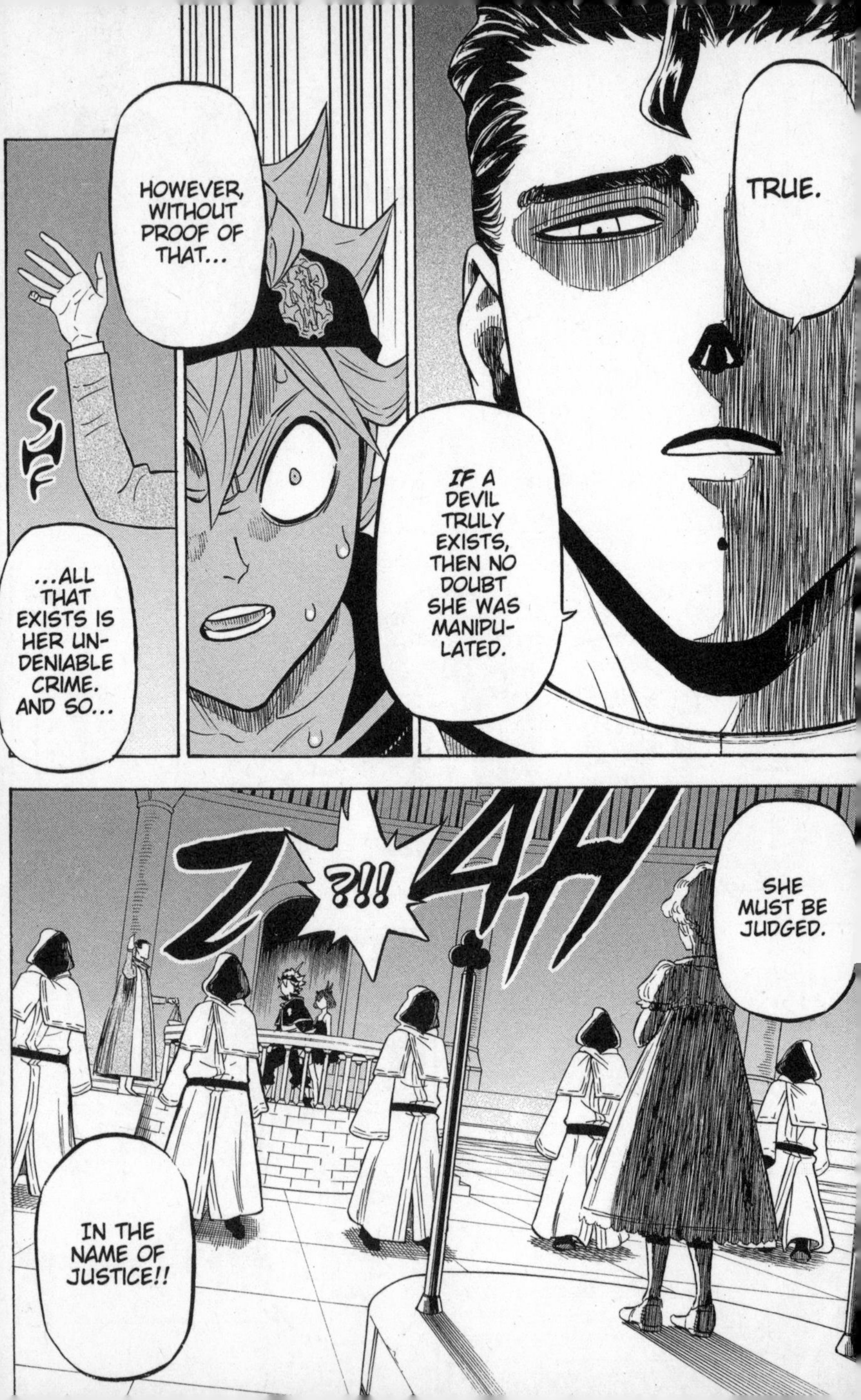
TRUE.
IF A DEVIL TRULY EXISTS, THEN NO DOUBT SHE WAS MANIPULATED.
HOWEVER, WITHOUT PROOF OF THAT...
...ALL THAT EXISTS IS HER UNDENIABLE CRIME. AND SO...
SHE MUST BE JUDGED.
?!!
IN THE NAME OF JUSTICE!!

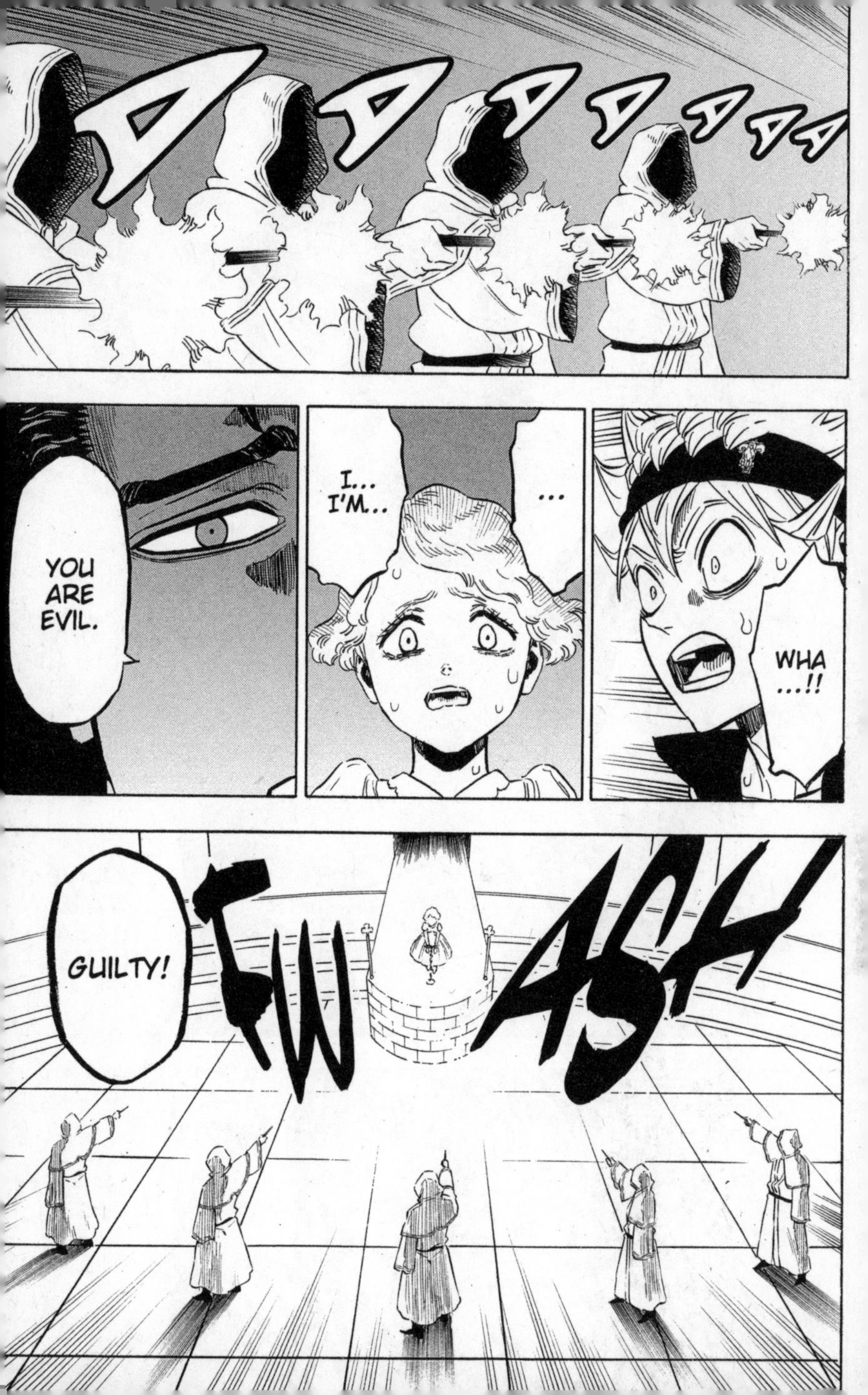
AAAAAAAA
WHA...!!
...
I... I'M...
YOU ARE EVIL.
GUILTY!
FWASH

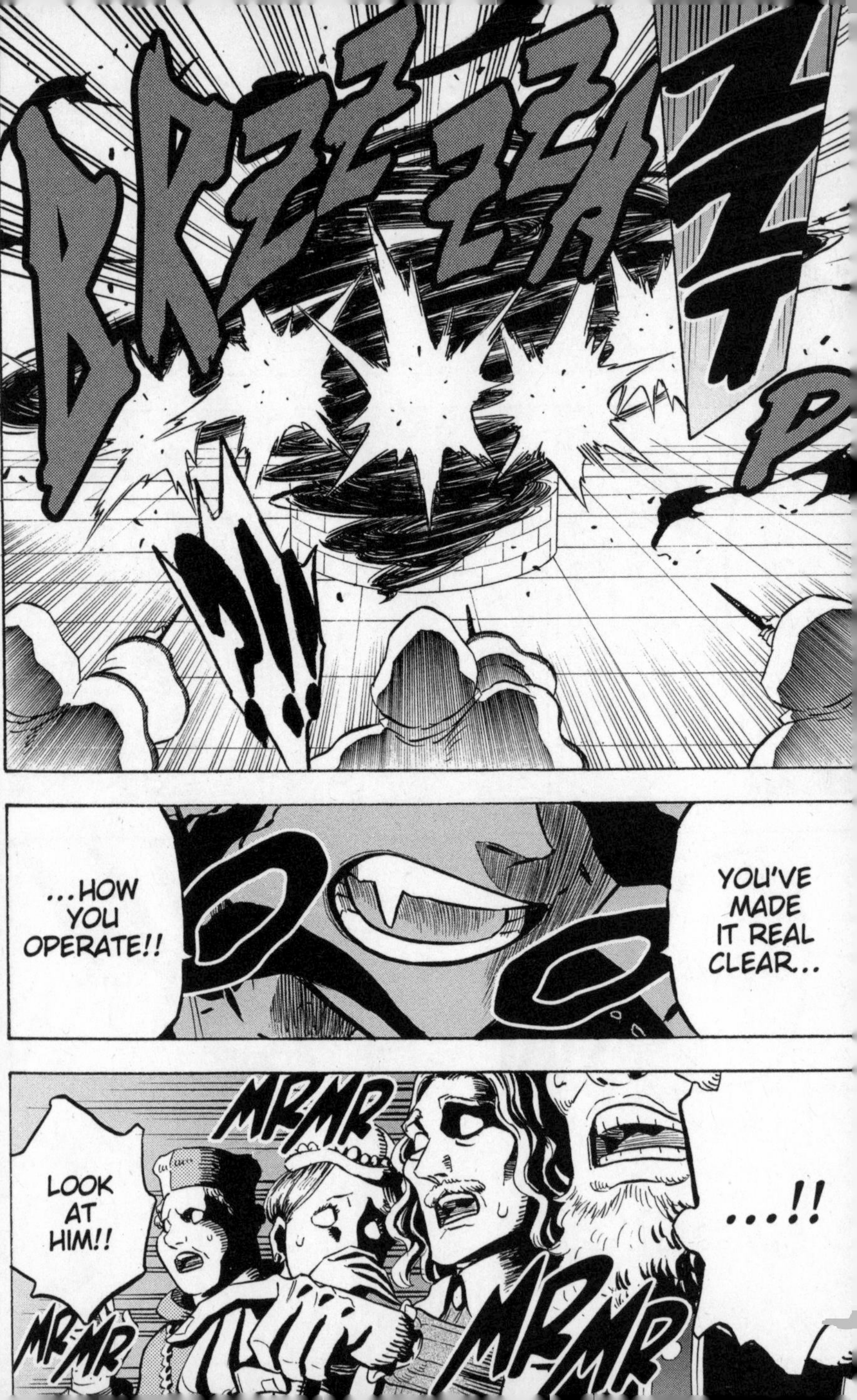
DRZZZZAT
YOU'VE MADE IT REAL CLEAR...
...HOW YOU OPERATE!!
...!!
MR MR
LOOK AT HIM!!
MR MR
MR MR

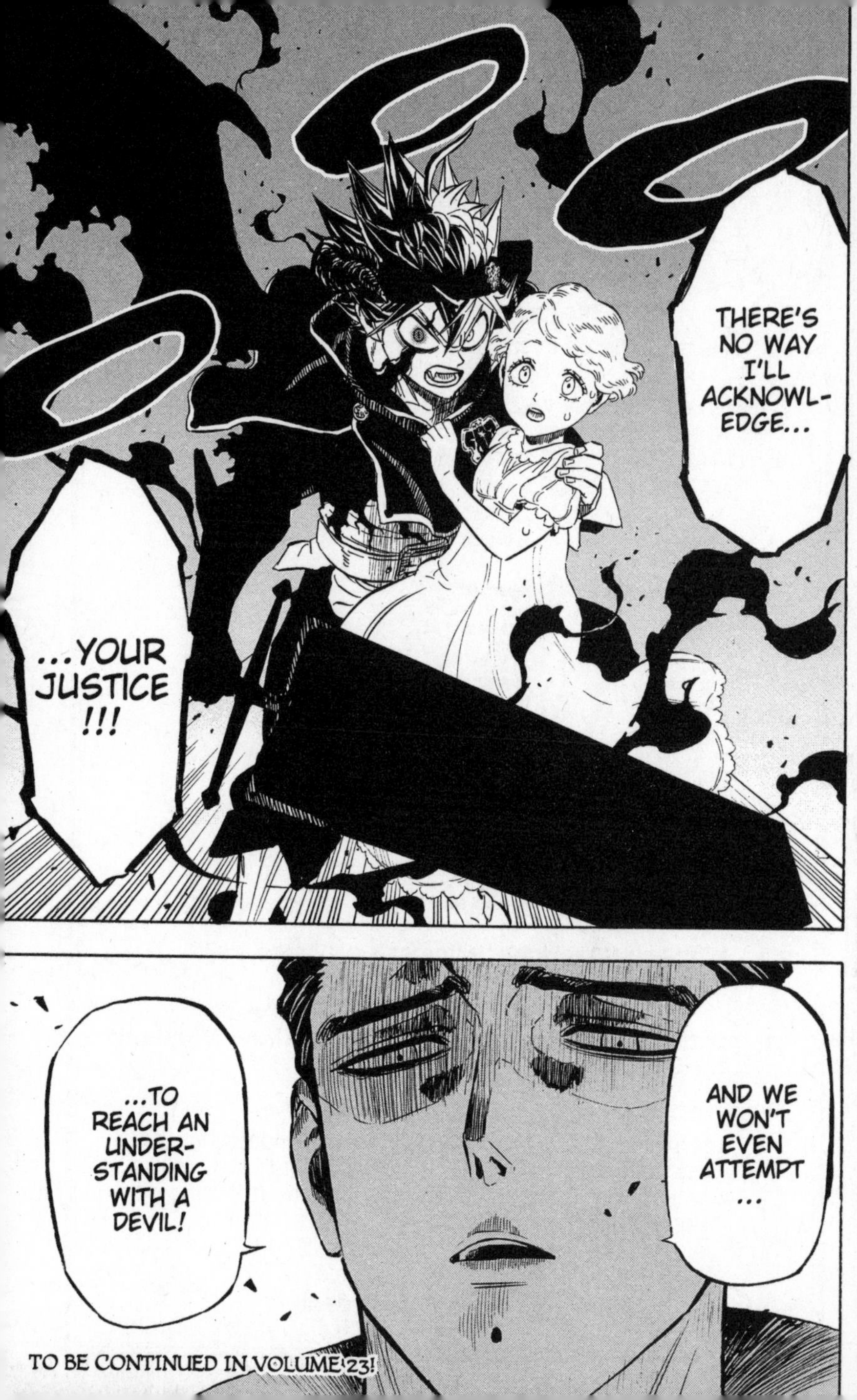
THERE'S NO WAY I'LL ACKNOWL-EDGE...
...YOUR JUSTICE !!!
AND WE WON'T EVEN ATTEMPT ...
...TO REACH AN UNDER-STANDING WITH A DEVIL!
TO BE CONTINUED IN VOLUME 23!

The Assorted Questions Brigade

Good day! Good evening! Good morning!

It's time for the letters corner.

This time, there's even a question about that one academy!
All right, let's get to it!

Q: In the side story *Royal Clover Academy*, please tell me which subjects the people in the teaching positions are in charge of. (*Skymoon*, Aichi / *I Want To Support My Favorite*, Miyagi)

A:

Augustus Kira	Director		
Julius	Principal	Marx	Vice-Principal

Fuegoleon	Japanese
Mereoleona	Health and P.E.
Yami	Health and P.E.
Jack	Math
Rill	Art
Dorothy	Biology
Langris	Foreign Languages
Teresa	Japanese
Revchi	Janitor

Nozel	Chemistry
Charlotte	Math
William	Foreign Languages
Gueldre	Civics
Kaiser	Geography and History
Kirsch	Music
Zora	Student Teacher
Lily	School Nurse

It's about like that!

Q: Whose bust is bigger, Mimosa's or Vanessa's? (*Hexagon*, Fukuoka)

A: Between those two, it's Mimosa. Right now, Mimosa is the bustiest character in the series!

Q: I really love Alecdora Sandler, and compared to his first appearance, I think he's lost weight, and his cheeks have gotten gaunter. Is it from stressing out over Yuno? (*Itsuki*, Kyoto)

A: ....Yes! It's Yuno-induced stress!!!

The Blank Page Brigade

This volume's topic:
What summer memory has stayed with you?

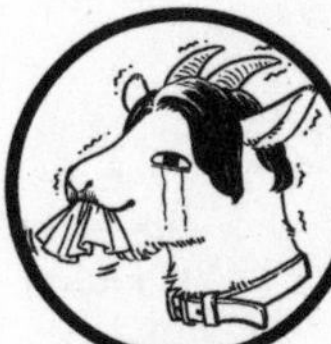

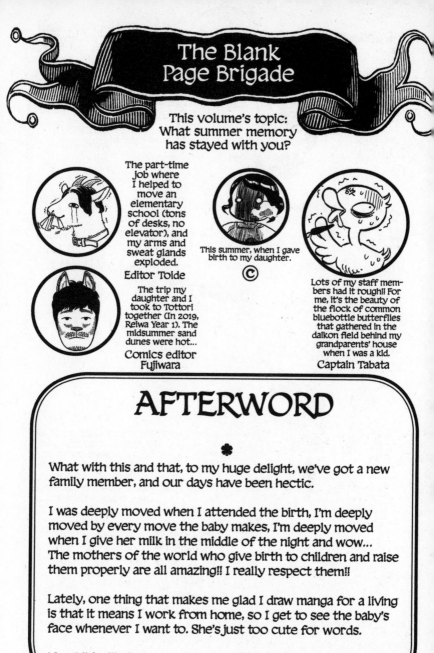

The part-time job where I helped to move an elementary school (tons of desks, no elevator), and my arms and sweat glands exploded.

Editor Toide

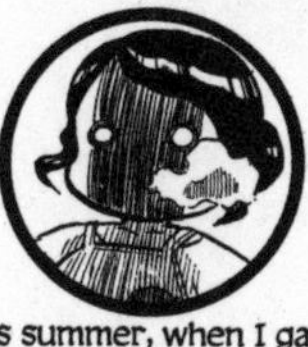

This summer, when I gave birth to my daughter.

©

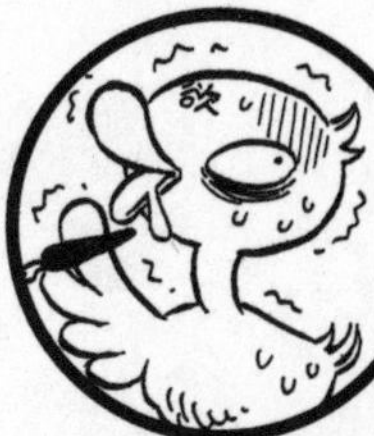

Lots of my staff members had it rough!! For me, it's the beauty of the flock of common bluebottle butterflies that gathered in the daikon field behind my grandparents' house when I was a kid.

Captain Tabata

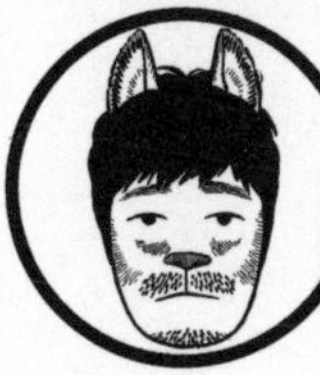

The trip my daughter and I took to Tottori together (In 2019, Reiwa Year 1). The midsummer sand dunes were hot...

Comics editor Fujiwara

AFTERWORD

What with this and that, to my huge delight, we've got a new family member, and our days have been hectic.

I was deeply moved when I attended the birth, I'm deeply moved by every move the baby makes, I'm deeply moved when I give her milk in the middle of the night and wow... The mothers of the world who give birth to children and raise them properly are all amazing!! I really respect them!!

Lately, one thing that makes me glad I draw manga for a living is that it means I work from home, so I get to see the baby's face whenever I want to. She's just too cute for words.

My child will give me energy, and I'll work hard on the manga!!

I've only got vague memories of what I did, but my summers in high school, which were definitely fun...

UwaAAaaaaAAAaaugh! (A scream at the cruelty of time)

Yōtarō Hayakawa

My first summer in high school, when I fell out of a boat and almost drowned.

Hayato Gotō

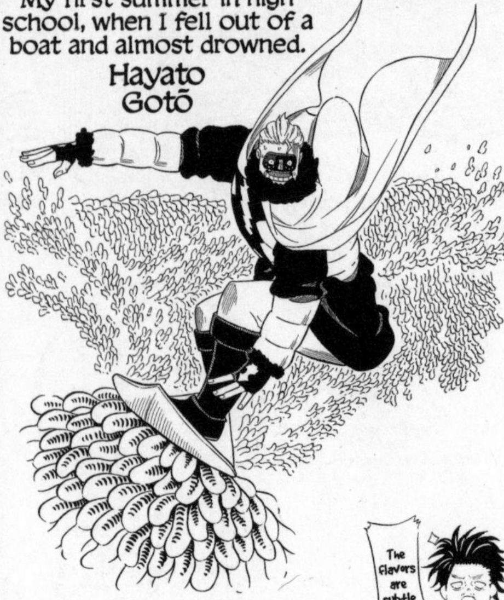

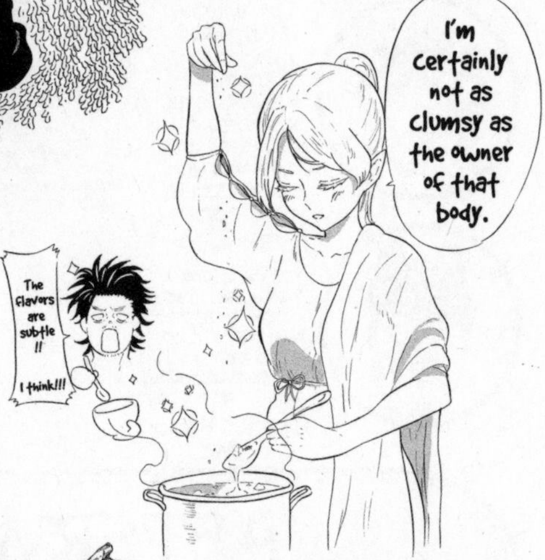
I'm certainly not as clumsy as the owner of that body.
The flavors are subtle!!
I think!!!

The terribly busy summer I spent at a blazing hot workplace where even turning the air conditioning up to MAX did nothing, working on a weekly series (which got canceled).

Teruaki Mizuno

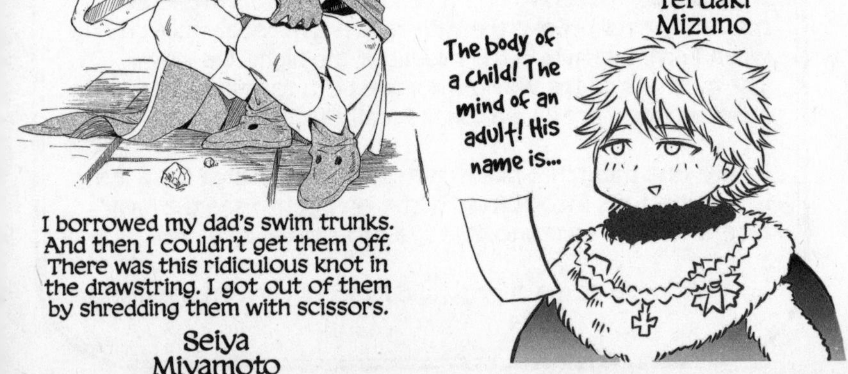
The body of a child! The mind of an adult! His name is...

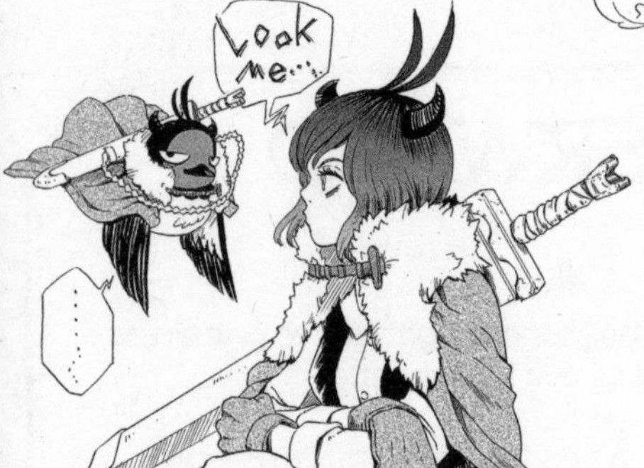
Look me...

I borrowed my dad's swim trunks. And then I couldn't get them off. There was this ridiculous knot in the drawstring. I got out of them by shredding them with scissors.

Seiya Miyamoto

My first summer in middle school, when I went to an amusement park pool with a group of friends (guys and girls), and I was the only one in a too-tight school swimsuit.

Kazuhiro Wakao

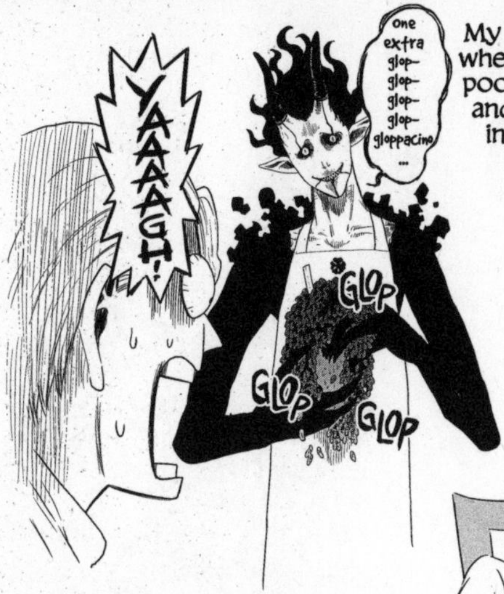
one extra glop- glop- glop- glop- gloppacino ...
YAAAAGH!
GLOP
GLOP
GLOP

The summer I threw myself into club activities in a boiling hot gym.

Yagasa

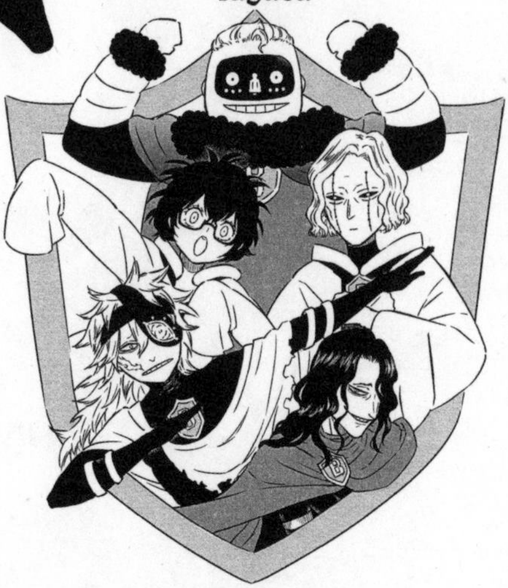

My first summer in grade school, when I made a whole lot of shiny-smooth mud balls over summer vacation.

Sōta Hishikawa

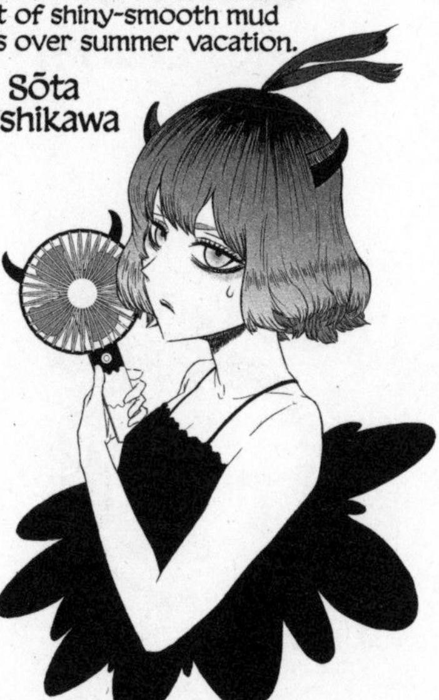

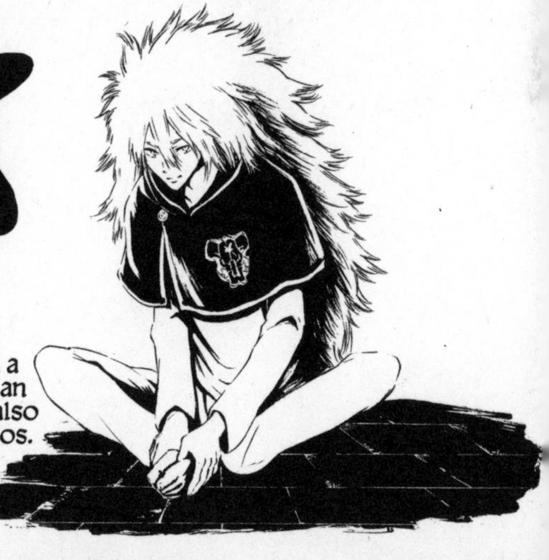

The hellish summer when I passed out while working on a weekly serial and almost got an ambulance called for me, and also ate too much and gained 15 kilos.

Masayoshi Satoshō

Special Bonus Materials

Charmy's trip around the world!
~Appetite transcends national borders~

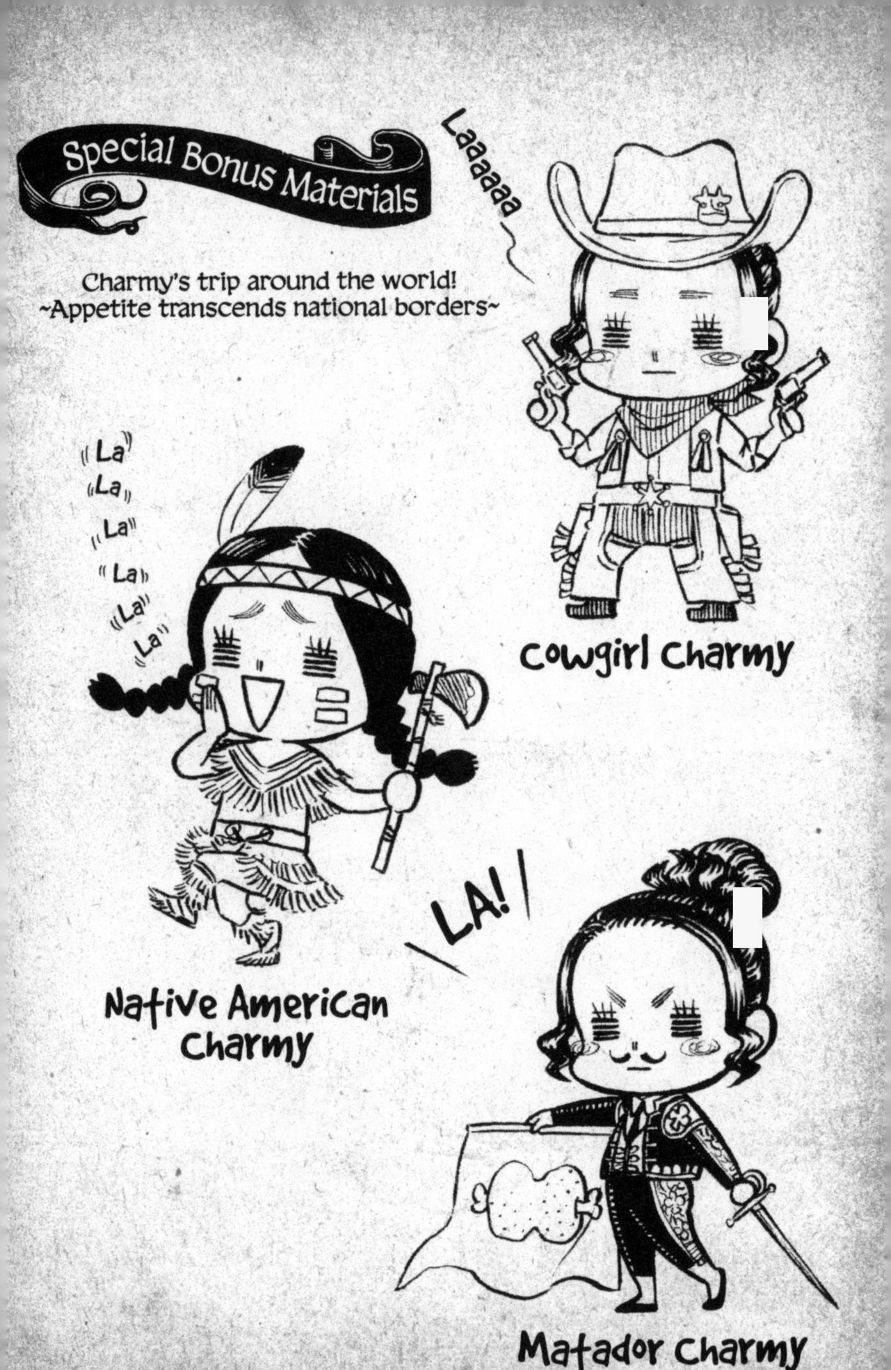
Laaaaaa
Cowgirl Charmy
La La La La La La
Native American Charmy
LA!
Matador Charmy

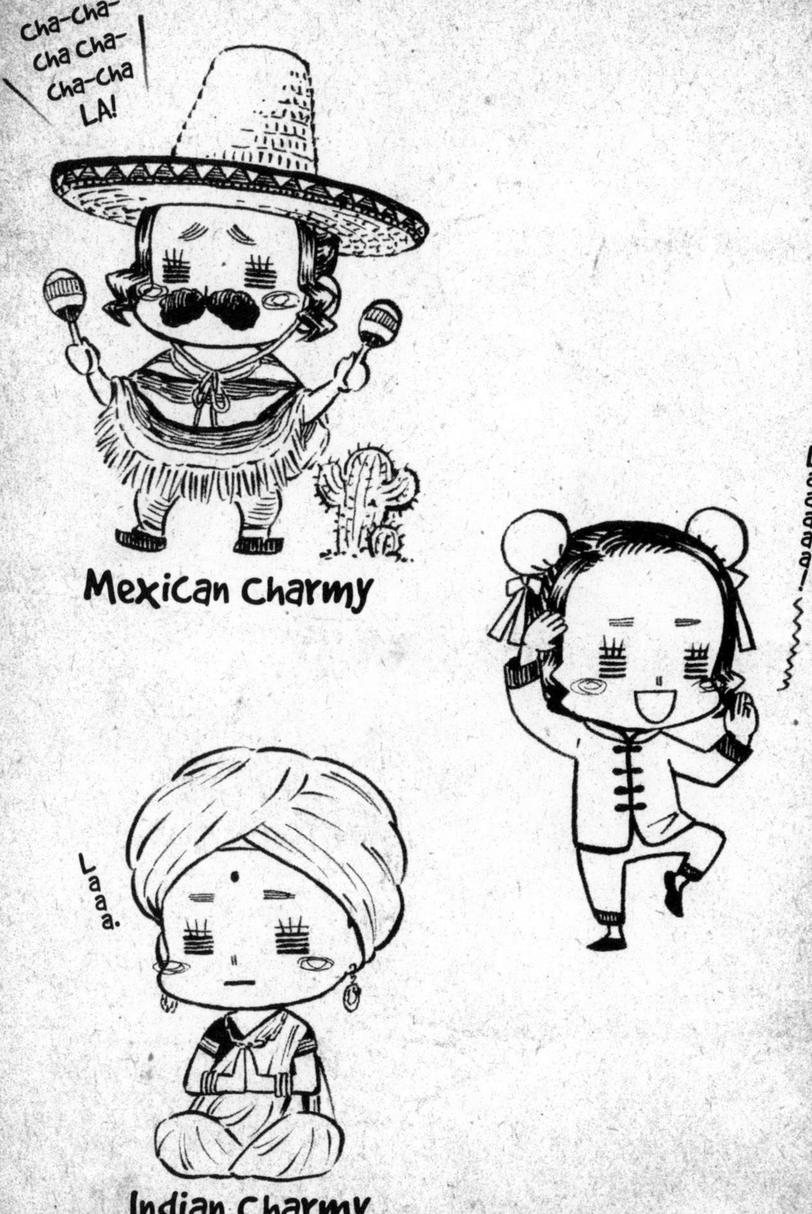
Cha-Cha-
Cha Cha-
Cha-Cha
LA!
Mexican Charmy
Laaaaaa!
Laaa.
Indian Charmy

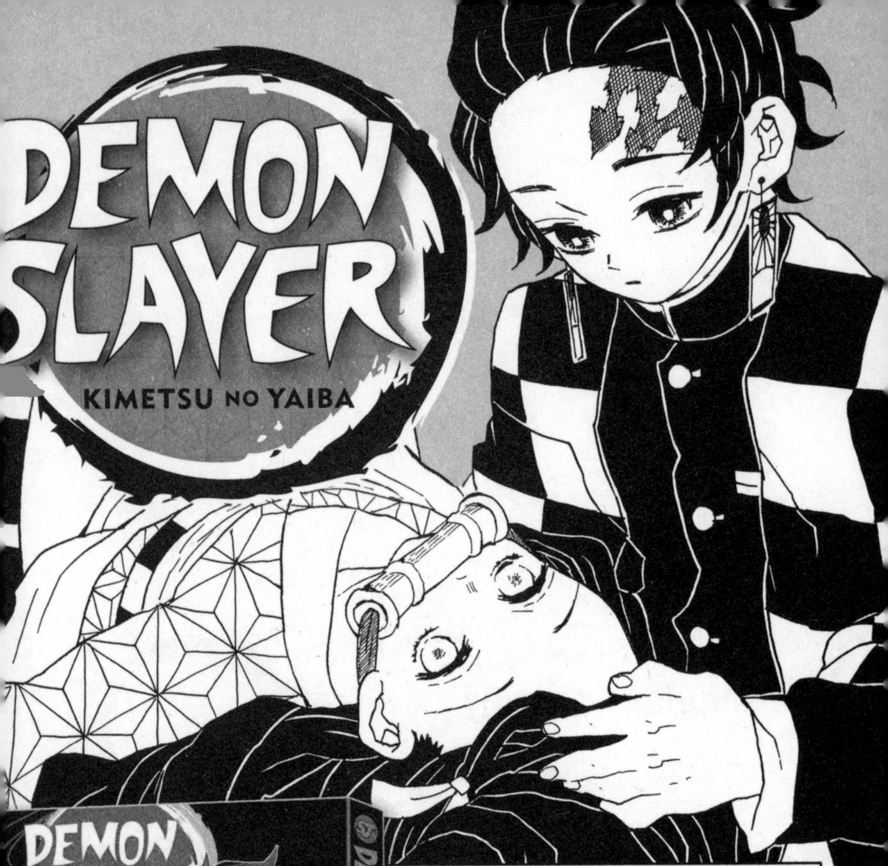
DEMON SLAYER
KIMETSU NO YAIBA

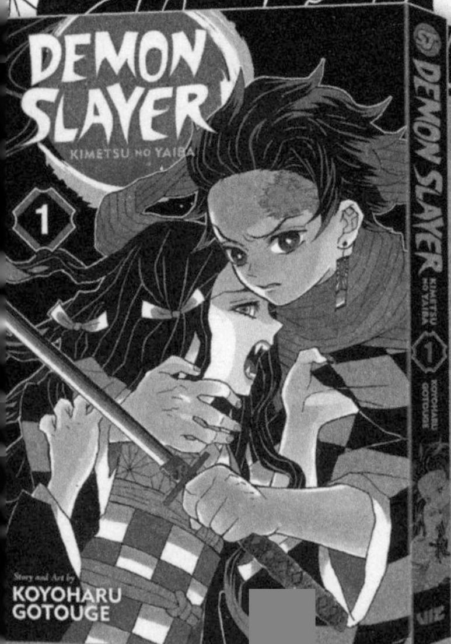
DEMON SLAYER
KIMETSU NO YAIBA
1
Story and Art by
KOYOHARU GOTOUGE
DEMON SLAYER
KIMETSU NO YAIBA
1
KOYOHARU GOTOUGE

Story and Art by

KOYOHARU GOTOUGE

In Taisho-era Japan, kindhearted Tanjiro Kamado makes a living selling charcoal. But his peaceful life is shattered when a demon slaughters his entire family. His little sister Nezuko is the only survivor, but she has been transformed into a demon herself! Tanjiro sets out on a dangerous journey to find a way to return his sister to normal and destroy the demon who ruined his life.

RATED T TEEN

VIZ

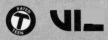

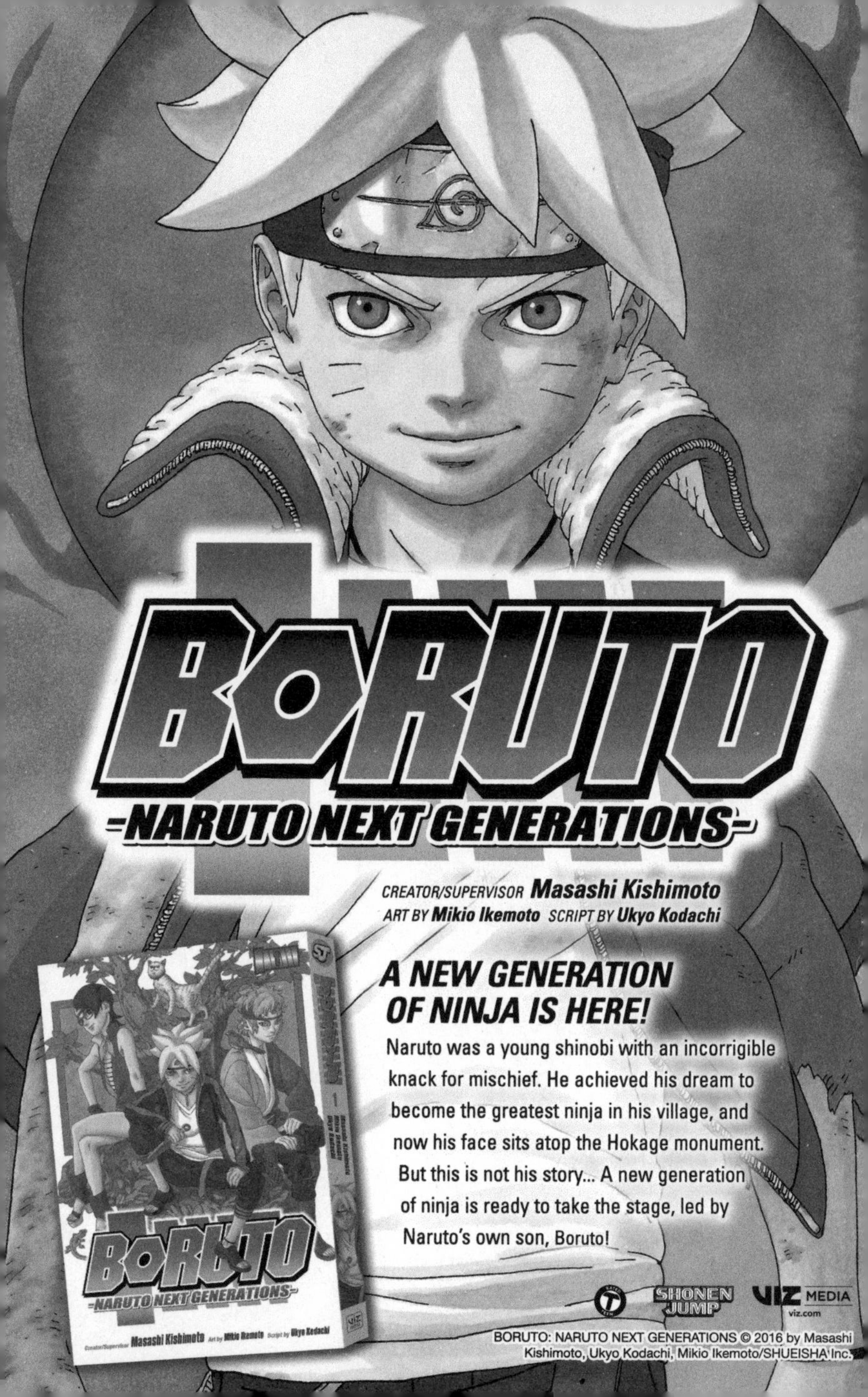
BORUTO
-NARUTO NEXT GENERATIONS-
CREATOR/SUPERVISOR Masashi Kishimoto
ART BY Mikio Ikemoto SCRIPT BY Ukyo Kodachi
A NEW GENERATION OF NINJA IS HERE!
Naruto was a young shinobi with an incorrigible knack for mischief. He achieved his dream to become the greatest ninja in his village, and now his face sits atop the Hokage monument. But this is not his story... A new generation of ninja is ready to take the stage, led by Naruto's own son, Boruto!
BORUTO
-NARUTO NEXT GENERATIONS-
Masashi Kishimoto
SHONEN JUMP
VIZ MEDIA
viz.com
BORUTO: NARUTO NEXT GENERATIONS © 2016 by Masashi Kishimoto, Ukyo Kodachi, Mikio Ikemoto/SHUEISHA Inc.

ASTRA
LOST IN SPACE

AN EIGHT TEENAGERS FIND THEIR WAY
HOME FROM 5,000 LIGHT-YEARS AWAY?

's the year 2063, and interstellar space travel has
ecome the norm. Eight students from Caird High
chool and one child set out on a routine planet camp
xcursion. While there, the students are mysteriously
ansported 5,000 light-years away to the middle of
owhere! Will they ever make it back home?!

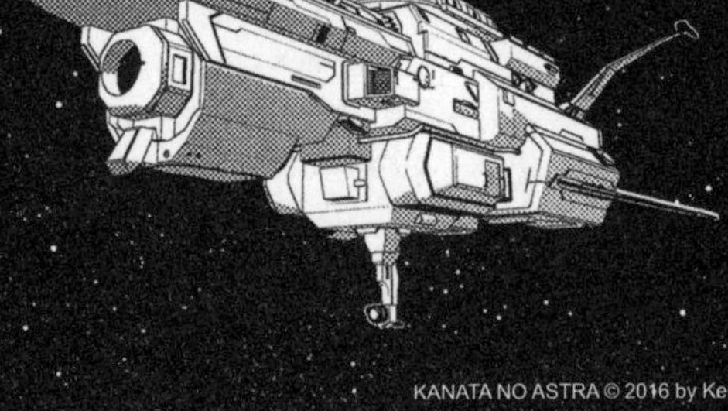

ASTRA
LOST IN SPACE

Story and Art by KENTA SHINOHARA

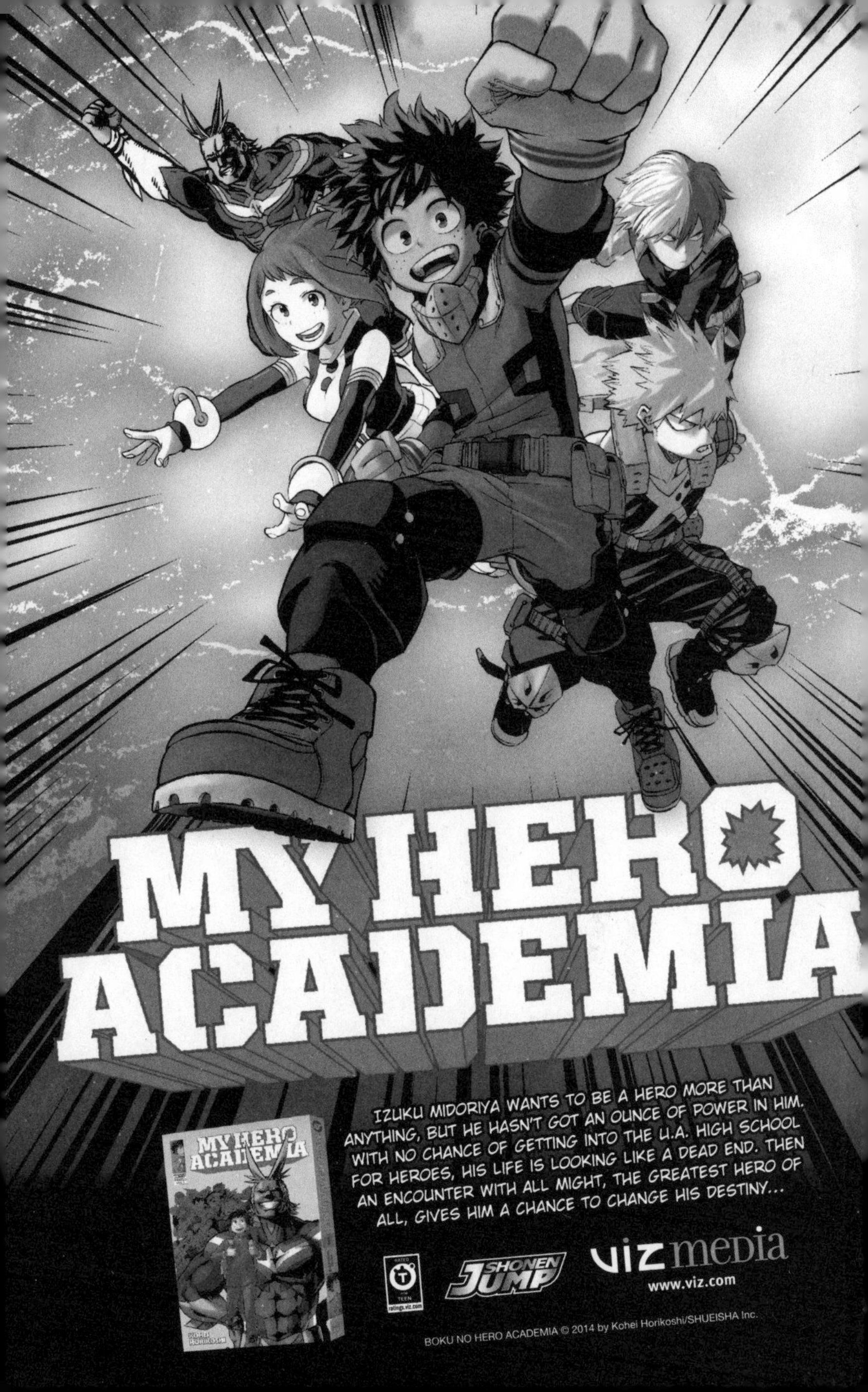
MY HERO ACADEMIA
IZUKU MIDORIYA WANTS TO BE A HERO MORE THAN ANYTHING, BUT HE HASN'T GOT AN OUNCE OF POWER IN HIM. WITH NO CHANCE OF GETTING INTO THE U.A. HIGH SCHOOL FOR HEROES, HIS LIFE IS LOOKING LIKE A DEAD END. THEN AN ENCOUNTER WITH ALL MIGHT, THE GREATEST HERO OF ALL, GIVES HIM A CHANCE TO CHANGE HIS DESTINY...
RATED T TEEN ratings.viz.com
SHONEN JUMP
VIZ media
www.viz.com
BOKU NO HERO ACADEMIA © 2014 by Kohei Horikoshi/SHUEISHA Inc.

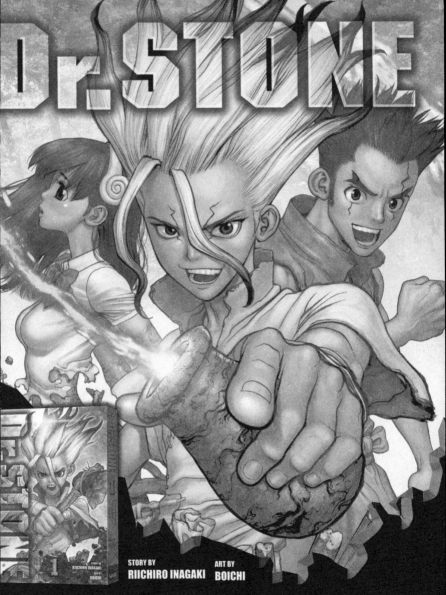

DR. STONE

STORY BY
RIICHIRO INAGAKI

ART BY
BOICHI

ne fateful day, all of humanity turned to stone. Many millennia ter, Taiju frees himself from petrification and finds himself urrounded by statues. The situation looks grim—until he runs nto his science-loving friend Senku! Together they plan to restart ivilization with the power of science!

Stop

YOU'RE READING THE WRONG WAY!

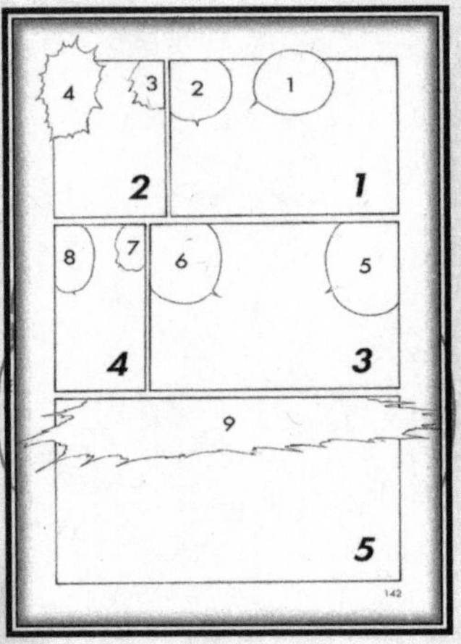

1
2
1
3
4
2
5
6
3
7
8
4
9
5
142

BLACK CLOVER
reads from right to left, starting in the upper-right corner. Japanese is read from right to left, meaning that action, sound effects, and word-balloon order are completely reversed from English order.